MCSA/MCSE: Windows Server 2
Security Administration Study (

MW00568884

Implementing and Administering Security in a Microsoft Windows Server 2003 Network

Exam 70-299

OBJECTIVE	CHAPTER
IMPLEMENTING, MANAGING, AND TROUBLESHOOTING SECURITY POLICIES	
Plan security templates based on computer role. Computer roles include SQL Server computer, Microsoft Exchange Server computer, domain controller, Internet Authentication Service (IAS) server, and Internet Information Services (IIS) server.	1
Configure security templates.	
Configure registry and file system permissions.	1
Configure account policies.	1
Configure .pol files.	1
Configure audit policies.	1
Configure user rights assignment.	1
Configure security options.	1
Configure system services.	1
Configure restricted groups.	1
Configure event logs.	1
Deploy security templates.	1
Plan the deployment of security templates.	1
Deploy security templates by using Active Directory–based Group Policy Objects (GPOs).	1
Deploy security templates by using command-line tools and scripting.	1
Troubleshoot security template problems.	1
Troubleshoot security templates in a mixed operating system environment.	1
Troubleshoot security policy inheritance.	1
Troubleshoot removal of security template settings.	1
Configure additional security based on computer roles. Server computer roles include SQL Server computer, Exchange Server computer, domain controller, Internet Authentication Service (IAS) server, and Internet Information Services (IIS) server. Client computer roles include desktop, portable, and kiosk.	
Plan and configure security settings.	2
Plan network zones for computer roles.	2
Plan and configure software restriction policies.	2

SYBEX

SYBEX

MCSA/MCSE:
Windows Server 2003 Network Security Administration
Study Guide

MCSA/MCSE:
Windows® Server 2003 Network Security Administration
Study Guide

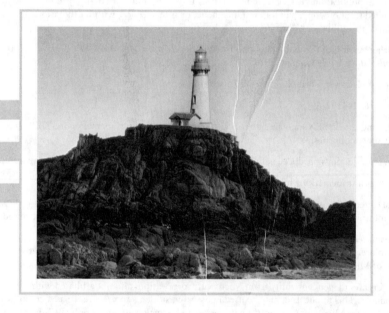

Russ Kaufmann

Bill English

San Francisco • London

SYBEX®

Associate Publisher: Neil Edde
Acquisitions and Developmental Editor: Maureen Adams
Production Editor: Mae Lum
Technical Editors: Craig Vazquez, Chris N. Crane, J. Kevin Lundy
Copyeditor: Sarah Lemaire
Compositor: Craig Woods, Happenstance Type-O-Rama
Graphic Illustrator: Interactive Composition Corporation
CD Coordinator: Dan Mummert
CD Technician: Kevin Ly
Proofreaders: Laurie O'Connell, Nancy Riddiough
Indexer: Nancy Guenther
Book Designers: Bill Gibson, Judy Fung
Cover Designer: Archer Design
Cover Photographer: Photodisc, Victor Arre

An earlier version of this book was published under the title *MCSA/MCSE: Windows 2000 Network Security Administration Study Guide* © 2003 SYBEX Inc.

Library of Congress Card Number: 2003100046

ISBN: 0-7821-4332-6

SYBEX

To Our Valued Readers:

Thank you for looking to Sybex for your Microsoft certification exam prep needs. We at Sybex are proud of the reputation we've established for providing certification candidates with the practical knowledge and skills needed to succeed in the highly competitive IT marketplace.

With its release of Windows Server 2003, and the revised MCSA and MCSE tracks, Microsoft has raised the bar for IT certifications yet again. The new programs better reflect the skill set demanded of IT administrators in today's marketplace and offers candidates a clearer structure for acquiring the skills necessary to advance their careers.

Sybex is proud to have helped thousands of Microsoft certification candidates prepare for their exams over the years, and we are excited about the opportunity to continue to provide computer and networking professionals with the skills they'll need to succeed in the highly competitive IT industry.

The authors and editors have worked hard to ensure that the Study Guide you hold in your hand is comprehensive, in-depth, and pedagogically sound. We're confident that this book will exceed the demanding standards of the certification marketplace and help you, the Microsoft certification candidate, succeed in your endeavors.

As always, your feedback is important to us. Please send comments, questions, or suggestions to support@sybex.com. At Sybex, we're continually striving to meet the needs of individuals preparing for IT certification exams.

Good luck in pursuit of your Microsoft certification!

Neil Edde
Associate Publisher—Certification
Sybex, Inc.

Acknowledgments

As with every book I've worked on, there are many more people whose efforts are reflected in these pages but whose names are not on the cover. Without their help, this book would not be in your hands.

I'd also like to thank my co-author, Russ Kaufmann, who came into this project after it started and did a bang-up job with his chapters even though he experienced several setbacks that were out of his control. Russ, thanks for writing this book with me and for being such a good friend. I would be honored to work with you again.

Neil Salkind, my agent from StudioB, did his usual great job in pulling together the contractual elements that enabled me to co-author this book. Thanks, Neil, for being such an outstanding agent.

As always, my wife Kathy supported me in this project. Thanks, Kathy, for your love and friendship.

Finally, I'd like to thank Jesus Christ, who gave me the talent and opportunity to write this book and without whom I'd be lost forever.

Bill English
Nowthen, Minnesota

It seemed to me that this project would never end. Just when I thought I was back on schedule, or even ahead of schedule, something else would come up to twist and turn my life into new shapes. Construction at my home was one of the biggest obstacles. Power outages, wires shorted out by nails, network lines dug up in the yard, huge amounts of dust clogging fans and causing circuits to overheat, and having to move the servers and all of the network infrastructure from place to place within the house all contributed to massive amounts of gray hair. Then, to top it off, we had an addition to the family: Raymond, a very large, bouncing baby boy of about 132 lbs. was added to our family. Okay, he is not a baby; he is my 14-year-old nephew. We love him a lot, but adding him to the family came with huge amounts of stress. Between everything, it was amazing that I was able to work at all. It is truly amazing how many obstacles get in the way of completing a project like this one.

I would like to thank the people at Sybex for their hard work. Thanks to the understanding of Mae Lum and Maureen Adams, we were able to get it all done. Mae and Maureen were fantastic in keeping the material organized and keeping a semblance of a schedule. Craig Vazquez did a great job combing through the material and checking it for technical accuracy. Kevin Lundy stepped in and was great in updating some content to keep things on schedule. The entire Sybex team did a wonderful job.

I would like to thank my agents, Neil Salkind and Laura Lewin, who somehow kept me from flipping out and checking into the local mental ward. I swear, if just one more deadline popped up out of nowhere I was going to... Never mind, it all worked out. They really did save the day on more than one occasion. Thanks, guys!

I have to give special thanks to Bill English. Okay, I really don't have to do it, but he has earned it. Bill made this revision possible by driving the first edition of this book to its completion. Without Bill English being involved, I would have never taken on the first edition, much less this revision. I really hope that I have the opportunity to work with him again in the future. Not only is he a colleague that I admire, he is a friend whom I can depend on again and again.

Ben Smith and David Lowe of Microsoft were extremely helpful during this process. Whenever I was not exactly sure what Microsoft was looking for with the test objectives, each of them took the time to help me out. Ben provided many answers to technical questions during the process. David, while not directly involved in answering my questions, was a fantastic conduit to information. Without his help, I would have had to spend several days hunting down answers.

Another person who deserves his own paragraph in the acknowledgments is Brian Komar. You should recognize Brian from his many contributions to our community: TechNet articles, Microsoft Official Courseware contributions, MEC and TechEd speeches, and several books. Brian was extremely helpful. I am not saying this just because I owe him a box of golf balls.

There are others who deserve acknowledgment for this project even though they did not do any of the work. My family helped in so many ways that I cannot name them all. My special thanks go to my wife of over twenty years, Annabelle, and my two children, David and Eric. Without their support, I would never have completed my part of this project.

This book has been a great experience for me, and I have to thank everyone involved for its success. I hope to have a chance to work with all of you again in the future.

Russ Kaufmann
Westminster, Colorado

Sybex would like to thank copyeditor Sarah Lemaire, Happenstance Type-O-Rama, and indexer Nancy Guenther for their valuable contributions to this book.

Contents at a Glance

Contents

Table of Exercises

Introduction

The Microsoft Certified Systems Associate (MCSA) and Microsoft Certified Systems Engineer (MCSE) tracks for Windows Server 2003 are the premier certification for computer industry professionals. Covering the core technologies around which Microsoft's future will be built, the MCSE program is a powerful credential for career advancement.

This book has been developed to give you the critical skills and knowledge that you need to prepare for one of the elective requirements of the MCSE certification program: *Implementing and Administering Security in a Microsoft Windows Server 2003 Network* (Exam 70-299).

As security becomes more and more important in today's network infrastructure, your abilities to design and implement security using Microsoft's operating systems grow in importance as well. In the future, it may very well be that significant career advancement will be tethered to how well you understand security issues.

The Microsoft Certified Professional Program

Since the inception of its certification program, Microsoft has certified almost 1.5 million people. As the computer network industry grows in both size and complexity, this number is sure to grow—and the need for *proven* ability will also increase. Companies rely on certifications to verify the skills of prospective employees and contractors.

Microsoft has developed its Microsoft Certified Professional (MCP) program to give you credentials that verify your ability to work with Microsoft products effectively and professionally. Obtaining your MCP certification requires that you pass any one Microsoft certification exam. Several levels of certification are available based on specific suites of exams. Depending on your areas of interest or experience, you can obtain any of the following MCP credentials:

Microsoft Certified Desktop Support Technician (MCDST) Microsoft's newest certification track, MCDST, is aimed at an entry-level audience looking to start their IT career by troubleshooting and maintaining client desktops. Students need to take two exams to obtain this certification.

Microsoft Certified System Administrator (MCSA) on Windows Server 2003 The MCSA certification targets system and network administrators with roughly 6 to 12 months of desktop and network administration experience. You must take and pass a total of four exams to obtain your MCSA: three core exams and one elective exam.

 If you are already certified as an MCSA on Windows 2000 and want to earn the MCSA on Windows Server 2003, you should refer to the Microsoft website (www.microsoft.com/learning/mcp/mcsa/windows2003/upgrade.asp) for upgrade exam information.

Microsoft Certified Systems Engineer (MCSE) on Windows Server 2003 The MCSE certification track is designed for network and systems administrators, network and systems analysts, and technical consultants who work with Microsoft Windows 2000 Professional, Windows XP

Professional, Windows 2000 Server, and Windows Server 2003. You must take and pass seven exams to obtain your MCSE: five core exams, one design exam, and one elective exam.

 If you are already certified as an MCSE on Windows 2000 and want to earn the MCSE on Windows Server 2003, you should refer to the Microsoft website (www.microsoft.com/learning/mcp/mcse/windows2003/upgrade.asp) for upgrade exam information.

Microsoft Certified Application Developer (MCAD)   The MCAD certification track is designed for application developers and technical consultants who primarily use Microsoft development tools. Currently, you can take exams on Visual Basic .NET or Visual C# .NET. You must take and pass three exams to obtain your MCAD: two core exams and one elective exam.

Microsoft Certified Solution Developer (MCSD) for Microsoft .NET   The MCSD certification track is designed for software engineers and developers and technical consultants who primarily use Microsoft development tools. Currently, you can take exams on Visual Basic .NET and Visual C# .NET. You must take and pass five exams to obtain your MCSD: four core exams and one elective exam.

Microsoft Certified Database Administrator (MCDBA) on SQL Server 2000   The MCDBA certification track is designed for database administrators, developers, and analysts who work with Microsoft SQL Server. As of this printing, you can take exams on either SQL Server 7 or SQL Server 2000, and on either Windows 2000 Server or Windows Server 2003. You must take and pass four exams to achieve MCDBA status: three core exams and one elective exam.

Microsoft Certified Trainer (MCT)   The MCT certification track is designed for any IT professional who develops and teaches Microsoft-approved courses. To become an MCT, you must first obtain your MCSE, MCSD, or MCDBA. Then you must take a class at one of the Certified Technical Training Centers. You will also be required to prove your instructional ability. You can do this in various ways: by taking a skills-building or train-the-trainer class, by achieving certification as a trainer from any of several vendors, or by becoming a Certified Technical Trainer through CompTIA. Last of all, you need to complete an MCT application.

How Do You Become an MCSA or MCSE on Windows Server 2003?

Attaining any MCP certification has always been a challenge. In the past, students have been able to acquire detailed exam information—even most of the exam questions—from online "brain dumps" and third-party "cram" books or software products. For the new Microsoft exams, this is simply not the case.

Microsoft has taken strong steps to protect the security and integrity of the MCSA and MCSE tracks. Now, prospective students must complete a course of study that develops detailed knowledge about a wide range of topics. It supplies them with the true skills needed, derived from working with Windows 2000, Windows XP, Windows Server 2003, and related software products.

The Windows Server 2003 MCSA and MCSE programs are heavily weighted toward hands-on skills and experience. Microsoft has stated that "nearly half of the core required exams' content demands that the candidate have troubleshooting skills acquired through hands-on experience and working knowledge."

Fortunately, if you are willing to dedicate the time and effort to learn Windows 2000, Windows XP, and Windows Server 2003, you can prepare yourself well for the exams by using the proper tools. By working through this book, you can successfully meet the exam requirements to pass the Windows Server 2003 Network Security Administration exam.

This book is part of a complete series of MCSE Study Guides, published by Sybex, which together cover the core MCSE as well as numerous elective exams. Check out www.sybex.com for information on all our MCSA and MCSE titles.

MCSA Exam Requirements

Candidates for MCSA certification on Windows Server 2003 must pass four exams, including one client operating system exam, two networking system exams, and one elective.

MCSE Exam Requirements

Candidates for MCSE certification on Windows Server 2003 must pass seven exams, including four networking system exams, one client operating system exam, one design exam, and one elective.

 For a more detailed description of the Microsoft certification programs, including a list of current and future MCSA and MCSE electives, check Microsoft's website at www.microsoft.com/learning. Additional exams in the electives area will be added by Microsoft in the future as new and upgraded products are released.

The Windows Server 2003 Network Administration Exam

The Implementing and Administering Security in a Microsoft Windows Server 2003 Network exam covers concepts and skills related to installing, configuring, and managing security in a Windows Server 2003 environment. It emphasizes the following:

- Understanding concepts related to baseline security
- Implementing and staying current on service packs and hotfixes from Microsoft
- Troubleshooting secure communication channels
- Working with remote authentication and remote access security
- Implementing and managing a PKI and EFS infrastructure

Although you won't see it in the exam objectives, this exam is heavily weighted toward using Group Policies to implement many of these concepts. A good understanding of Group Policies from your Windows Server 2003 training will go a long way toward helping you pass this exam.

Microsoft provides exam objectives to give you a general overview of possible areas of coverage on the exams. For your convenience, this Study Guide includes objective listings at the beginning of each chapter in which specific Microsoft exam objectives are discussed. Keep in mind, however, that exam objectives are subject to change at any time without prior notice and at Microsoft's sole discretion. Please visit Microsoft's website (www.microsoft.com/learning) for the most current listing of exam objectives.

Types of Exam Questions

In an effort to both refine the testing process and protect the quality of its certifications, Microsoft has focused its Windows 2000, Windows XP, and Windows Server 2003 exams on real experience and hands-on proficiency. There is a greater emphasis on your past working environments and responsibilities and less emphasis on how well you can memorize. In fact, Microsoft says an MCSE candidate should have at least one year of hands-on experience.

Microsoft will accomplish its goal of protecting the exams' integrity by regularly adding and removing exam questions, limiting the number of questions that any individual sees in a beta exam, limiting the number of questions delivered to an individual by using adaptive testing, and adding new exam elements.

Exam questions may be in a variety of formats. Depending on which exam you take, you'll see multiple-choice questions, as well as select-and-place and prioritize-a-list questions. Simulations and case study–based formats are included as well. You may also find yourself taking what's called an *adaptive format exam*. Let's take a look at the types of exam questions and examine the adaptive testing technique, so you'll be prepared for all the possibilities.

Starting with the release of Windows Server 2003 exams, Microsoft is providing a detailed score breakdown. The numerical score is broken down by objective section.

For more information on the various exam question types, go to www.microsoft.com/learning/mcpexams/policies/innovations.asp.

Multiple-Choice Questions

Multiple-choice questions come in two main forms: One is a straightforward question followed by several possible answers, of which one or more is correct. The other type of multiple-choice question is more complex and is based on a specific scenario. The scenario may focus on several areas or objectives.

Select-and-Place Questions

Select-and-place exam questions involve graphical elements that you must manipulate to successfully answer the question. For example, you might see a diagram of a computer network, as shown in the following graphic taken from the select-and-place demo downloaded from Microsoft's website.

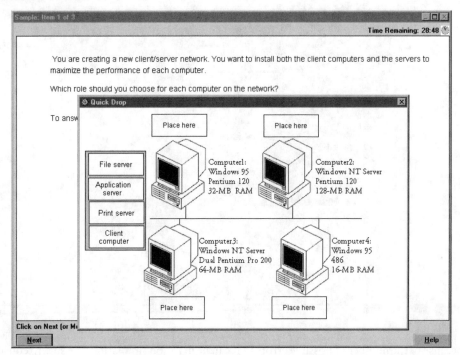

A typical diagram shows computers and other components next to boxes that contain the text "Place here." The labels for the boxes represent various computer roles on a network such as a print server and a file server. Based on information given for each computer, you are asked to select each label and place it in the correct box. You need to place *all* the labels correctly. No credit is given for the question if you correctly label only some of the boxes.

In another select-and-place question, you might be asked to put a series of steps in order by dragging items from boxes on the left to boxes on the right and placing them in the correct order. One other type of select-and-place question requires that you drag an item from the left and place it under an item in a column on the right.

Simulations

Simulations are the kinds of questions that most closely represent actual situations and test the skills that you use while working with Microsoft software interfaces. These exam questions include a mock interface on which you are asked to perform certain actions according to a given scenario. The simulated interfaces look nearly identical to what you see in the actual product, as shown in this example:

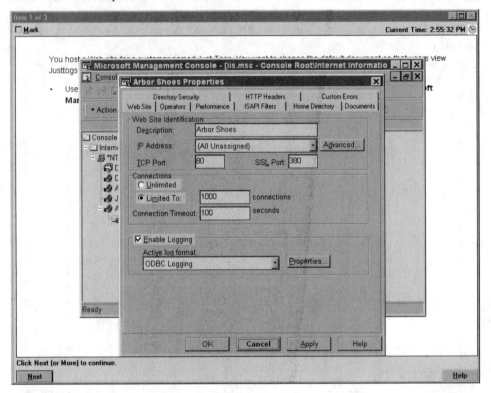

Because of the number of possible errors that can be made on simulations, be sure to consider the following recommendations from Microsoft:

- Do not change any simulation settings that don't pertain to the solution directly.

- When related information has not been provided, assume that the default settings are used.

- Make sure that your entries are spelled correctly.

- Close all the simulation application windows after completing the set of tasks in the simulation.

The best way to prepare for simulation questions is to spend time working with the graphical interface of the product on which you will be tested.

Case Study–Based Questions

Case study–based questions first appeared in the MCSD program. These questions present a scenario with a range of requirements. Based on the information provided, you answer a series of multiple-choice and select-and-place questions. The interface for case study–based questions has a number of tabs, each of which contains information about the scenario.

At present, this type of question appears only in most of the Design exams.

 Microsoft will regularly add and remove questions from the exams. This is called *item seeding*. It is part of the effort to make it more difficult for individuals to merely memorize exam questions that were passed along by previous test-takers.

Exam Question Development

Microsoft follows an exam-development process consisting of eight mandatory phases. The process takes an average of seven months and involves more than 150 specific steps. MCP exam development consists of the following phases:

Phase 1: Job Analysis   Phase 1 is an analysis of all the tasks that make up a specific job function, based on tasks performed by people who are currently performing that job function. This phase also identifies the knowledge, skills, and abilities that relate specifically to the performance area being certified.

Phase 2: Objective Domain Definition   The results of the job analysis phase provide the framework used to develop objectives. Development of objectives involves translating the job-function tasks into a comprehensive package of specific and measurable knowledge, skills, and abilities. The resulting list of objectives—the *objective domain*—is the basis for the development of both the certification exams and the training materials.

Phase 3: Blueprint Survey   The final objective domain is transformed into a blueprint survey in which contributors are asked to rate each objective. These contributors may be MCP candidates, appropriately skilled exam-development volunteers, or Microsoft employees. Based on the contributors' input, the objectives are prioritized and weighted. The actual exam items are written according to the prioritized objectives. Contributors are queried about how they spend their time on the job. If a contributor doesn't spend an adequate amount of time actually performing the specified job function, their data is eliminated from the analysis. The blueprint survey phase helps determine which objectives to measure, as well as the appropriate number and types of items to include on the exam.

Phase 4: Item Development   A pool of items is developed to measure the blueprinted objective domain. The number and types of items to be written are based on the results of the blueprint survey.

Phase 5: Alpha Review and Item Revision During this phase, a panel of technical and job-function experts reviews each item for technical accuracy. The panel then answers each item and reaches a consensus on all technical issues. Once the items have been verified as being technically accurate, they are edited to ensure that they are expressed in the clearest language possible.

Phase 6: Beta Exam The reviewed and edited items are collected into beta exams. Based on the responses of all beta participants, Microsoft performs a statistical analysis to verify the validity of the exam items and to determine which items will be used in the certification exam. Once the analysis has been completed, the items are distributed into multiple parallel forms, or *versions*, of the final certification exam.

Phase 7: Item Selection and Cut-Score Setting The results of the beta exams are analyzed to determine which items will be included in the certification exam. This determination is based on many factors, including item difficulty and relevance. During this phase, a panel of job-function experts determines the *cut score* (minimum passing score) for the exams. The cut score differs from exam to exam because it is based on an item-by-item determination of the percentage of candidates who answered the item correctly and who would be expected to answer the item correctly.

Phase 8: Live Exam In the final phase, the exams are given to candidates. MCP exams are administered by Prometric and Virtual University Enterprises (VUE).

Tips for Taking the Windows Server 2003 Security Administration Exam

Here are some general tips for achieving success on your certification exam:

- Arrive early at the exam center so that you can relax and review your study materials. During this final review, you can look over tables and lists of exam-related information.

- Read the questions carefully. Don't be tempted to jump to an early conclusion. Make sure that you know *exactly* what the question is asking.

- Answer all questions. Remember that the adaptive format does *not* allow you to return to a question. Be very careful before entering your answer. Because your exam may be shortened by correct answers (and lengthened by incorrect answers), there is no advantage to rushing through questions.

- On simulations, do not change settings that are not directly related to the question. Also, you can assume default settings if the question does not specify or imply which settings are used.

- For questions that you're not sure about, use a process of elimination to get rid of the obviously incorrect answers first. This improves your odds of selecting the correct answer when you need to make an educated guess.

Exam Registration

You can take the Microsoft exams at any of more than 1000 Authorized Prometric Testing Centers (APTCs) and VUE Testing Centers around the world. For the location of a testing center near you, call Prometric at 800-755-EXAM (755-3926) or call VUE at 888-837-8616. Outside the United States and Canada, contact your local Prometric or VUE registration center.

Find out the number of the exam that you want to take and then register with the Prometric or VUE registration center nearest you. At this point, you will be asked for advance payment for the exam. The exams are $125 each, and you must take them within one year of payment. You can schedule exams up to six weeks in advance or as late as one working day prior to the date of the exam. You can cancel or reschedule your exam if you contact the center at least two working days prior to the exam. Same-day registration is available in some locations, subject to space availability. If same-day registration is available, you must register a minimum of two hours before test time.

You can also register for your exams online at www.prometric.com or www.vue.com.

When you schedule the exam, you will be provided with instructions regarding appointment and cancellation procedures, ID requirements, and information about the testing center location. In addition, you will receive a registration and payment confirmation letter from Prometric or VUE.

Microsoft requires certification candidates to accept the terms of a Non-Disclosure Agreement before taking certification exams.

Is This Book for You?

If you want to acquire a solid foundation in administering security for a Windows Server 2003 network, and your goal is to prepare for the exam by learning how to use and manage this operating system, this book is for you. You'll find clear explanations of the fundamental concepts that you need to grasp and plenty of help to achieve the high level of professional competency that you need to succeed in your chosen field.

If you want to become certified as an MCSE or MCSA, this book is definitely for you. However, if you just want to attempt to pass the exam without really understanding how to administer security for a Windows Server 2003 network, this Study Guide is *not* for you. It is written for people who want to acquire hands-on skills and in-depth knowledge of this topic.

How to Use This Book

What makes a Sybex Study Guide the book of choice for more than 100,000 MCSEs? We took into account not only what you need to know to pass the exam, but what you need to know to take what you've learned and apply it in the real world. Each book contains the following:

Objective-by-objective coverage of the topics that you need to know   Each chapter lists the objectives covered in that chapter, followed by detailed discussions of each objective.

Assessment Test   Directly following this introduction is an Assessment Test that you should take. It is designed to help you determine how much you already know. Each question is tied to a topic discussed in the book. Using the results of the Assessment Test, you can figure out the areas where you need to focus your study. Of course, we do recommend that you read the entire book.

Exam Essentials   To highlight what you learn, you'll find a list of Exam Essentials at the end of each chapter. The Exam Essentials section briefly highlights the topics that need your particular attention as you prepare for the exam.

Glossary   Throughout each chapter, you will be introduced to important terms and concepts that you will need to know for the exam. These terms appear in italic within the chapters. At the end of the book, a detailed Glossary gives definitions for these terms, as well as for other general terms that you should know.

Review questions, complete with detailed explanations   Each chapter is followed by a set of review questions that test what you learned in the chapter. The questions are written with the exam in mind, meaning that they are designed to have the same look and feel as what you'll see on the exam. Question types are just like the exam, including multiple choice.

Hands-on exercises   In each chapter, you'll find exercises designed to give you the important hands-on experience that is critical for your exam preparation. The exercises support the topics of the chapter, and they walk you through the steps necessary to perform a particular function.

Real World Scenarios   Because reading a book isn't enough for you to learn how to apply these topics in your everyday duties, we have provided Real World Scenarios in special sidebars. These explain when and why a particular solution would make sense, in a working environment that you'd actually encounter.

> The topics covered in this Study Guide map directly to Microsoft's official exam objectives. Each exam objective is covered completely.

This book provides a solid foundation for the serious effort of preparing for the exam. To best benefit from this book, you might want to use the following study method:

1. Take the Assessment Test to identify your weak areas.

2. Study each chapter carefully. Do your best to fully understand the information.

3. Complete all the hands-on exercises in the chapter, referring to the text as necessary so that you understand each step.

4. Read over the Real World Scenarios sidebars in the chapters to improve your understanding of how to use what you learn in this book.

5. Study the Exam Essentials at the end of each chapter to make sure you are familiar with the areas that you need to focus on.

6. Answer the review questions at the end of each chapter. If you prefer to answer the questions in a timed and graded format, install the test engine from the book's CD and answer the chapter questions there instead of in the book.

7. Take note of the questions that you did not understand and study the corresponding sections of the book again.

8. Go back over the Exam Essentials.

9. Go through the Study Guide's other training resources, which are included on the book's CD. These include electronic flashcards, the electronic versions of the chapter review questions and of the Assessment Test, and the two bonus exams.

To learn all the material covered in this book, you will need to study regularly and with discipline. Try to set aside the same time every day to study and select a comfortable and quiet place in which to do it. If you work hard, you will be surprised at how quickly you learn this material. Good luck!

What's on the CD?

With this new book in our best-selling MCSA and MCSE Study Guide series, we are including an array of training resources. The CD includes bonus exams and flashcards to help you study for the exam. We have also included the complete contents of the Study Guide in electronic form. The CD's resources are described in the following subsections.

The Sybex Ebook for Windows Server 2003 Network Security Administration

Many people like the convenience of being able to carry their whole Study Guide on a CD. They also like being able to search the text via computer to find specific information quickly and easily. For these reasons, the entire contents of this Study Guide are supplied in PDF on the CD. We've also included Adobe Acrobat Reader, which provides the interface for the PDF contents as well as the search capabilities.

The Sybex Test Engine

These are a collection of multiple-choice questions that will help you prepare for your exam. There are three sets of questions:

- Two bonus exams designed to simulate the actual live exam
- All the questions from the Study Guide, presented in a test engine for your review
- The Assessment Test

Here is a sample screen from the Sybex MCSE test engine:

Chapter Test: Chapter 1

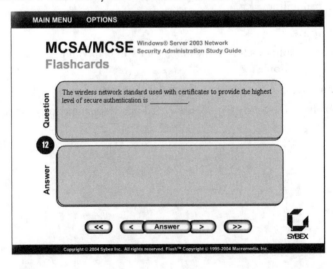

| ☐ Mark | Time Left: 1 hr 19 min(s) | Question: 8 of 20 |

You want to enforce a minimum password length of eight characters. You create a new Group Policy object, open the Account Polices node, and select the Minimum Password Length setting. What should you do after double-clicking this setting? (Choose all that apply.)

☐ **A.**   Click the Reset All Passwords To This Length check box.

☐ **B.**   Click the Define This Policy Setting In This Template check box.

☐ **C.**   Clear the Define This Policy Setting In This Template check box.

☐ **D.**   Clear the Reset All Passwords To This Length check box.

☐ **E.**   Select 8 as the number of characters for the minimum password length.

Your Answer:

(<) (>) (Show Answer)   (Finish) 🏠 (?)

Sybex Flashcards for PCs and Handheld Devices

The "flashcard" style of question is an effective way to quickly and efficiently test your understanding of the fundamental concepts covered in the exam. The Sybex Flashcards set consists of approximately 150 questions presented in a special engine developed specifically for this Study Guide series. Here's what the Sybex Flashcards interface looks like:

MAIN MENU   OPTIONS

MCSA/MCSE Windows® Server 2003 Network Security Administration Study Guide
Flashcards

Question

The wireless network standard used with certificates to provide the highest level of secure authentication is _____.

12

Answer

(<<) (<) (Answer) (>) (>>)

SYBEX

Contacts and Resources

To find out more about Microsoft Education and Certification materials and programs, to register with Prometric or VUE, or to obtain other useful certification information and additional study resources, check the following resources:

Microsoft Training and Certification Home Page

`www.microsoft.com/learning`

This website provides information about the MCP program and exams. You can also order the latest Microsoft Roadmap to Education and Certification.

Microsoft TechNet Technical Information Network

`www.microsoft.com/technet`

800-344-2121

Use this website or phone number to contact support professionals and system administrators. Outside the United States and Canada, contact your local Microsoft subsidiary for information.

Prometric

`www.prometric.com`

800-755-3936

Contact Prometric to register to take an MCP exam at any of more than 800 Prometric Testing Centers around the world.

Virtual University Enterprises (VUE)

`www.vue.com`

888-837-8616

Contact the VUE registration center to register to take an MCP exam at one of the VUE Testing Centers.

MCP Magazine Online

`www.mcpmag.com`

Microsoft Certified Professional Magazine is a well-respected publication that focuses on Windows certification. This site hosts chats and discussion forums and tracks news related to the MCSE program. Some of the services cost a fee, but they are well worth it.

Windows & .NET Magazine

`www.windows2000mag.com`

You can subscribe to this magazine or read free articles at the website. The study resource provides general information on Windows 2000, Windows XP, and Windows Server 2003.

Cramsession on Brainbuzz.com

`cramsession.brainbuzz.com`

Cramsession is an online community focusing on all IT certification programs. In addition to discussion boards and job locators, you can download one of several free cram sessions, which are nice supplements to any study approach that you take.

Assessment Test

1. A security template is _____.
   A. A method of applying security settings to a Group Policy
   B. A way to discover the current security settings
   C. A set of guidelines published by Microsoft for securing a server
   D. A physical layout of the server room's security system

2. A Group Policy contains which of the two following configuration settings?
   A. Network
   B. System
   C. User
   D. Computer

3. A limitation of L2TP/IPSec is _____.
   A. It is unable to traverse NAT implementations.
   B. It isn't as secure as PPTP.
   C. It works only with Windows XP Professional clients.
   D. It requires that Active Directory be in native mode.

4. Which of the following are EFS features in Windows XP Professional? (Choose all that apply.)
   A. Sharing EFS files with multiple users
   B. Encrypting offline files
   C. Using web folders for encrypted files
   D. Encryption without an enterprise certificate authority

5. Which of the following terms describes the process of tracking noteworthy events on your network?
   A. Process tracking
   B. Auditing
   C. Resource recovery
   D. Countermeasure

6. Which of the following is a popular Microsoft tool designed to secure an Internet Information Services (IIS) 5 website? (Choose all that apply.)
   A. URLScan
   B. IIS Lockdown
   C. Security Toolbox
   D. Snort

7. When you have confidence that a message could only have been sent by the person claiming to be the sender, you have _____.

   A. Nonrepudiation

   B. Integrity

   C. Confidentiality

   D. Anti-replay

8. Your co-worker states that he is still able to successfully use a certificate that was revoked yesterday. What is the most likely reason?

   A. A new CRL with the information for his certificate has not been published yet.

   B. The CRL distribution point (CDP) is offline.

   C. The revocation must still be in the pending requests folder on the CA.

   D. The CA's chain must be broken.

9. When you have confidence that a message has not been altered in transit, you have _____.

   A. Nonrepudiation

   B. Integrity

   C. Confidentiality

   D. Anti-replay

10. The Microsoft server software used with 802.1x to authenticate wireless users to your Active Directory is called _____.

   A. Kerberos Server

   B. Key Distribution Center (KDC)

   C. RADIUS Server

   D. Internet Authentication Server (IAS)

11. Which of the following operating systems support Kerberos v5? (Choose all that apply.)

   A. Windows 9x

   B. Windows 9x with the Directory Services client

   C. Windows NT 4 Workstation

   D. Windows 2000 Professional

12. The graphical tool used to determine which service packs and hotfixes are missing from a Windows Server 2003 computer is called _____.

   A. HFNetChk

   B. EventComb

   C. MBSA

   D. Server Monitor

13. The method of incorporating service pack updates into the base set of installation files is called _____.

    A. Service pack installation

    B. Hotfix installation

    C. Windows updates

    D. Slipstreaming

14. The method of ensuring that the latest service packs and hotfixes are automatically updated on all your Windows Server 2003 computers is called _____.

    A. Service pack installation

    B. Hotfix installation

    C. Slipstreaming

    D. Software Update Services

15. The process of inserting a digital signature into each packet is called _____.

    A. Slipstreaming

    B. Digital signing

    C. SMB signing

    D. Encryption

16. When a person sends a message as if they are another person, this process is called _____.

    A. Eavesdropping

    B. Impersonation

    C. Nonrepudiation

    D. Confidentiality

17. Another term for the network name in wireless networks is _____.

    A. Security set identifier (SSID)

    B. Wired Equivalent Privacy (WEP)

    C. Wireless access point (WAP)

    D. Beacon

18. Which of the following authentication methods can Windows 2000 Professional clients use? (Choose all that apply.)

    A. CHAP

    B. MS-CHAP

    C. MS-CHAPv2

    D. EAP

19. When the computer portion of a Group Policy is applied last, this process is called _____.

    A. Reverse Policy Assignment

    B. Loopback

    C. Missing Policy Assignment

    D. Impersonation

20. Before data can be securely exchanged between two computers, what must be accomplished?

    A. Negotiation of a common dialect

    B. Negotiation of a session key

    C. Negotiation of the window size

    D. Negotiation of a security association

21. A limitation of PPTP is _____.

    A. It is Microsoft-specific.

    B. It isn't as secure as L2TP/IPSec.

    C. It works only with Windows XP Professional clients.

    D. It requires server and client certificates.

22. When an encrypted packet is sent to an endpoint, it is said to be in _____.

    A. Tunnel mode

    B. Transport mode

    C. Mixed mode

    D. Native mode

23. Which two of the following are methods to test an IPSec policy assignment?

    A. Net View

    B. PING

    C. Telnet

    D. IPSec Monitor

    E. Network Monitor

    F. MBSA

24. A warning message in the System Log indicates that _____.

    A. An event of no importance has occurred. You can safely ignore the message.

    B. An event of importance has occurred. You should investigate.

    C. A serious catastrophe has occurred. You should shut down the servers and plan on being fired.

    D. Without knowing a warning message's contents, you cannot discern if it is important or not.

25. Secure Sockets Layer (SSL) can be used with which of the following technologies? (Choose all that apply.)

    A. SMTP

    B. HTTP

    C. FTP

    D. IMAP4

26. A certificate contains which of the following pieces of information? (Choose all that apply.)

    A. Expiration date

    B. Issuing certificate authority name

    C. Length of the key

    D. CRL publication interval

27. If you want to audit access to objects that exist in the configuration partition, you should enable _____.

    A. Directory Services auditing

    B. Object Access auditing

    C. Process auditing

    D. Logon auditing

28. To view the packets that have passed between two computers, which of the following tools should you use?

    A. Systems Management Server

    B. Microsoft Security Baseline Analyzer

    C. Network Monitor

    D. IPSec Monitor

29. To summarize a group of Application Logs across multiple Windows Server 2003–based computers, which of the following tools should you use?

    A. MSBA

    B. Network Monitor

    C. IPSec Monitor

    D. EventComb

30. The physical address of a network device is referred to as its _____ address.

 A. Media access control (MAC)

 B. Security set identifier (SSID)

 C. Host name

 D. NetBIOS name

31. Which of the following are user certificate types? (Choose all that apply.)

 A. EFS

 B. S/MIME

 C. Computer

 D. IPSEC

32. Wired equivalent privacy (WEP) can be broken using new technologies and is being replaced by _____.

 A. Pre-Shared Key mode (PSK)

 B. Wi-Fi protected access (WPA)

 C. Media access control (MAC) filtering

 D. Security set identifier (SSID) beaconing

33. You need to deploy 802.1x authentication for your wireless network. Which of the following are required to support 802.1x authentication? (Choose all that apply.)

 A. Windows XP Professional clients

 B. Active Directory

 C. RADIUS

 D. 802.11g wireless access points

34. Public key cryptography uses which kind of keys?

 A. Symmetric keys

 B. Asymmetric keys

 C. Shared secret keys

 D. Pairs of shared secret keys

35. A wireless access point (WAP) that is deployed on your network by unauthorized personnel is often called a _____.

 A. User deployed WLAN (wireless local area network)

 B. Wi-Fi protected access (WPA) point

 C. User supported WAP

 D. Rogue WAP

Answers to Assessment Test

1. **A.** You can think of a template as having predetermined settings that can be applied to multiple objects, either at the same time or at different times. You can use a template to build a Group Policy. Only answer A matches the purpose and use of a template. For more information, see Chapter 1.

2. **C, D.** When you take a long step back from Windows Server 2003 you'll find that there are really two parts to a GPO: one for the computer and the other for the user. For more information, see Chapter 1.

3. **A.** L2TP is unable to work through NAT. For more information, see Chapter 8.

4. **A, B, C.** Windows XP Professional offers some improvements on EFS from Windows 2000 Professional, including sharing EFS-encrypted files, encrypting offline files cached on a laptop, using web folders for storing encrypted files, using 3DES, and the ability to reset passwords without breaking EFS by using a special reset disk. For more information, see Chapter 10.

5. **B.** Auditing is the process by which you define the kinds of events that you want to display in the Security Log. Process tracking is one type of event that can be audited. For more information, see Chapter 11.

6. **A, B.** You use the IIS Lockdown tool to configure IIS to work with only some types of requests based on the type of website that you want to lock down. This tool is rather useful and is popular too. URLScan runs as part of IIS Lockdown. For more information, see Chapter 2.

7. **A.** Nonrepudiation describes the assurance that the person who claims they sent the message is the same person who actually sent the message. Although similar, the terms in the other answers really have different foci. For more information, see Chapter 9.

8. **A.** If the CRL does not list his certificate as being revoked, the certificate is assumed to be good. The next time the CRL is published, the certificate will be on it, and it will no longer work. For more information, see Chapter 9.

9. **B.** Unlike nonrepudiation, which assures that the sender really sent the message, integrity assures that the message itself has not been altered in transit. It is important to have integrity so that you know that the message received was the same as the message sent. For more information, see Chapter 9.

10. **D.** IAS works with your wireless users to ensure that they can be authenticated to Active Directory. Although your server may use Kerberos as the authentication protocol, the point that wireless users interact with is the IAS. For more information, see Chapter 2.

11. **D.** Only Windows 2000 and later support Kerberos authentication. For more information, see Chapter 7.

12. **C.** Microsoft Baseline Security Analyzer is the graphical equivalent to HFNetChk. MBSA does more than just identify computer missing service packs and hotfixes. MBSA also scans computers for known vulnerabilities. For more information, see Chapter 3.

13. D.   None of the other answers deal with service pack file incorporation into the source install files. Slipstreaming is a method for ensuring that the latest version of each file is installed the first time, and it eliminates the need to install a service pack after the initial operating system installation. For more information, see Chapter 3.

14. D.   This free software—Software Update Services (SUS)—is designed to ensure that your servers and workstations are kept up-to-date with the latest hotfix installations. Employing this tool helps you close known vulnerabilities quickly. For more information, see Chapter 3.

15. C.   Although digital signatures can sign an entire message as a single package, SMB signing signs each packet while it is in transit between two points. This type of signature gives added security and assures nonrepudiation. For more information, see Chapter 4.

16. B.   Impersonation is the process of acting and looking like another person on the network. Successful impersonation damages nonrepudiation. For more information, see Chapter 9.

17. A.   The SSID is used by wireless access points to identify different wireless networks. For more information, see Chapter 5.

18. A, B, C, D.   Windows 2000 Professional supports all of these authentication methods. For more information, see Chapter 7.

19. B.   Loopback is the process of ensuring that the computer portion of a GPO that would not have been assigned based on the user's logged-in security context is still assigned. This usually happens in the context of having multiple GPOs assigned or inherited by a given object in the folder. For more information, see Chapter 1.

20. D.   A security association (SA) is the term used to describe the process of two computers negotiating all the aspects of security so that they can talk to each other. The other three answers are all part of the SA negotiations. For more information, see Chapter 4.

21. B.   L2TP is more secure than PPTP. For more information, see Chapter 8.

22. A.   You'll see these two terms—*tunnel mode* and *transport mode*—on the exam. Just remember that in tunnel mode the packet is encrypted all the way to its final destination endpoint. In transport mode, this is not the case. For more information, see Chapter 4.

23. B, D.   How do you know that an IPSec policy assignment is really working? You can use either PING (Packet Internet Groper) or IPSec Monitor. For more information, see Chapter 4.

24. B.   Check event logs every day. Warning messages can be especially problematic if they are difficult to troubleshoot. Although you can skim past the blue information icons, be sure to stop and read the warning and error messages. For more information, see Chapter 11.

25. A, B, D.   SSL can be used with SMTP, HTTP, and IMAP4 to secure these protocols. For more information, see Chapter 6.

26. A, B, C.   Certificates do not list the CRL publication interval because it can be changed on the CA well after certificates have been issued. For more information, see Chapter 9.

27. A.   Directory Services auditing audits events related to objects in Active Directory. Object Access auditing can refer to objects outside AD such as a printer. For more information, see Chapter 11.

28. C.   Network Monitor is Microsoft's sniffer. It can capture packets that flow on the network line for later analysis. For more information, see Chapter 11.

29. D.   EventComb is the tool used to coalesce multiple log entries. For more information, see Chapter 11.

30. A.   The MAC address of network devices is a combination of a manufacturer identifier and a manufacturer-assigned address that is supposed to be unique among all other network devices. For more information, see Chapter 5.

31. A, B.   EFS and S/MIME are user certificate templates and are stored in the user profile. For more information, see Chapter 10.

32. B.   WPA is considered a replacement for WEP. WPA provides encryption for wireless networks that is not susceptible to the same attacks as WEP. For more information, see Chapter 5.

33. A, B, C.   802.1x authentication requires Windows XP Professional client operating systems, a Windows Active Directory domain, a certificate authority to issue certificates, a RADIUS server, and remote access policies. For more information, see Chapter 5.

34. A.   Public/private keys use asymmetric keys. When one key is used to encrypt, the other key is used to decrypt. For example, if you send an e-mail to somebody encrypted with their public key, they use their private key (the matching one of the pair) to decrypt the e-mail. For more information, see Chapter 6.

35. D.   Unauthorized wireless access points are often called rogue access points. These devices can cause considerable problems with existing wireless networks and are considered security risks. For more information, see Chapter 5.

Chapter 1

Configuring, Deploying, and Troubleshooting Security Templates

THE MICROSOFT EXAM OBJECTIVES COVERED IN THIS CHAPTER:

✓ **Plan security templates based on computer role. Computer roles include SQL Server computer, Microsoft Exchange Server computer, domain controller, Internet Authentication Service (IAS) server, and Internet Information Services (IIS) server.**

✓ **Configure security templates.**

  ▪ Configure registry and file system permissions.

  ▪ Configure account policies.

  ▪ Configure .pol files.

  ▪ Configure audit policies.

  ▪ Configure user rights assignment.

  ▪ Configure security options.

  ▪ Configure system services.

  ▪ Configure restricted groups.

  ▪ Configure event logs.

✓ **Deploy security templates.**

  ▪ Plan the deployment of security templates.

  ▪ Deploy security templates by using Active Directory–based Group Policy Objects (GPOs).

  ▪ Deploy security templates by using command-line tools and scripting.

✓ **Troubleshoot security template problems.**

- Troubleshoot security templates in a mixed operating system environment.
- Troubleshoot security policy inheritance.
- Troubleshoot removal of security template settings.

Windows Server 2003 provides a rich set of security features that enable administrators to secure information and activity on their Windows Server 2003–based networks. Through the use of Group Policy Objects (GPOs), you can push configurations out to each Windows-based machine on the network to help ensure network-wide security. You can quickly create GPOs to perform this task by applying a template. A template is a preconfigured set of values that can be used to create a GPO. Security templates are text-based .inf files that allow the administrator to create security configurations once and then apply those configurations to multiple servers. Templates also reduce the amount of administrative effort required to secure a group of Windows Server 2003 servers, Windows 2000 workstations and servers, and Windows XP Professional workstations. These templates are administered through the Microsoft Management Console (MMC) and are applied to multiple servers using one or more Group Policies.

Because this exam emphasizes the use of GPOs, we are going to spend some time going over how GPOs work and how you can deploy them effectively. We understand that this may be a review for many of you. If you are comfortable and confident in your GPO skills and depth of understanding, you can skip this section and start with the "Working with Security Templates" section later in this chapter.

This book jumps right in with the specific information you will need to pass the exam. If you need to get up to speed with the basics, try *Network Security JumpStart* by Matt Strebe (Sybex, 2002). For more information on general networking theory and concepts, try *Mastering Network Security, 2nd Edition* by Chris Brenton and Cameron Hunt (Sybex, 2002).

However, if you feel you need a refresher on Group Policies, read this section. You will need this information to do well on the exam and to better understand how to implement security in a Windows Server 2003 environment.

Group Policy Objects and Windows 2003 Server

Policies are not new to Microsoft products. Since the release of Windows 95, policies have been a way to ensure that Registry settings are configured correctly across multiple computers with a single administrative act. In previous versions of Windows, policies were difficult to configure and did not meet the needs of most businesses when they were configured. Policies did not address as many configurable settings in earlier versions.

You can use GPOs to define a user's work environment and then implement changes to that environment without the user needing to reboot their workstation. In almost every case, you can deploy a GPO without users even knowing that it has been deployed. The only way that users will know that there is a GPO deployed is if its settings conflict with a configuration that the user is trying to set. User and computer settings are defined once in a GPO, and then the object is used to push those settings out to the computers and user accounts you designate. Windows Server 2003 continually enforces the settings in the GPO. As updates to the settings in the GPO are configured, these updates are pushed out to the Windows Server 2003 and Windows XP Professional computers on your network.

 In addition to handling security concerns, you can use Group Policies to reduce lost productivity—which is often due to user error—by removing unnecessary programs and abilities that ship standard with the Windows Server 2003 platform. This also can lower the overall total cost of ownership (TCO).

GPOs are linked to a site, a domain, or an organizational unit (OU) container. When linked to a site or a domain container, GPOs allow you to centralize settings for an entire organization. When GPOs are linked to an OU container, you can apply different settings to different sets of user and/or computer accounts. In both cases, GPOs can be filtered to prevent some users and computers from having the GPO applied to them.

GPOs also ensure that users have the desktop environment necessary to perform their job effectively. You can configure settings to ensure that certain shortcuts, drive mappings, and other configurations exist whenever the user is logged on. Furthermore, you can automate software installations, negating the need to send a technician to the desktop to install or update software packages.

Corporate security and business policies can also be enforced through the use of GPOs. For example, you can ensure that security requirements for all users match the security required by corporate policy.

Configuring Group Policies

When a GPO is first opened, you'll find several types of settings that you can configure:

Administrative Templates   These are Registry-based settings for configuring application and user desktop environments. For example, these settings can be used to configure which shortcuts and objects will appear on the user's desktop environment. They can also be used to redirect the My Documents location to the user's home directory on a remote file server.

Security   Your choices here are local computer, domain, and network settings. These settings control user access to the network, account and audit policies, and user rights. For example, these settings can be used to configure the account policies, manage the event logs, and even manage client behavior when there are multiple wireless networks available to the client computer.

Software Installation   These settings centralize software management and deployment. Applications can be either published or assigned. Applications can also be deployed based upon security group memberships as well as to individuals.

Scripts   These settings specify when Windows computers run a specific script. Scripts can be run at four different times using GPOs:

- Computer startup: Startup scripts are run as the operating system boots up. All scripts will run, and when they are complete, the user will be prompted with the security window to press Ctrl+Alt+Delete.

- User logon: Logon scripts are run after the user submits their username and password to the network. Once all scripts have been completed, the user desktop appears and the user is able to start interacting with the interface.

- User logoff: Logoff scripts are run after the user has logged off the computer. Once all logoff scripts are complete, the computer will prompt the user with the security window to press Ctrl+Alt+Delete.

- Computer shutdown: Shutdown scripts are run when the computer is being shut down or restarted. Once the scripts and the other shutdown processes are complete, the user will be prompted with the "It is now safe to turn off your computer" message. If the computer has the proper power configuration components, it will automatically shut down and power itself off. If the user was restarting the computer, all shutdown scripts must run before the server will prompt for the power to turn off the power.

Remote Installation Services   These settings control the options available to users when running the Client Installation Wizard by Remote Installation Services (RIS). RIS can be configured with several options for client computer installations. For example, a client computer using RIS can automatically be supplied with a computer name or the user can be allowed to select their own computer name.

Internet Explorer Maintenance   These settings let you administer and customize Internet Explorer (IE) configurations on Windows Server 2003, Windows 2000, and Windows XP computers. IE can be configured for all users, or select network users, with a standard home page for the browser and standard favorites lists. GPOs can also be used to provide security configuration information and other important information such as the proxy settings.

Folder Redirection   These settings store specific user profile information and take a shared folder on a server and make it look like a local folder on the desktop of the computer. The Folder Redirection option in a GPO is very important, because now network users can be forced to use network storage locations instead of local storage locations on their computers. By forcing storage to centralized server locations, the data can be properly backed up and scanned for viruses on a regular basis. The data can be protected more efficiently if it is stored on a server.

Now, a GPO comprises two elements: the *Group Policy Container (GPC)* and the *Group Policy Template (GPT)*. The GPC is located in *Active Directory (AD)* and provides version information used by the domain controllers to discern which GPO is the most recent version. If a domain controller (DC) does not have the most recent version, it relies on replication with other DCs to obtain the latest GPO and thereby update its own GPC.

The GPT is a folder hierarchy in the shared `sysvol` folder on domain controllers. The GPT contains the settings that are applied to the computers on your network. Computers connect to the `sysvol` folder on the DC to read the settings in the GPT before applying them to their local Registry. The GPT is named after the Globally Unique Identifier (GUID) of the GPO. When the GPO is created, it is assigned a new GUID, and the GPT name is the GUID of the GPO.

Each GPO has two sets of configuration settings: one for computers and the other for users. This basic architecture has not changed since Windows 95, which used `user.dat` and `system.dat` as the basis for forming the policy file. This was also the case in Windows 98, but many additional configuration settings are available in Windows 2000 and Windows Server 2003.

The configuration settings for computers specify the following:

- Operating system behavior
- Desktop behavior
- Security settings
- Computer startup and shutdown scripts
- Application assignments, options, and settings

The configuration settings for users specify the following:

- Operating system behavior
- User-specific desktop settings
- User-specific security settings
- Assigned and published applications
- Folder redirection options
- User logon and logoff scripts

When a GPO is linked to a site, a domain, or an OU container, the user and computer accounts hosted in that object are affected by the policy. GPOs can be linked to more than one container such that the following statements are true:

- You can link one GPO to multiple sites, domains, and/or OUs.
- Linking at the site or domain level gives you centralized administrative abilities.
- Linking at the OU level decentralizes your administration, yet maintains uniformity for those objects affected by the GPO.
- You can link multiple GPOs to a single site, domain, and/or OU.
- Creating multiple GPOs allows you to easily administer each group of settings you want to apply.
- Link inheritance is maintained in AD; lower-level objects inherit the upper-level settings from a GPO. For example, all OUs in a domain inherit the settings of a GPO linked to the domain object.
- You cannot link GPOs to default AD containers, including the Users, Computers, and Builtin containers.

After a GPO is created, it is not required to be linked to an object. GPOs can simply be created and then linked later to the desired object when the GPO's settings are needed. In addition, when you work on GPOs from a domain controller, by default, you work in the memory space of the domain controller that has been assigned the Flexible Single Master Operations (FSMO) role of primary domain controller (PDC) emulator. The PDC emulator looks and feels like a PDC to Windows NT backup domain controllers (BDC) and Windows NT workstations. The FSMO role of PDC emulator is implemented for legacy compatibility purposes. You will use *Active Directory Users and Computers (ADUC)* to link a GPO to a domain or an OU. You will use *Active Directory Sites and Services (ADSS)* to link a GPO to a site. You must be a member of the Enterprise Admins security group to link a GPO to a site object.

 If you would like to learn more about the PDC and BDC roles in Windows NT 4.0, please consult *Mastering Windows NT Server 4, 7th Edition* by Mark Minasi (Sybex, 2000).

Applying Group Policies

To be successful in the real world, as well as on the exam, you'll need to understand how GPOs are applied in AD. GPO inheritance constitutes the order in which policies are applied. GPOs are first applied to the site container, then to the domain container, and then to the OU container. As policies are applied, they override the previous policy, meaning that a policy setting at the OU level overrides the policy setting at the domain level and policy settings at the domain level override policy settings at the site level. In other words, the most recently applied policy, the one that is applied last, has the greatest priority in setting the final configurations for objects hosting in the linked container.

However, bear in mind that inheritance is at work too. An OU could be inheriting multiple policies that have been linked to the site, domain, and upper-level OU objects. The policies are applied, even though no policy has been directly linked to the OU.

You'll also need to understand how GPOs are processed, which is different from how they are inherited or linked. When we talk about policies being processed, we are talking about the order in which policies are applied when multiple policies are linked to the same container. And because there are two parts to every GPO, it is important to understand which part of the GPO is processed first.

The computer settings of a GPO are processed and applied before the user settings. When the Windows computer processes computer settings, the startup scripts run. When a user logs on, the logon scripts are processed. The reverse happens when a user cleanly shuts down a workstation; logoff scripts run first, and then shutdown scripts run.

If multiple polices are linked to the same container, the default setting is to process all policies synchronously. You can change the processing of a GPO to asynchronous by using a Group Policy setting for both computers and users. In asynchronous processing, all policies are processed simultaneously using multiple threads. In synchronous processing, one policy must finish processing before the next policy can begin processing. Also in synchronous processing, the desktop for the user does not appear until all policies are processed and applied. If you decide to use asynchronous processing, you might possibly sacrifice reliability in each policy being enforced correctly system-wide. Best practice is to leave policy processing at the default of synchronous.

Windows Server 2003, Windows 2000, and Windows XP clients refresh their policies every 90 minutes with an additional, randomized offset of 30 minutes to ensure that the domain controller doesn't become overloaded with policy calls from clients in the same site. Domain controllers refresh every 5 minutes within the same site. Thus, new policy settings are applied more quickly to domain controllers than to workstations. Updates for domain controllers must be done quickly to make sure that new account policies and other security settings are implemented across the organization.

When multiple policies are applied to a single container, they are applied in the order listed in the Group Policy tab of the object's properties, from bottom to top. The GPO at the top of the list is applied last and thus can overwrite earlier settings; it has top priority in the application of the settings to the workstation or server. An exception occurs to the application priority when the most recent setting processed results in conflicts between the user and computer settings. In this case, the computer setting overrides the user settings.

 As long as there are no conflicts or overwrites during the application of multiple policies, the settings in all policies linked to a given container are cumulative for all objects that reside in that container.

Modifying Group Policy Inheritance

Policy inheritance is not absolute, however. Inheritance can be blocked and modified. You can prevent a child container from inheriting any GPOs from the parent containers by enabling Block Inheritance on the child container. Enabling Block Inheritance lets you set new policies for the child container. However, you need to bear the following in mind:

- You cannot selectively choose which GPOs to block. It is an all-or-nothing proposition.

- GPOs can be configured with the No Override setting, which means that the GPO is applied even if inheritance is blocked. You can use this setting to push down necessary settings even if an OU administrator doesn't like the settings. GPOs that represent critical, corporate-wide rules should have the No Override option enabled.

- The No Override option is really set on the link, not on the GPO itself. Thus, if you have a GPO that is linked to multiple containers, you can configure the No Override option on each container and gain administrative flexibility to decide to which containers the GPO will always be applied.

If you want to block some GPOs on a child container but apply others, the best practice is to block inheritance and then create new links on the child container to the desired GPOs.

You can also link a GPO to a container and then filter the application of the GPO to certain objects within the container. By default, for any given container, the GPO settings are applied to all objects within the container. However, you might not want this. You might want certain objects not to inherit the settings. Well, you can control or filter the application of those settings by using the *Discretionary Access Control List (DACL)* in the properties of the objects you want to filter.

You can modify the default permissions in three ways:

- You can explicitly deny the Apply Group Policy permission for the group that contains the user or computer account for whom you want to filter.

- You can remove Authenticated Users *Access Control Entry (ACE)* from the DACL. When you do so, Authenticated Users have no explicit permission on the GPO. However, if you remove Authenticated Users, you will need to create a security group for the other accounts in the container to whom the GPO should apply and then use that group account in place of the Authenticated Users security group account.

- You can use Windows Management Instrumentation (WMI) filters to identify which users or computers will receive the GPO. WMI filters can be created and then imported to any number of GPOs. Because WMI filters are so powerful, there are many different conditions that can be part of the query. For example, a GPO can be used to install a new application. The application, though, might require a certain service pack level. With WMI filtering, WMI can determine which computers have the appropriate service pack and then allow the GPO to be applied to just those computers.

You can also set a Loopback processing mode, which essentially ensures that the computer GPO is applied last rather than the user GPO. This setting might be useful if applications that are assigned to a user should not be automatically available on a server. Hence, you use the Loopback processing mode to ensure that the computer portion of the GPO is applied last.

Now that we've reviewed GPOs, we'll look at security administrative templates for much of the rest of this chapter. Templates are a collection of settings that modify the Registry on the target computer. You use administrative templates to configure user and computer Registry-based settings that control the user's desktop environment. Specifically, the template settings modify the HKEY_LOCAL_MACHINE and HKEY_CURRENT_USER Registry trees.

Microsoft provides a number of preconfigured templates for security purposes that we will discuss in detail. It is important to understand what these templates do and their purposes because they will be a focus on this exam.

Working with Security Templates

You create and modify *security templates* using the Security Template snap-in of the MMC. The way to access the templates is to create a new MMC and add the security template to the new MMC. Follow these steps:

1. Choose Start ➢ Run to open the Run dialog box.

2. In the Open box, enter **mmc.exe** to run a new MMC.

3. Choose File ➢ Add/Remove Snap-In to open the Add/Remove Snap-In dialog box.

4. Click the Add button to open the Add Standalone Snap-In dialog box, shown in Figure 1.1, and select Security Templates from the list of snap-ins.

5. Click Add to add the snap-in to the MMC, and then click Close to close the Add Standalone Snap-In dialog box.

6. Click OK in the Add/Remove Snap-In dialog box to add Security Templates to the new MMC, as shown in Figure 1.2.

FIGURE 1.1   The Add Standalone Snap-In dialog box

FIGURE 1.2   The Security Templates snap-in added to a new MMC

You'll notice in the Security Templates MMC that the templates reside (by default) in the C:\WINNT\Security\Templates folder. If you were to look at this folder, you'd see a listing of .inf files that you can easily open in any text editor. What the Security Templates snap-in really does is provide a graphic front end to what would be a taxing task of modifying these .inf files.

If you select any template in the left pane of the MMC, you'll see seven objects in the right pane, as shown in Figure 1.3. You might remember seeing some of these objects before as nodes in a GPO.

FIGURE 1.3 The seven objects that can be secured in a Windows Server 2003 security template

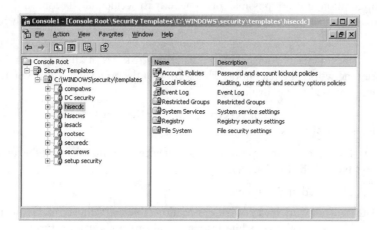

Here is an explanation of each of these objects:

Account Policies This area covers a cluster of policies that pertain to user accounts. Even account policies are specified at the domain level; domain controllers receive their account policies settings from the domain controller OU. Account policies include the following three individual policies:

Password policy With this policy, you can set restrictions on password length, age, uniqueness, and complexity.

Account lockout policy With this policy, you set the rules for account lockout, including duration and method of releasing the account after it has been locked out.

Kerberos policy This policy governs such settings as the ticket lifetime and the maximum tolerance for computer time differences.

Local Policies This object includes a cluster of policies that focus on auditing local and/or network access to the server. *How* events are audited is also included in this policy. This template includes the following three policies:

Auditing policy This policy specifies which events are recorded for later reference.

User rights policy With this object, you specify rights for user accounts and security groups. For example, with the Add Workstations To A Domain User right, users can add new computers to the domain without administrator intervention.

Security options policy This policy holds a wide-ranging set of configurable values, including the logon banner and SMB (Server Message Block) signing. Other important settings in this section allow renaming the guest account and renaming the administrator account.

Event Log This object contains configurable options on how the application, security, and system event logs behave. In particular, it specifies how large the logs can become, whether they can be overwritten automatically, and how long the logs should be maintained online.

Restricted Groups   This setting allows the administrator to define membership in the built-in security groups or other administrator-defined security groups that are given elevated privileges. With proper configuration, it is not possible for somebody to accidentally become a domain administrator group member or for an existing domain administrator to be accidentally removed from the group.

System Services   This policy lets you specify the security attributes of all system services, including file, print, network, and telephone. This section of the policy will allow you to define which services are supposed to run or not run.

Registry   This object contains the security settings for your Registry keys and lets you set auditing values and access permissions.

File System   This object allows for the configuration of access permissions and the auditing of specific folders and files on the local server.

Two facts should be noted at this point:

- These templates will not work on a FAT (file allocation table) partition, so make sure that you are running NTFS (New Technology File System) on all partitions on the server that you want to secure.

- Never deploy these templates on production systems without first testing them in a lab environment. Unintended access or denials can occur if you don't first test these templates on an offline server to observe their effects.

The names of the .inf files might appear confusing at first, but after you work with them for a while, they'll make more sense. Let's now take a look at each template type and the .inf files that are included in each type.

Default Security Templates

Microsoft has some predefined templates that you can use as is or customize to meet your specific needs. Some of these templates only modify existing templates, and others install an entire set of values on the computer.

The security templates provide Windows Server 2003, Windows 2000, and Windows XP settings for workstations, servers, and domain controllers. You can use these templates to reverse unwanted behavior that is a result of a customized template being applied. You can also use these templates to apply an initial set of security values to any computer that has been installed or upgraded to Windows Server 2003. These templates contain settings for the following areas as well as for others:

- Account policies
- Local policies
- Event log maintenance
- Basic permissions for system services
- Access permissions for files

These policies do not include configuration values for user rights assignments so that these policies will not overwrite any assignments made by an installed application. Because the members of the Windows Server 2003 Users group have stricter permissions than members of the Windows NT Users group, Windows NT applications that are not certified for Windows Server 2003 may not run under the security context of the Windows Server 2003 Users group. You can fix this by doing one of the following:

- Add all user accounts to the Power Users group (not recommended for most security environments due to the added permissions enjoyed by the Power Users group).
- Apply the compatible security template (`compatws.inf`).
- Upgrade the application to be Windows Server 2003 certified.

Each of these security templates can also be applied to Windows 2000 family products. It is possible that there are some settings that are available in the templates that do not exist in Windows 2000 products. In these cases, the Windows 2000 computer will not be able to enforce those particular settings.

Incremental Templates

Windows Server 2003 ships with several templates that modify only existing security settings. When working with these templates, you'll need to first have a default template applied. These templates include only modifications. They do not include the default settings, and they elevate security settings from the default settings found in the default templates.

Secure templates   Two templates fall into this area: `securews` (workstations and servers) and `securedc` (domain controllers). These templates provide increased security for the operating system. Resources secured by permissions are not covered in these templates. These templates do remove members of the Power Users group from the DACL on resources.

High security templates   The `hisecws` (workstation and server) and `hisecdc` (domain controller) templates increase security for parameters that affect network protocols such as SMB Signing. Use this template only in pure Windows Server 2003, Windows 2000, and Windows XP environments; applying this template will likely degrade the performance of your servers. Moreover, this template removes the Terminal Server Security Identifier (TS SID) from your system and removes members from the Power Users group and gives them permissions similar to that for the Users group.

Compatible template   This template (`compatws`) is for workstations and servers. Because the permissions for the Users group in Windows Server 2003 were tightened, you might need to "loosen" them just a bit to allow older applications to run on your servers and workstations. This template makes these applications "compatible" with the Windows Server 2003 and Windows XP operating systems so that these older applications can run as they did under older operating systems.

Other templates   You might run across a few other templates that provide a specific function. First, the `setup security` template resets all values to default, which means that you'll be taking your server or workstation back to the state it was in when first installed.

The `rootsec` template is used to secure the system root on a Windows Server 2003 Professional computer. The `DC security` template is used to reset all values to their defaults on domain controllers.

Configuring Templates

You can select numerous options in each section to increase security on your systems. However, because it would be of little value to discuss each and every one in detail, we'll discuss at a high level how you configure each area.

Account Policies

To modify any of the account policies settings, expand the Account Policies settings node inside the Group Policy that you want to configure. Beneath this node, you'll see three policies that you can configure: password, account lockout, and Kerberos. When you select a policy, the actual settings appear in the right pane (see Figure 1.4).

To configure an individual setting, double-click it in the right pane to open a dialog box that is specific to that setting. However, you'll also be given the choice to either enable or disable the setting by selecting or clearing the Define This Policy Setting In The Template check box. In Figure 1.5, you can see that a minimum password length of seven characters is being enforced.

FIGURE 1.4   Individual security policy settings under the Account Policies node

FIGURE 1.5   The individual policy setting dialog box for setting a minimum password length

Once you define the setting and click OK, the MMC displays the new configuration in the Computer Setting column in the right pane (see Figure 1.6).

FIGURE 1.6   The results of the new minimum password setting displayed in the Computer Setting column in the Security Templates MMC

In Exercise 1.1, you will configure an account policy.

EXERCISE 1.1

Configuring an Account Policy

1.   Open the Active Directory Users And Computers MMC.

2.   Open the properties of the domain or OU that you wish to apply the account policy against.

3.   Click the Group Policy tab.

4.   Click Edit to open the Group Policy dialog box.

5.   Navigate to the Account Policies section of the Group Policy.

6.   Make your configuration changes in either the Password or Account Lockout policy or both.

7.   Close the Group Policy dialog box.

8.   Click OK to close the Properties dialog box.

.pol Files

Down-level client operating systems—including Windows NT 4.0 and Windows 9x operating systems—use `.pol` files to maintain their profile information. Windows 9x clients use a `config.pol` file, and Windows NT 4.0 clients use an `ntconfig.pol` file. The two `.pol` files are not the same and cannot be interchanged.

The `.pol` file is used to store information such as which shortcuts appear on the Desktop and which applications appear in the Start menu. The `.pol` file also provides control for access to Control Panel and the command prompt, restricting access for the user to certain settings such as the Desktop wallpaper, among many others.

The `.pol` files are created using the System Policy Editor that matches each operating system. The `.pol` files can also be copied from the client machine and hosted on domain controllers to provide support for roaming users that benefit from having their profile available to them, no matter which computer they use. Of course, the Windows 9x profile is available only to Windows 9x clients, and the Windows NT 4.0 profile is available only to Windows NT 4.0 clients.

Once the `.pol` files have been created, they are placed in the NETLOGON share point (`c:\winnt\system32\repl\import\scripts`) on the primary domain controller (PDC). They are replicated from the PDC to all backup domain controllers (BDCs) so that the user can access the `.pol` file, no matter which server logs them in. However, in Windows Server 2003, there is no BDC, so you need to configure the replication from the domain controller (DC) hosting the PDC emulator role to all other domain controllers.

Audit Policies

Auditing is both a proactive and reactive security measure. It informs administrators of events that might be potentially dangerous and leaves a trail of accountability that can be referenced in the future. By default, all auditing is turned off; if you want to use this feature, you'll need to turn it on. The easiest way to do this is through a security template that is applied to all your servers.

Before you can configure a template for auditing, you must first plan your audit policy. The following categories are available for auditing:

- Account logon events
- Account management
- Directory service access
- Logon events
- Object access
- Policy change
- Privilege use
- Process tracking
- System events

On non–domain controller computers, you'll use either Computer Management or a GPO to enable auditing on the local machine. On a domain controller, you'll use a Group Policy to edit the audit policy.

When developing your audit policy, you'll need to account for three elements:

- Who will be audited
- Whether to audit failed events, successful events, or both
- What type of object access will be audited

When you want to audit an individual resource such as a folder or printer, you'll need to enable object access auditing on the computer hosting the resource. Then you'll need to go to the resource's Properties dialog box and enable auditing there as well. Hence, when auditing for object access, there is always a two-step process that doesn't exist with other event categories.

The results of your auditing policy are displayed in the Security Event Log. This log displays detailed information about the chosen events.

 The "Event Logs" section of this chapter discusses how to use security templates to configure the behavior of all logs on your Windows Server 2003 servers, Windows 2000–based servers, and Windows 2000 and Windows XP Professional workstations.

The auditing options are as follows:

Audit account logon events   Tracks events related to user logon and logoff activity system-wide. Events are recorded on the domain controllers in your domain even if they occur on member servers or workstations.

Audit account management   Tracks account management actions in Active Directory Users And Computers. Any time that a user, a computer, or a group account is created, modified, or deleted, an event can be generated and placed in the log file.

Audit directory service access   Tracks access to Active Directory by users or computers. You will need to configure the object's properties to audit either success or failed events.

Audit logon events   This is the same as Windows NT's Logon and Logoff audit category. User logon and logoff activities are recorded in the local server's logs. This policy records only activity for the local server to which the policy is applied.

Audit object access   Tracks access to objects on non–domain controllers. You will need to configure the object's properties to audit either success or failed events.

Audit policy change   Tracks changes to user rights, auditing, and trust relationships.

Audit privilege use   Tracks the use of user rights and privileges, such as when a user shuts down a server.

> The audit privilege use policy does not track the following user rights: bypass traverse checking, debug programs, create a token object, replace process-level token, generate security audits, back up files and folders, and restore files and folders. If you want to track backup and restore activities, you'll need to override this default behavior by enabling Audit Use Of Backup and Restore Privilege under the Security node nested inside the Local Policies node.

Audit process tracking   Tracks each process running on the server and the resources that it uses.

Audit system events   Tracks system events such as startup, shutdown, and restart. It also tracks actions that affect system security or changes to the security log.

To turn on auditing, navigate to the desired template, drill down to the Audit Policy node as shown in Figure 1.7, and make your selections.

FIGURE 1.7   Audit log selections for a security template

To enable auditing for object access, you'll need to access the folder or file properties directly and enable it. To do so, follow these steps:

1. Open the object's Properties dialog box.

2. Click the Security tab.

3. Click the Advanced button to open the object's Access Control Settings dialog box, as shown in Figure 1.8.

4. Click the Auditing tab, click Add, select the accounts that you want to audit, and then click OK.

In the Auditing Entry For *name_of_object* dialog box (see Figure 1.9), you can select exactly which actions you want to audit and how to apply your selections. The information in the Auditing Entry dialog box will depend on the object, because the auditing options are different for folders, files, and printers.

You have two other options that you can use to specify the objects to which your auditing policy should be applied. At the bottom of the Auditing Entry dialog box, you'll see an Apply These Auditing Entries To Objects And/Or Containers Within This Container Only check box. Select this check box to specify that the auditing policy you are implementing be applied only to objects that reside within the target container (or folder).

At the bottom of the Auditing tab in the Access Control Settings dialog box, you can push down the auditing configurations you've selected to all child objects of the target object you are configuring by selecting the Replace Auditing Entries On All Child Objects With Entries Shown Here That Apply To Child Objects check box.

Selecting this check box does not override settings on individual child folders after the values have been applied. For example, if you have a parent folder named `Payroll` and a subfolder named `ShopWorkers`, you can set auditing on both folders by making your configuration choices on the `Payroll` folder and then selecting the Replace Auditing Entries On All Child Objects With Entries Shown Here That Apply To Child Objects check box. Thereafter, if you make further selections on the `ShopWorkers` folder, you'll find that those choices will be added to the settings being pushed down from the `Payroll` folder.

FIGURE 1.8   The Access Control Settings dialog box, open at the Auditing tab

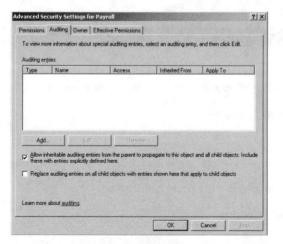

FIGURE 1.9   Selecting auditing options for a folder

You can also block auditing inheritance from parent objects by clearing the Allow Inheritable Auditing Entries From The Parent To Propagate To This Object And All Child Objects check box. This allows you to either copy or remove the current auditing policies and create a new set of policies for an individual folder or for a new hierarchy of folders. However, this can be overridden by selecting the Replace Auditing Entries On All Child Objects With Entries Shown Here That Apply To Child Objects check box on a parent folder.

To enable auditing for an Active Directory object, you'll need to access the object in Active Directory Users And Computers and open the object's Properties dialog box. From there, create a new Group Policy and create your audit policy for that object. If necessary, you can block policy inheritance so that you can create a new, fresh policy on an individual AD object.

In Exercise 1.2, you will configure an audit policy.

EXERCISE 1.2

Configuring an Audit Policy

1.   Select a target container upon which to configure the audit policy, such as an OU.

2.   Open the container's Properties dialog box.

3.   Click the Group Policy tab.

4.   Highlight the Group Policy that you want to use and click Edit to open the Group Policy.

5.   Navigate to the Audit Policy node under the Local Policies node.

6.   Double-click an individual policy setting.

7. Click the Define These Policy Settings check box.

8. Make your configuration choices.

9. Click OK to close the Policy Settings dialog box.

10. Close the Group Policy dialog box by selecting Close from the Group Policy menu.

11. Click OK to close the container's Properties dialog box.

User Rights Assignment

You use the User Rights Assignment node to assign user and/or group rights to perform activities on the network (see Figure 1.10). To configure user rights, select the User Rights Assignment node and then double-click the right that you want to configure in the right pane. Select the Define The Policy Settings In The Template check box, and then add the users and/or groups to the setting. Click OK to display the new settings next to the right in the Computer Setting column in the right pane.

In Exercise 1.3, you will configure a user rights policy.

EXERCISE 1.3

Configuring a User Rights Policy

1. Select a target container upon which to configure the user rights, such as an OU.

2. Open the container's Properties dialog box.

3. Click the Group Policy tab.

4. Select the Group Policy that you want to use and click Edit. This will open the Group Policy.

5. Navigate to the User Rights Assignments node under the Local Policies node.

6. Double-click an individual policy setting.

7. Click the Define These Policy Settings check box.

8. Click Add to open the Add User Or Group input box. Select the user and/or group accounts that you want to apply this policy setting to by clicking the Browse button. This will open the Select Users Or Groups box.

9. Click OK to close the Select Users Or Groups box after making your selection.

10. Click OK to close the User And Group Names box.

11. Click OK to close the policy setting.

12. Close the Group Policy dialog box by selecting Close from the Group Policy menu.

13. Click OK to close the container's Properties dialog box.

FIGURE 1.10   The User Rights Assignment node and settings in the Security Templates console

Security Options

The Security Options node provides many options to strengthen security on your network. The options are too numerous to list here, but some of the highlights include the following:

- Do Not Display Last Username In Logon Screen

- Automatically Logoff Users When Logon Time Expires

- Message Text For Users Attempting To Logon

- Force Communications Between Servers To Be Digitally Signed

You set options in this node in the same way that you assign user rights.

In Exercise 1.4, you will configure the last logged-on username so that it does not appear in the Logon dialog box. This practice is highly encouraged on production networks. After all, an intruder only needs only two pieces of information to break into most networks: a valid user account and the password. By leaving the logged-on username configured in the default setting, an intruder will be able to acquire a valid username with very little effort.

EXERCISE 1.4

Configuring the Last Logged-On Username So That It Doesn't Appear in the Logon Dialog Box

1.   Select a target container upon which to configure the account policy. In this example, you'll select the domain object.

2.   Open the container's Properties dialog box.

3.   Click the Group Policy tab.

4. Select the Group Policy that you want to use and click Edit to open the Group Policy.

5. Navigate to the Security Options node under the Local Policies node.

6. Double-click Do Not Display Last Logged On Username In Logon Screen policy setting to open this policy setting.

7. Select the Define This Policy Setting check box.

8. Make your desired configuration choices.

9. Click OK to close the policy setting.

10. Close the Group Policy dialog box by selecting Close from the Group Policy menu.

11. Click OK to close the container's Properties dialog box.

System Services

You use the System Services node to configure the startup and access control settings for each of the system services such as the Server service, Workstation server, DHCP (Dynamic Host Configuration Protocol) server, and so forth.

Setting a system service policy can be both useful and destructive. Make sure that the services configured in your template don't conflict with any of the roles that your servers or workstations are performing.

To configure a system service setting, select the System Services node in the left pane (see Figure 1.11). Double-click the target service in the right pane. Click the Define This Policy In The Template check box to open the security dialog box for this service. Edit the security as needed and then select the startup mode for the service. Click OK to configure a policy for a system service.

FIGURE 1.11   The System Services node in the Security Template console

In Exercise 1.5, you will configure a policy for a system service.

Configuring a System Service Security and Startup Policy

1. Select a target container upon which to configure the account policy, such as an OU.

2. Open the container's Properties dialog box.

3. Click the Group Policy tab.

4. Select the Group Policy that you want to use and click Edit to open the Group Policy.

5. Navigate to the System Services node under the Security Settings node.

6. Double-click an individual security policy setting.

7. Select the Define These Policy Settings check box. The Security tab for this setting will automatically appear.

8. Make your configurations by clicking the Browse button to add user and/or group accounts from the Select Users, Groups Or Computers dialog box. If you are happy with the Everyone Group as the only choice, then you need not click the Add or Remove buttons. Once you've made your selections, they will appear on the Security tab of the service. Click OK to close the Security tab.

9. Select the Service Startup Mode that you need for this service and click OK to close the policy setting.

10. Close the Group Policy dialog box by selecting Close from the Group Policy menu.

11. Click OK to close the container's Properties dialog box.

Registry and File System Permissions

You use the Registry node to configure both access control entries and auditing values for specific Registry keys. To modify the Registry settings, first select the Registry node in the left pane. Some templates may not display anything in the right pane, but those that can modify the Registry entries will display a list of Registry settings in the right pane. The hisecdc template does not show the registry settings (see Figure 1.12). Use the compatws template, for example, to show the registry settings.

In the left pane, right-click Registry and then select Add Key and browse the registry to the section you would like to select. Click OK. Verify that the security settings are appropriate and click OK again. In the Add Object window, you can configure the settings for the new permissions for that Registry key (see Figure 1.13). From here, you can configure the key and then do the following:

- Add permissions to existing permissions on the key and subkeys.

- Replace existing permissions on all subkeys.

You can also select to not allow permissions to be replaced on this key. This selection is most helpful *after* the desired permissions have been applied to the key or if you want to essentially block permission inheritance on a particular key.

To change the permissions on the key, click the Edit Security button and make your selection.

If you right-click the Registry node, you can add a key and then configure permissions on that individual key. By designating individual keys, you can set and then block permissions for an individual key in the Registry and ensure that those permissions will persist after other settings have been applied.

File system permissions work exactly the same way as described for the Registry permission settings, except you will be working on file and folder hierarchies and not on Registry keys. The look and feel of the dialog boxes is the same under the File System node as it is for the Registry node.

FIGURE 1.12   The Registry node in the Security Templates console

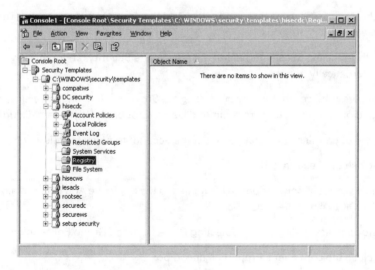

FIGURE 1.13   The Add Object dialog box

In Exercise 1.6, you will configure a Registry setting for a security policy.

EXERCISE 1.6

Configuring a Registry Setting Policy

1. Select a target container upon which to configure the Registry setting, such as a domain.

2. Open the container's Properties dialog box.

3. Click the Group Policy tab.

4. Select the Group Policy that you want to use and click Edit to open the Group Policy.

5. Navigate to the Registry Settings node under the Security Settings node.

6. Right-click the Registry Settings node and select Add Key from the context menu. This will open the Select Registry Key box.

7. Select a key from the list to be entered into the policy. The Security tab for this key's properties will automatically appear.

8. Make your security choices for this key by clicking the Browse button on the Security tab to select user and/or group accounts from the Add Users, Groups Or Computers dialog box.

9. Select the type of permission(s) that you want the account to enjoy for this key.

10. Click OK to close the Security tab.

11. Configure how you want permissions to be applied to the key in the Add Object dialog box and then click OK to close the dialog box.

12. Close the Group Policy dialog box by selecting Close from the Group Policy menu.

13. Click OK to close the container's Properties dialog box.

Restricted Groups

You use the Restricted Groups node to define who should and should not belong to a specific group. When a template with a restricted Group Policy is applied to a system, the Security Configuration Tool Set adds and deletes members from specified groups to ensure that the actual group membership coincides with the settings defined in the template.

For example, you might want to add the Enterprise Admins to all Domain Admins security groups or to add the Domain Admins group to all Local Administrators groups on your workstations and servers.

To create a restricted Group Policy, right-click the Restricted Groups node and choose Add Group from the shortcut menu. Select the group that you want to modify by either entering the group's name or browsing to find and select the group. Then click OK.

You'll see the group in the right pane. Right-click the group and select Security from the shortcut menu to open the Configure Membership tab, as shown in Figure 1.14. You can configure the membership of this group or configure the groups of which this group will be a member. Make your choices about membership and then click OK. The group membership policy will now be set.

 Real World Scenario

Using Security Policies to Configure Settings for DNS Dynamic Updates

You have decided that you want to prevent your Windows XP and 2000 Professional workstations from registering an A (host) and PTR (pointer) record with your DNS (Domain Name Service) server. You'd like to rely on your Domain Host Configuration Protocol (DHCP) server to perform the registrations for your workstations. How would you go about this?

Well, the way to do this is to configure the following Registry key on each workstation:

HKLM\System\CurrentControlSet\Services\Tcpip\Parameters\DisableDynamicUpdate

How would you configure this Registry key network-wide? Create a GPO and apply it to the OU that hosts your workstations. Modify the GPO to include this registry key. Wait two hours to ensure that the Registry key has been applied to all your workstations. Thereafter, when the workstations reboot, the DHCP server will register their DNS settings.

FIGURE 1.14   The Configure Membership tab

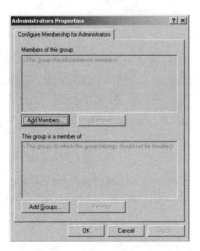

In Exercise 1.7, you will add the Domain Administrators Global Security group to a new security group that you have created. For this exercise to work properly, you'll first need to create a new security group.

EXERCISE 1.7

Adding the Domain Administrators Global Security Group to a New Security Group That You Have Created

1. Select a target container upon which to configure the account policy, usually a domain container.

2. Open the container's Properties dialog box.

3. Click the Group Policy tab.

4. Select the Group Policy that you want to use and click Edit to open the Group Policy.

5. Navigate to the Restricted Groups node.

6. Right-click the Restricted Groups node and choose Add Group from the shortcut menu to open the Add Group box. Click the Browse button to open the Select Groups box and select the Domain Administrators Security Global Group.

7. Click OK to close the Select Groups box.

8. Click OK to close the Add Group box.

9. Right-click the Domain Administrators group in the right pane of the Group Policy and select Security from the context menu to open the Configure Membership For Guests dialog box.

10. In the This Group Is A Member Of section, click Add to display the Group Membership box. If you don't know the name of the group that you wish to use, click Browse to display the Select Group selection box and select the group from this box.

11. Click OK to close the Select Groups box.

12. Click OK to close the Group membership box.

13. Click OK to close the Configure Membership box.

14. Close the Group Policy dialog box by selecting Close from the Group Policy menu.

15. Click OK to close the container's Properties dialog box.

Event Logs

The settings for the event logs are configured under a common policy, regardless of the log type. As you can see in Figure 1.15, you can set the log size, guest access, the log retention period, and other options unique to log files in Windows Server 2003, Windows 2000 Server and Professional, and Windows XP Professional. To change the configurations on these settings, simply double-click the setting in the right pane and make your configuration choices. Changing these settings works the same as it does for account and local polices, described earlier in this chapter.

FIGURE 1.15   Event log settings in the Security Template console

Deploying Security Templates

After you configure your security templates to your requirements, you'll need to deploy them. This section describes two ways to do so, using group policies and using scripts.

Using Group Policies to Deploy Templates

The best way to deploy security templates is to use a GPO. As mentioned earlier in this chapter, a GPO is a collection of policy settings that is applied in a uniform manner across a set of objects. You can import security templates into a GPO and then apply that GPO to a site, a domain, or an OU.

If you need to apply security settings to one or more Windows Server 2003 computers in a workgroup setting, the only way to do so is to use a local policy template and apply it to the local system directly. Use this method when you are in a workgroup environment, when your Windows Server 2003 server is on a non-Microsoft network, or when no Active Directory is present.

The effective policy applied to a Windows Server 2003, Windows 2000, and Windows XP computer is really the culmination of several policies applied in a particular order. The policies on a Windows 2000 computer are processed in the following order:

1. Local policy of the computer
2. Policies applied at the site level
3. Policies applied at the domain level

4. Policies applied at the parent OU level

5. Policies applied at the child OU level

The policy applied last takes precedence. Hence, policies processed at the local OU level override any policy settings defined at other levels. The only exception to this is domain controllers, whose account policy settings defined in the default domain controller's policy override any account policy setting from other GPOs. Hence, domain controllers use the account policies defined in the default domain controller's policy regardless of the account policies set on the domain.

To assign a GPO to a container in Active Directory, follow these steps:

1. Navigate to the container and open its Properties dialog box.

2. Click the Group Policy tab then click Edit to open the Group Policy.

3. Navigate to the Security Settings node and then right-click the node and select Import Policy from the shortcut menu (see Figure 1.16) to open the Import Policy From selection box.

4. Select the template that you wish to import and click Open. You will be returned to the group policy focused on the Security Settings node.

5. Select Close from the Group Policy menu. You've just applied a template to multiple computers using a GPO.

Remember that domain controllers update their GPO assignments every 5 minutes, whereas servers and workstations update every 90 minutes, with a random offset of 30 minutes.

FIGURE 1.16   Selecting Import Policy from the shortcut menu

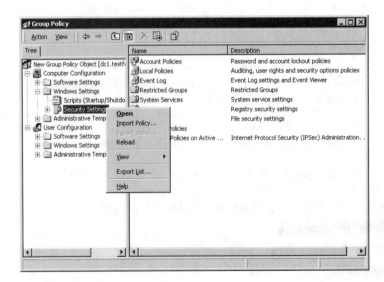

To import a policy template for an individual server, use the Local Security Policy console on the Administrative Tools menu.

Using Scripts to Deploy Templates

You can also use the command-line version of the *Security Configuration and Analysis tool (secedit.exe)* to deploy security templates. Specifically, you use `secedit /configure` to apply a stored template to one or more computers. Here are the switches and what they mean:

/db filename Use this switch, which is required, to specify the location of the database file that you want to use. The database referred to here is one that is created using the Security Configuration and Analysis tool (SCA). We'll discuss how to do this shortly.

/cfg filename This switch can only be used in conjunction with the /db switch. Use this switch to import a template into an existing database.

/overwrite This switch can only be used when the /cfg switch is used. This switch specifies whether the template in the /cfg switch should be appended to current settings or whether the template should overwrite current settings in the selected database. If you don't use this switch, the template settings are appended to the current settings.

/areas area1, area2 Use this switch to specify which security areas should be applied with this command. If you don't use this switch, you apply all the areas of the template. Separate area designations using a single space. Here are the area names and their meanings:

SECURITYPOLICY Apply the local and domain policies.

GROUP_MGMT Apply Restricted Group settings.

USER_RIGHTS Apply User Logon Rights settings.

REGKEYS Apply Registry settings.

FILESTORE Apply File System settings.

SERVICES Apply System Services settings.

/logpath Use this switch to specify the path and name of the log file in which you want to record the results of this command.

/verbose Use this switch if you want to know everything there is to know about the progress of your command and how it is working or not working.

/Quiet This switch suppresses both screen and log file output.

If this is the first time you're applying the template to one or more computers, your database is named `basic.sdb`, and the path to the database is `x:\securitydbs`, use this syntax:

```
Secedit /configure /db x:\securitydbs\basic.sdb
```

If this is not the first time you're applying the template to one or more computers, and you want to use a new template to overwrite the existing configurations in basic.sdb, and the new template file is named highsecurity.inf, use this syntax:

```
Secedit /configure /db x:\securitydbs\basic.sdb /cfg
f:emplates\highsecurity.inf /overwrite
```

To create a new database in the SCA tool, follow these steps:

1. Create a new MMC with the SCA snap-in.

2. Open the snap-in.

3. Right-click Security Configuration And Analysis and choose Open Database from the shortcut menu to open the Open Database dialog box.

4. In the File Name box, enter a name for the database. The example in Figure 1.17 named the new database HighSecurity.

5. Click Open to open the Import Template dialog box, as shown in Figure 1.18.

FIGURE 1.17   The Open Database dialog box

FIGURE 1.18   Associating the hisecdc template with the HighSecurity database

6. Select the template to apply to the database (in this example, the `hisecdc` template is selected) and then click Open again.

7. By default, the database is saved in the `My Documents\security` folder of the user account under which you are logged on when the database is created. You can, of course, move the database to another location for easier path administration when using the `secedit` command.

Troubleshooting Security Templates

When troubleshooting security settings, you need to understand which GPO has been applied and at what level that GPO resides. You can determine where a GPO has been applied in the overall folder structure in two ways: look at each site, domain, and OU container or use the `gpresult` resource kit utility. Let's look at each technique briefly.

If you want to know which objects a particular GPO has been assigned to, open the Properties dialog box of the GPO in either Active Directory Users And Computers or Active Directory Sites And Services. This dialog box has three tabs: General, Links, and Security. On the Links tab, click Find Now to find all the objects to which this GPO has been explicitly applied. Containers that are inheriting the GPO will not appear on this list.

The `gpresult` resource kit is a command-line tool that quickly runs through Active Directory and displays the results for your currently logged-on user account as well as the computer at which you are logged on. For your purposes, look to the end of this report and find all the GPOs that have been applied to this computer and user and what areas were affected (see Figure 1.19). Use this information to direct your efforts when troubleshooting the deployment of *security templates*.

FIGURE 1.19   The results of running the `gpresult` utility at the command prompt

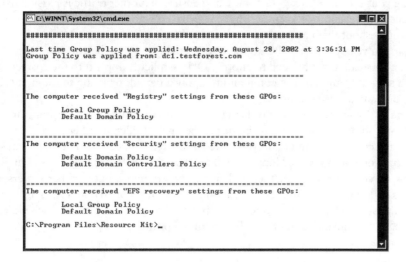

One of the most common scenarios when troubleshooting templates is that once applied, they don't do what you thought they would do. If this happens, bear in mind the following:

- Deleting the Group Policy will not remove the configurations.
- Appending a policy to current configurations will not remove the configurations.
- You will need to overwrite the configurations with the correct configurations.

To overwrite the configurations with a new policy, you can use the secedit command. A more labor-intensive method is to manually make the changes in the currently applied GPO. At this workstation, use the secedit /refresh command to force this new policy to be applied immediately. Either way, you'll need to somehow rewrite the settings that are amiss in your overall security configuration.

Troubleshooting Group Policy–Applied Templates

Not only do you need the skills necessary to apply security templates via GPOs or command-line tools, but you also need to know how to troubleshoot security templates when something doesn't work as expected.

This section covers some basic troubleshooting tips for GPOs and discusses the "gotchas" for applying GPOs in a mixed client environment and after a server's operating system has been upgraded to Windows Server 2003 from Windows NT 4.

A GPO can be applied incorrectly for a number of reasons, but they can be distilled into two common occurrences:

- Network problems are preventing the GPO from being applied.
- The policy was assigned to the wrong AD container and therefore is not being applied to the desired objects in AD.

First, eliminate all your network connectivity issues. Check DNS to ensure proper name resolution, ping your servers, check your cables, and ensure that other traffic is passing over your network. Check the event logs to ensure that there are no warning or stop error messages. If there are, troubleshoot them as needed.

Second, if you've applied the GPO to the wrong container—maybe you wanted to apply it to one OU and instead it was applied to another OU—explicitly apply it to the correct OU and then use the secedit /overwrite command to apply a default template to the first OU to remove the unwanted configurations.

If you find that your policies are not being applied after waiting an appropriate amount of time, use the secedit command to refresh the policies in the folder. In other words, if the policy is applied to the correct container and you have eliminated connectivity issues, perhaps the problem is that you haven't waited long enough for the policy to be applied on its own. Remember that domain controllers update their policies every 5 minutes, but member servers and workstations update every 90 minutes, with a randomized offset of 30 minutes. Hence, you may need to run the secedit command to force the policies to refresh before their scheduled interval. The secedit command is run from the command prompt.

Troubleshooting after Upgrading Operating Systems

Remember that Windows NT 4 policies will not migrate to Windows Server 2003 or Windows 2000, so any `*.pol` files that were created in your Windows NT 4 domain will not be migrated.

In addition, after you upgrade a Windows NT 4 server to Windows Server 2003, group policies are not automatically applied to that server. Hence, after upgrading a Windows NT 4 server to Windows Server 2003, apply the proper templates to the server to apply at least a baseline of values to the server.

Troubleshooting Mixed Client Environments

If you have a mix of Windows 9x, Windows NT, Windows 2000, and Windows XP clients on your network, pushing out security templates via group policies will not be easy. But you can enable a policy setting to allow the use of Windows NT 4–style policies for your legacy clients.

When configured this way, legacy clients will connect to the Netlogon share to find their `.pol` file and apply it during logon or logoff. However, if you change the policy, your legacy clients will need to log off and log back on to effect those changes right away. Unlike a Windows 2000 client that refreshes its policy settings every 90 minutes, legacy clients apply policies only during logon or logoff. This inefficient method can create some real headaches for administrators who might be more comfortable having their policy changes applied without client intervention.

If the new policies conflict with the old settings, some clients can be in conflict with others; for example, some clients can access a resource and others cannot.

The only real solution here is to adapt to the legacy clients and implement changes during times when you know your legacy clients will soon be logging off or on to the network.

Summary

This chapter started with an overview of Group Policies and then discussed what security templates are, how you can modify them, and how you can use them to update a GPO. You learned about the various security templates, including the basic and incremental templates. You also learned how to create a new template using the SCA tool, as well as how to troubleshoot templates.

You also learned that you can use the SCA tool to create new templates for GPOs. You saw how to use the `secedit` command-line utility to push out new policies to workstations and servers using customized templates.

This chapter also covered troubleshooting policies, which can be a bit tricky. The main thing to remember is that most problems occur from either applying the policy to the wrong container or configuring the wrong settings on the container. The best practice is to always apply a new template to an offline server first to observe the results of the policy before applying it to your production servers.

Exam Essentials

Know how to configure security templates.   Be sure that you understand which templates to use when configuring a new template. Be sure that you understand which templates write an entire set of configuration values and which ones merely write new information and assume that a base set of values is already in place.

Know the methods for deploying templates.   Be sure to understand that templates can be deployed in several different ways. You can deploy policies by importing them into an existing or a new Group Policy Object, or you can deploy them by using the `secedit /configure` command. You can use the `secedit` command to push out templates immediately. You can use a Group Policy to push out changes that don't need to be pushed out immediately.

Understand the potential hazards of working in mixed client environments.   Understand that you can enable the functionality of a Windows NT 4 policy in a Windows 2000 Server environment using a Group Policy. However, be aware of the timing differences between legacy systems and Windows 2000 Professional systems. Such differences can result in significant headaches when trying to reconfigure policies on your network.

Review Questions

1. You have 50 Windows 2000 Professional computers and four Windows 2000 domain controllers. Seven of your workstations are running an old application that has not been upgraded to be Windows 2000 compatible. You need to enable this application to run on those seven Windows 2000 Professional computers. What actions should you take? (Choose all that apply.)

   A. Apply the `basicws.inf` template. Modify the local policies to allow the application to run.

   B. Apply the `compatws.inf` template to the computers OU.

   C. Apply the `compatws.inf` template.

   D. Move the seven computers into their own OU and apply the `compatws.inf` template to this new OU.

2. You are developing a new security template to be used on all workstations in the engineering lab. You have been told that these computers must have the strongest security settings possible. Which template should you use as the starting point for your customer template?

   A. Use the `compatws.inf` template.

   B. Use the DC `security.inf` template.

   C. Use the `hisecdc.inf` template.

   D. Use the `hisecws.inf` template.

3. You imported the `hisecws.inf` template to all of your Windows XP and Windows 2000 Professional workstations. Ever since you imported this template, everyone who uses `ACT-T.exe` reports problems trying to run the application. ACT-T is a custom application written for use by Windows 95 clients. What should you do?

   A. Create a new Group Policy to apply security at the Local Policies level for all workstations that need to run the application.

   B. Create a new OU named ACT-T. Create a new Group Policy to apply the `hisecdc.inf` template to the new OU. Move all workstations that need to run the application to the new OU.

   C. Create a new OU named ACT-T. Create a new Group Policy to apply the `compatws.inf` template to the new OU. Move all workstations that need to run the application to the new OU.

   D. Convert the new application to work with Windows Terminal Server in Windows 2000 and then apply the `notssid.inf` template.

4. The Maximum Lifetime For User Ticket Renewal is an example of what kind of policy setting?

   A. Password

   B. Local

   C. Kerberos

   D. User Rights Assignment

   E. System Services

5. You have a new Windows Server 2003. On this server, you have an industry-specific application that needs a unique set of system rights applied. You have applied those rights correctly. Now you want to install a new security template. You decide to first apply the `hisecws.inf` template. What will be the result of this action on the permissions that you've created for your application?

   A. Permissions will be modified.

   B. Permissions will not be modified.

   C. Permissions will be retained.

   D. Permission will be overwritten.

6. You have a special legacy application that needs to run on your Windows Server 2003 server. You do not want to apply the `compatws.inf` template. What should you do?

   A. Add all the user accounts that need to use this application to the Power Users security group.

   B. Give the Everyone security group Write permissions to the Netlogon share.

   C. Give the Authenticated Users security group Read permissions to the `Sysvol` folder.

   D. Add all the user accounts that need to use this application to the Authenticated Users security group and then add this group to the Power Users security group.

7. You want to implement a high degree of security on three of your Windows Server 2003 member servers. Which template should you use?

   A. `hisecws.inf`

   B. `hisecdc.inf`

   C. `DC security.inf`

   D. `rootsec.inf`

8. You want to enforce a minimum password length of eight characters. You create a new Group Policy object, open the Account Polices node, and select the Minimum Password Length setting. What should you do after double-clicking this setting? (Choose all that apply.)

   A. Click the Reset All Passwords To This Length check box.

   B. Click the Define This Policy Setting In This Template check box.

   C. Clear the Define This Policy Setting In This Template check box.

   D. Clear the Reset All Passwords To This Length check box.

   E. Select 8 as the number of characters for the minimum password length.

9. You want to enable auditing on the company's payroll printer. You believe that a malicious user is attempting to use the printer to print bogus payroll checks. You want to find out who this user is before they are successful. What is the best way to do this? (Choose all that apply.)

   A. Enable failed logon events.

   B. Enable failed object access.

   C. Enable successful object access.

   D. Enable privilege use tracking.

   E. Audit the Authenticated Users security group in the printer's Properties dialog box.

   F. Audit the Power Users security group in the printer's Properties dialog box.

10. You need to audit all successful and failed logon attempts for 40 Windows Server 2003 member servers and 15 Windows Server 2003 domain controllers. Which option should you use to ensure that all servers are covered by your policy?

    A. Account Logon Events

    B. Account Management

    C. Directory Service Access

    D. Logon Events

    E. Privilege Use

11. You need to audit who is backing up and restoring files as part of a larger effort to track user activity on your network and ensure overall security. What action should you take?

    A. Audit Privilege Use.

    B. Audit Process Tracking.

    C. Enable Audit Use Of Backup And Restore Privilege under the Security node.

    D. Enable Audit Use Of Backup And Restore Privilege under the Local Policies node.

12. You have a folder named `Confidential Memos` that is accessed only by executives in your company. Inside this folder are two other folders: `Current Memos` and `Past Memos`. You need to ensure that auditing is set on all three folders and their files so that your manager can track who is accessing these folders and their contents. What actions should you take? (Choose all that apply.)

    A. Enable successful object access on the domain GPO.

    B. Enable Authenticated Users group in the Properties dialog box of the `Confidential Memos` folder.

    C. Select Reset Auditing Entries On All Child Objects in the `Confidential Memos` folder.

    D. Select Apply These Auditing Entries To Objects And/Or Containers Within This Container Only.

13. Your manager has told you that a new Authorized Users message must appear when users log on to your Windows Server 2003 network. Which node will you need to look inside to find the Message Text For Users Attempting To Logon setting?

    A. Local Policies

    B. User Rights Assignment

    C. System Services

    D. Security Options

14. You have opened the `hisecdc.inf` template in the Security Template snap-in. You attempt to modify a permission setting on a Registry value. You discover that the Registry entries are missing. What is the problem?

    A. You are working with a template that won't display the Registry entries.

    B. You are working with a corrupt template. Copy an uncorrupted version of the template from another Windows 2000 server.

    C. You need to refresh your view to display the Registry entries.

    D. You need to be logged on as a member of the Enterprise Administrators security group to see these Registry entries.

15. When applying an audit policy on your network, what part of the object is modified?

    A. The object's properties

    B. The object's System Access Control List

    C. The object's Discretionary Access Control List

    D. The object's advanced properties

16. Which of the following are methods for deploying a security template to one or more computers? (Choose all that apply.)

    A. Systems Management Server

    B. Group Policy Object

    C. `secedit /export`

    D. `secedit /configure`

17. In your site Group Policy, you selected to remove the Run command from the Start menu. In your computer's OU Group Policy, you deselected to have the Run command removed from the Start menu. In your domain Group Policy Object, you selected Not Defined for the Remove The Run Command From The Start Menu. What is the effective result of these three policies?

    A. The Run command will appear on the Start menu.

    B. The Run command will not appear on the Start menu.

    C. The Run command will appear but will be grayed out on the Start menu.

    D. The Run command will not appear on the Start menu but will be published in Add/Remove Programs in Control Panel.

18. You've just implemented a change to your domain security policy. The Group Policy is being applied to the domain controllers OU and is also linked to the computers OU. After 45 minutes, you discover that only a few of the Windows 2000 Professional workstations on your network have the new settings applied. What should you do?

A. Use the `secedit /export` command to force all the workstations to update with the new security settings.

B. Use the `secedit /configure` command to force all the workstations to update with the new security settings.

C. Reboot the PDC emulator, because this domain controller is the default domain controller on which all group policies are initially applied and modified. Rebooting the server will apply the Group Policy to all the machines on your network.

D. Do nothing. This is expected behavior.

19. You configured new account policy settings in the domain Group Policy Object. You find that it is not being applied to your Windows Server 2003–based computers on your network. You run the `secedit /refresh` command on each domain controller and wait two hours. Network connectivity issues are not preventing non-policy traffic from working on your network. The policy settings are still not being applied. What should you do?

A. Apply the account policy settings at the site level.

B. Make sure that you have saved the Group Policy settings correctly by rebooting your PDC emulator.

C. Apply the account policy settings at the domain controllers OU.

D. Ensure that you have refreshed all the workstations on your network by running the `secedit /refresh` command in their logon script. Have all users log off and log back on.

20. You have a user whom you have explicitly denied access to a folder on a Windows Server 2003 member server. How will Windows Server 2003 apply that configuration when the user attempts to open that folder? (Choose all that apply.)

A. By reading the SACL

B. By reading the DACL

C. By reading the ACL

D. By reading the Access Token

Answers to Review Questions

1. C, D. The compatws.inf template is written to "loosen" permissions on Windows 2000 computers and servers to allow older applications to work correctly. If you applied this template to the computers OU, all 50 computers would have their permissions loosened. Best practice is to move the seven computers to their own OU and have them apply the template to their own OU.

2. D. The hisecws.inf file is the most secure of the existing templates for use with workstations. The compatws template is the least secure. The DC security and the hisecdc templates are for domain controllers and are not meant to be used for workstations.

3. C. The best solution is to apply the compatws template to the workstations running the legacy application. Local Policies will be overwritten by GPOs; the hisecdc template is for domain controllers; and using Windows 2000 is not a good solution because it requires a new server and configuration of terminal services, which is cost prohibitive and actually means taking a step backward in operating systems.

4. C. The Kerberos protocol uses tickets, session tickets, ticket-granting tickets, and user tickets.

5. C. The default security templates do not include configuration values for user rights assignments, including rights assignments created by an application that is installed on Windows 2000 Server.

6. A. The Power Users group enjoys additional permissions that will allow a legacy application not written for Windows 2000 to run on the Windows 2000 platform.

7. A. Even though hisecws.inf may indicate that this is a template for workstations, it is also the template used for member servers (not domain controllers).

8. B, E. By default, all settings are not selected in a new GPO. Therefore, you first need to define the setting in the Group Policy template and then indicate the number of characters that you want to use in the setting.

9. B, E. Because you know that the user has not been successful at printing any checks, it would be better to see who is attempting to print to the printer unsuccessfully. Auditing the Authenticated Users group will include all users who have logged on to your domain.

10. A. This option tracks events related to user logon and logoff activity domain-wide, and the events are recorded on the domain controllers.

11. C. The Audit Privilege node does not track user activity related to backup and restore procedures. Therefore, under the Security node, you'll need to enable Audit Use Of Backup And Restore Privilege.

12. A, B, C. The last option is set only when you want to limit the scope of the policies being applied to the local container and its objects. If more folders are created under the Confidential Memos folder and you have this folder selected, these folders will not inherit the policy settings.

13. C. This node includes many options that you can select to strengthen security on your network.

14. A. Some templates won't display the Registry entries. If you need to configure permissions on Registry entries for a new policy template, you'll need to work with a template that will display these entries.

15. B. Auditing places entries in the System Access Control List.

16. B, D. You can use the Group Policy Object or the `secedit / configure` command to deploy a security template. The `secedit /export` command is used to export a security template stored in a security database to a stand-alone template. You can use Microsoft's Systems Management Server to deploy a `secedit` script, but that would be unnecessary.

17. A. The most local policy is applied last, and because the policy for the OU deselects this restriction, the Run command will appear.

18. D. The workstations are configured to update every 90 minutes, with a random offset of an additional 30 minutes. That the policy has not been applied after 45 minutes to most workstations is not a problem, and you should take no action.

19. C. Domain controllers receive their account policy settings only from the Group Policy object that is applied to the domain controllers OU. Your domain controllers will not recognize account policies applied at any other level or object.

20. B, D. The Windows 2000 operating system will find the explicitly denied access configuration in the discretionary portion of the ACL. The user's SID, which is found in the Access Token, will be compared to the list of SIDs in the DACL. If there is a match, the match will be enforced. Because the user has been denied access, the user's SID will be found at the top of the DACL and marked as Denied Access. The Local Security Services on the Windows 2000 server will enforce this setting first, meaning that all other settings in the ACL will be ignored.

Chapter

2

Configuring Security Based on Computer Roles

THE MICROSOFT EXAM OBJECTIVES COVERED IN THIS CHAPTER:

✓ **Configure additional security based on computer roles. Server computer roles include SQL Server computer, Exchange Server computer, domain controller, Internet Authentication Service (IAS) server, and Internet Information Services (IIS) server. Client computer roles include desktop, portable, and kiosk.**

- Plan and configure security settings.

- Plan network zones for computer roles.

- Plan and configure software restriction policies.

- Plan security for infrastructure services. Services include DHCP and DNS.

You can apply security templates to your servers all day long, but if you don't understand the unique needs of your servers, you'll miss some important configurations that should be set for these servers.

As part of this exam, you'll be expected to understand these needs and know how to tweak the configurations on these servers to ensure that they are as secure as reasonably possible. These server platforms include

- SQL Server
- Exchange Server
- Internet Information Services
- Windows domain controller
- Wireless client computers

This chapter also covers the security considerations for non-Windows clients.

Exam questions will probably incorporate this information into larger questions that will require you to integrate multiple server platforms into an overall security solution. So don't think you can skip this chapter. You'll find this information peppered throughout the exam.

The information on securing a domain controller can legitimately be applied to the other server roles discussed in this chapter. Hence, although items such as SMB signing are discussed in the "Windows Domain Controller Security" section, those items can be applied to other server roles as well.

SQL Server Security

Microsoft has released several versions of SQL Server in recent years. This section focuses on SQL Server 2000 (referred to as "SQL" in this chapter.)

SQL Server 2000 is based on the Windows security model. Therefore, a good understanding of the Windows security features is necessary to understanding how to secure SQL. However, SQL also has its own security features, which we'll discuss first. We'll then discuss how Windows security supports SQL security.

Security Features in SQL Server 2000

When installing SQL right out of the box, it is important to understand that the (default installation is extremely vulnerable) It is important to understand the security options available during installation and how they are affected by later Service Pack installations. SQL starts with an option to use one of two different authentication models:

- Windows Only—In Windows Only mode, only users who are authenticated via NT LAN Manager (NTLM) and have been granted access to SQL Server are allowed access to SQL Server. (Note: While it is possible for SQL 2000 to utilize Kerberos authentication, it is not configured by default and must be enabled with the SQL Server 2000 resource kit utility SETCERT.)

- (Windows and SQL Server (Mixed)—In Mixed mode, users can be authenticated via NTLM as in Windows Only or can supply a username and password that is validated by SQL Server. This mode is very vulnerable, because there is no account lockout policy within SQL Server and the passwords are stored with easily reversible encryption. There is a special account in SQL Server called SA (system administrator) that is granted all access to SQL Server functionality. It is possible for this account to be created with a blank password. As a matter of fact, it is the default configuration in previous versions of SQL Server. Due to the existence of this account and the fact that other accounts are stored with such simple encryption, it is highly recommended that this mode not be used unless absolutely necessary.

Once SQL is installed, it is vital that it be updated using the latest Service Pack available. Starting with Service Pack 3, SQL requires that the SA account password is not blank. The Service Pack application is vital because otherwise it is possible to have a blank password for the SA account. You should immediately be worried any time you are told that a blank password is the default. Because the SA is the most powerful of SQL accounts, it is vital that it is properly secured. It is very common that the password for the SA account is never set properly during installation, unless SQL is installed by a well-trained database administrator (DBA). The Windows NT Authentication mode uses the security context of the user for validation to a domain controller before allowing setup to continue. In Mixed mode, this does not happen.

The Windows NT Authentication mode can take advantage of the Kerberos authentication system in Windows 2000 and Windows Server 2003. A token is requested on behalf of the user for authentication to the SQL server. The SIDs (security identifiers) returned from the domain controller are checked against the `sysxlogins` master database. If a match is found, that match is enforced. If a match is not found, the user cannot log in to the SQL server. For user accounts created on the SQL server itself, the Windows NT Authentication mode allows for password expiration, auditing, account lockouts, and password attributes.

SQL secures the folders that it installs to allow access to only the SQL service accounts and the built-in Administrators group. In addition, the SQL Registry key (`HKLM\Software\Microsoft\MSSQLServer\MSSQLServer`) will have restricted access to only the service accounts for the SQL server that are selected during the setup process.

SQL also works with *Security Account Delegation* or *Delegation Authentication*, which is the ability to pass security credentials across multiple computers and applications on behalf of a user or a service account. This is a feature of Kerberos that is turned on by default in Windows. If a user has authenticated to ServerX and ServerX needs to access ServerY to fulfill a request by the client, ServerX requests a ticket on behalf of the client, and the client is authenticated on ServerY. This process is transparent to the user. This property is on all accounts in the folder, which can be turned on or off. NTLM does not support forwarding of credentials, but Kerberos does. This feature is thought to be a big improvement over Windows NT 4 Server and NTLM.

A word of caution is in order here when discussing Security Account Delegation. Essentially you are opening an impersonation of a user account via a service account. The decision to enable this feature should not be entered into lightly, because this opens a security hole in your organization. For example, a hacker could take control of a service account and then impersonate user accounts to perform malicious activities. While not easy to do, it is certainly not outside the realm of possibility either.

The SQL Server security model is a relatively simple model that makes heavy use of a concept known as ownership chaining. Objects in SQL Server databases are "owned" by database users, and the owner of any object is allowed to perform any action whatsoever on that object. (Permissions are never checked when an object owner accesses an object.) If the owner of object A creates another object that references object A (for example, a stored procedure accesses a database table), any user who has access to the new object need not have access to object A in order to use the new object. This is what is known as an unbroken ownership chain. This concept is not limited to a single database. For example, if a user has access to an object in Database A, and that object accesses a table in Database B, the user in Database A need not have any access whatsoever in Database B in order to access the object. This concept is known as cross-database ownership chaining. Starting with Service Pack 3, cross-database ownership chaining is turned off by default.

Windows Security and SQL Server

From a security standpoint, you'll probably want to turn off delegation by default and then enable it for certain service and user accounts. When delegation is turned on, you are enabling delegation for all services that run under the Local System account on the computer. If an unwary administrator installs an untrusted service on the computer and configures it to run as Local System, it too is going to be able to gain access to local and network resources while impersonating other users. A better practice is to configure services that use delegation to run under their own domain user accounts managed by domain administrators. Service accounts can be used to more effectively control the access of specific services running on a computer, especially when multiple services are running on the same computer.

To configure a user account for delegation, follow these steps:

1. In Active Directory Users And Computers, right-click User and choose Properties from the shortcut menu to open the Properties dialog box, which is shown in Figure 2.1.

2. Click the Account tab.

3. Notice in Figure 2.1 that the Account Is Sensitive And Cannot Be Delegated check box is cleared by default; it should remain that way.

4. Click OK.

FIGURE 2.1   The user's Properties dialog box, open at the Account tab

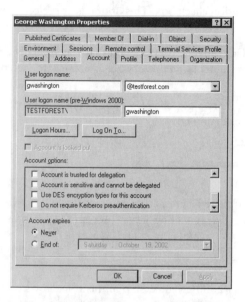

Now if this is a service account, you'll have an additional choice to make. The options you select depend on whether the service runs under a computer's Local System account or under its own domain user account. If the service is configured to run under the Local System account, the computer on which the service runs must be trusted for delegation. To configure this setting, follow these steps:

1.   In Active Directory Users And Computers, right-click the Computer object and choose Properties from the shortcut menu to open the Properties dialog box, shown in Figure 2.2.

FIGURE 2.2   A computer's Properties dialog box, open at the General tab

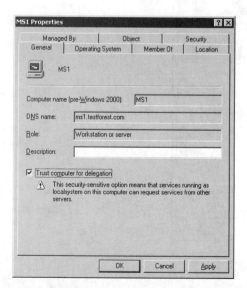

2. Click the General tab.

3. Click the Trust Computer For Delegation check box. This option is not selected by default.

4. Click OK.

If the service is configured to run under a separate user account that was specially created for the service, the user account of the service must be enabled to act as a delegate. To enable this account, follow these steps:

1. In Active Directory Users And Computers, right-click User and choose Properties from the shortcut menu to open the Properties dialog box.

2. Click the Account tab (see Figure 2.3).

3. Click the Account Is Trusted For Delegation check box.

4. Click OK.

If you have multiple SQL servers or if there is interaction between the SQL Server and another application on another server, consider enabling Service Account Delegation. Doing so will decrease response times to the user and create a better end-user experience.

The BulkAdmin Role

The BulkAdmin role is new in SQL Server 2000. Membership in this role allows users to load data from any file on the network or computer that can be accessed by the SQL service account. Do not add users to this role unless you are certain that they need it, because malicious users with this role can potentially corrupt large portions of a database by performing a bulk insert of bogus items.

FIGURE 2.3   The Properties dialog box for a service account, open at the Account tab

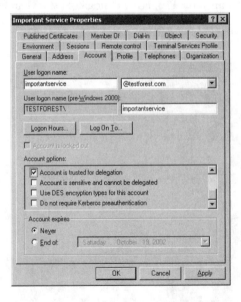

The Encrypting File System and SQL Server 2000

SQL Server 2000 works with the Windows operating system to protect data files via the *Encrypting File System (EFS)*. However, to use this correctly, you must assign an individual user account to the SQL Server 2000 service so that it doesn't run under the Local System account. Once you encrypt the account, if you need to change the service account for SQL Server 2000, you must first decrypt the files under the old service account, change the account, and then encrypt the files under the new service account.

Many DBAs recommend against implementing EFS because of its impact on performance. The encryption and decryption processes are CPU intensive, and they significantly slow down the performance of SQL servers. Also, keep in mind that physical security is vital when dealing with business databases, and that physical security needs to include backup and restore functions. If backups of the data can be removed from the premises, then the data is not secure.

Exchange Server Security

Most viruses enter a network through e-mail. This is why protection of your Exchange Server is so important, both from an external and an internal viewpoint. Exploitation of the SMTP (Simple Mail Transfer Protocol) service on an Exchange 2000 or Exchange Server 2003 server (or *any* SMTP server for that matter such as SMTP as a component of IIS) can lead to significant loss of production as well as exposure to liability should unwanted or offensive content arrive in a person's inbox.

Because each Exchange Server database is exposed via the *Exchange Installable File System (ExIFS* or just *IFS)*, each item in the store can be accessed both through a URL and through *server message blocks (SMBs)*. This means that folders in an Exchange Server store can be shared to users on the local network and accept mapped drive assignments. Moreover, this means that if you open the NetBIOS ports on your firewall (something that is *not* recommended), then hackers could have a direct line into your Exchange databases. In addition, every item in the database can be accessed through a browser over port 80 using a service known as *Outlook Web Access (OWA)*.

Like SQL, Exchange also takes advantage of the Active Directory user and group accounts. Each item in the store, whether in a mailbox or a public folder, can be secured using regular NTFS (New Technology File System) permissions. What this means is that items found in a public folder can be filtered using NTFS permissions so that only those users who have explicit access to the item can access it. In fact, the ability to select who can *view* an item is also available to an Exchange Server administrator.

Securing the SMTP Service

The SMTP service is the most important service to secure. Port 25 is one of the most often attacked ports by hackers; hence, it is important to ensure that you have taken steps to guard inbound and outbound e-mail. SMTP is attacked by sending unsolicited commercial e-mail

(UCE), which puts an extra load on the server similar to a denial of service (DoS) attack. SMTP can also be attacked by using unsecured SMTP servers as relay servers. UCE can be bounced off of unsecured SMTP servers and sent to other recipients outside of the organization. Not only does relaying UCE cause an additional load on the SMTP server, it can also lead to unsecured SMTP servers being placed on block lists so that other SMTP servers will not accept messages, even if they are valid business messages.

In most organizations, sexual harassment policies forbid certain types of conduct and conversation. These policies can be violated by pornographic spam arriving in a user's inbox. The exposure to liability for an employer in this instance is real in that it causes an uncomfortable work environment. It is also bad for business in that it places extra messages in everyone's mailboxes, which increases the size of mailboxes and increases the work of individuals who need to clean out unwanted e-mail. To ensure that this does not become a problem, install content scanning and anti-spam filters on your SMTP gateway server that will block e-mail messages based on their content both in the subject line and in the body of the message. Also, make sure that no other SMTP server in the organization can be used to send or receive e-mail between the organization and the Internet. You can make sure that rogue SMTP servers are unable to communicate with the Internet by configuring the firewall and external routers to send all inbound port 25 traffic to the SMTP gateway server (or other protected servers running content scanning and spam-filtering software) and configuring the firewall and external routers to accept outbound port 25 traffic only from the SMTP gateway server.

In addition, e-mail messages should be scanned for viruses before they arrive in a user's inbox. Always ensure that antivirus scanning is turned on and is updating its definitions on a regular basis. The combination of content scanning, spam filtering, and virus scanning will help ensure that your e-mail arrives clean of unwanted content and viruses.

> Many third-party content and virus-scanning products are available for Exchange 2000 and Exchange Server 2003. You can find more information at www.msexchange.org.

Securing Outlook Web Access

You can secure OWA in two ways: by using a front-end server and by using *Secure Socket Layer (SSL)*.

In Exchange 2000 and Exchange Server 2003, you can place front-end Exchange servers in your *DMZ (de-militarized zone)* and transfer user calls for content from their inbox or a public folder to back-end database servers sitting inside your firewalls. This architecture provides a couple of benefits. First, users don't connect directly to the back-end database servers. Their calls for information are proxied to the back-end servers by the front-end servers. Because the front-end servers do not have any databases sitting on them, this architecture is more secure. For instance, you can require users to use SSL to connect to the front-end server and then require *IPSec (Internet Protocol Security)* to connect to the back-end server using an internal username and password from your local domain controller. If the front-end servers are brought down by a malicious user, you've really lost nothing (other than HTTP [Hypertext Transfer Protocol] access) because the databases sit on the back-end server.

The term *DMZ* is often replaced with secured subnet, screened subnet, or partitioned subnet in some documentation. In all cases, these terms refer to the use of firewalls to provide a certain level or protection for computers that reside in the network segment defined by the firewalls.

Second, the front-end/back-end (FE/BE) architecture allows you to expose your entire Exchange Server deployment under a single name, IP address, and port number combination. Essentially, this hides your internal Exchange Server layout while providing services to your users through OWA. Securing OWA with SSL will protect all OWA traffic from external malicious users who attempt to listen in on e-mail messages.

Securing Outlook Web Access, URLScan, and IIS Lockdown

You can also "lock down" your OWA website using the URLScan and IIS Lockdown tools. The advantage of doing this is that because OWA runs inside IIS, these tools can treat OWA as another website. These tools are explained in detail in the "IIS 5 Server Security" and "IIS 6 Server Security" sections later in this chapter.

Securing Public Folder Information

Items held in public folders are secured using NTFS file permissions. When it comes to securing information in a public folder, consider using these permissions to lock down folders and/or files that should be viewed and read only by certain individuals or groups. For instance, if you have ten items in a public folder and you want Sue to view only five of them, remove Sue from the permissions on the other five folders. This should result in Sue being able to see only the five remaining items.

Windows Domain Controller Security

Because Windows domain controllers (DCs) perform authentication and other network services, it is important to understand the actions you can take to secure a domain controller. Remember that implementing a security solution is always a tradeoff between security and ease of use. The more secure a resource is, the more difficult it is to use that resource. Good security usually means limited ease of use. The challenge to every security architect is to find a balance between the two.

Domain controllers are vital to networking services that allow member servers and network clients to operate efficiently. One of the first tasks when securing a domain controller is to find out who the DC is talking to and who is talking to it.

Using Digital Signatures for Communication

If you want to ensure that the Windows DC is talking only to those servers and clients that are a part of the domain, you can require that network traffic be digitally signed (called *SMB signing*) for both servers and clients before a DC will accept an incoming transmission. Implementing digital signing helps to prevent impersonation of clients and servers or "man-in-the-middle" attacks. When enabled, SMB packet signing is required, meaning that a digital signature is placed in each packet and must be verified by both the client and the server before data transfer can occur.

If you require servers to have their communication digitally signed but you don't at least enable this setting on the clients, no data transfer can occur. To require digital signing between servers and clients, apply a Group Policy to the Domain Controller OU in Active Directory Users And Computers. (See Figure 2.4, where these various options are illustrated.) Be sure to enable Digitally Sign Client Communication (Always) and Digitally Sign Server Communication (Always). You will also need to do this on the OU or OUs that are hosting the client workstation accounts. Of course, for signing to work properly, you will need certificate services running on your network, and all servers and workstations will need to obtain a certificate from the certificate authority. The settings for implementing digital signing are spread out between domain member, Microsoft network client, and Microsoft network server.

FIGURE 2.4   Apply a Group Policy to the Domain Controller OU in Active Directory Users And Computers.

When SMB signing is implemented, you'll experience a performance overhead of up to 15 percent in order to sign and verify each packet between the client and server. This extra overhead can cause serious performance problems for some systems and cause users to complain about the performance of their workstations.

Securing DNS Updates

A second way to secure a Windows domain controller is to require secure updates to your DNS (Domain Name System) records if you are running Active Directory–integrated DNS zones. When a client or a server then attempts to update the DNS records in Active Directory, a security session must first be established based on security tokens between the client and the server:

1. The client generates the initial token and sends it to the server.

2. The server processes the token and, if necessary, returns a subsequent token to the client.

3. This negotiation continues until it is complete and a security context has been established.

The security context has a finite lifetime during which it can be used to create and verify the transaction signature on messages between the two parties. The lifetime depends on the protocol being used. In Windows 2000 and Windows Server 2003, the lifetime is equal to the maximum service ticket lifetime—any time greater than 10 minutes and less than the maximum user ticket lifetime; the default is 10 hours.

Restricting Anonymous Access

Windows 2000 and Windows Server 2003 allow anonymous users to perform certain activities on the network such as enumerating names of domain accounts and network shares. You might decide that such enumeration without authentication represents a security risk. To mitigate this risk, configure the Network Access: Do Not Allow Anonymous Enumeration Of SAM Accounts, and the Network Access: Do Not Allow Anonymous Enumeration Of SAM Accounts And Shares. When these options are configured, Anonymous user accounts will be able to access only resources to which they have been granted explicit permissions. Specifically, the Do Not Allow Anonymous Enumeration Of SAM Accounts removes the Everyone group and replaces it with the Authenticated users group.

To configure this setting, you'll need to use a Group Policy that is applied at the domain level. As you can see in Figures 2.5 and 2.6, these settings are actually configured under the Network Access section.

To configure these settings, follow these steps:

1. Double-click the Network Access: Do Not Allow Anonymous Enumeration Of SAM Accounts setting to open the Security Policy Setting dialog box.

FIGURE 2.5 Additional Restrictions For Anonymous Connections policy under the Security Options node

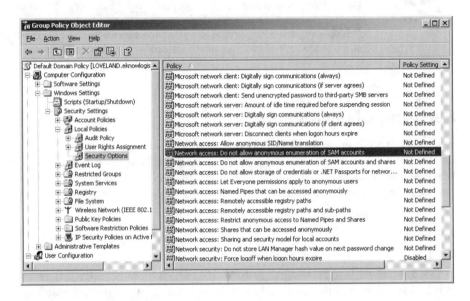

FIGURE 2.6 Configuring the No Access Without Explicit Anonymous Permissions policy setting

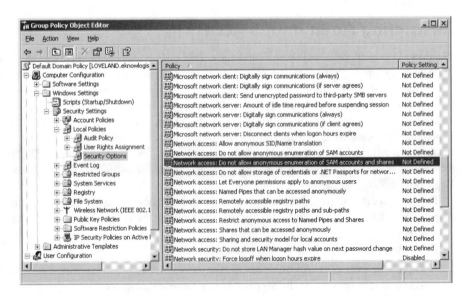

2. Check the Define This Policy Setting check box.

3. Select the radio button Enabled to configure the option. Click OK.

4. Double-click the Network Access: Do Not Allow Anonymous Enumeration Of SAM Accounts And Shares setting to open the Security Policy Setting dialog box.

5. Check the Define This Policy Setting check box.

6. Select the radio button Enabled to configure the option. Click OK.

7. Click File and Exit to close the Group Policy Object Editor window.

Once configured, these policy changes require that Anonymous accounts be granted explicit permissions to a resource before the resource can be exposed to the account.

Enabling NTLMv2 for Legacy Clients

If you are running a mixed-client environment with Windows NT 4 and/or Windows 9*x* workstations, you can force these clients to use the NTLMv2 authentication protocol instead of the older NTLM protocol. Remember that these clients cannot authenticate using Kerberos, so forcing NTLMv2 is the best you'll get.

The difference between NTLMv2 and NTLM is that v2 introduces a secure channel that protects the authentication process, whereas NTLM does not. To enable NTLMv2, you'll need to install Service Pack 4 or later on the Windows NT workstations and install the Directory Service Client on the Windows 9*x* workstations.

Hardening the TCP/IP Stack

You can help prevent successful *denial of service (DoS)* attacks by hardening the TCP/IP (Transmission Control Protocol/Internet Protocol) stack on any server that is connected to the Internet. You modify the Registry to harden the stack. You will perform this work under the `HKLM\System\CurrentControlSet\Services\Tcpip\Parameters` key. Each key mentioned here will be added as a subkey to this key. All keys discussed here are DWORD type keys.

    Be sure to back up the Registry before making any changes.

- The `SynAttackProtect` key allows you to configure TCP/IP to time out more quickly in the event of a SYN attack. Zero (0) is the default setting, and two (2) is the highest setting. Two is the recommended setting.

- The `EnableDeadGWDetect` Registry key allows TCP to perform dead gateway detection. With this setting enabled, TCP may ask IP to find another gateway to use if the current selected gateway is experiencing problems. This is a True/False setting, so 1 = True and 0 = False. The upshot here is that a server under attack may connect to an undesired gateway if this Registry key is set to True. Hence, the recommended setting is False. The default setting is True.

- The `EnablePMTUDiscovery` Registry key allows TCP to discover the largest packet size along the entire path that will be accepted without fragmentation. The value of doing this is that packets will be sent in a size acceptable to each router along the path and won't need fragmentation, increasing the transmission speed of the packets to the destination. However, if this feature is enabled, an attacker could set the discovery size so low that your TCP/IP stack is unnecessarily overworked when transmitting data. Hence, the best practice is to enter this Registry key and then set the value to zero (0) for False instead of one (1) for True. The default for this key is one (1).

- The `KeepAliveTime` Registry key controls how often TCP attempts to verify that an idle connection is still alive by sending a KeepAlive packet to the client. If the client is still there, the client will respond. If there is no response, the connection is killed. The default setting for this key is 7,200,000 milliseconds, or 2 hours. The recommended setting is 300,000 milliseconds, or 5 minutes. The reasoning is that if the packets are sent more often and there is no response, idle connections are killed more quickly.

While tedious and detailed, actions like this can help ensure that your domain controller is not brought down by a DoS attack. You can use a Group Policy Object (GPO) to push out these Registry settings to all your servers instead of modifying each server individually.

Disabling Auto Generation of 8.3 Filenames

The disable auto generation feature is turned on by default in Windows 2000 Server and is there to allow for legacy compatibility with 16-bit applications. When this feature is enabled, an attacker needs only 8 characters to refer to any file in the folder structure. Unless you are running 16-bit applications, it is recommended that you turn off this feature. To do this, add `NtfsDisable8dot3NameCreation (DWORD)` as a subkey to the `HKLM\System\CCS\Control\FileSystem` key with a value of one (1). Any existing 8.3 names will remain intact after this key is applied to your system. However, you may decide that you want to keep 8.3 names to support down-level client operating systems, and for the ease of use of 8.3 naming when using the command prompt and when writing scripts.

Disabling LM Hash Creation

By default, Windows 2000 Server creates a hash of each password for the older LAN Manager (LM) and Windows NT (NTLM) and NTLMv2 authentication schemes. The LM hash is the weakest of all the hashes and can be vulnerable to a brute force attack. If you are running Windows 2000 only on your network, disable the LM hash creation. To do this, add the `NoLMHash (DWORD)` key as a subkey to the `HKLM\System\CCS\Control\LSA` key and set the value to one (1).

Securing Built-in Accounts

A number of built-in accounts cannot be deleted in Windows 2000 Server, but you can rename them. Be sure to rename the Guest and Administrator accounts and do not enable the Guest account unless you have a specific reason for doing so. This advice is also true of the local Administrator account on member servers and workstations. Accounts can be renamed using a

> ### 🌐 Real World Scenario
>
> #### Recovering an Infected FTP Site
>
> Administrators make mistakes all the time. A common mistake is to set up and configure a temporary FTP site. Setting up the site is not the mistake as much as forgetting that it is there.
>
> If you ever check your firewall logs, you will see that there is a great deal of activity every day, where all that is happening is that somebody or their unattended script is probing the firewall to see if there are any open ports and responses on common ports. If you forget the FTP site is there, those automated scripts running all over the Internet will not be so kind. Your site will be found, and it will be filled with stolen software or content such as movies or music files.
>
> It is almost a joke today: "What is the fastest way to fill up a hard drive?" The answer is "Publish it as an FTP site with write permissions."
>
> The main problem with these files is that they are all long-name files with invisible characters and are almost impossible to delete.
>
> So if it happens to you, what next? Just follow these steps:
>
> 1. Shut down the FTP service and disable it.
>
> 2. At a command prompt, navigate to the FTProot directory.
>
> 3. At the command prompt, run **dir /x** and expose all the 8.3 names.
>
> 4. Delete the files using their 8.3 names, and you will have removed the content.
>
> Without 8.3 names, it is almost impossible to delete all of those files on the hard drive. The only other way to get rid of them is to reformat the hard drive and start over. Of course, you will note to yourself and your peers, "Never publish an FTP site with write permissions."

Group Policy. To do so, use the Rename Administrator Account policy under the Security Options node (see Figure 2.7). Just double-click the policy setting, and inside the Security Policy Setting dialog box, select the Define This Policy Setting check box. Once selected, you'll be able to input the new name of the administrator account. Then click OK and exit the Group Policy.

Infrastructure Security

Securing network infrastructure resources should be a part of your implementation plan. Dynamic Host Configuration Protocol (DHCP) and Domain Name Service (DNS) are the two major services that can be compromised and used to insert an unauthorized computer into the company network. DHCP and DNS are vital to most organizations, and they are also open to several types of attacks.

FIGURE 2.7   Renaming the Administrator account

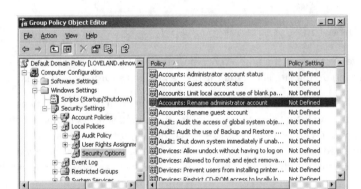

DHCP

Most companies implement DHCP and do not give it a second thought after DHCP has been fully implemented and is in production. DHCP is considered to be an essential service for most companies, because maintaining and supporting static IP addresses can take a significant amount of administrator time and administrative effort to keep it current.

However, the very convenience that DHCP offers is also fraught with security risks. If you look at the requirements for an intruder to access your company network, it comes down to just a few requirements. A potential intruder just needs to know

- The IP addresses being used on the network segment that is being targeted

- The subnet mask used

Other information that can make life even easier for a potential intruder would include the following:

- A route table for the company network segments

- The default gateway used to access other subnets on the network

- The domain name being used

- The location of the DNS servers

- The location of any WINS servers

You should recognize all of this information as information that DHCP usually provides to DHCP client computers on the company network. DHCP can be a double-edged sword in that it provides a great convenience for network administration, but it also provides intruders with information that makes it easy for them to attack the network.

DHCP is susceptible to the following types of attacks:

- Rogue servers can issue improper information to DHCP clients.

- DHCP servers can overwrite DNS information.

- DHCP servers can create authorized DNS entries.
- Unauthorized DHCP clients can obtain IP configuration information.

DHCP is a significant security risk in that there are no protections against many of these attacks against the service. You can choose to limit the ability of DHCP to create and update DNS account information on behalf of DHCP clients. However, that is about the extent of the security steps that can be taken to properly secure DHCP. If you feel that DHCP is being used by unauthorized computers, you can use the DHCP logs to check and find the unauthorized computers on the network. Microsoft also strongly suggests that you do not install DHCP on a domain controller. Keeping DHCP off of domain controllers ensures that the domain controller always has ownership of its own host and service records.

DNS

Windows 2000 and Windows Server 2003 Active Directory domains are dependent on a properly functioning DNS server. DNS—like many other services—is susceptible to attacks by malicious users and intruders. In particular, DNS is susceptible to the following types of attacks:

- Modification of host and service records
- Unauthorized zone transfers
- Exposure of the IP addresses in use
- Denial of service (DoS) attacks

Securing DNS from these potential weaknesses requires making some changes to your DNS configurations. In particular, many DNS functions that were meant to ease administration have become weaknesses. The best example is the support of dynamic DNS, which allows new client computers to enter host and service account information in DNS without any sort of approval being required. It is possible—through modification of existing records or overwriting existing records—for an intruder or malicious user to impersonate a server or client computer on the network. You can imagine the possible damage that could be caused if certain servers were impersonated successfully.

Allowing unauthorized computers to perform zone transfers with an existing DNS server allows an attacker to gain access to all of the IP configuration information and hostnames on the network. With this IP and host information, it is possible for an attacker to easily develop a network diagram of the company network and use it for attacks.

Improperly configured DNS servers can lead to the entire networking structure of the internal network being made available to external users. If the DNS information for the internal network is made available to the external part of the network, then others can query the DNS service and gain detailed information about the internal network.

DNS, like most services, is susceptible to DoS attacks. The major problem with a Windows 2000- and Windows Server 2003–based network is that without a properly functioning DNS service, it is very difficult for network authentication to take place and very difficult for hostname resolution. With Active Directory so dependent on DNS, any attacks that render it unavailable can shut down the company network by making file, printing, and other services unavailable as well.

Luckily, it is possible to reduce the exposure of DNS to many of these attacks. Some solutions include the following:

Implement Active Directory–integrated DNS zones.   By storing DNS information in Active Directory, it is possible to maintain multiple instances of DNS and securely update replication between DNS servers.

Implement separate DNS servers for external and internal networks.   By implementing a split DNS solution, it is possible to provide DNS services for internal network resources without exposing them in any way, shape, or form to attackers outside the company network. External DNS records are extremely static and very limited, so they can be maintained using manual methods that are more secure than dynamic DNS.

Limit the servers that are allowed to request and receive zone transfers.   DNS servers have the ability to provide a list of other authorized DNS servers on the network that are authorized to transfer zone information. This method is one of the best to use when not using Active Directory–integrated DNS zones. When using standard primary and secondary zones, you can limit the servers that can transfer DNS zone information and stop unauthorized DNS servers from receiving zone transfers.

Implement IPSec for DNS.   Using IPSec, DNS servers can be configured to require secure communications, and client computers can be configured as IPSec clients that attempt to use IPSec when communicating with servers that are IPSec-enabled. With IPSec configured, any clients wishing to use DNS must first establish and negotiate a security association with a DNS server. IPSec can then secure all traffic between the DNS client and the DNS server by providing mutual authentication. You need to properly configure IPSec filters to allow for all appropriate types of network traffic between clients and servers protected using IPSec configurations. This can make IPSec difficult to implement. Also, implementing IPSec on such a large scale within the organization can have a significant performance impact. IPSec is covered in Chapter 4, "Configuring IPSec and SMB Signing."

IIS 5 Server Security

Port 80 is the most often attacked port on the Internet. Therefore, the likelihood of your IIS server being attacked is rather high. To make your IIS server as secure as possible, Microsoft has provided the IIS Lockdown tool. IIS Lockdown is a flexible tool that lets you specify the nature of your web server and then remove any functionality that is not required. The changes made by the IIS Lockdown tool to secure the web server can also be made manually. A manual security checklist with manual steps can be found at www.nsa.gov for IIS 5.

 Before implementing the IIS Lockdown tool (or any recommendation in this chapter) in your production environment, be sure to test thoroughly any changes you want to make in a lab environment.

The IIS Lockdown tool is available as part of the Security Toolkit from Microsoft's security website (`www.microsoft.com/security`). After you download the tool, follow these steps:

1. Run the tool, accept the license agreement, and click Next to open the Select Server Template screen, as shown in Figure 2.8.

2. In the Server Templates list, select the type of server that you want to lock down and click Next to open the Internet Services screen, shown in Figure 2.9.

3. To view the individual template settings, click the View Template Settings check box. This forces the tool to display the screens shown in Figures 2.9, 2.10, and 2.11. If this box is not checked, the tool will go directly to the URLScan screen, shown in Figure 2.12.

FIGURE 2.8 The Select Server Template screen in the IIS Lockdown Wizard

FIGURE 2.9 The Internet Services screen in the IIS Lockdown Wizard

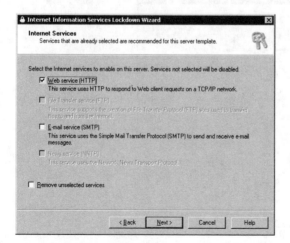

4. Select which services to enable on the server. If you select the Remove Unselected Services check box, those services not selected are removed instead of disabled. For a static web server, select the Web Service (HTTP) option only.

5. Click Next to open the Script Maps screen, shown in Figure 2.10. The default selection for a static web server is to disable support for all script maps.

6. Click Next to open the Additional Security screen, shown in Figure 2.11. This screen allows you to remove unnecessary directories and change permissions for anonymous users. For a static web server, all choices are selected by default.

FIGURE 2.10 The Script Maps screen in the IIS Lockdown Wizard

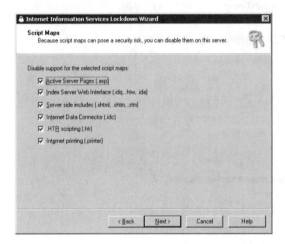

FIGURE 2.11 The Additional Security screen in the IIS Lockdown Wizard

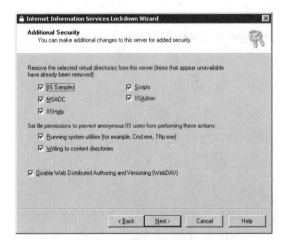

7. Click Next to open the URLScan screen, shown in Figure 2.12. The default selection is to install the URLScan tool. Before you do so, you should understand how that tool works and operates. Practice installing the tool in a lab environment and then put the tool through some serious tests. We'll discuss the URLScan tool later in this chapter.

8. Click Next to open the Ready To Apply Settings screen, shown in Figure 2.13. This screen displays a summary of the actions that the tool will perform.

9. Click Next to start the IIS Lockdown tool. Instead of getting a progress bar, you'll see a listing of the actions that the tool is performing as they are being performed, as shown in Figure 2.14.

FIGURE 2.12   The URLScan screen in the IIS Lockdown Wizard

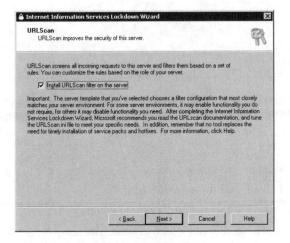

FIGURE 2.13   The Ready To Apply Settings screen in the IIS Lockdown Wizard

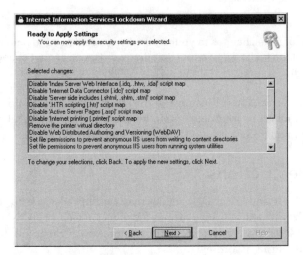

FIGURE 2.14 The Applying Security Settings screen in the IIS Lockdown Wizard

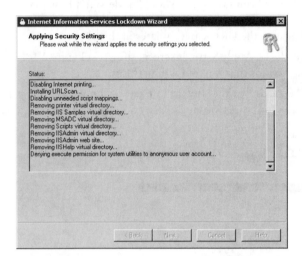

You can use the IIS Lockdown tool to lock down any number of server scenarios that rely on offering services through port 80, including OWA, SQL, SharePoint Portal Server, and Small Business Server. If you want to lock down an OWA server using IIS Lockdown, the tool will do the following:

- Leave HTTP and SMTP running on the OWA server.

- Leave the .asp script map enabled; all others are disabled.

- Leave WebDAV (Web Distributed Authoring and Versioning) enabled.

To uninstall IIS Lockdown, simply run the tool a second time. The settings for the tool are on the server in the `oblt-log.log` file in the `%windir%\system32\inetsrv` folder and can be used to "reverse" the installation. Once IIS Lockdown is uninstalled, your server will be back to the state it was before running the tool.

 If you want to make changes to your web server, you'll need to uninstall and then reinstall the IIS Lockdown tool. In other words, you cannot change the configuration of the server without first uninstalling the current settings.

Figure 2.8, shown earlier in this chapter, lists most of the server types that this tool locks down. But the IIS Lockdown tool is not your only option in securing IIS. You can take further steps to secure your servers running IIS.

IP Address/DNS Restrictions

If possible, you can set the exact IP address or DNS names that are allowed access to your web server. Obviously, for publicly oriented websites, such as e-commerce websites, this is impractical. But for other sites that host sensitive or restricted information, you might be able to specify the clients for the website and set this accordingly.

Disabling the IIS Anonymous Account

It is pretty much common knowledge that the default IIS Anonymous account is named IUSR_ *computername*. A better way to handle anonymous access is to disable this account, create a new account, and use the new account as the anonymous account for your website(s). Make the account adhere to strong password guidelines, which will make it more difficult for a hacker to guess the name and password combination.

The URLScan Tool

HTTP access to your websites can be analyzed and suspicious traffic can be rejected *before* that traffic hits IIS services. URLScan protects a server from attacks by filtering and rejecting certain packets that you define. When URLScan is first installed, it rejects the following request types:

- CGI (.exe) pages
- WebDAV
- FrontPage server extensions
- Index Server
- Internet printing
- Server-side includes

This tool is configured via the urlscan.ini file, which is installed in the %windir%\system32\ intesrv\urlscan folder. There are several sections to this file, and a typical section is shown in Figure 2.15.

FIGURE 2.15   The urlscan.ini file displaying the DenyVerbs section

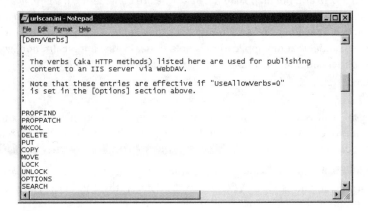

The Options section of the `urlscan.ini` file defines how valid and invalid requests are handled. The Options section includes the following:

UseAllowVerbs   Allowed values for the UseAllowVerbs option are either one (1) or zero (0). The default is one. When set to one, the tool rejects any request containing an HTTP verb that is not explicitly listed in the AllowVerbs section of the file. This section is case-sensitive. If this option is set to zero, the tool rejects any request that contains verbs in the DenyVerbs section of the file. This section is not case-sensitive.

UseAllowExtensions   Allowed values for the UseAllowExtensions option are either one (1) or zero (0). The default is zero. When set to the default, the tool rejects any request in which the file extension associated with the request is listed in the DenyExtensions section of the file. When set to one, the tool rejects any request in which the file extension associated with the request is not listed in the AllowExtensions section of the file.

NormalizeURLBeforeScan   Allowed values for this option are either one (1) or zero (0). The default is one. When set to the default, the tool analyzes all packets after IIS has normalized the URL request. When set to zero, the tool analyzes all requests in their raw form. This option will open your server to canonicalization attacks.

Canonicalization

Canonical means the simplest or most standard form of something. *Canonicalization* is the process of converting something from one representation to its simplest form.

Web applications must deal with lots of canonicalization issues, from URL encoding to IP address translation. For example, a URL canonicalization vulnerability results when a security decision is based on a URL and not all possible URL forms are considered. If a URL is allowed access, it is possible to send a URL that appears as if it is pointing to one resource when, in fact, it is pointing to a different resource. When security decisions are based on canonical forms of data, it is therefore essential that the application is able to deal with canonicalization issues accurately. Only experienced administrators should configure the application.

VerifyNormalization   Allowed values for the VerifyNormalization option are either one (1) or zero (0). The default is one. When set to the default, this tool verifies the *URL normalization* and helps defend against canonicalization attacks. The best practice is to leave this at the default value.

AllowHighBitCharacters   Allowed values for the AllowHighBitCharacters option are either one (1) or zero (0). The default is zero. When set to the default, this tool rejects any request in which the URL contains a character not found in the ASCII character set.

AllowDotInPath   Allowed values for the AllowDotInPath option are either one (1) or zero (0). The default is zero. When set to the default, the tool rejects any URL that contains multiple dots (.). When set to one, the tool does not check for multiple instances of dots. In default mode, the tool rejects names with dots such as `http://mail.domainname.com/exchange`.

RemoveServerHeader   Allowed values for the RemoveServerHeader option are either one (1) or zero (0). The default is zero. When set to the default, the tool allows server headers in all server responses. When set to one, the tool removes the server header from all server responses.

EnableLogging   Allowed values for the EnableLogging option are either one (1) or zero (0). The default is one. When set to the default, the tool logs its actions in the `urlscan.log` file. When set to zero, no logging is performed.

PerProcessLogging   Allowed values for the PerProcessLogging option are either one (1) or zero (0). The default is zero. When set to the default, the tool does not associate the log filename with each process that is being logged. When set to one, the tool appends the process ID of the IIS process hosting `URLScan.dll` to the log filename.

AlternativeServerName   The AlternativeServerName option works in concert with the RemoveServerHeader option. When RemoveServerHeader is set to zero, the string of characters entered here replaces the default header in all server responses.

AllowLateScanning   Allowed values for the AllowLateScanning option are either one (1) or zero (0). The default is zero. When set to one, the tool registers itself as a low-priority filter, which means that other tools can scan and modify the incoming URL before URLScan. When set to the default, the tool scans in high-priority mode.

PerDayLogging   Allowed values for the PerDayLogging option are either one (1) or zero (0). The default is one. When set to the default, a new log file is created for each day when the first log entry is written for that day. If there are no entries, no log file is generated.

RejectResponseUrl   The input values for the RejectResponseUrl option are a string of characters in the form `/path/filename.ext`. This is the URL that is run when the tool rejects a request. The URL must be local.

UseFastPathReject   Allowed values for the UseFastPathReject option are either one (1) or zero (0). The default is zero. When set to the default, this option is ignored. But when set to one, the tool ignores the settings in the RejectResponseUrl and displays a 404 response to the client when it rejects a request.

The `urlscan.ini` file also contains sections for the following:

- Allowed verbs
- Denied verbs
- Denied headers
- Allowed extensions
- Denied extensions

If you install URLScan on each IIS web server, it acts as an endpoint intrusion detection system (IDS). If you install URLScan on an ISA (Internet Security and Acceleration) server, it can act as a network-based IDS for all IIS servers on your network. At the network perimeter, you can block all types of requests instead of letting those requests traverse your network and then get blocked at the server level.

Although the IIS Lockdown tool works at the service level, URLScan works at the URL level to help secure your website. When you select one of the templates during the installation of IIS

Lockdown, a preconfigured `urlscan.ini` file is also installed, easing the burden of administration for you. And if necessary, you can go back and tweak the `urlscan.ini` file to work exactly the way you need it to work.

IIS 6 Server Security

With the release of Windows Server 2003, IIS 6 is now available. IIS 6 is a distinct improvement over IIS 5 in reliability, performance, and security. As you install IIS Lockdown and URLScan, you will notice that they are designed for use with IIS 5. Microsoft made a dramatic change in the philosophy around Windows server development; security now takes priority over ease of use. The Windows Server 2003 team worked hard to make IIS more secure with version 6. In particular, IIS 6 now comes completely locked down when installed. You do not need to lock down IIS 6 with any special utilities. While a version of URLScan is provided for IIS 6, it not needed in most cases. IIS 6 is completely locked down and will support only static HTML files when first installed. If you want to support ASP files, for example, you need to configure IIS 6 to enable ASP file support.

Open the Internet Information Services (IIS) Manager by choosing Start ➤ Administrative Tools ➤ Internet Information Services (IIS) Manager. Once you have opened the MMC snap-in, expand the server name and click Web Service Extensions, as shown in Figure 2.16.

 Real World Scenario

Securing an IIS 5 Website Using the Anonymous Account

Let's say you want to present company files on the Internet for general public consumption, such as product and general information documents. Obviously, you want this site to be secure and yet accessible via the Anonymous account. Follow these steps:

1. Install the IIS Lockdown and URLScan tools.

2. Select the Static Web Site option in IIS Lockdown and accept the defaults in the `urlscan.ini` file.

3. Use a Group Policy to disable the Anonymous account membership in the Everyone and Network user security groups.

4. Explicitly give permissions to the Anonymous user account to the resources that will be presented in the website.

5. Rename the Anonymous user account with a name that "blends in" with the other names in your Active Directory so that a hacker cannot readily discern which accounts are intended for web access and which are not.

6. Require SSL for client connectivity if you want to ensure that data communications between your visitors and the web server are encrypted. With public documents, this might not be a desired outcome, but it is certainly available if you want to use it.

FIGURE 2.16   Internet Information Services (IIS) Manager

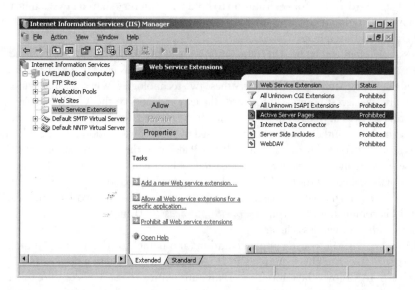

To add support for ASP pages, click Active Server Pages and click the Allow button. IIS 6 will reconfigure itself to support ASP content. To configure support for WebDAV and other extensions, you should follow the same procedure to allow their use on the IIS 6 server.

Securing Mobile Communications and Internet Authentication Service (IAS) Server

There is little doubt that wireless communication has exploded in the last few years. Along with this explosion, however, are real security concerns that have not been fully resolved. Like the other types of servers in this chapter, these technologies also raise specific security concerns, which include the following:

- No per-packet authentication.

- Vulnerability to disassociation attacks.

- No central authentication support.

- RC4 stream cipher is vulnerable to plain-text attacks.

- Some *WEP (Wired Equivalent Privacy)* keys are derived from passwords.

- No support for advanced security such as smart cards, biometrics, and so on.

- Key management issues such as rekeying global keys and no dynamic, per-station unicast key.

The WEP algorithm defines the use of a 40-bit secret key for authentication and encryption. The 802.11 standard allows for each station to hold two different shared keys: a unicast session key and a multicast/global key. The WEP is a symmetric algorithm in which the same key is used for both cipher and decipher.

Wireless technology can be used in conjunction with an IAS or any *Remote Authentication Dial-In User Service (RADIUS)*. Because most wireless communications need to access resources sitting on a cabled network, there is a need to marry these two technologies. When a wireless user connects to the network, the access point (AP) forwards the user's identity to the RADIUS server to initiate authentication services in Active Directory. Once authenticated, the RADIUS server sends back to the user via the AP an authentication key to be used to access information on the cabled network. The key is sent in encrypted form, of course. The AP also uses the authentication key to securely transmit per-station unicast session and multicast/global authentication keys to the user's device. The user's device, called a station (STA), then has keys available to transmit information back and forth between itself and the AP for access to information on the cabled network. Hence, the RADIUS server works in conjunction with your *certificate authority (CA)* and the AP to provide secure communications with your wireless clients.

The IAS service is Microsoft's implementation (and name) for the industry-standard RADIUS service. IAS can check Active Directory for a wireless client's request for authentication. The use of IAS allows the remote access user authentication services to the cabled network.

You can take some steps to further secure your IAS server. First, as the number of wireless client types increases, it is reasonable to assume that not every client will want to authenticate to the IAS server using the same methods. This situation already exists for Windows 9x clients, which use NTLM, and Windows 2000 and later clients, which use Kerberos. The best practice here is to create a different user account for each client-authentication method. This way, if a password on one account is compromised, it is only compromised for that client, not for all the clients that the user is using.

Second, ensure that you are allowing all wireless traffic to come through on a specific IP address. This allows you to hide your internal IP scheme and use a single namespace for resolution outside your network.

Finally, you can use the remote access account lockout feature in Windows 2000 and Windows Server 2003 to configure the number of times that a user's authentication can fail before future connection attempts using that account are denied.

 The Remote Access Account Lockout feature is not related at all to the Account Locked Out setting in the Properties dialog box for a user account.

To configure the Remote Access Account Lockout feature, you edit the Registry on the server providing user authentication. To enable account lockout, you must set the MaxDenials entry in the Registry (`HKLM\SYSTEM\CurrentControlSet\Services\RemoteAccess\Parameters\AccountLockout`) to one (1) or greater. This setting specifies the maximum number of failed attempts before the account is locked out. The default setting is that this feature is zero (0), or disabled. If you set it to three (3), the account will lock out after three failed authentication attempts. If you set it to five (5), the account will lock out after five failed authentication attempts.

The window of time in which the specified number of failed authentication attempts is set is called the ResetTime (mins). You can find this entry in the Registry under the HKLM\SYSTEM\ CurrentControlSet\Services\RemoteAccess\Parameters\AccountLockout key. The default is set to 0xb40, or 2880 minutes (48 hours). You can increase or decrease this value as necessary.

If you need to manually reset a user account that has been locked out before the failed attempts counter automatically resets the account, delete the following Registry subkey that corresponds to the user's account name:

HKLM\SYSTEM\CurrentControlSet\Services\RemoteAccess\Parameters\
AccountLockout\domain name:*user name*

Applying Security to Client Operating Systems

When it is time to apply additional security to client operating systems, you can either walk around and touch each desktop, or you can use some type of method that automatically applies the settings to each desktop. The best (and easiest) way to apply security to a group of desktops is to use the Group Policy feature in Windows 2000 and Windows Server 2003.

You can use Group Policy Objects (GPOs) to apply additional security to clients by configuring a template and then applying that template to a GPO. You then assign the GPO to a site, a domain, or an OU container, and the clients inherit the settings. Now, each operating system is unique and has its own needs. Let's take a look at these needs.

Unix Clients

Unix clients can authenticate using the Kerberos version 5 protocol. They can also use the Windows 2000 and Windows Server 2003 domain controllers as their Kerberos *Key Distribution Center (KDC)*. If they already have a KDC they are using, an inter-realm Kerberos trust can be created between their KDC and a domain controller (DC). Either way, their account will need to be created in Active Directory in order for them to gain access to Windows resources. Account mappings may need to be created between the Unix KDC and the DC. Such mappings associate the Windows account SID with a defined account in the Unix domain.

Older Unix clients that use the Common Internet File System (CIFS) such as Samba can use the NTLM protocol to authenticate with AD. In addition, Unix clients can use certificates for SSL and Transport Layer Security (TLS) connections. All that is needed is a trusted CA by both the Unix and the Windows servers.

Finally, remember that clear-text passwords can be secured using either SSL or IPSec (Internet Protocol Security). You'll need to secure clear-text passwords because Unix clients use them in several utilities. To set clear-text authentication, enable the Send Unencrypted Password To Connect To Third-Party SMB Servers setting under the Security Node in the Local Policies node of the GPO template (see Figure 2.17). Once this policy is set, you can use IPSec or SSL to secure the transmission.

FIGURE 2.17 The policy setting for clear-text authentication

You secure FTP and Telnet traffic using IPSec. You secure HTTP traffic using SSL.

If your Unix clients need to use their native NFS (Network File System) for file services, you can design a secure resource topology in Windows by installing Services for Unix. In this scenario, the Unix clients authenticate to their own NIS (Network Information Service) server. In order for them to access files on the Windows server, you need to map the user identifier (UID) and group identifier (GID) from the NIS server to an account in AD. This mapping assigns the Unix account an SID from the domain and allows the Unix client to access files and servers in the domain. You'll set permissions on NFS resources by using the AD accounts.

NetWare Clients

Microsoft provides three services to help NetWare clients interoperate with Windows 2000 and Windows Server 2003:

Client Services for NetWare   This service allows Windows clients to access resources hosted on a Novell NetWare server. The clients have direct access to file services, print services, and Novell Directory Services (NDS). Do not install this if you are going to install Gateway Services for NetWare.

If you need to manage a large number of accounts for both AD and NDS, consider using the Microsoft Directory Synchronization Service to synchronize accounts between AD and NDS/3.*x* binderies. It is important to note that while NetWare 4 and later versions can emulate the 3.*x* bindery, it is not a recommended long-term solution. Many companies will implement the bindery emulation during migrations from NetWare to Windows, but they will not do so for long-term integrations.

Later versions of NetWare do not require any special client software installations on Windows clients.

Gateway Services for NetWare (GSNW)   GSNW provides a single gateway through which Windows clients can access NetWare resources. Essentially, a Windows server acts as a proxy agent for requested resources to the Windows clients. Do not install this service if you are going to install Client Services for NetWare on all your workstations.

Authentication for this service uses a single account that must be a member of the NTGATEWAY group on the NetWare server. This account must be given permission to the NetWare resources if Windows clients are going to be able to access these resources. If this account is given Supervisor rights on the NetWare box, you could have a potential security hole if that account is compromised. Guard this account, and ensure that the password is changed regularly.

Services for NetWare   This add-on product from Microsoft provides several utilities to help Novell and Microsoft platforms coexist:

Microsoft Directory Synchronization Services (MSDSS)   This service provides two-way directory synchronization between AD and Novell Directory Services (NDS).

Microsoft File Migration Utility   This tool enables the migration of files from a NetWare server to a Windows 2000 server while preserving the directory structure and file permissions.

File and Print Services for NetWare   This service enables Windows to provide file and print services to NetWare clients. The Windows server will look and feel like a NetWare server to the NetWare clients.

There are security holes with the NWLink protocol, Microsoft's implementation of IPX/SPX (Internetwork Packet Exchange/Sequenced Packet Exchange). NetWare servers that use IPX/SPX advertise themselves to the network using the Service Advertising Protocol (SAP), which provides basic server information to everyone on the network, including attackers. For this reason, strive to use only TCP/IP on your network.

Macintosh Clients

By default, Macintosh clients use nonencrypted passwords. This should remain the case only for anonymous-accessed resources such as public websites or public files. If you install File Services for Macintosh (FSM), you can have Macintosh clients that do not have accounts in AD authenticate as a guest user. This is best used for resources that do not require auditing or have liberal permission sets.

In addition, if you install FSM, you can instruct your Mac clients to authenticate using Apple Standard Encryption, which allows passwords up to only 8 characters. You can also specify that they use the Microsoft User Authentication Module (MS-UAM). Using MS-UAM, passwords can be a maximum of 14 characters, but it does require the AppleShare client 3.8 or later to be installed on the Mac client.

For file security, set up volume passwords, which is somewhat analogous to share-level permissions. To access the volume, users must first supply the appropriate password.

As far as printing is concerned, there are no print permissions using the AppleTalk protocol. There is no user-level security for Macintosh printers.

Summary

This chapter focused on securing different server platforms and securing non-Windows clients. Specifically, it focused on how to secure the following:

- SQL Server 2000
- Exchange Server
- Internet Information Services
- Internet Authentication Service Server
- Wireless clients

This chapter also discussed how to secure a website using the IIS Lockdown and URLScan tools. Because these tools are unique to IIS, any server platform that uses IIS can (potentially) benefit from using them.

Non–Windows 2000 clients need to be secured too, so we discussed how to secure a Unix client on your Windows 2000 network. Probably the best interoperability with Windows 2000 exists from the Unix world.

We also discussed the interoperation with NetWare and how to secure these platforms when they must coexist. You learned that Microsoft has released a directory synchronization tool to ease administration when many accounts need access to both NetWare and Windows 2000.

Finally, you learned to password-protect Macintosh volumes and to use the MS-UAM protocol for Macintosh clients.

Exam Essentials

Be able to list two or three actions that you would take to secure each server platform discussed in this chapter. Know what actions are recommended for each server and why you need to take them. Also, remember the interaction of the RADIUS server with wireless clients and the IAS server. You might also remember that you can use the IIS Lockdown tool for Exchange 2000 Server OWA.

Understand how IIS Lockdown and URLScan work together with IIS 5. The IIS Lockdown tool works at the service level to add and remove services based on the configuration or template that you choose when working with the tool. Once set, configuration choices must be uninstalled before they can be modified. The URLScan tool applies settings from the urlscan.ini file to incoming web services requests. Be sure you know that URL normalization and day-to-day security of your website is much more a function of the URLScan tool than the IIS Lockdown tool.

Understand how IIS 6 changes do not require IIS Lockdown and URLScan. IIS Lockdown and URLScan are basically built into the IIS 6 structure. IIS 6 installs in a completely locked-down state and requires administrator effort to add functionality to IIS 6.

Understand how to secure each client type in a Windows environment.   Because so many of you run a mixed-client environment, it is important to understand how to secure each client type. You would also do yourself some favors by understanding the differences among the three NetWare services that Microsoft provides.

Review Questions

1. You have just installed SQL Server 2000 using Windows Authentication Mode. Which of the following statements is true?

   A. The SA account defaults to a predetermined password.

   B. NTLM becomes the default authentication protocol.

   C. Password expiration and account lockout are enabled.

   D. The SQL Server 2000 Registry keys will not be secured.

2. You are running 50 Windows 2000 Professional workstations and 30 Unix workstations. Mary, a user on a Windows 2000 Professional workstation, authenticates at Server1, a DC in the `administration.testforest.com` domain. She needs access to a SQL Server 2000 database that resides on a member server, SQL1. After authenticating to the network, Mary can access the SQL server. While working with data from the SQL server, she clicks a link that takes her to a secure intranet website on WS1. What will be the default behavior among these servers?

   A. SQL1 will request a ticket from Server1 on behalf of Mary for authentication to WS1.

   B. Mary's security credentials will be sent to WS1 from Server1, and SQL1 will not be involved in her authentication to WS1.

   C. Mary's security credentials will need to be created on WS1 after WS1 verifies her token with Server1.

   D. Mary's security credentials follow her everywhere in the forest. There is no need for SQL1 and WS1 to communicate directly.

3. When discussing Delegation Authentication, the best practice from a security standpoint is to do what?

   A. Leave the default settings alone.

   B. Modify the default settings.

   C. Change the default Delegation Authentication settings so that DA is enabled only for individual computers and user accounts.

   D. Remove Delegation Authentication and then install it on individual servers and workstations that need it.

4. You are the administrator of a Windows 2000 network. You have 200 Windows 2000 Professional workstations, 20 Windows 2000 Server Member Servers, and 5 Windows 2000 DCs. You want to make authentication to each server as fast and transparent as possible to your end users. You also want communication between your servers to be as secure as possible. What should you do? (Choose all that apply.)

   A. Leave Delegation Authentication at the default configuration.

   B. Require digital signatures on all communication between servers.

   C. Enable Delegation Authentication on each server.

   D. Require digital signatures on all client communication.

5. You are the administrator of a SQL Server 2000 server. You have used the Encrypting File System (EFS) to encrypt SQL-specific files. You then change the service account for your SQL server. You discover that you cannot access the encrypted files. What should you do?

A. Reinstall the SQL binary files. This will reset the SQL server to the default, and the files will be decrypted during the installation.

B. Use the Local System account to decrypt the files. You can then encrypt them again using the new system account.

C. Log on locally as the administrator. Use this account to decrypt the files.

D. Change the service account to the old server account, and then decrypt the files. Change the server account again to the new account. Encrypt the files.

6. Items in an Exchange 2000 Server store can be accessed using which of the following methods? (Choose all that apply.)

A. URL

B. SMB

C. MAPI

D. HTTP

E. HTTPS

F. FTP

G. Microsoft Office Application

7. Which of the following steps can you take as an Exchange 2000 Server administrator to further secure port 25 on your TCP filter? (Choose all that apply.)

A. Install URLScan to scan incoming OWA requests.

B. Install antivirus scanning of e-mail in the DMZ.

C. Install IIS Lockdown to remove unnecessary services.

D. Install content scanning of e-mail in the DMZ.

8. You are the system administrator for a large network of 2000 Windows 2000 Professional workstations, 50 Windows 2000 servers, and 300 Unix workstations. You have one intranet web server, WS1. You also have one Outlook Web Access (OWA) server. Your users use OWA to access their e-mail from the Internet. Because of heavy demand, you need to install a second OWA server. The OWA servers do not host any mailboxes or public folders. You also want your users to continue using the same URL they have been using to access OWA, but you want user calls balanced between the two servers. What should you do? (Choose all that apply.)

A. Move your OWA servers to the DMZ.

B. Transfer the databases to other Exchange 2000 servers.

C. Use a DNS alias to load-balance client calls between the two servers.

D. Install two Exchange 2000 Server front-end servers in your DMZ.

E. Install Network Load Balancing to load-balance client calls between the two front-end servers.

F. Use SSL for client connections to the front-end servers.

G. Use IPSec to secure communication between the front-end and back-end servers.

9. You are the administrator for an OWA server. The server was installed using default settings. You want to further secure this server. Which two tools would you use to do this?

    A. Network Load Balancing

    B. URLScan

    C. IIS Lockdown

    D. SSL

10. Which of the following will help prevent impersonation on your network? (Choose all that apply.)

    A. User authentication

    B. IIS Lockdown

    C. SMB signing

    D. Removing Delegation Authentication

11. You are the system administrator for 20 Windows 2000 servers and 2000 Windows 98 workstations. You also have 300 Unix workstations and two Novell NetWare file servers. You want to increase security for all client logon traffic. All clients connect to both Windows 2000 servers and the two Novell NetWare file servers. What actions should you take? (Choose all that apply.)

    A. Enable NTLMv2 for the Unix workstations.

    B. Enable NTLMv2 for the Windows 98 workstations.

    C. Use only TCP/IP protocol on your network.

    D. Use Directory Synchronization Services.

12. You are the system administrator of a network consisting of 600 Windows 2000 Professional workstations and 30 Windows 2000 servers. One of your servers, Web1, hosts your company's e-commerce website. You discover that this server has been compromised using the Anonymous user account. You want to quickly secure this server and all resources to which the Anonymous user account has permissions. What should you do? (Choose all that apply.)

    A. Require SSL for all connections to your e-commerce website.

    B. Enable auditing for all packets on your router.

    C. Configure the No Access Without Explicit Anonymous Permissions Group Policy setting. Apply to all servers on your network.

    D. Run the IIS Lockdown and URLScan tools.

    E. Rename the Anonymous user account.

13. You find that your web server is receiving a large number of SYN packets. You suspect that you are being hit with a DoS attack. What should you do?

    A. Audit the packets and perform reverse DNS on the attacker's IP address. Block all packets from this IP address at the router.

    B. Configure the SynAttackProtect key on your web server to cause your web server to time out more quickly when it receives too many SYN packets.

    C. Configure the EnablePMTUDiscovery key on your web server to cause your web server to time out more quickly when it receives too many SYN packets.

    D. Block the sender's IP address in the Properties dialog box for your web server.

14. You are the system administrator for 10 Windows 2000 servers. You have no 16-bit applications running on your servers. What should you do to increase security?

    A. Modify the `NtfsDisable8dot3NameCreation` Registry key.

    B. Remove the `NtfsDisable8dot3NameCreation` Registry key.

    C. Uninstall the thunking process by removing the `win32onwin16.dll` file.

    D. Do nothing. There is no security issue.

15. You are the system administrator for a network with 800 Windows 2000 Workstations and 40 Windows 2000 servers. You want to increase your password security. What actions should you take? (Choose all that apply.)

    A. Require complex passwords.

    B. Do not allow users to publicly expose their passwords.

    C. Disable LM hash creation.

    D. Do not allow users to use recently used passwords.

16. You have run the IIS Lockdown tool on your web server. You need to deliver dynamic, streaming content from your web server and use the FTP service for file transfers. You also need to reconfigure the settings for the IIS Lockdown tool to allow this new content to be delivered efficiently. What should you do?

    A. Edit the `urlscan.inf` file. Reinstall IIS Lockdown.

    B. Edit the `protocol.ini` file. Reinstall IIS Lockdown.

    C. Edit the `urlscan.ini` file.

    D. Uninstall and then reinstall the IIS Lockdown tool.

17. You need to launch a private website that will be accessed by 20 of your users and 10 partners from other companies. It is required that this site be highly secure. What actions should you take? (Choose all that apply.)

    A. Accept connections only from predetermined IP addresses and DNS names.

    B. Disable anonymous connections. Require user authentication.

    C. Use SSL for all client communications.

    D. Install the IIS Lockdown and URLScan tools.

18. You have been charged with designing a secure solution for wireless access to your network. Although you don't have any wireless users right now, your manager wants to update the remote sales force to use wireless PCs and connect to inventory data on your intranet without plugging into their customers' networks to gain Internet access. How should you design this network? (Choose all that apply.)

    A. Require SSL connectivity between the wireless workstation and the intranet server.

    B. Install an access point on your network.

    C. Install Internet Authentication Service.

    D. Require IPSec at the network layer between the users and the access point.

    E. Have the web server trust an internal CA, and have your wireless users trust an external CA.

    F. Have everyone trust the same CA.

    G. Disable LM hash.

19. You are the administrator for 3000 users who are running a mix of Windows 98, Windows NT 4, Windows 2000, and Unix workstations. You also have 400 wireless workstations in your warehouses and portable buildings. Many of the wireless users also log on to the network from their desktops. What should you do to increase security?

    A. Disable Routing And Remote Access for the wireless workstations.

    B. Require each user to use a different account for each device they use to log on to the network.

    C. Enable Routing And Remote Access for the wireless workstations. Require IPSec.

    D. Set the KeepAlive time to 120 seconds.

20. You are the administrator of a network that has 30 Windows 2000 workstations and 30 Macintosh clients. You want to secure the Macintosh clients' passwords as much as possible. What actions should you take? (Choose all that apply.)

    A. Require Kerberos for all Macintosh clients.

    B. Install File Services for Macintosh.

    C. Specify that the Microsoft User Authentication Module be used.

    D. Do nothing. Kerberos is the default authentication protocol for Macintosh clients.

Answers to Review Questions

1. C. When you install SQL Server 2000 using Windows Authentication Mode, the security context of the user is used for validation to a DC before allowing setup to continue. Kerberos becomes the default authentication protocol, and the directories and Registry keys are secured in this mode as well.

2. A. Security Account Delegation, or Delegation Authentication, is the ability of one server to request a ticket on behalf of a user or service account when that user is currently connected to the local server but needs to connect to another server. Answer A is the only answer that fits the description of this behavior. Delegation Authentication is enabled by default in Windows 2000 Server.

3. C. The best practice is to turn off Delegation Authentication by default and then enable it for certain services and user accounts. This will guard against an easily hacked service account name and password combination being used to access the server via impersonation.

4. A, B. What is described in the question is Delegation Authentication, and it is enabled by default on all Windows 2000 servers. Requiring digital signatures, among the other answers, is the best way to secure communication between your servers. Answer D would not be appropriate because client-to-server communication was not a focus of this question.

5. D. SQL 2000 Server works with the Windows 2000 Server EFS, but it encrypts files under its service account name and password assignment. If you change this account without decrypting any encrypted files, this data will be totally lost to you until they are decrypted. The only way to decrypt the files is to use the account under which they were encrypted for the decryption process.

6. A, B, C, D, E, G. Because of the ExIFS, every item in an Exchange 2000 Server store can be accessed using a number of different protocols. This allows for flexibility in how information is managed and stored. However, the different access points also create security concerns in that the information must be secured on multiple fronts. Items are secured using Windows 2000 Server user and group accounts and NTFS permissions.

7. B, D. Two actions you can take on inbound SMTP mail are to run that mail through both a content scanner and an antivirus scanner. Doing both will protect your mail from viruses, unwanted attachments, and unwanted content. The URLScan and IIS Lockdown tools are suited for HTTP and port 80, not SMTP and port 25.

8. D, E, F, G. You might be surprised that you don't have to move any databases to achieve this solution. Because the OWA servers are not hosting any mailboxes or public folders, all you need to do is configure them to be front-end servers and then install security for communication between the clients and the front-end server and again between the front-end servers and back-end servers. The best security for information between the front-end servers and your clients is SSL. IPSec can be used for calls between the servers. Because you are using front-end servers, you'll need to install Network Load Balancing to load-balance calls between these two servers. By default, Network Load Balancing uses a single IP address and namespace.

9. B, C. Although using SSL is a way to secure client-to-server communication over port 80, only URLScan and IIS Lockdown are tools that secure the server directly.

10. C, D. SMB signing, when required, is a method to ensure that all communication on your network is digitally signed at the packet level. In addition, Delegation Authentication is a type of impersonation that servers perform on behalf of clients. This can be removed to eliminate the possibility of an attacker using this feature to impersonate another user.

11. B, C, D. Because Unix workstations can use Kerberos, enabling NTLMv2 would be a step back for them. By using only TCP/IP, you eliminate IPX/SPX from the network and its need to use SAP to advertise the presence of each server to the clients on the network. And in installations in which a large number of clients need to authenticate to both NetWare and Windows 2000 Server, directory synchronization can increase security by using the same accounts in both directories.

12. C, E. Because the compromise occurred using the Anonymous user account, first limit what this account can do and its group memberships. By default, the Anonymous account is a member of the Everyone and Network security groups. Enabling this policy setting will require that you explicitly set permissions to all resources for the Anonymous user account. Although you might be able to think of other things that should be done in this scenario, only answers C and E directly mitigate against the threat of a compromise using the Anonymous account.

13. B. Because this is a SYN attack, configure the SynAttackProtect Registry key on your web server. Obviously, you might take other actions, but this one will help mitigate against the DoS attack on that individual server.

14. A. If you have no Windows 16-bit applications, turn off the 8.3 auto generation of filenames. With this feature turned on, an attacker needs only eight characters to refer to a filename. With this feature turned off, the attacker will need the entire filename in order to use a file.

15. A, B, C, D. Because most resources are password-protected, this is one of the favorite techniques that an attacker uses to compromise your network. All these measures will help increase the password security on your network. And all of them are recommended, except for the LM hash answer, which you must leave enabled if you have legacy clients, such as Windows NT 4 or Windows 98 clients.

16. D. If you were just allowing more verbs on your website, answer C might suffice. However, if you need to redo the service structure on your website after running the IIS Lockdown tool, you'll need to uninstall and then reinstall the tool choosing the option during installation to secure this new type of server.

17. A, B, C, D. All these actions will help secure your website. By accepting connections from only certain IP addresses or DNS names, you significantly limit who can even connect to the web server. And then requiring user authentication will mean that hackers must not only spoof an IP address, but also compromise a username and password combination and then impersonate a user to gain access to the website.

18. A, B, C, F. To connect, wireless workstations need an access point. You can use SSL for port 80 connections between the workstation and the access point. To authenticate on the network, a RADIUS server can be employed to proxy the authentication requests from your users to the DC. Because all this communication will occur using encryption and signatures, you'll need a CA available that both sides trust.

19. B. Because each wireless device may have a different way to authenticate on the network, you should require a different username and password combination for each client device. This is because client devices will vary in their security when passing the password from the client to the access point.

20. B, C. The default password security for Macintosh clients is 8 characters and clear-text passwords. When you install File Services for Macintosh, you can then select the MS-UAM, which allows for password characters up to 14 characters in length.

Chapter

3

Installing, Managing, & Troubleshooting Hotfixes & Service Packs

✓ **Analyze security configuration. Tools include Microsoft Baseline Security Analyzer (MBSA), the MBSA command-line tool, and Security Configuration and Analysis.**

✓ **Plan the deployment of service packs and hotfixes.**

  ▪ Evaluate the applicability of service packs and hotfixes.

  ▪ Test the compatibility of service packs and hotfixes for existing applications.

  ▪ Plan patch deployment environments for both the pilot and production phases.

  ▪ Plan the batch deployment of multiple hotfixes.

  ▪ Plan rollback strategy.

✓ **Assess the current status of service packs and hotfixes. Tools include MBSA and the MBSA command-line tool.**

  ▪ Assess current patch levels by using the MBSA GUI tool.

  ▪ Assess current patch levels by using the MBSA command-line tool with scripted solutions.

✓ **Deploy service packs and hotfixes.**

  ▪ Deploy service packs and hotfixes on new servers and client computers. Considerations include slipstreaming, custom scripts, and isolated installation or test networks.

  ▪ Deploy service packs and hotfixes on existing servers and client computers.

Probably the best way to keep your servers secure on an ongoing basis is to install the latest service packs and hotfixes. Because new vulnerabilities are discovered every day, new hotfixes (sometimes referred to as "patches") are released to shut down each vulnerability. A *hotfix* is nothing more than a small piece of code that has been rewritten to eliminate the vulnerability in the software product. In the past, Microsoft used to issue patches several times during the month, and it was sometimes difficult to keep up with the patches. Because many patches required restarting servers, this caused a great deal of stress for many businesses. When should they apply the fix? If they did it right away, they would have to take system outages and interrupt business in many cases. If they waited until there were several patches to apply all at once, they would have to assume the risk of being attacked and not having the proper patches installed to protect the company systems. What made it even worse was the amount of testing required, because each patch had to be tested before it could be deployed.

Microsoft will keep you informed of these updates if you subscribe to their security notification e-mail service at www.microsoft.com/security.

Starting in October 2003, Microsoft changed the way that it deployed hotfixes by reducing the number of hotfix release dates. New security bulletins are released the second Tuesday of each month. However, there will be exceptions to the monthly updates, depending upon the risk associated with the fix. The goal of the new combined releases each month is to reduce the amount of testing that each company will need to perform and to reduce the number of system outages that may be required throughout the year in the event that a patch requires a reboot of the system.

This chapter focuses on service packs and hotfixes. We'll look at installing, managing, and troubleshooting them. And we'll discuss the tools that are available to help in this process.

Determining the Current Status of Hotfixes and Service Packs

If you need to see the current status of a service pack that is installed on an individual workstation or server, right-click My Computer, choose Properties to open the System Properties dialog box, and click the General tab (see Figure 3.1).

However, if you need to find out the service pack level of many workstations or servers at the same time, you have to run the Microsoft Baseline Security Analyzer (MBSA) tool. When you're working at the enterprise level, it's possible that some service pack and/or hotfix installations won't be distributed to every computer at the same time. It's also possible that some workstations or servers will be missed when using manual installation techniques. Hence, you may need to poll a group of target computers to determine their service pack level and then get all the updates and hotfixes installed in a uniform manner across the enterprise.

We'll discuss the MBSA tool later in this chapter, but first, let's go over how to install a service pack and a hotfix.

Installing Service Packs and Hotfixes

To install a new service pack on a Windows workstation or server, you first need access to the service pack file. Microsoft wraps service packs into a single installation file (see Figure 3.2) that, when invoked, expands into the local `temp` directory (see Figure 3.3) on the computer and then begins the installation process (see Figure 3.4). Microsoft also does this for hotfixes and updates.

FIGURE 3.1   The System Properties dialog box, open at the General tab

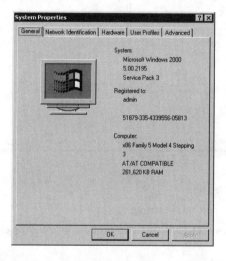

FIGURE 3.2   Notice that the Windows service pack is encapsulated in a single file, which is highlighted in this illustration.

FIGURE 3.3   After the service pack file is invoked, the file is verified and then expanded in the temp directory.

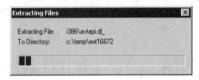

FIGURE 3.4   After the file has been expanded, the Setup Wizard opens and starts the service pack installation.

To complete the installation, follow these steps:

1. At the Welcome screen, click Next to open the licensing screen.

2. If you agree to the terms of the license, select the I Agree radio button and then click Next to open the Select Options screen:

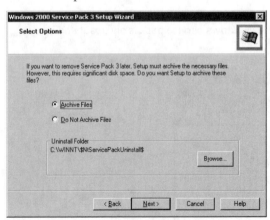

3. Choose whether to archive the files that the service pack will overwrite and then click Next to start the installation.

Archiving the files means that the earlier versions will be retained and the current service pack can be uninstalled to revert to the earlier version in case the current service pack causes problems that cannot be resolved. If you choose not to archive the files, the service pack cannot be uninstalled. Remember that archiving the files requires more disk space.

The Setup Wizard first runs some diagnostic routines to determine how much disk space your computer has (see Figure 3.5) and to find out about some of the environment variables. It then begins the process of installing the updated files to your hard drive. If you selected to archive your files, the Setup Wizard first backs up all the files that it intends to overwrite before installing the updated files from the `temp` directory.

FIGURE 3.5   The Setup Wizard checks for adequate disk space.

Once the Setup Wizard has completed, you are given a choice on the Finish screen to either reboot the computer now or reboot later. What this allows you to do is to install the service pack during the day and then reboot the computer later when client use is at low demand. Earlier versions of service packs did not include this feature. But remember, you must reboot the server in order for the new files that were installed to be registered and used. Until you reboot, you are operating under the old service pack, even though the new one has been installed.

In Exercise 3.1, you will install a new service pack for Windows 2000. The process is very similar for both Windows Server 2003 and Windows XP Professional.

EXERCISE 3.1

Installing a Service Pack for Windows 2000

1. Double-click the service pack file.

2. Wait for the file to be verified and then expanded in the `temp` directory.

3. At the Welcome screen, click Next to open the licensing screen.

4. Read the licensing agreement, click the I Agree radio button, and then click Next.

5. Make your archiving selection on the Select Options screen and click Next to start the installation.

6. Wait for the Setup Wizard to run.

7. Click Finish.

8. Reboot your computer.

Using the MBSA Tool

The Microsoft Baseline Security Analyzer (MBSA) tool is the replacement for the Microsoft Personal Security Advisor (MPSA) and is designed to perform much of what the Microsoft Network Security Hotfix Checker (HFNetChk) tool performs, but with a graphical front end (we like that!) and expanded capabilities.

You can scan one computer or a group of computers and check the installed operating system and the service pack level to determine which hotfixes are installed. You can find out about misconfigurations and missing hotfixes that have been recommended by Microsoft.

 You can download the MBSA tool free of charge from Microsoft's security website at www.microsoft.com/security or www.microsoft.com/mbsa, which will redirect your browser to the MBSA site.

MBSA can scan the following platforms:

- Windows Server 2003
- Windows 2000
- Windows NT 4
- Windows XP Professional
- Windows XP Home Edition

You can run MBSA from any Windows Server 2003, Windows 2000, or Windows XP platform, but you cannot run it from a Windows NT 4 computer. MBSA uses the HFNetChk tool to discover security updates that have been applied to a given computer or group of computers. How does MBSA know if all the required security updates have been installed? Well, it downloads an XML

(Extensible Markup Language) file from Microsoft that contains all the hotfix updates that should be applied to each platform. It then checks for Registry keys, file version numbers, and checksums for each file or key that should have been installed with the hotfix. If there is a match to the XML file, the hotfix is presumed to be installed. If not, MBSA notifies you of this misconfiguration.

Each hotfix is stored under the Registry key `HKLM\Software\Microsoft\WindowsNT\`
`CurrentVersion\Hotfix\Q######`. Each hotfix has its own name with the syntax *Q######_ XXX_YYY_ZZZ_LL*`.exe`:

- *Q######* is the number of the Knowledge Base article that discusses the hotfix.
- *XXX* indicates the platform or operating system to which this hotfix should be applied.
- *YYY* indicates the service pack level the system should be at before installing the hotfix.
- *ZZZ* indicates the hardware platform for which this hotfix was written.
- *LL* indicates the language of the hotfix.

MBSA scans not only for Windows Server 2003 and Windows 2000 hotfixes, but also for hotfixes associated with Windows XP, IIS (Internet Information Services), SQL Server 7 and 2000, and Internet Explorer 5.01 and later. This tool also checks for simple passwords and informs you if the passwords are either simple or blank.

Installing MBSA

To install the MBSA tool, follow these steps:

MBSA will not install via Windows Terminal Services.

1. Download MBSA from Microsoft's website.
2. Double-click the `mbsasetup.msi` file to start Microsoft Baseline Security Analyzer Setup.
3. At the Welcome screen, click Next to open the licensing agreement screen.
4. Read the licensing agreement, agree to it, and then click Next to open the User Information screen:

5. Enter your name and organization information, choose whether you want the tool available for all users of the computer or just you, and then click Next to open the Destination Folder screen.

6. Specify where you want the MBSA files installed and then click Next to open the Choose Install Options screen. You can choose to do the following:

   - Launch the application after it is installed.

   - View the Readme file after installation.

   - Place a shortcut to MBSA on the Desktop after installation.

7. Make your selections and then click Next to open the Select Features screen:

8. If you are unsure whether you have enough disk space to install MBSA, click the Disk Cost button to display a screen that shows you the amount of space that MBSA will consume and the amount of free disk space you will have after installation (see Figure 3.6).

FIGURE 3.6   Click the Disk Cost button to display information about drive space.

The Select Features screen really doesn't give you much in terms of additional features. About all you can select here is whether you want the MBSA installed on the local hard drive or whether you want all the features installed on the local hard drive. This is a bit of playing with semantics, because both choices lead to the same end.

9. Click Next, and Setup tells you that it is ready to install the application.

10. Click Next to begin the installation.

In Exercise 3.2, you will install the MBSA tool.

EXERCISE 3.2

Installing the MBSA Tool

1. Double-click the mbsasetup.msi file to start Microsoft Baseline Security Analyzer Setup.

2. At the Welcome screen, click Next to open the licensing agreement screen.

3. Agree to the licensing agreement and then click Next to open the User Information screen.

4. Specify whether you want the tool available for everyone or only yourself, fill in the identifying information, and then click Next to open the Destination Folder screen.

5. Select your destination folder and click Next to open the Choose Install Options screen.

6. Make your install option choices and click Next to open the Select Features screen.

7. Click Next, and Setup tells you that it is ready to start the installation.

8. Click Next again to start the installation.

9. Click Finish.

When you first run the MBSA tool, you'll see a rather nifty opening splash screen, as shown in Figure 3.7.

FIGURE 3.7   The opening menu screen for the MBSA tool

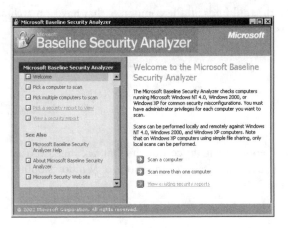

From this point, you can scan one or multiple computers, view security reports, or access online help.

We think it would be worthwhile, as a running example here, to scan both test computers in the testforest.com domain. It will be interesting to see how the default installation of Windows 2000 compares with the service packs and hotfixes that Microsoft recommends. By the way, we already have Service Pack 3 installed on our domain controller, DC1. So what we'll do is click the Pick Multiple Computers To Scan link to display in the right pane input fields that let you enter a domain name and/or range of IP (Internet Protocol) addresses (see Figure 3.8).

FIGURE 3.8   Configuring MBSA to scan the testforest.com domain

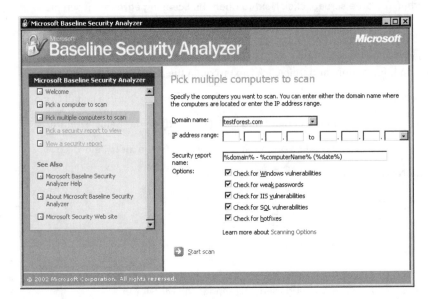

Armed with this information, the tool finds all the computers that have a match and then scans them for the selected items, which include the following:

- Windows vulnerabilities
- Weak passwords
- IIS vulnerabilities
- SQL vulnerabilities
- Hotfixes

After the tool runs, it displays a report listing the computers that it scanned and its evaluation of their security status. Needless to say, the default installations of Windows 2000 will incur a Severe Risk assessment (see Figure 3.9).

FIGURE 3.9   The results of running the MBSA tool on the two servers in the testforest.com domain

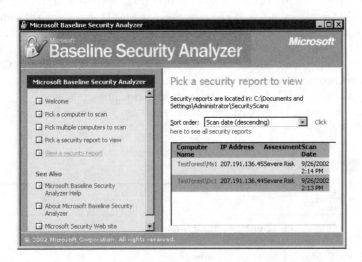

Clicking an individual computer in the report displays a detailed report for that computer (see Figure 3.10). If you run this tool on a default installation of Windows 2000 Server, you'll find that the default is really not very secure!

Although the MBSA tool has lots of whistles and bells, you can also use the HFNetChk tool to take care of many of the same tasks.

FIGURE 3.10   An individual server report from the MBSA tool

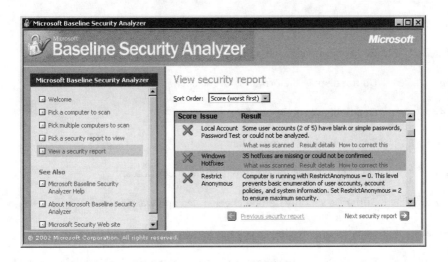

The HFNetChk Tool and MBSA

MBSA uses a command-line tool to expose all of the options previously available through HFNetChk to scan the target computer(s). You now use the mbsacli.exe command-line utility to access the information that used to be acquired through HFNetChk. The mbsacli.exe utility has a large list of options that make it extremely flexible. The reason you'll probably want to run MBSA as opposed to mbsacli.exe from the command line is that MBSA has a GUI front end that makes it easier to manage and navigate. The command-line interface of mbsacli.exe allows for it to be used in scheduled tasks and as part of many different scripts.

To view the syntax for mbsacli.exe, type **mbsacli.exe /?** at a command prompt. Table 3.1 describes each of the switches.

TABLE 3.1   The HFNetChk Switches

/hf Switch	Description
/c	Scan a single computer by computer name.
/i	Scan a single computer by IP address.
/r	Scan multiple computers by scanning a range of IP addresses.
/d	Scan all computers in a domain.
/n	Select which scans to not perform. By default, all checks are run, including OS, SQL, IIS, Updates, and Password. Multiple selections can be made by using the + symbol (no spaces).
/o	Output is in XML file format.
/f	Redirect output to a file.
/qp	Do not display the progress of the scan.
/qe	Do not display the error list.
/s 0	Do not display the report list.
/s 1	Do not suppress the security update check notes.
/s 2	Suppress security update check notes and warnings.
/nosum	Security update checks will not test file checksums.
/sus	Check only security updates approved at the specific Software Update Services (SUS) server. The /sus switch includes the /nosum switch. Include /sum to override the /nosum that is implied.

TABLE 3.1 The HFNetChk Switches *(continued)*

/hf Switch	Description
/e	List errors from the latest scan.
/l	List all reports available.
/ls	List reports from the latest scan.
/lr	Display the overview report.
/ld	Display a detailed report.
/v	Display the security update reason codes.
/hf	Run the mbsacli in HFNetChk mode.
-h	Specify the NetBIOS computer name to scan. The default location is the local host. You can scan multiple host names if you separate each host name entry with a comma, as follows: hfnetchk -h *computer1,computer2,server1,server2.*
-fh	Specify the name of a file that contains NetBIOS computer names to scan. There is one computer name on every line, with a maximum of 256 in every file.
-i	Specify the IP address of the computer to scan. Similar to NetBIOS names, you can scan multiple IP addresses if you separate each IP address entry with a comma.
-fip	Specify the name of a file that contains IP addresses to scan. There is one IP address for every line, with a maximum of 256 for each file.
-r	Specify the IP address range to be scanned, beginning with *ipaddress1* and ending with *ipaddress2* inclusive, for example: hfnetchk -r 172.16.1.1-172.16.1.35.
-d	Specify the domain name to scan. All computers in the domain are scanned.
-n	Specify all computers on the local network to be scanned. This switch is similar to the -d switch for a domain, but all computers from all domains in My Network Places are scanned.
-history	Display hotfixes that have been explicitly installed. Explicitly installed hotfixes are individually installed, as opposed to being installed in a group via a rollup package.
-b	Scan your computer for hotfixes that are marked as baseline critical by the Microsoft Security Response Center (MSRC). To perform a baseline scan, your computer must be running the latest service pack that is available for your operating system.

TABLE 3.1   The HFNetChk Switches *(continued)*

/hf Switch	Description
-t	Display the number of threads that are used to run the scan. Possible values are from 1 through 128. The default value is 64. You can use this switch to throttle down (or up) the speed of the scanner.
-o	Specify the desired output format. The (tab) outputs in tab-delimited format. The (wrap) outputs in a word-wrapped format. You'll use the tab output when scanning more than 255 hosts. The default is wrap.
-x	Specify the XML data source for the hotfix information. The default file is the Mssecure.cab file from Microsoft's website.
-s	Eliminate the NOTE and WARNING messages in the output of the tool. The number 1 = NOTE messages only. The number 2 = both NOTE and WARNING messages. The default is no suppression.
-nosum	Prevent the tool from performing checksum validation for the hotfix files. The checksum information is found in the Mssecure.xml file for all hotfixes.
-z	Prevent the tool from performing Registry checks.
-v	Display the reason that a scan did not work in wrap mode.
-f	Specify the name of a file to output the results to.
-u	Specify the username to use when scanning local or remote computer(s). You must use this switch with the -p (password) switch.
-p	Specify the password to use to help create the security context under which the tool will run. This switch must be used with the -u switch.
-about	Display information about HFNetChk.
-?	Display a help menu.

You can find a public newsgroup dedicated to the HFNetChk tool at microsoft.public .security.hfnetchk on the news.microsoft.com website.

HFNetChk is a good tool to use for scanning individual computers or a range of computers. However, it can be used only to scan for security updates and service packs. MBSA not only provides a graphical user interface (GUI), it also provides much great functionality. MBSA can scan Windows computers for security practices such as identifying weak passwords and missing passwords. MBSA can also be used to scan IIS and SQL servers for common configuration problems. Microsoft Office, Outlook, and Internet Explorer can also be scanned for security configuration problems using MBSA. The current release of MBSA, V1.2, combines the functionality of earlier versions of MBSA with HFNetChk in a single product.

A new feature of MBSA is that it will use your current SUS server to identify the hotfixes and service packs that have been approved for the company. The results of the MBSA scan will identify only approved fixes that have not been implemented.

If you want a quick and clean report on which updates are installed on a single computer or a range of computers, HFNetChk is a great tool to use. The differentiating factor between using HFNetChk vs. MBSA is not the number of computers scanned, but the desired information. If you want just a report listing the updates that are not installed, HFNetChk is the tool to use. If you want to check for other items, such as IIS and SQL vulnerabilities, use MBSA.

Slipstreaming

Slipstreaming is a method for incorporating a service pack into the base install files on an installation point so that when a new installation occurs, the service pack is automatically installed. Slipstreaming removes the need to install the service pack separately.

To slipstream a service pack into a distribution share point, take these steps:

1. Create a distribution folder where you want the installation files to be held.

2. Copy the I386 folder contents from the Windows 2000 CD-ROM. Be sure to copy all of the subfolders too.

3. Run the service pack with the following syntax:

   `Update.exe -s:c:\<folder_name>`

This command copies all the service pack files over the original installation files. Then, whenever a new installation is performed using these files, the service pack that was slipstreamed into the installation point is automatically installed.

In Exercise 3.3, you will slipstream Service Pack 3 into a Windows 2000 installation share point. The process is similar for Windows Server 2003.

EXERCISE 3.3

Creating a Slipstreamed Installation Share Point

1. Create a distribution folder on your server.

2. Copy the contents of the I386 folder into the folder you just created.

3. Place the CD for Service Pack 3 in your CD-ROM drive.

4. Run this command: **update.exe -s:c:\<*name_of_distribution_folder*>**.

5. Allow enough time for the installation to finish.

Using Remote Installation Services (RIS)

We've chosen not to describe in detail how to create a RIS image and how to deploy it. This is a long, involved topic that would provide great background information, but probably not prepare you for the exam topic discussed in this chapter. You can't use RIS to keep your new workstations up-to-date with the latest service packs. This is not a solution for workstations that have already been deployed. Instead, this is a solution for creating a new workstation with the latest service packs and hotfixes when initially installing the workstation's operating system.

When new hotfixes become available, you can install these fixes on test servers and workstations. Once installed, you can then run Sysprep and store the new baseline image for future server and workstation installations using third-party image distribution software. If the image is a Windows 2000, Windows XP Professional, or Windows Server 2003 image, you can use RIS as a means of distribution. The basic steps to using RIS are:

1. Install the RIS service on a server using the Add or Remove Software applet in Control Panel.

2. During installation, point the RIS service to the location where the source files are for the proper operating system. RIS can be used to deploy Windows 2000 Professional and Windows XP Professional, for example. Both appear on the selection menu if you configure both sources. Authorize the RIS server in the DHCP MMC console.

3. Use a PXE (preboot execution environment) version .99c or later enabled network card or a RIS boot disk that supports many popular network cards that are not PXE to boot the computer to the network.

4. Enter the proper information during installation to complete the installation of the operating system.

You can also use RIS to build a number of reference computers and then run RIPrep on the reference computers to load the images—including all new software and configurations—onto the RIS server. The images then appear on the menu for RIS clients. RIPrep is a good solution for creating images for deployment by RIS. However, there are many third-party applications that are much better than RIS.

The good part of this is that new workstations can be installed completely updated with all the latest service packs and patches. The downside is that you'll need to keep re-creating the image, which means rebuilding a source workstation every time a new service pack or hotfix becomes available. This is probably a solution for larger environments only, in which the time spent rebuilding the source image is less than the time spent updating new computers after they have been deployed.

Working with Custom Scripts

If you are running a scripted installation of Windows Server 2003, Windows 2000, or Windows XP, you can include in a script the hotfixes and updates. For both hotfixes and service packs, the -q switch allows the installation to run in quiet mode, which means that no user interaction is required for the installation to complete. Because every installation can be scripted, there are ways to ensure that a full, unattended installation occurs without any user intervention and with every update and fix installed.

Here are the command-line switches for update.exe:

-u   Unattended mode.

-f   Force other applications to close at shutdown.

-n   Do not back up files for uninstall.

-o	Overwrite OEM files without prompting.
-z	Do not restart the computer after installation has completed.
-q	Quiet mode—no user interaction.
-s:<foldername>	Use integrated installation mode.

Here are the command-line switches for `hotfix.exe`:

-y	Uninstall hotfix.
-f	Force other applications to close at shutdown.
-n	Do not back up files for uninstall.
-z	Do not restart the computer after installation has completed.
-q	Quiet mode—no user interaction.
-m	Unattended mode.
-l	List installed hotfixes.

> If you have installed multiple hotfixes that replace the same file and you want to roll back your installation, you'll need to uninstall the hotfixes in reverse order of how they were installed.

You can also include the QChain tool in your scripts to ensure that you don't have version conflicts between hotfixes when they are installed with only one reboot. Be sure to read the section on QChain later in this chapter, as this is an outstanding tool that helps install multiple updates with only one reboot of the server.

Working on Isolated Networks

In a nutshell, Microsoft feels that the best way to keep your system up-to-date is to use their Software Update Services. This service (discussed in detail later in this chapter) allows you to set up a dedicated server to download and locally host new updates from Microsoft. This server will also manage offering these updates to the computers on your network.

However, if you are on an isolated network, meaning that you have *no* Internet connectivity, you'll need to install the updates and fixes using an alternative method. This means that you might need to order the service pack CD-ROMs or find an offsite location with good Internet connectivity, download the updates, burn them to a CD-ROM, and then bring them into your network, or find another way to import the updates into your network.

Software Update Services lets you manually download updates. In a highly secure environment, it might be wise to completely disconnect the network from the Internet and connect only the Software Update Services server long enough to download the updates. Although more time-consuming for the administrator, this ensures that your network has all the updates installed, yet is only connected for discrete periods of time to the Internet.

Installing on New Clients and Servers

If you don't use RIS or any imaging system to install new clients and server, but yet you want to ensure that the initial installation contains all the latest service packs and hotfixes, this section is for you. Essentially, what you'll be doing is using an .ini file to specify the hotfixes that you want to run after you've installed a slipstreamed version of Windows 2000 Server or Professional, Windows XP Professional, or Windows Server 2003.

Follow these steps:

1. Create a distribution share point on your network and slipstream the latest service pack into the Windows installation files.

2. Prepare the hotfixes for installation. Because the Windows Setup program requires the 8.3 naming convention for all files and folders in the distribution folder, you must change the hotfix filenames from Q######_XXX_YYY_ZZZ_LL to Q######.

3. Open the dosnet.inf file located in the I386 folder on your distribution share point.

4. Add svcpack under the [OptionalSrcDirs] section. Save this file.

5. Create a svcpack folder under the I386 folder on your distribution share point and copy the sp3.cat file to this folder.

6. Copy the hotfix(es) to this folder using the 8.3 naming convention.

7. Expand the hotfix and then copy the hotfix binary files to the I386 folder. There is no need to copy hotfix.exe, hotfix.inf, spmsg.dll, or the symbol files.

8. Under the I386 folder, delete the svcpack.inf file.

9. Create a new svcpack.inf file and include the following information:

    ```
    [Version]
    Signature="$Windows NT$"
    [SetupData]
    CatalogSubDir="i386/svcpack"
    [ProductCatalogsToInstall]
    sp3.cat
    [SetupHotfixesToRun]
    Q######.exe </switches you want to use>
    ```

As the number of hotfixes increases or changes, all you need to do is expand the hotfix, copy the binary files to the I386 folder, ensure that the old binary files are deleted, and note the new hotfix in the SetupHotfixesToRun section of the svcpack.ini file.

Once complete, you can then use the regular setup commands to run this command in unattended mode.

If you don't want to slipstream the installation files, you can install Windows 2000 and later, integrated with the latest service pack. To do this, follow these steps:

1. Copy the installation files for Windows to a distribution share point.

2. Expand the service pack files to another distribution share point.

3. Run the update.exe program in integrated mode using the following syntax:

    ```
    Update.exe -s:x:\Windows
    ```

- The -s switch specifies integrated mode.

- x:\ is the drive letter of the partition holding your Windows installation files.

- \Windows is the name (and path) of the folder holding the installation files.

After Update.exe builds the integrated installation, you can deploy Windows to your users' computers from the distribution share point in either attended or unattended mode.

Managing Service Packs and Hotfixes

To say on top of the latest security issues from Microsoft, you can check several resources:

- Sign up to receive the latest Microsoft security bulletins from the Microsoft Security Bulletin Service. Whenever a new bulletin is released, you will receive an e-mail outlining the security problem and a link to the fix(es) for the problem.

- Microsoft Software Update Services sends automatic notifications to your servers and workstations when security updates are posted to Microsoft's website. Microsoft has also released free software that lets an individual server on your network act as a Windows Update server. This is a nifty way to keep your network up-to-date with the latest security fixes and updates. We'll discuss this server and Windows Update a bit later in this chapter.

- Windows BugTraq is an independent website that maintains a mailing list that reports reproducible security bugs in Windows NT, Windows 2000, Windows XP, Windows Server 2003 and related applications. You can find this website, shown in Figure 3.11, at www.ntbugtraq.com.

- You can use the MBSA, discussed earlier in this chapter.

These four resources, when combined, can provide a powerful solution for keeping your workstations and servers up-to-date. This section focuses largely on the Software Update Services, because this is a free software package that you can deploy on your servers and workstations.

FIGURE 3.11   The home page for ntbugtraq.com

Software Update Services: Keeping Servers and Clients Up-to-Date

You can find the Software Update Services software at `www.microsoft.com/windowsserversystem/sus/default.mspx`. This software will help you manage and distribute critical Windows updates and fixes. What this software relieves you of is the responsibility of having to constantly check for new updates or download those updates when they become available. SUS does this automatically. And only one server requires access to the Internet; the rest of your servers and workstations can be on an isolated network without Internet connectivity.

Here are the features of SUS:

Content synchronization between your SUS server and the Windows Update service at Microsoft   The synchronization feature resides on the SUS server and retrieves the latest updates from Microsoft. As new updates are added to the Windows Update service at Microsoft, the SUS server automatically downloads and stores those updates locally. You can schedule this automatic downloading, or you can download manually.

Intranet-hosted Windows Update server   Because the updates are downloaded to your SUS server, what you'll essentially have is a Windows Update server on your own network. This local server will handle the updates from Microsoft to all the servers and workstations on your network.

The opportunity to test new updates before deployment   Because the updates are downloaded to the SUS server, you can test the effects of installing each update before deploying it on your network. You can schedule the updates to run on your network, and you can deploy them according to the options that you select.

Integration with the Automatic Updates feature   Automatic Updates is a Windows feature that can be set up to automatically check for updates published on Windows Update. SUS can publish downloaded updates, and the clients can obtain their updates from your local SUS server instead of from Microsoft's Windows Update server.

The SUS solution has both server- and client-side software that is intended to run on only Windows 2000, Windows XP Professional, and Windows Server 2003.

 If you are operating in a mixed environment of Windows Server 2003, Windows 2000, Windows NT, Windows 9x, Unix, Novell, Macintosh, and/or DOS, you'll need to find other ways to install the updates. For example, you can use Microsoft's Systems Management Server.

The SUS solution has three main components:

- *Windows Update Synchronization Service*, which downloads content to your server running SUS
- The installation of an SUS website that services update requests from clients
- The installation of an SUS administration web page

From a client perspective, the SUS solution provides a number of features that are attractive, including the following:

- Background downloads
- Chained installations

- Built-in security
- Manageability
- Multilanguage support

Creating an SUS Server

After you download the software, you will need to install it. Your server must meet the following requirements:

- A P700 processor or higher
- 512MB RAM
- 6GB of available disk space
- Windows 2000 with Service Pack 2 or later
- Windows Server 2003
- Not a domain controller
- Not a Small Business Server (SBS)
- NTFS file system

To install the SUS software on a server, follow these steps:

1. Double-click the `sussetup.msi` file (a newer version with Service Pack 1 is `sus10sp1.exe` from Microsoft's website) to start an inventory of your server, which will give you context-sensitive error messages such as not enough memory, not enough available disk space, or domain controller status.

2. When the inventory is complete (it's performed transparently in the background), you'll see the Welcome screen to the Microsoft Software Update Services Setup Wizard.

3. Click Next to open the licensing agreement screen.

4. Agree to the licensing terms and then click Next to open the Installation Choices screen.

5. You can choose to perform a typical or a custom installation. We'll demonstrate a custom installation. However, the typical selection is just fine if you want to perform the installation quickly with default settings. Select Custom and then click Next to open the Choose File Locations screen:

You can select the location for the updates to be stored by specifying the path when you click the Browse button. The default is c:\sus\. Most administrators will want to select a path other than the root drive.

You can also specify whether you want the updates pushed down to each computer on your network and then installed locally or whether you want all the computers to connect to your internal SUS and install the updates from that server.

6. Make your selection and then click Next to open the Language Updates screen.

7. You can select all languages, which is the default, you can select English, or you can specify another language. Again, just make your choices and then click Next to open the Update Approval Settings screen.

8. Here, you can tell SUS whether you want to manually approve new updates or have the tool automatically approve the updates. If you select the manual choice, you'll have the opportunity to test the updates in your environment before they are deployed on your network. In this example, select the Manual option and then click Next to open the Client URL Information screen.

9. This screen gives you the default URL that your clients should connect to for updates. The default URL is http://<servername>. This screen is for information only, and when you click Next, the installation will commence.

Setup will run the IIS Lockdown tool. This means that URLScan will be automatically installed as well. Once this tool has been installed and installation is complete, you'll see a screen indicating the URL for administration of the tool, which is, by default, http://<servername>/susadmin.

FIGURE 3.12   The home page for the administration of Software Update Services

Configuring the Software Update Services

Once installed, SUS needs to be configured. To do this, you have to be running Internet Explorer 5.5 or later. Go to `http://<servername>/susadmin` (see Figure 3.12). You'll also find a shortcut to this site under the Administrative Tools.

> You must be logged on as a local administrator to view the administration website for Software Update Services.

Click the Set Options link in the left pane to open the Set Options page (see Figure 3.13) on which you can configure a proxy server for SUS. Enter the information that's needed. In addition, on this page, you can specify the name of the server that your clients use to connect to the server.

Notice that you are entering the NetBIOS name of the computer. If you need to use DNS, enter the fully qualified domain name (FQDN) for the server or enter its IP address. Finally, you can select to have this server synchronize directly with Microsoft's Windows Update server or synchronize with another update server that is hosted locally on your network. The second option allows you to deploy a farm of update servers on your network to provide load balancing for numerous client connections. This would only be applicable in large environments. Again, if you are using DNS for name resolution on your network, you'll want to enter the FQDN of the server from which this server should obtain its updates. Otherwise, NetBIOS name resolution is assumed.

You can configure the synchronization schedule of the server with the Windows Update server at Microsoft by clicking the Synchronize Server link in the left pane of the home page (see Figure 3.12, shown earlier). On the Synchronize Server page are two buttons: Synchronize Now and Synchronization Schedule. Click the Synchronize Now button if you want your server to synchronize itself with Microsoft's Windows Update server. This is best used when the server is first installed and you want to get all the updates downloaded right away to your SUS server. When you click this button, the Windows catalog is downloaded first and then the updates. A progress bar informs you of the progress of the downloads. The catalog is important to download because the SUS server will compare its version of the catalog with the version on the Windows Update server. Should they match, there are no updates to download. However, if there is not a match, the server will download the missing updates and make them available to the other computers on your network.

After all the updates are downloaded, you are prompted to click OK and approve the updates. Remember that updates cannot be installed on computers on your network until they are approved. When this package is initially downloaded, you'll need to click a number of check boxes to approve the updates that you want installed on your network if you selected the Manually Approve option. This can be time-consuming because there is no Select All button in the user interface. Also, if you did not select a specific language to install, all language versions will be downloaded. You'll need to scroll through that list and select the updates that you want installed and the language that you want to use as well.

Clicking the Synchronization Schedule button displays a simple schedule page that allows you to set a basic synchronization schedule so that you don't have to manually update the SUS server. The best practice here is to download updates when the server is not being backed up.

Installing the SUS Client

Except for your SUS servers, all your other computers will be SUS clients. If you are running Service Pack 2 or earlier for Windows 2000 or Windows XP Professional without Service Pack 1, you can install the SUS client, wuau22.msi. However, the SUS client is included in Service Pack 3 for Windows 2000 and Service Pack 1 for Windows XP Professional, so by installing this service pack, you also install the SUS client. Windows Server 2003 ships with the SUS client installed.

FIGURE 3.13   The Set Options page for Software Update Services

Now, you might think that if you open the client, you can make your configuration choices there. Not true. Instead, you will configure the client via Group Policy Objects (GPOs).

When Service Pack 3 is installed in Windows 2000, for example, a wuau.adm file is also installed, which can be imported as a template into a GPO. Once installed, the GPO can be applied to the client computers. After you add the .adm template to the GPO, you can find the Windows Update node under the Administrative Templates section.

See Chapter 2, "Configuring Security Based on Computer Roles," for information about how to add templates to GPOs.

To install the SUS client, you'll apply a GPO that has imported the wuau.adm. Here are the steps to follow to install the SUS client:

1. Under the Windows Update node inside the Administrative Templates of your Windows 2000 GPO, double-click the Configure Automatic Updates setting to open the Configure Automatic Updates Properties dialog box:

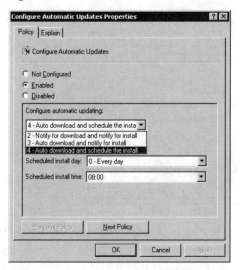

2. Notice that you can configure the update method, how the updates are applied to the client, and a schedule of when you want the updates installed. Make your selections and click OK, or if you want to go to the next policy, click the Next Policy button.

 In Windows Server 2003 GPOs, you will find the proper settings in the Computer Configuration\Administrative Templates\Windows Components\Windows Update node.

If you select Notify For Download And Notify For Install or Auto Download And Notify For Install options in the Configure Automatic Updating section, you need to understand that these options work only with a logged-on administrative user account. User accounts that are not members of the local administrative group will not receive these notifications.

The other policy setting in the Windows Update node is Specify Intranet Microsoft Update Service Location Properties. Double-click this setting to open the Specify Intranet Microsoft Update Service Location Properties dialog box, as shown in Figure 3.14.

In this dialog box, you can specify the update server from which your clients will download and install the updates. You'll also need to specify the statistics server. This server is the server to which clients will upload their statistics information so that from the SUS Admin page, you can determine aggregate numbers about updates on your network.

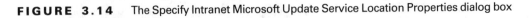

FIGURE 3.14   The Specify Intranet Microsoft Update Service Location Properties dialog box

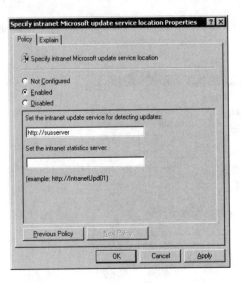

The statistics server must be running IIS. Statistics are stored in the IIS logs. The client returns to the statistics server the following information:

- During self-update: self-update pending
- After self-update: success or failure
- During detection: initialization success or failure
- After detection: detection success or failure
- After download: download success or failure
- After installation: installation success or failure

If you plan to use a server other than your SUS server as a statistics server, you need to copy the `\<website root>\Vroot\wutrack.bin` file to the root of your statistics server. This file is necessary to log SUS stats to the statistics server. Moreover, if you want only SUS statistics to appear in the logs (instead of all the HTTP traffic), you need to turn off logging in the website Properties dialog box. Then right-click `wutrack.bin` and choose Log Visits from the shortcut menu.

When Automatic Updates is configured through Group Policies, the policy will override the preferences set by the local administrator for the Windows client. If the policy is removed, the settings for the local client are used once again.

The nice thing about using GPOs to configure the clients is that by applying different settings to different OUs (organizational units), different SUS servers can be specified for a group of computers and thereby load-balance calls to your SUS servers.

If you are not running Service Pack 3 for Windows 2000, you'll need to deploy the SUS client. This is also true for Windows XP Professional, which requires SP1 in order to have the SUS client included. You can add the SUS client in several ways. First, you can use IntelliMirror (for

Active Directory clients only) by configuring a GPO and creating a new software installation package. Assign the software package instead of publishing it and then allow time for the policy to replicate throughout the forest. Ensure that you configure the package to install at boot time. Then reboot your client computers.

You can also deploy the SUS client using the Critical Update Notification (CUN) service. Set this Registry key as follows:

```
HKLM\Software\Microsoft\Windows\CurrentVersion\WindowsUpdate\CriticalUpdate
```

Create a `SelfUpdServer` key as a REG_SZ and enter the following value:

```
http://<Servername./SelfUpdate/CUN5_4
```

Do the exact same thing under the following key:

```
HKLM\Software\Microsoft\Windows\CurrentVersion\WindowsUpdate\
CriticalUpdate\Critical Update SelfUpdate
```

To confirm that this has been successful, find the `wuaueng.dll` file and check its version number, which should be equal to or later than 5.4.3626.2.

SUS and Disaster Recovery

To successfully recover your SUS server in the event of a disaster, you need to back up the website directory in which the SUS administration website was created, the SUS directory that contains the content, and the *IIS metabase*.

You can back up the IIS metabase from within the IIS MMC (Microsoft Management Console). In the IIS console, follow these steps:

1. Select the server to back up.
2. Choose Action ➢ Backup/Restore Configuration to open the Configuration Backup dialog box.
3. Enter a configuration backup name and then create the backup.

You can now use your backup software to back up the metabase backup file.

Deploying SUS in the Enterprise

If you are using a proxy server to access the Internet, be sure to configure your proxy server on the Set Options page in the SUS Admin website. If you need to bypass the proxy server for local addresses, select the Bypass Proxy Server For Local Addresses check box. If your proxy server requires a user ID and password to access the Internet, select the Use The Following User Credentials To Access The Proxy Server check box and enter the needed credentials. You can also specify that basic authentication is used if your proxy server requires basic authentication.

You can deploy a farm of SUS servers to ensure that there is load-balancing of client requests for updates. You can synchronize content between servers running SUS or from a manually configured distribution point. Such a farm is useful when you have multiple SUS servers and you don't want all of them going to the Internet to update their content. In addition, if you have sites that do not have Internet access, or if you want to pull content only from a test lab (after the updates have been tested) into your production environment, synchronizing content between SUS servers is an excellent solution.

The server that obtains the updates from Microsoft's website is considered the *Parent server*. Other servers on your network that update their information from the Parent server are considered Child servers. On the *Child server*, click the Set Options link in the home page of Software Update Services to display the Set Options page. Enter the correct server name and select the Synchronize From A Local Software Update Services Server radio button (see Figure 3.15). Moreover, if you select the Synchronize List Of Approved Items Updated From This Location (Replace Mode) check box, the Child server synchronizes the list of approved items along with the content. However, if you make this selection, you will not be able to alter the list of approved items on the Child server because that list is the same list as the one on the Parent server. If you need to make changes to this list, make your changes on the Parent server.

When you first install SUS, a default distribution point is created under the virtual root /Content folder. If you want to manually create a content distribution point, you must create a folder named Content and copy all the items from the Content folder on the source SUS server to the distribution server. You then create an IIS virtual root called http://<*servername*>/ content and point that root to the Content folder. Remember that you can only deploy content that has been synchronized via SUS to other manually created content distribution points.

In larger environments, you can configure the SUS farm in conjunction with Network Load Balancing (NLB) to balance client connectivity to the Child servers. In this scenario, you'll have only one server downloading content from Microsoft's website; then the Child servers will synchronize their content and offer it to your users. NLB works best when there is good connectivity between all your Child servers and your clients. The nice thing about using NLB is that you can assign the same IP address and host name to all the Child servers in the cluster (*cluster* is the term used by NLB to designate which servers are load-balanced by this service) and thus publish only one URL for all users to connect to. In large environments, this eliminates the necessity of having to create different GPOs and move computer accounts to different OUs to achieve load balancing across Child servers.

When working with Child servers, each server should store its content locally. In addition, you'll need to ensure that you have all the locales selected that will meet the needs of your users and choose the same locales for all the servers in the NLB cluster. Finally, each Child server in the cluster should obtain its downloads from the same source, whether that is a manual distribution point or another SUS server.

Troubleshooting SUS

Two logs are provided to the administrator to help determine SUS errors and activities: the synchronization log (see Figure 3.16) and the approval log. You can view both logs from the SUS Admin web page. You can use the logs to determine the point of failure and then use this information to further troubleshoot the problem.

In addition, the synchronization service generates event log messages for every synchronization action performed by the server and notes any major errors that were encountered. Moreover, a Monitor Server page (see Figure 3.17) in the SUS Admin website keeps information about available updates. This page displays the current contents of the metadata cache on the IIS server. From this page, you can find out how many updates are available for each platform on your network. You'll also see the last time the cache was updated next to each platform.

FIGURE 3.15   The Set Options page of the Microsoft Software Update Services website

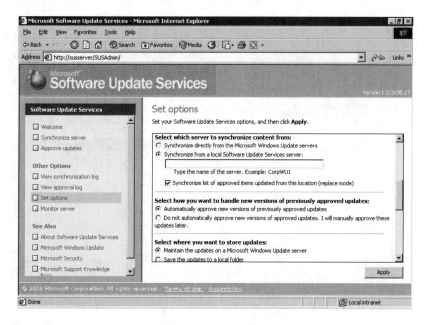

FIGURE 3.16   The synchronization log on a SUS server

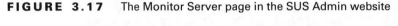

FIGURE 3.17   The Monitor Server page in the SUS Admin website

The white paper "Deploying Microsoft Software Update Services" contains a list of all the event log messages and error codes for the Software Update Services. If you are working with SUS, it is a good idea to print a copy of this paper and have it available for reference. You should also read through this paper to prepare for the exam.

 You can find the white paper "Deploying Microsoft Software Update Services" at www.microsoft.com/windowsserversystem/sus/default.mspx.

 Real World Scenario

Using SUS to Deploy Updates to 20,000 Windows Workstations

You work in a large installation of 20,000 workstations, with 10,000 Windows 2000 Professional workstations, 5000 Windows NT 4 workstations, and 5000 Windows 98 workstations. In addition, there are 400 Windows 2003 servers. Generally speaking, your company deploys roughly 550 new workstations each month. Because building new workstation images for all three workstation platforms every time a new update is released is too time-consuming, your CIO has directed you to develop a plan to install new workstations in unattended mode with all the updates and service packs. All new workstations are Windows 2000 Professional workstations.

Moreover, your CIO is tired of trying to keep all the security updates installed on the servers and workstations. Your CIO has stated that the servers can be rebooted only once—when hotfixes are installed. He wants to ensure that the servers are up as much as possible, and he has made a requirement that no workstation can be connected to the network at any time without the latest updates and service packs installed.

The solution for this scenario is as follows:

1. Use slipstreaming to update the I386 installation folder for Windows 2000 Professional.

2. Create an unattended script to install the Windows 2000 Professional workstation operating system. Fold the script into a batch file that includes the unattended script commands for the operating system, plus all the hotfix commands that run with QChain.

3. Run the batch file on the new workstation and allow the operating system to install with the hotfixes.

4. Reboot the Windows 2000 Professional workstation. It should now be up-to-date and ready to connect to the network.

To keep the Windows NT 4 and Windows 98 workstations up-to-date, install the SMS (Systems Management Server) client and require the SMS client to install the new updates as they are released to the network. Do not allow your users to decline the installation. Because some users rarely reboot their workstations, force the SMS packages to install at logon.

For your Windows 2000 and Windows Server 2003 servers and current Windows 2000 Professional and Windows XP Professional workstations, take the following steps:

1. Install a dedicated SUS server and have that server download the updates from Microsoft's website.

2. Make this first SUS server a Parent server.

3. Build a farm of five Child SUS servers that synchronize their content with the Parent server.

4. Use NLB to balance calls between the Child SUS servers and publish a single URL for SUS connectivity.

5. Create a GPO that instructs all the Windows 2000 computers to download and install the updates from the SUS server farm.

6. Make sure that the schedule for the updates does not occur when backups, indexing, or other regular database maintenance utilities are running.

Ensure that your servers install updates at a time when they can be rebooted with minimal user interruption, usually overnight.

Systems Management Server (SMS)

Remembering that GPOs can be used along with SUS to distribute the proper client software and configuration settings, one of the main uses of Systems Management Server (SMS) when it comes to software distribution for security needs is to push out updates to older Windows clients. This includes Windows NT 4 and Windows 9*x* clients. You can set up software packages to install when the user logs on and even give the user a choice as to when the software is installed. Using SMS, you can also schedule software to be installed when users are not logged on to your network.

If you need to upgrade computers that have an operating system already installed, you can use SMS. However, you cannot use SMS to perform the operating system installation. You must use other means to install the operating system on your client computers.

QChain

QChain.exe is a command-line utility that gives you the ability to install multiple hotfixes with only one reboot of the server, even if each individual hotfix would require a reboot on its own. The updates are "chained" together into a single installation, and then the server is rebooted only once. This allows more uptime for each server.

If you try to install multiple hotfixes before rebooting a server without QChain, you can run into a situation in which one hotfix replaces a file in the Pending File Rename queue that another hotfix already placed in the queue. The potential to overwrite a more recent version of a file with an older version is great, and you can end up with version conflicts.

The answer to this problem is to use QChain. To install multiple hotfixes with only one reboot, first run each hotfix with the -z switch to instruct the hotfix to not reboot after installation. After you install all the hotfixes, run QChain.exe and then reboot the computer.

 Knowledge Base article Q296861 provides sample code for performing this operation using a simple batch file.

As you might have noticed by now, you can ensure that all the hotfixes are installed with one administrative act in two ways: you can use QChain, or you can use the method described earlier in this chapter that incorporates an .ini file, a distribution share point, and the manual expanding of hotfix files into the I386 distribution folder.

Which is better? Well, it all depends on your environment, but here are some guidelines:

When you need short installation times for your workstations, manually expand the hotfix binary files into the *I386* distribution folder.   If you are going to use imaging to create a new workstation, it makes sense to take the time to manually expand each hotfix back into the I386 distribution folder and then create a new image for use on your new computers. Although it's time-consuming to expand each hotfix, this method ensures that the installation of the image doesn't take long and is up-to-date the moment the computer has complete installation.

When you need to ensure that your servers are up as much as possible, use QChain. Because multiple hotfixes can be installed with only one reboot, it makes sense to use QChain to install hotfixes on your Windows 2000 or Windows NT 4 servers.

When you install new workstations using unattended mode but don't want to run a batch file after installation to install the updates, manually expand the hotfix binary files into the *I386* distribution folder.   Then add command lines in the Cmdlines.txt file to run the hotfixes during Windows 2000 Setup. Using this method, only one command—the unattend command—will have to be run because the hotfixes are already present in the I386 distribution folder. Just run the setup as you normally would, and the installation of each workstation will be up-to-date.

In Exercise 3.4, you'll use QChain to install a series of hotfixes.

EXERCISE 3.4

Using QChain to Install a Series of Hotfixes

1. Place the hotfixes that need to be installed in the same folder location as the QChain utility.

2. Create a batch file that runs each hotfix as follows:

```
@echo off

setlocal

set PATHTOFIXES=<directory_path_to_fixes>

%PATHTOFIXES%\q######.EXE -Z -M

%PATHTOFIXES%\q######.EXE -Z -M

%PATHTOFIXES%\q######.EXE -Z -M

%PATHTOFIXES%\q######.EXE -Z -M

%PATHTOFIES%qchain.exe
```

3. Run the batch file.

4. Reboot the computer.

Troubleshooting the Deployment of Service Packs and Hotfixes

In our experience working with SUS, it's best to install the server software on a new installation of IIS. The best solution is to use a Windows Server 2003 server as the installation server for SUS. If you have previously installed a heavily dependent software product such as Microsoft's SharePoint Portal Server, uninstalled it, and then tried to install SUS, chances are good that SUS will install. But you won't be able to display the home page from which to perform administration, and SUS is likely to perform oddly in other areas.

Hence, it is a good idea that before you install SUS, you uninstall IIS, then reinstall IIS, and then reinstall the latest service pack. We think you'll bypass a number of difficult-to-troubleshoot issues using this method. The best solution is to perform a completely new build of the server.

Other troubleshooting scenarios will crop up, and it is impossible to discuss each possible scenario in this chapter. However, some common scenarios deserve attention, and we'll discuss them next. Some of these common scenarios have to do with third-party compatibility, some with SUS itself, and others with version conflicts.

Third-Party Application Compatibility Issues

You need to ensure that after SUS is installed, your third-party applications continue to run. The best practice is to install those applications on a test server and then install SUS and observe any negative effects before doing this on a production server. Another best practice is to quarantine SUS services on an individual server that is performing no other role. Doing this will ensure that your third-party applications are not interrupted with the introduction of SUS into your environment.

However, if you are not so fortunate as to have a plethora of servers sitting around, be aware of the changes that will be made to IIS when SUS is installed:

- The `AspProcessorThreadMax` Registry key is set to one (1).
- The `AspThreadGateEnabled` Registry key is set to TRUE.
- ASP (Active Server Pages) files are enabled.
- IDQ (Internet data query), SHTML (Secure Hypertext Markup Language), SHTM (secure HTM file), STM (server-side include file), IDC (Internet database connector), printer, and HTR (hard return) mappings are all disabled.
- Sample web files and the scripts virtual folder are removed.
- The MSDAC (Microsoft Data Access Components) virtual directory is removed.
- WebDAV (Web Distributed Authoring and Versioning) is disabled.
- IIS anonymous user is prevented from executing system utilities.
- IIS anonymous user is prevented from writing web content.

 The IIS Lockdown tool is not applied when SUS is installed on a Windows Server 2003 server because IIS 6 defaults to secure mode.

If any of your third-party applications need any settings different from those listed here, don't install SUS on that server.

Permissions

Some hotfixes and service packs will require administrative privileges on the local computer to successfully install. SUS is a great way to ensure that these updates and service packs are installed properly without having to log on to each workstation as an administrator and run the updates. For new computers, you can either manually expand the hotfix binaries into the I386 distribution folder or use QChain to install the hotfixes using a batch file.

Another way to ensure that you don't run into permissions issues is to use SMS to install on legacy platforms such as Windows NT 4 and Windows 9x.

Version Conflicts

Version conflicts sometimes arise when you install incompatible service packs or hotfixes on the same computer. This is most often the case when multiple hotfixes are installed without the use of QChain. The best way to ensure that you don't have version conflicts between hotfix installations is to use QChain.

Less often, but still not uncommon, is the scenario in which you attempt to install an earlier version of a service pack over a later version. Microsoft does not allow this to happen because the service packs check the current service pack level of the workstation or server that is being run and return the error you see in Figure 3.18, for example, if the current service pack level is greater than the one being installed. Similar messages will be generated based upon the operating system that is being patched.

FIGURE 3.18   The Service Pack Setup error message

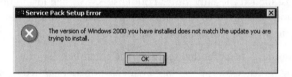

Summary

In this chapter, we discussed a number of different issues, including how to use the MBSA tool to determine which updates need to be installed on each computer on your network and how to use SUS to ensure that these updates are automatically downloaded and installed throughout your environment.

We also discussed the HFNetChk tool, which is used in conjunction with MBSA to poll the target computers to determine what hotfixes, if any, need to be installed on them. HFNetChk can be run by itself, but is more useful when run inside MBSA.

We spent a fair amount of page space on the Software Update Services, which replaces the Critical Notification Service. If you are working with an older version of the test's domains and objectives, you'll see the Critical Notification Service mentioned. We did not neglect to cover this. On the contrary, SUS replaces this service and is the preferred method to ensure that you have all the updates and hotfixes installed on each Windows 2000, Windows XP, and Windows Server 2003 computer on your network.

For legacy platforms, use SMS to install updates on computers that already have an operating system. For new computers, use slipstreaming and perhaps some scripting to run a batch of hotfixes using the QChain tool. However, when compared to SUS, slipstreaming and writing scripts seems rather time-consuming. If you are in an environment that doesn't allow any computer to not have the latest updates installed—even for a short period of time—slipstreaming and scripts using QChain will be the best way to ensure that new computers are up-to-date right from the start.

Exam Essentials

Know how to install Software Update Services. You'll need to understand how to install the SUS server software. You'll also need to remember that the client software needs to be installed on all Windows 2000 computers that are running Service Pack 2 or earlier and that it is included in Service Pack 3 and later versions of Windows.

Know how to use NLB to balance client demand for updates from an SUS server farm. Essentially, NLB balances calls between IIS servers placed in a single NLB cluster. In large environments, calls for updates to SUS servers can be high, and this would indicate a need for NLB.

Know when to use QChain, when to use SMS, and when to manually expand hotfix binaries into the *I386* distribution folder to install hotfixes. QChain gives you the ability to install multiple hotfixes with only one reboot. This can be advantageous on both servers and workstations if a number of hotfixes need to be installed at the same time. You'll use SMS when installing updates on legacy platforms, and you'll manually expand the hotfix binaries when you need to keep your source installation files up-to-date for new workstation installations.

Know how to use the MBSA tool and its expanded features. Remember that the MBSA tool uses HFNetChk to find out which target computers have which updates installed. But MBSA has expanded features that allow you to perform an expanded diagnosis of your workstations and servers.

Remember that version conflicts can occur without the use of QChain. QChain gives you the ability to install multiple hotfixes and not experience version conflicts between individual binary files. If multiple hotfixes are installed with only a single reboot, the possibility exists for the wrong version of an individual file to be installed last, thereby creating a version conflict. QChain solves this problem for you.

Review Questions

1. You recently installed a service pack on your Windows Server 2003 server. You now need to uninstall this service pack. Which installation choice should you have made to allow for the removal of the service pack?

    A. The -q switch

    B. Archive files

    C. Unattended mode

    D. Native mode

2. You have just been hired as the new system administrator for a company with 20 Windows Server 2003 server computers, 400 Windows XP Professional workstations, and 100 Windows 98 workstations. You need to quickly find out what service packs and hotfixes are installed on each computer. You want a complete report for your network. What action should you take?

    A. Run the HFNetChk tool.

    B. Run the MBSA tool.

    C. Run Update.exe.

    D. Run hotfix.exe.

3. You need to install the MBSA tool. The server you want to install this tool on is located in another building, so you connect to that server using the Terminal Services client. You proceed through the Setup process and receive an unspecified error. After the error, Setup will not continue. What should you do?

    A. Update your Terminal Services client and rerun Setup.

    B. Turn off antivirus scanning during the installation.

    C. Ensure that the Setup file is not infected with a virus.

    D. Walk to the server and install MBSA in person.

4. When using MBSA to scan for multiple computers, which two options are available to specify the target computers?

    A. One or more IP subnets

    B. One or more IP addresses

    C. Domain name

    D. Forest name

5. You have recently acquired a small competitor who has five Windows 2000 Professional workstations and one Windows 2003 Server computer. You want to quickly find out what service packs and hotfixes need to be installed on these six computers. What action should you take?

    A. Run MBSA.

    B. Run HFNetChk.

    C. Run Update.exe.

    D. Run hotfix.exe.

6. Which command should you run to slipstream a service pack into a distribution point for Windows 2003 Server?

    A. Update.exe -q

    B. Update.exe - m

    C. Update.exe -1

    D. Update.exe -s

7. You have 400 new Windows 2000 Professional workstations that you need to deploy. You want to deploy them with the latest updates installed with the initial installation. You are not using imaging to create these new computers. What method should you use?

    A. Slipstream the service packs and hotfixes into the source files and then perform the installations on the workstations.

    B. Create a batch file that will run unattend.exe, update.exe, and hotfix.exe.

    C. Update your test workstation. Then run Sysprep and install the new image to each workstation.

    D. Run a basic installation of Windows 2000 Professional. Then allow the Software Update Services server to update the workstation automatically.

8. You are the administrator of a highly secure network. One requirement of this network is that it be isolated from all external connectivity, including dial-up and dedicated technologies. However, you need to ensure that all the servers and workstations have the latest updates from Microsoft. Every update must be tested before being deployed on your network, and you must import the updates in the most secure method possible. What actions should you take to ensure that all workstations and servers are kept up-to-date with the latest updates, service packs, and hotfixes? (Choose all that apply.)

    A. Install a dedicated Software Update Services server.

    B. Connect this server to the Internet only long enough to download the latest updates from Microsoft.

    C. Install a Parent Software Update Services server.

    D. Connect this Parent server to the Internet only long enough to download the latest updates from Microsoft.

    E. Test the updates on an isolated network in a lab environment.

    F. Synchronize an internal Child server with the Parent server.

9. You are the administrator for a network of 600 Windows 2000 Professional workstations and 50 Windows 2000 Server computers. Each Windows 2000–based computer is running Service Pack 2. You want to deploy the Software Update Services client and upgrade each computer to Service Pack 3. What action or actions should you take? (Choose all that apply.)

    A. Use a Group Policy to install the Software Update Services client on each computer.

    B. Use a Group Policy to install Service Pack 3.

    C. Use SMS to install the Software Update Services client on each computer.

    D. Use SMS to install Service Pack 3 on each computer.

    E. Reboot the computers.

10. Which of the following are the three main components for the Software Update Services?

   A. Critical Notification Service

   B. Windows Update Synchronization Service

   C. Software Update Services website

   D. Software Update Services Administration website

   E. Windows Update service

11. You are the administrator of a network with 200 Windows 2000 Professional workstations, 7 Windows 2000 Server computers that are domain controllers, and 4 Windows Server 2003 computers. You want to install the Software Update Services. What should you do?

   A. Install the Software Update Services on the root domain controller.

   B. Install the Software Update Services on any domain controller.

   C. Create a new domain controller and install the Software Update Services.

   D. Install the Software Update Services on one of the Windows Server 2003 computers.

12. You are the administrator of your network. There are 1000 Windows 2000 Professional workstations on your network and 150 Windows 2000 Server computers on your network. All computers are running Service Pack 3. You need to ensure that all software updates from your Software Update Services server are installed on all workstations and servers on your network with as little administrative effort as possible. What actions should you take? (Choose all that apply.)

   A. Create a new GPO and assign it to the Domain object.

   B. Open the Configure Automatic Update dialog box and select the Auto Download And Notify For Install option.

   C. Open the Configure Automatic Update dialog box, and select the Auto Download And Schedule The Install option.

   D. Create a new GPO and assign it to the Domain Controllers Organization Unit object.

   E. Specify an Intranet Update server and Intranet Statistics server in the Specify Intranet Microsoft Update Service Location Properties dialog box.

13. You are the administrator for 400 Windows 2000 Professional workstations and 35 Windows 2000 Server computers. Some of your workstations are not receiving software updates from your Software Update Services server. You want to log update activities only. Which two actions should you take?

   A. Turn on logging in IIS on the Software Update Services website.

   B. Turn off logging in IIS on the Software Update Services website.

   C. Enable logging on the `wutrack.bin` file.

   D. Disable logging on the `wutrack.bin` file.

14. You are the administrator for 50 Windows 2000 Professional workstations, 6 Windows XP Professional workstations, 10 Windows 2000 Server computers, and 4 Windows Server 2003 computers. All Windows 2000 computers are running Service Pack 3, and Windows XP Professional computers are running Service Pack 1. You have successfully installed a Software Update Services server and have successfully used a GPO to configure the clients to download their updates from the SUS server. You now have decided to have all your Windows 2000–based computers obtain their updates directly from Microsoft's website. You disable the policy settings in the Windows Update node in the Group Policy Object. What will be the result of this action?

   A. Current updates will be uninstalled.

   B. Current updates will be unaffected, but new updates will not be downloaded.

   C. Current updates will be unaffected; new updates will require an administrative intervention to install them.

   D. New updates will be successfully downloaded with no more intervention.

15. You are running a mixed environment of Windows 2000 Professional and Windows NT 4 workstations. You need to deploy the Software Update Services client. One group of Windows 2000 Professional clients in the East OU is running Service Pack 1. All other Windows 2000 clients are running Service Pack 3. The Windows NT 4 clients are running Service Pack 6a. You are not running Systems Management Server. How should you deploy the Software Update Services client? (Choose all that apply.)

   A. Create a software package and use Group Policies to push the client down to the Windows 2000 computers in the East OU.

   B. Use the Critical Update Notification service to set the Registry entries on your Windows NT 4 workstations.

   C. Use the Windows Update service to set the Registry entries on your Windows NT 4 workstations.

   D. Create a software package and publish it to all workstations in your domain.

16. What must you restore in order to fully restore a Software Update Services server? (Choose all that apply.)

   A. IIS metabase

   B. IIS database

   C. Extensible Storage Engine

   D. The Content folder

   E. Software Update Services websites

17. You need to push out software updates to a group of Windows 98 clients. What is the best way to accomplish this task?

   A. Create a Group Policy Object and assign the software package to the workstations.

   B. Use Systems Management Server to push out each update's installation at logon.

   C. Use QChain to push out the installation packages.

   D. Use the Critical Update Notification service to push out the update installations.

18. You have six hotfixes you need to install on 26 Windows-based workstations. What should you do?

   A. Create a script that installs each hotfix individually and then runs QChain.

   B. Create a script that installs each hotfix serially and then runs QChain.

   C. Expand each hotfix into the I386 folder and run `Update.exe -q`.

   D. Expand each hotfix into the I386 folder, and then run `winnt32.exe -q`.

19. You have to install 400 new Windows 2000 Professional workstations each month and rebuild 100 deployed workstations. You need to perform these installations in the fastest time possible, but install all the latest updates as well. You cannot use imaging to perform this task. What should you do?

   A. Run an unattended installation and then run a batch file that installs all the hotfixes using QChain.

   B. Slipstream the latest service pack into the source files and then use QChain to install necessary hotfixes.

   C. Slipstream the latest service pack into the source files and then manually expand each hotfix into the source files.

   D. Assign a software package to the desktop that will install the operating system with the necessary hotfixes.

20. You have recently installed eight hotfixes on your Windows 2000 server. Now some third-party programs won't run correctly. You are also receiving version conflict errors in the event logs. What should you have done to prevent this?

   A. Run the `wutrack.bin` file.

   B. Run RIS to install the hotfixes.

   C. Run QChain to install the hotfixes.

   D. Installed each hotfix individually and then performed one reboot of your server.

Answers to Review Questions

1. B. During the installation of a service pack, you can choose to archive the files that will be over-written. When you do this, the old files are placed in a special folder and kept there in the event that you want to uninstall the service pack. During the uninstallation process, the current files are replaced with the old, saved files and then deleted.

2. B. Although the HFNetChk tool will give you a list of all the updates and hotfixes that have not been installed on your servers and workstations, only the MBSA tool will give you a complete report that includes IIS and SQL server platforms as well as other items such as weak passwords and platform-specific vulnerabilities. To get the most complete report, you need to run MBSA. Update.exe is the command used to install a service pack, and hotfix.exe is the command used to install a hotfix.

3. D. You cannot install the MBSA tool using the Terminal Services client.

4. B, C. When running the MBSA tool, you can group your target computers based on either domain name or IP address range. Because all four octets of the IP address range are available for configuration, it would not be fair to say that you can specify only an IP subnet. You need to specify the exact starting and ending IP addresses, even if this means specifying the starting and ending address for a given subnet.

5. B. HFNetChk is a great tool for pinpointing which updates need to be applied to the scanned computers. If you don't need the additional scanning options that MBSA offers, use the HFNetChk tool.

6. D. The -s switch is the integrated mode switch. You can also think of this as the slipstream switch. When you specify a folder path and name after the -s switch, the service pack files are expanded and then copied over the current installation files. Then, when the installation is run from these files, the service pack will be installed along with the rest of the operating system.

7. A. Only answer A meets every need of the scenario described in this question. Answer D would be correct if the scenario described did not require the updated files to be installed at the time of initial installation. The batch file also doesn't meet the requirements of the scenario because this is a series of individual installations.

8. C, D, E, F. By installing a Parent server, you can accomplish two goals at the same time. First, you can further protect the isolated network by placing a firewall between the Parent and Child servers and ensure that the Child server is never connected to the Internet. Second, you can use the Parent server and another workstation as a test bed to test the updates before they are synchronized to the internal Child server. Also, this architecture keeps the SUS server on the isolated network from ever having any direct Internet connectivity.

9. B, E. When Service Pack 3 is installed on a Windows 2000–based computer, the Software Update Services client is installed as well. Although you can use SMS to perform the same function, pushing out a software update and assigning it to the workstation or server at the next reboot is the easiest way to get this software out to all your computers in a consistent and uniform manner.

10. B, C, D. The Critical Notification Service is the old iteration of the current Software Update Services. The Windows Update service is the client-side service that works with the Windows Update service from Microsoft's website. The Windows Update service on the client is installed with the operating system and exists whether the Software Update Services client is installed or not.

11. D. You cannot install the Software Update Services on a domain controller or a Small Business server. In addition, the server must have at least a PIII/700 processor, 512MB RAM, and 6GB of disk space. You must also be running Windows 2000 Server with Service Pack 2 or later (which includes Windows Server 2003) and be using the NTFS file system. Only answer D meets some of the criteria for server requirements for Software Update Services.

12. A, C, E. Answer B is incorrect because the Notify option means that someone must log on as an administrator and approve the installation. Answer D is incorrect because a policy applied only to the domain controllers OU would be applied only to the domain controllers and not to the computer accounts that exist in other OUs. A policy applied to the domain object will be inherited by all your computers in all OUs. The correct answers outline the basic steps that you need to take to make sure that the software updates are pulled from your local SUS server and not from the Windows Update server on the Internet.

13. B, C. In order to log only SUS traffic on the SUS server, you'll need to turn off IIS logging of that website and then enable logging on the `wutrack.bin` file.

14. D. When Automatic Updates are configured through Group Policies, the policy will override the preferences set by the local administrator. However, if the policy is removed, the old settings will take effect and be used once again.

15. A, B. For Windows NT 4 workstations, you can use the CUN to set Registry entries on each workstation that will tell the workstation to pull its updates from your internal SUS server. For the Windows 2000 workstations in the East OU, a Group Policy that assigns the package to the computer is the easiest way to install the client.

16. A, D, E. The three main parts to back up on an SUS server are the websites, the metabase, and the update content. Obviously, you'll need to restore this information to fully restore an SUS server.

17. B. When working with legacy clients, it is best to use SMS to push out update installations and assign the installation to run at a specific time. Because many people leave their computers turned on most of the time, you can select to have the software installed at logon.

18. B. QChain is designed to run after a series of hotfixes has been installed. Only answer B fits the purpose for running QChain.

19. C. What you are doing in answer C is updating the source installation files with the latest service pack and hotfixes. Because you can't use imaging here, the fastest way to get all these updates installed on new workstations is to use a combination of slipstreaming and hotfix expansion into the source files.

20. C. QChain is designed to eliminate version conflicts between system files that have been updated by different hotfixes. RIS installs an entirely new operating system, and the `wutrack.bin` file is designed to help track calls between SUS servers and SUS clients.

Chapter

4

Configuring IPSec and SMB Signing

THE MICROSOFT EXAM OBJECTIVES COVERED IN THIS CHAPTER:

✓ **Plan IPSec deployment.**

- Decide which IPSec mode to use.
- Plan authentication methods for IPSec.
- Test the functionality of existing applications and services.

✓ **Configure IPSec policies to secure communication between networks and hosts. Hosts include domain controllers, Internet web servers, databases, e-mail servers, and client computers.**

- Configure IPSec authentication.
- Configure appropriate encryption levels. Considerations include the selection of perfect forward secrecy (PFS) and key lifetimes.
- Configure the appropriate IPSec protocol. Protocols include AH and ESP.
- Configure IPSec inbound and outbound filters and filter actions.

✓ **Deploy and manage IPSec policies.**

- Deploy IPSec policies by using Local policy objects or Group Policy objects (GPOs).
- Deploy IPSec policies by using commands and scripts. Tools include IPSecPol and NetSh.
- Deploy IPSec certificates. Considerations include deployment of certificates and renewing certifications on managed and unmanaged client computers.

✓ **Troubleshoot IPSec.**

- Monitor IPSec policies by using IP Security Monitor.

- Configure IPSec logging. Considerations include Oakley logs and IPSec driver logging.

- Troubleshoot IPSec across networks. Considersations include network address translation, port filters, protocol filters, firewalls, and routers.

- Troubleshoot IPSec certificates. Considerations include enterprise trust policies and certificate recovation list (CRL) checking.

Network analyzers, protocol sniffers, and packet-capturing applications have changed security requirements for most organizations as they have become more common and more people understand how to use them. With a network analyzer, network traffic can be captured and then later analyzed and interpreted. The network traffic that can be captured includes security-specific information such as usernames and passwords, plus confidential information such as payroll information being sent or retrieved from an accounting server.

This chapter focuses on Internet Protocol Security (IPSec) protocol: how you implement, manage, and troubleshoot it. IPSec is an important tool for ensuring that IP traffic is encrypted over untrusted networks such as the Internet, and even internal networks that contain unauthorized users of the information that you are protecting. We'll cover the considerations you must make for using IPSec in a variety of environments.

Server Message Block (SMB) signing is also an integral part of securing your network, so we'll go over SMB in this chapter as well.

Finally, we will cover a couple of important issues regarding Network Monitor and network analyzers in general.

Understanding IPSec

Internet Protocol Security (IPSec) is an open framework for ensuring private, secure communications over IP (Internet Protocol) networks using cryptographic security services. IPSec is a method widely employed to ensure that IP traffic is encrypted over untrusted networks such as the Internet.

IPSec guards against several types of network attacks:

Eavesdropping   When you use TCP/IP (Transmission Control Protocol/Internet Protocol) in its native format, information passed between computers is sent in clear text, which allows an attacker to "listen in" or read the traffic by simply copying the packets from the network line to their own computer. The ability to monitor and capture packets is generally thought to be the largest internal security concern for network administrators.

Data modification   Because an attacker can read clear-text data, it would stand to reason that the attacker could also alter the data without the sender or receiver of that data knowing that it had been altered. Altering data can result in incorrect and perhaps illegal activities such as altering amounts ordered, messages sent, or sums of money. The ability to modify data can lead to a number of different types of attacks:

Identity spoofing or impersonation If you can alter the contents of packets passed on the network, it's possible to spoof the sender's IP address or impersonate a different sender to the recipient of the message. This means that messages can be sent to a recipient that appear as if they came from a person who never sent them. In addition, real messages can be altered to have a different, malicious meaning. Such ability to disrupt real, authentic communication can wreak havoc on an organization.

Password attacks Older applications may not protect passwords well. And if you're using Basic Authentication, all passwords are passed in clear-text format. The ability to intercept a password and then use it to gain access to secure data could place the attacker in a powerful position and put the organization in a vulnerable position.

 Some extremely common applications will work only with clear-text passwords. FTP and Telnet are perfect examples of applications that support only basic authentication, where usernames and passwords, as well as all data, travel in the clear. It is extremely important to remember that if you must use such applications, you should use a separate set of usernames and passwords that are not used on the rest of the network.

Even passwords that are not passed in the clear are susceptible to password attacks. LM (LAN Manager) and NTLM (NT LAN Manager) usernames and passwords can be broken using tools available on the Internet. Even NTLM version 2 is not secure enough for many organizations. Protecting against password attacks is extremely important. The next username and password that get broken could be your own.

Denial of service attacks *Denial of service (DoS)* attacks result in servers going down or being unavailable because of all the SYN packets it is trying to service. Resources can be blocked by a DoS attack and your IS staff's time totally consumed in stopping the attack. Meanwhile, the attacker can concentrate on other secure targets and work unhindered while the IS staff defends against the DoS attack.

Compromised-key attack In this type of attack, an attacker copies a key off the network line and then breaks the key and uses it to gain access to secured resources. Such keys are referred to as *compromised keys* because they can no longer ensure the integrity of the data sent or secured.

IPSec is a real defense against these types of attacks. It provides a key line of defense against private network and Internet attacks.

IPSec has two basic foci. The first is to protect the packets sent across the line, and the second is to defend against network attacks. Both goals are achieved though the use of a public key infrastructure for users on the network, users on the Internet, and users accessing the network remotely through dial-up technologies. Because IPSec operates at the network layer, it provides a method of secure data transmission that is transparent to most applications. Deploying IPSec requires no changes to existing applications or operating systems, and IPSec policies can be centrally managed through Group Policies or locally on a computer.

The use of IPSec provides the following security benefits:

Nonrepudiation   This means that the sender of the message is the only one who could have sent the message. Nonrepudiation is accomplished through the use of digital signatures, by which the sender's private key is used to sign the message.

Antireplay   IPSec ensures that each packet is unique. No packet can be captured, opened, modified, and then sent again, or replayed.

Integrity   IPSec ensures that the packet was not modified during transit and that the information contained in the packet is the information the sender intended to place in the packet before sending it. Because only the sender and receiver have the key to encrypt and decrypt the packet, it stands to reason that only the sender and receiver can read its contents, ensuring the integrity of the packet's contents.

Confidentiality   At first glance, you might be tempted to think that confidentiality and integrity are the same thing, but they are not. Whereas integrity ensures that the packet's contents have not been altered, confidentiality ensures that only the sender and receiver can read the packet's contents. This is accomplished through the use of data encryption, which is accomplished by a key that is known only to the sender and receiver of the data.

IPSec encrypts the data in packets for secured transmission. The Data Encryption Standard (DES) is one encryption method used by IPSec. IPSec's implementation of DES has the ability to frequently regenerate encryption keys during a communication. This prevents the entire data set from being encrypted by the same key and thus (potentially) having the entire data set compromised if the key is compromised.

IPSec supports the use of an advanced form of DES, called *3DES*, which processes each block of data three times in the following manner:

- Encryption on the block with key 1
- Decryption on the block with key 2
- Encryption on the block with key 3

The receiving computer reverses this process to decrypt the packet.

> **NOTE**   Windows 2000 and Windows Server 2003 use the United States *Data Encryption Standard (DES)* to encrypt data in its IPSec implementation.

Within the IPSec policies, you can also control how often a new key is generated during the communication between both computers. This regeneration of a new key is called *dynamic rekeying*. As computers send messages back and forth, their messages are divided into blocks, which are then encrypted to ensure confidentiality and integrity. Dynamic rekeying allows you to use a different key to encrypt each block of data; even if one key is compromised, only that portion of the overall communication is compromised. This is a secure method of transmitting data.

IPSec can share keys between communicating computers without sending the key across the network line. Windows 2000 and Windows Server 2003 use the *Diffie-Hellman (DH) algorithm* to perform this function. First, the two communicating computers publicly exchange some keying information, which Windows protects with a hash function signature. Second, with this shared information, each computer can generate the identical shared key. Now each computer can use the key to communicate using IPSec. After the DH material exchange, identities are authenticated. Notice that the DH algorithm does not perform authentication; it merely provides a method of creating an environment using keys in which authentication and communication can take place.

Before data can be securely exchanged, the two computers must set up a *security association (SA)*, which is an agreement about how to protect information during transit. If your policies allow unsecured communications with non–IPSec-based computers, a *soft* SA is established. However, if the client is compatible with your IPSec policies and can securely communicate with your server, a *hard* SA is established with the client. Once IPSec SAs are established (one in each direction) between the client and server, they remain in effect for one hour after the last packet is sent between them. After that hour, the client drops the association and returns to the "respond only" state.

To build this contract, the two computers must engage in a key exchange resolution, called the *Internet Key Exchange (IKE)*.

IKE is a two-phase process. The first phase is a policy negotiation phase in which four parameters are agreed on:

- The encryption algorithm—either DES or 3DES
- The hash algorithm—either MD5 (Message Digest 5) or SHA (Secure Hash Algorithm)
- The authentication method—either certificate, preshared key, or Kerberos
- The exchange of DH material for key generation

In the second phase, the computers agree on the following parameters:

- The IPSec protocol—either AH or ESP
- The hash algorithm—either MD5 of SHA
- The algorithm for encryption, if requested—either DES or 3DES

As part of the second phase, session key material is refreshed again, and a new pair of keys is generated. The generation of new keys prevents bogus session material from being inserted into the data stream by an attacker.

After these two phases are completed, the SA is said to be set up, and IPSec is ready to send secured data back and forth between the two computers. In the following sections, you'll learn how to use IPSec and then discuss what happens when things go wrong.

Configuring and Administering IPSec Authentication

IPSec is implemented in Windows 2000 and Windows Server 2003 via the use of Group Policies. The policy rules are enforced by the IPSec driver, which is responsible for matching every incoming and outgoing packet against the security settings defined in the IPSec Group Policy.

These policies are managed from the IP Security Policy Management template underneath the Security Settings template in the object's Group Policy (see Figure 4.1).

FIGURE 4.1   The IP Security Policy Management template in the default Group Policy

You can also create a custom MMC (Microsoft Management Console) that focuses only on the IP Security Policy Management node. After adding this node to the MMC, you'll need to select the computer for which you want to manage the IPSec policies as follows (see Figure 4.2):

- If you want to manage only the computer on which you are running the console, leave the default, which is the Local Computer option.

- If you want to manage the IPSec policies for any domain member server, select Manage Domain Policy For This Computer's Domain.

- If you want to manage the IPSec policies for a remote domain that the local computer is not a member of, select Manage Domain Policy For Another Domain.

- If you want to manage the IPSec policies for a single, remote computer, select Another Computer.

After making your selection, you can save the MMC for future use.
In Exercise 4.1, you will create a custom IPSec MMC.

EXERCISE 4.1

Creating a Custom MMC for IPSec Management

1. Choose Start ➢ Run to open the Run dialog box and in the Open box, type **MMC** and press Enter to open the Microsoft Management Console (MMC).

2. Choose File ➢ Add/Remove Snap-in to open the Add/Remove Snap-in dialog box.

3. Click Add to open the Add Standalone Snap-in dialog box.

4.   Select the IP Security Management snap-in and then click Add to open the Select Computer selection box.

5.   Make your selection on the Select Which Computer This Snap-in Will Manage.

6.   Click Finish to close the Select Computer selection box.

7.   Click Close to close the Add Standalone Snap-in dialog box.

8.   Click OK to close the Add/Remove Snap-in dialog box.

9.   Save the MMC Console.

Three predefined IPSec policies are installed with Windows 2000 and Windows Server 2003 (see Figure 4.1, earlier in this chapter). These policies can be left alone or modified as needed or used to help define a custom security template for future use. The policies are as follows:

Client (Respond Only)   This policy is for computers that do not require secure communications. If secure communications are requested, this policy instructs the computer to respond in a positive fashion. Computers using this policy can communicate using IPSec with other computers that request IPSec or require IPSec and can also communicate with other computers that do not use IPSec.

Server (Request Security)   This policy is for computers that would like to use secure communications, if possible. These computers will accept unsecured traffic, but they will always attempt to secure subsequent communications by requesting security from the sending computer. If the sending computer does not respond positively, all communications are sent without using IPSec.

FIGURE 4.2   Management selections for IPSec policies when creating a customized IPSec MMC

Real World Scenario

Using IPSec to Protect Payroll Information

Many companies have their employees sign a non-disclosure agreement (NDA) that covers many issues around their salary, benefits, and working conditions.

Your manager comes to you and says, "Last year, right after we did performance appraisals and provided raises for some employees, we had a large number of employees come into the Human Resources manager's office complaining about pay discrepancies. This should not have happened because nobody is supposed to talk about pay. I'm pretty sure that they must have gotten this information from the network." You reply that you will look into it and try to provide a solution.

You investigate and find out there are three employees in Accounting who key in the new salary information and the rest of the confidential employee service information for pay and benefits. These employees update a database on the Accounting server.

You set up a network packet sniffer and capture traffic from the computers in Accounting to the Accounting server. You find that it's pretty easy to decipher the information and see the data being entered.

You configure the Accounting server to use the Secure Server (Require Security) IPSec policy. You also configure the Accounting client computers to use the Client (Respond Only) IPSec policy. You again test the connections between the Accounting client computers and the Accounting server. You are no longer able to capture and decipher information about user salary.

You report back to your manager that you have resolved the problem.

Secure Server (Require Security)   This policy requires computers to use IPSec and secure their communications. Computers assigned to this policy always reject unsecured communications, and outgoing traffic is always secured.

To assign a policy to a given computer, you must enable that policy. Enabling the policy means that it is assigned to the object that it is modifying. You can either assign or unassign a policy, but you cannot assign more than one policy to any given object. Hence, you cannot assign both Client (Respond Only) and Server (Request Security) to the same Active Directory object. Instead, all you can do is assign one of the three policy settings to any given object.

Tunnel Mode versus Transport Mode

IPSec can be configured for either transport or tunnel mode. The *transport mode* authenticates and encrypts data moving between computers. This is the default mode for IPSec in Windows 2000 and Windows Server 2003.

To specify transport mode, open the Properties dialog box of the policy setting that you want to modify. Click the rule that you want to modify and click Edit to open the Edit Rule Properties dialog box. On the Tunnel Setting tab, select This Rule Does Not Specify An IPSec Tunnel (see Figure 4.3).

In Exercise 4.2, you will set your IPSec policy to run in transport mode.

EXERCISE 4.2

Setting IPSec to Run in Transport Mode

1. Open the Group Policy in the Properties dialog box of the object that you want to modify.

2. Navigate to the IP Security Policies In Active Directory node.

3. Select the setting in the right pane for which you want to set transport mode.

4. Open the setting's Properties dialog box.

5. Select the rule that you want to modify and click Edit to open the Edit Rule Properties dialog box.

6. Click the Tunnel Setting tab.

7. Select This Rule Does Not Specify An IPSec Tunnel.

8. Click OK.

9. Close the Properties dialog box and exit the Group Policy object.

Unlike transport mode, which secures the packet from the source to the destination, *tunnel mode* places a secure, existing packet inside a new IP packet that is sent to a tunnel endpoint. The tunnel endpoint is probably not the final destination of the inside packet, but it is the final destination of the outside packet. The outside packet is stripped off at the tunnel endpoint, and the internal packet can be further routed to the final destination.

Tunnel mode does not provide security within each network that the packet will traverse. It simply provides security to the packet itself and guarantees that security to the endpoint (IP address) that you specify.

FIGURE 4.3 Setting IPSec to run in transport mode

IPSec tunnel mode is not designed to be used for virtual private network (VPN) remote access.

In Exercise 4.3, you will set IPSec to run in tunnel mode.

EXERCISE 4.3

Setting IPSec to Run in Tunnel Mode

1. Open the Group Policy in the Properties dialog box of the object that you want to modify.

2. Navigate to the IP Security Policies In Active Directory node.

3. Select the setting in the right pane in which you want to set tunnel mode.

4. Open the setting's Properties dialog box.

5. Select the rule that you want to modify and click Edit to open the Edit Rule Properties dialog box.

6. Click the Tunnel Setting tab.

7. Select The Tunnel Endpoint Is Specified By This IP Address.

8. Enter the IP address of the device that will act as the endpoint for the tunnel.

9. Click Apply.

10. Close the Properties dialog box and exit the Group Policy object.

Transport mode and tunnel mode are not available for the Client (Respond Only) setting. In addition, if you need to set up multiple tunnels, you will need to configure multiple rules, because each tunnel requires its own rule in the policy setting. Finally, Windows 2000 and Windows Server 2003 support multiple tunnel mode connections, but only one tunnel at a time.

Configuring an IPSec Rule

You can create customized IPSec policies, each with its own set of rules. Each policy can host more than one rule, and it is important to understand how these rules work because these rules govern how and when a policy is invoked. Any number of rules can be active simultaneously. You can create or modify existing rules to meet your requirements. Filters are applied in the order of most-specific filters first.

A rule consists of the following components:

Tunnel endpoint   A tunnel endpoint defines the IP address to which the tunnel will guarantee secured communications. There must be two rules to define an IPSec tunnel—one rule for each direction.

Network type   Use this setting to select the scope of the rule. You can select All Network Connections, Local Area Network (LAN), or Remote Access (see Figure 4.4).

Authentication method   You select the authentication method in the Authentication Methods tab. The default is Kerberos, as shown in Figure 4.5. If you click Add, you can select the other supported authentication methods in Windows, which are shown in Figure 4.6 and then described.

FIGURE 4.4   Configure the scope of the rule in the Connection Type tab.

FIGURE 4.5   The Authentication Methods tab

FIGURE 4.6   Supported authentication methods that can be selected for any given rule

Windows Default (Kerberos)   This is the default for Windows 2000 and Windows Server 2003. This selection uses the Kerberos V5 authentication protocol. Any Kerberos-compliant clients can use Kerberos V5, even if they are not Windows-based clients. However, every client must be a member of a local or trusted domain.

Use A Certificate From This Certificate Authority (CA)   This selection requires that a trusted CA be available and that both the sender and the receiver use a certificate issued by the trusted CA.

Use This String To Protect The Key Exchange (Preshared Key)   This setting specifies a secret, shared key that both computers will use to encrypt and decrypt the packets. Obviously, this selection requires manual preconfiguration prior to its use.

Once a particular method is selected using the wizard, you can go back into the authentication methods tab for the policy and add another method for authentication.

IP filter list   This selection defines which traffic will be secured by this rule. You can use the defaults of All ICMP Traffic (Internet Control Message Protocol) or All IP Traffic, or you can select the type of traffic that you want to include in the rule.

The filter is rather granular, allowing you to make selections in two areas: addressing and protocols. In addressing, you can select to filter traffic against any of the following defined addresses in Windows Server 2003 (see Figure 4.7):

- My IP address
- Any IP address
- A specific IP address
- A specific IP subnet
- DNS Servers <dynamic>
- WINS Servers <dynamic>

- DHCP Servers <dynamic>
- Default Gateway <dynamic>

To access the tab in Figure 4.7, first highlight the filter list that you wish to edit in the IP Filter List tab (either All ICMP Traffic or All IP Traffic) and then click the Edit button. This invokes the IP Filter List dialog box. Click the Edit button on this box, and the Filter Properties dialog box illustrated in Figure 4.7 opens.

In the Protocol tab, you can select to filter traffic against the following defined protocols and either any port number or a predefined port number (see Figure 4.8):

- Any
- EGP (Exterior Gateway Protocol)
- HMP (Host Monitoring Protocol)
- ICMP (Internet Control Message Protocol)
- Other
- RAW (protocol 255)
- RVD (MIT Remote Virtual Disk Protocol)
- TCP (Transmission Control Protocol)
- UDP (User Datagram Protocol)
- XNS-IDP (Xerox NS IDP)

Filter action   The filter action lists the security actions that will occur when traffic matches the IP filter. These actions appear on the Filter Action tab in the Edit Rule Properties dialog box. There are three basic default settings (see Figure 4.9):

- Permit, which permits unsecured IP packets to pass.
- Request Security (Optional), which means that the server will request secure methods of communicating but will transfer data in an unsecured manner too.

FIGURE 4.7   The Addresses tab in the Filter Properties dialog box

FIGURE 4.8   The Protocol tab in the Filter Properties dialog box

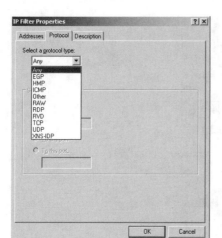

- Require Security, which means that the server will accept unsecured connections but then will require clients to communicate using only secured methods. This selection instructs the server to not communicate with untrusted clients.

What is interesting here is how granular the filter action can be. Figure 4.10 shows the default settings for the Request Security (Optional) security methods, which can be navigated to by clicking the Protocol tab in the Filter Properties dialog box. Notice that this method allows unsecured communications, but that each connection is responded to with IPSec. What this means is that the server attempts IKE with each computer that connects to it in an attempt to communicate using IPSec.

FIGURE 4.9   The Filter Action tab in the Edit Rule Properties dialog box

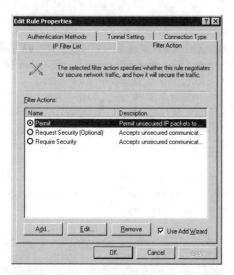

FIGURE 4.10 The default settings for the Request Security (Optional) security method

The Session Key Perfect Forward Secrecy setting is cleared by default. *Perfect forward secrecy (PFS)*, when selected, means that every time rekeying occurs, a new master key is also generated. Although this is the most secure setting possible, it also generates additional overhead for your server and should be selected only in highly secure environments. Because a new master key is generated, both server and client will need to renegotiate new key material, and this can create interoperability problems with some non-Microsoft products.

So when you put all of these parts together, you have the ability to create a rule that defines the following:

- The scope (tunnel endpoint and network type)
- The authentication method
- Which traffic to secure (the IP filter list)
- The actions to take when the rule is met (the filter action)

When taking the exam, it will be easy to get lost in the details of the question. Keep yourself focused on the larger picture and remember how to further secure traffic using an IPSec filter rule. For instance, if you need to secure traffic over the Internet, make sure that you have selected a tunnel endpoint. If you need to authenticate using certificates, you'll need a CA trusted by all parties involved in the process. If you want to secure only certain types of traffic, understand that you are working with the IP filter list to select a protocol and port combination. And if you want to tweak the actions to be taken when traffic meets the defined rules, you are working in the Filter Action area.

If, after applying a rule, you don't like the results, you can restore default policies. Right-click the IP Security Policies Local Machine, choose Restore Default Policies from the shortcut menu, and then click Yes from the pop-up IP Security Policy Management message box.

Using Command-Line Tools and Scripts

As with most Microsoft security components, IPSec can be deployed using a graphical user interface (GUI) or a command-line interface.

Netsh is an extremely powerful command-line utility that can be used for a wide number of network configuration changes, including IPSec. Netsh can be used to

- Add a filter.
- Add a policy.
- Add a rule.
- Delete a filter.
- Delete a policy.
- Delete a rule.
- Export a policy.
- Import a policy.
- Show configurations.
- Show statistics.

There are many other tasks that can be performed using Netsh. To go into them all would require several pages, and to remember the syntax would require several days of studying. What is important for you to know is that Netsh can be used to configure and manage IPSec policies for the organization.

Another tool that can be used at the command prompt for managing IPSec is the IPSecPol tool. You can download this tool from the Microsoft website. IPSecPol can perform every task that can also be performed using the IP Security MMC snap-in. The IPSecPol utility is modeled directly after the MMC snap-in and can be used in scripts to manage the IPSec implementation for the organization. The current version—1.00.0.0—can be deployed only on Windows 2000 operating systems.

IPSecCMD is similar to IPSecPol, except that it is for use on Windows XP Professional computers. IPSecCMD is run from the command prompt by administrators using a Windows XP Professional workstation instead of a Windows 2000 Professional workstation. IPSecCMD can be used to configure IPSec policies, filters, and filter actions.

Testing IPSec Policy Assignments

You can test your IPSec policy assignments in two ways: by using the `ping` command and by using the IP Security Monitor. The IP Security Monitor is a resource kit tool for Windows 2000, and a new version is included in Windows Server 2003 with a different interface.

The `ping` (packet internet groper) command sends four echo packets to the server and expects to receive four echo replies back. A server running under the default IPSec policies will respond to the `ping` command. However, if there are problems with establishing a secure channel, you will receive a response, "Negotiating IP Security." You can expect this response while the secure channel is established, before the echo packets are responded to by the server.

The IP Security Monitor in Windows 2000 (see Figure 4.11) is a handy tool that gives you statistics about what SAs have been established and with whom. Moreover, you'll find good information on basic IPSec statistics. The tool automatically refreshes every 15 seconds, but this option is configurable using the Options button.

FIGURE 4.11   The IP Security Monitor in Windows 2000

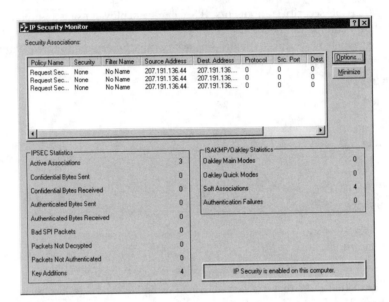

To run the IP Security Monitor in Windows 2000, choose Start ➢ Run, enter the following syntax in the Open box, and press Enter:

`Ipsecmon <computername>`

In the lower-right corner of the IP Security Monitor dialog box is a message indicating whether IPSec is enabled on the computer.

To run the IP Security Monitor in Windows Server 2003, as shown in Figure 4.12, you need to add it to a custom MMC. The console contains more information in a different format from the resource kit tool used in Windows 2000.

IPSec Policy Inheritance

IPSec policies follow the Group Policy inheritance model. Group Policies are applied in the following order:

- Site
- Domain
- OU

Policies applied last take precedence over policies applied first. However, you need to bear a couple of points in mind when it comes to policy inheritance and IPSec:

- IPSec policies assigned to a domain policy override any local IPSec policies when the computer is a member of the domain.
- IPSec policies assigned to an OU override domain-level policies.

Hence, if you need to assign a policy to a group of domain controllers but not to the other computers on your network, you want to do this at the OU level, not at the domain level.

FIGURE 4.12   The IP Security Monitor in Windows Server 2003

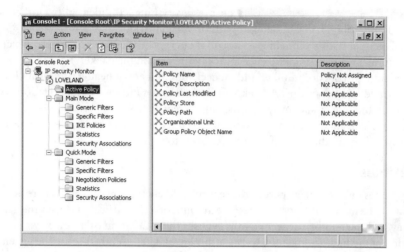

Configuring the Appropriate IPSec Protocol and Encryption Levels

At a high level, Hash Message Authentication Codes (HMACs) are used to sign packets to verify that the information sent is the same information received (think "integrity" here). The hash function is really an algorithm that combines with the sender's private key to produce a cryptographic checksum or message integrity code (MIC). Each party must compute this checksum to ensure that the data has integrity.

When configuring the IPSec protocol, you can select two functions:

MD5 *Message Digest 5 (MD5)* makes four passes over the data blocks, which results in a 128-bit key that is used for the integrity check. MD5 is the fifth iteration of the Message Digest hash function.

SHA The Secure Hash Algorithm (SHA) is closely modeled after MD5, but it produces a 160-bit key that is used for the integrity check. Obviously, the longer key length provides greater security, so SHA is considered stronger than MD5.

The IPSec protocols further protect each packet by adding their own security protocol header to each IP packet. There are two protocol header types: AH and ESP.

The Authentication Header (AH)

The *Authentication Header (AH)* does not encrypt the data, but it does provide authentication, integrity, and antireplay for the entire packet. Although the data is in clear text, an attacker cannot modify it. AH uses the HMAC algorithms to sign each packet to ensure integrity. In the AH, a checksum is inserted between the network and transport layer headers. If the receiving computer's checksum does not match that which is in the AH, the packet is discarded. Antireplay is achieved by inserting a sequence number in the AH. AH can be used with or without the Encapsulating Security Payload (ESP).

The Encapsulating Security Payload (ESP)

The *Encapsulating Security Payload (ESP)* ensures everything: confidentiality, authentication, integrity, and antireplay. ESP can be used with or without AH.

When ESP is used with a tunneling protocol, it encrypts the entire packet. However, in the absence of a tunneling protocol, ESP encrypts only the data in the packet, not the headers. Like AH, ESP provides a sequence number and a checksum in its own header and provides authentication in a trailer via the integrity check value (ICV) and a message authentication code that is used to verify the sender's identity and message integrity.

Because the ESP header is inserted between the IP and upper layer headers, the IP header itself is not protected, leaving this part of the packet open to attack.

Key Lifetimes

The Key Lifetimes field is used as part of the security and encryption of IPSec. There are two key settings that can be managed using policies: the amount of data traffic that causes the generation of a new key and the number of seconds that causes the generation of a new key.

Two different methods can be used to track the age of a key and then cause the generation of a new key. The first method generates a new key every 100MB by default, but the amount of data can be increased or decreased. The second method generates a new key every hour by default, and the amount of time can be changed. If both methods are used, the first method to reach its level causes the generation of a new key.

In the following graphic, the column for Key Lifetimes includes two numbers. The first number is the amount of data traffic that causes a new key to be generated, and the second number is the number of seconds that causes the key to be regenerated. In this example, 100,000KB is equal to 100MB and 3600 seconds is equal to one hour.

By default, the Key Lifetimes option is not used. However, you can implement it by selecting the security method that you wish to use and then clicking the Edit button.

Perfect Forward Secrecy (PFS)

Perfect forward secrecy (PFS) can also be implemented at this same screen. You can enable the check box, which then enables PFS for every computer that implements the IPSec policy. PFS is used when you want to negotiate a new master key every time the computers in an IPSec conversation start a new session.

Implementing PFS leads to higher security, because the master key information is constantly changing and updated with each session between IPSec-enabled computers. Using PFS has a high impact on computer performance, because it requires reauthentication for each session. PFS needs to be implemented only on the client or on the server, but it does not require both in order to work properly.

Deploying and Managing IPSec Certificates

Before you can run IPSec on your network, you need to issue two different certificate types: IPSec and Computer. Without these two certificates issued by the CA, IPSec cannot work.

The default setting of the Policy Module in the Microsoft Certificate Authority is to always issue a certificate upon request. But you will also need to configure a Group Policy so that your computers automatically request the certificates from the CA. Because the best practice is for all the computers in your domain to be issued certificates, the best practice here is to perform this task on the domain object.

Open your Group Policy, expand Computer Configuration, expand Security Settings, and then expand Public Key Policies. Right-click Automatic Certificate Request Settings, point to New, and select Automatic Certificate Request (see Figure 4.13) to start the Automatic Certificate Request Setup Wizard.

FIGURE 4.13   Selecting the Automatic Certificate Request menu option

Now follow these steps:

1. At the Welcome screen, click Next to open the Certificate Template screen, as shown in Figure 4.14.

FIGURE 4.14 The Certificate Template screen

2. Select the certificate from the template list and click Next to open the Certificate Template screen.

3. Select the CA from whom you want to have this certificate issued and then complete the wizard.

You'll now see the certificate in the right pane of the Group Policy window, indicating that this certificate will be automatically issued to every computer the next time the computers boot up and connect to the network (see Figure 4.15).

FIGURE 4.15 The IPSec certificate is now being automatically issued.

Notice the difference between the right pane of the screen in Figure 4.13 and the right pane of the screen in Figure 4.15. The IPSec certificate is now listed in the right pane.

You need to do this for both the IPSec and the Computer certificates. In addition, you have to specify the trusted root CA(s) for your network. You can specify more than one trusted root CA to accommodate remote users who may not be able to be issued a certificate from an internal Microsoft CA.

When you run through the wizard, you are prompted to specify the file that contains the certificate from the CA. Enter the path and filename, click Next, and finish the wizard. The certificate from the CA will now be trusted by all who have the Group Policy applied to them.

Renewing Certificates

When your users need to renew their certificates, they can do so by using the certificate website option that can be installed with Certificate Services. The default URL is *servername*/certsrv. If users navigate to that website, they can renew their certificate and continue to engage in secure communications using IPSec.

If your users are remote, you may need to open this website so that they can renew their certificates too. If they are trusting third-party CAs, they need to purchase their renewal certificates from the third-party vendor.

Remember that certificates need to be current and trusting the same CA as the server.

Securing Communication between Server Types with IPSec

Securing different server types requires an in-depth knowledge of the type of packet traffic that each server will experience. This section looks at the specific attention and hurdles different types of servers might require.

Securing Web Servers

Securing a web server using IPSec is going to be difficult if the website is public. Although you can configure IPSec to request secured communications, chances are good that most clients will not be IPSec-ready and will communicate using only unsecured transmissions. The proper way to secure web server traffic is to use SSL; this topic is covered in Chapter 6, "Deploying, Managing, and Configuring SSL Certificates."

However, if the website either is secured through authentication or is an extranet with defined, known users, you can require IPSec for communications between your server and the site's users.

If the secured server is directly accessible from the Internet, or if the first client packets contain sensitive data, the client must receive an IPSec policy so that it requests IPSec security for traffic when it attempts to communicate with the server. This is the best practice for a secure website, because a server set to request security instead of requiring security is easily open to a DoS attack. Remember that the server is set to request security, and then every client connection is responded to with an IKE request over port 500. Such additional traffic is unwarranted on the Internet and, through the smart use of a DoS attack, could render the server useless to legitimate client traffic.

One way to work with a secured website that has a defined group of users is to use a certificate known to everyone in advance and require that certificate for authentication. Doing this will prevent any unauthorized access to the website. Of course, if the certificate becomes compromised, another certificate needs to be generated and distributed to the users.

The best practice for unsecured Internet websites is to allow unsecured traffic. The best practice for secured websites is to require secure communications using IPSec or SSL because of its ease of use.

Securing E-Mail Servers

If your e-mail servers connect directly to the Internet to pass SMTP (Simple Mail Transfer Protocol) traffic, it is very unwise to require secured communications because most SMTP servers on the Internet are not configured for this type of communication. However, between your SMTP relay server in your DMZ (de-militarized zone) and your internal SMTP servers, you can require secure communication.

Doing this means that an attacker can compromise only your SMTP server in the DMZ, which is not a big loss because no critical data is sitting on that server. Because the internal SMTP servers will require secured communication before accepting mail, an attacker would need to impersonate the SMTP server in the DMZ with a valid certificate before being able to communicate directly with the internal SMTP server.

Securing Clients

Not all clients will be IPSec complaint. For these clients to successfully communicate with your IPSec servers, you need to ensure that you have assigned the Server policy, not the Secure Server policy. The Server policy always requests security, but allows unsecured communication with clients by falling back to clear-text communication if the client doesn't respond to the IKE request.

Note, however, that if a client does respond to the IKE request and then the negotiation fails, the client is blocked from communicating with the server for one minute, and thereafter another negotiation will commence.

When working with remote clients, it is important to remember two facts:

- You cannot use IPSec in a VPN solution for remote clients.
- The remote clients must trust the CA that your server is trusting for key generation.

This means that if you work with a number of remote clients, you may need to trust an external third-party CA instead of a local CA on your network. Although it is easier (and cheaper) to create an internal certificate server and make that server the root enterprise CA, it may not be the best way to ensure a common, trusted CA.

In addition, the list of authentication methods for remote clients must include certificates, and at least one valid certificate must be installed on each client and peer server. And finally, if you need to remotely administer a client computer, you must allow RPC TCP traffic in your IPSec rules for the internal network.

Troubleshooting IPSec

At a high level, IPSec problems can be grouped into several categories. IPSec won't work if the same CA isn't trusted. IPSec also won't work if different authentication methods are used in the rules for client and server. If you are working over the Internet, you must open port 500 and allow protocol IDs 50 and 51 for both inbound and outbound traffic. And finally, IPSec won't work for remote access clients unless they first tunnel into an RRAS (Routing and Remote Access Services) server using L2TP (Layer 2 Tunneling Protocol).

You may also find that you'll receive bad SPI (Security Parameter Index) messages in the event viewer. These messages may indicate that one party continued to send data after the SA expired. It may also indicate that the number of rekeys is too large compared to the amount of time that the SA has been active. You can reduce the bad SPI messages by setting longer key lifetime values in the policy.

IPSec Logging

IPSec information can be captured and made available to the event viewer through the system log, the application log, and the security log. To enable IPSec driver event logging, you need to use the Registry editor. As always, be very careful when using the Registry editor.

Using the Registry editor, set the `HKEY_LOCAL_MACHINE\System\CurrentControlSet\Services\IPSEC\DiagnosticMode` registry setting to 1. Changing this setting requires that you restart the computer for it to take effect.

Other logging can be implemented for IPSec using standard audit logging. Configure auditing to audit logon/logoff events to view security associations. Configure auditing to audit policy changes to view IPSec policy change events in the audit log.

The Oakley log can be enabled as well. The Oakley log provides detailed information about the implementation of IPSec, and it can be used to troubleshoot any IPSec problems that you might be having. The only way to enable the Oakley log is to use the Registry editor. In the Registry editor, set the `HKEY_LOCAL_MACHINE\System\CurrentControlSet\Services\PolicyAgent\Oakley\EnableLogging` Registry setting to 1. Once the Oakley log is enabled, it stores all ISAKMP main mode or quick mode negotiations in the `systemroot\Debug` folder using a file called `Oakley.log`. The Oakley log requires restarting the computer or restarting Routing and Remote Access and IPSec policy agent services. You can also use the `net stop policyagent` and `net start policyagent` commands at the command prompt.

Rule Configuration Issues

You need to verify several things when working with the rules. First, even if you have multiple rules, you must make certain that those rules allow the client and server to use the same authentication method. If not, the client and server will not be able to talk to each other. To avoid authentication method problems, don't use protocol- or port-specific filters for the purpose of negotiating security for traffic. Instead, use protocol and port filters for permitting and blocking actions.

Also, bear in mind that IPSec cannot be configured for one-way, secured traffic. If you create a rule that secures traffic from Server A to Client B, a rule needs to be created to secure traffic from Client B back to Server A. This is most easily done by creating two filters in the same filter list. However, what we've said here should not be confused with a one-way blocking rule. You can create a rule that blocks traffic in one direction, but this is different from creating a rule that secures traffic in one direction. To secure traffic more easily, you can select the Mirror check box (see Figure 4.7, earlier in this chapter), which automatically generates the rule that you are creating for both directions.

Certificate Configuration Issues

It is possible that certificates obtained incorrectly may result in a situation in which the certificate exists and is chosen for IKE authentication, but fails to work properly because the corresponding key in the key pair is not present on the local computer. You can see this by creating a new MMC that has the Certificates snap-in focused on the local computer. If the private key is not present, the certificate can't be used with IPSec.

In Exercise 4.4, you will create a new MMC that allows you to verify that a private key is installed.

EXERCISE 4.4

Creating a New MMC with the Certificate Snap-in

1. Open a new MMC.

2. Choose File ➢ Add/Remove Snap-in.

3. Click Add to open Add Standalone Snap-in.

4. Find the Certificates snap-in and click Add.

5. From the Certificates Snap-in dialog box that automatically opens, click the computer account for which this snap-in will manage certificates. Then click Finish to close this dialog box.

6. Click Close to close the Add Standalone Snap-in box.

7. Click OK to close the Add/Remove Snap-in dialog box.

8. Expand Certificates-User (local computer).

9. Expand Personal.

10. Click the Certificates folder.

11. In the right pane, double-click the certificate that you want to use to open it.

12. Verify that you see the text, "You have a private key that corresponds to this certificate."

Why might a private key fail? Well, for a couple of reasons. First, if the certificate in the personal folder doesn't have a corresponding private key, it is likely that the certificate enrollment process failed in some manner. Second, if the certificate was obtained from a Microsoft CA that was configured with the Strong Private Key Protection option, the user needs a PIN (personal identification number) to access the private key. Because the PIN cannot be supplied for IKE negotiation, this certificate can't be used for this purpose.

If the IKE negotiations are failing, enable auditing for success and failed events for the audit attribute Audit Logon Events. The IKE service reports entries in the security log, which gives you an explanation as to why the negotiations are failing.

If you feel you need to clear all IKE negotiations and start "fresh"—perhaps when secured communications suddenly fail—you can do so from a command prompt by typing the following command:

```
Net stop policyagent
```

To resume IKE negotiations, use the `Net Start` command, as follows:

```
Net start policyagent
```

Remember that when you stop the policy agent, all IPSec filters are deactivated for the time the service is stopped. In addition, your VPN tunnels are no longer protected with IPSec. In addition, RRAS is restarted as well.

If you have recently updated the policy settings and they don't seem to be taking effect, you can verify that the changes made to any policy have been updated in Active Directory by testing the policy's integrity. To do this, right-click the policy in the IP Security Settings For Active Directory, select Actions, point to All Tasks, and then click Check Policy Integrity.

Firewall and Router Configuration Issues

Firewalls generally reject IPSec packets by default. You'll need to configure your router or proxy server for some specialized filtering to ensure that packets secured with IPSec are not rejected. Here are some recommended filters for your router:

- Allow protocol ID 51 for inbound and outbound IPSec AH traffic.
- Allow protocol ID 50 for inbound and outbound ESP traffic.
- Allow UDP port 500 for inbound and outbound IKE traffic.

Without these ports and protocol IDs allowed, your firewall will not pass IPSec traffic.

Authentication Issues

You must use the same authentication methods for both rules between the client and server. Remember that there must be a rule for each direction, and if the authentication methods do not match, IPSec won't work. You must also verify that there is at least one compatible security method in both rules. Authentication can fail if the security methods do not match. If you are using IPSec tunneling, verify that the DNS name and IP address are correct and that the destination computer is up and running.

Common IPSec Event Log Entries

IPSec utilizes the Windows 2000 and Windows Server 2003 event logs to record events as they occur. These events can be used to assist in troubleshooting IPSec. In particular, there are events in the system log and events in the application log that are very valuable in troubleshooting IPSec (see Table 4.1).

TABLE 4.1   IPSec Event Log Entries

Event Log	Source	Category	Event ID	Meaning
System log	Policy agent	None	279	Identifies that an IPSec policy is in use on the computer. Also provides the source of the IPSec policy (local or domain) and the polling interval. Also shows when a change to an IPSec policy has been detected by showing "Updating IPSec Policy" in the event.
System log	Policy agent	None	284	Shows that the policy agent was unable to contact Active Directory.
System log	Policy agent	Logon/logoff	541	Shows that an IPSec security association has been established.
System log	Policy agent	Logon/logoff	542	Shows that an IPSec security association has ended.
Application log	Oakley	None	541	Shows that the client cannot generate high-security key material; the resulting negotiation agrees only on lower-level key material.
Application log	Oakley	None	542	Shows that client cannot perform encryption stronger than DES; the resulting negotiation agrees only on DES.

Domain Controllers and SMB Signing

If you want to secure communications at the packet level, then you need to use SMB signing. SMB signing can be an integral part of securing your network. *Server Message Blocks (SMB)* date from 1984 when IBM first introduced NetBIOS (Network Basic Input Output Service). In the years since, SMB has played a central role in passing information between computers and has been extended several times. The SMB protocol was developed jointly by Microsoft, Intel, and IBM. More recently, the *Common Internet File System (CIFS)*, an advanced version of the SMB protocol was introduced. We'll discuss CIFS later in this chapter.

SMB is an application-level protocol that is used to implement network session control, network file and print sharing, and messaging. Up to a point, SMB is analogous to the AppleTalk Session, Filing and Printer Access protocols, and Novell's NetWare Core Protocol (NCP).

At a granular level, SMB defines a series of commands that the client and the server use to coordinate passage of information between each other. The redirector packages network control block (NCB) requests or responses into an SMB structure, which are then sent over the network to the target machine. Like other protocols, such as SMTP, the commands passed back and forth between the client and the server are based on a request-response architecture. One computer initiates the connection and sends requests (the client), and the other computer responds to those requests (the server).

To make the initial connection with the correct server, a method of addressing was needed. Until the advent of CIFS, the SMB protocol used the NetBIOS name for addressing. One of the upgrades to SMB in CIFS is its ability to use DNS-based host names for addressing.

SMB Commands

The core SMB protocol commands execute basic functions. Here are some examples (in no particular order):

- Create Directory (SMBmkdir)
- Open File (SMBopen)
- Commit All Files (SMBflush)
- Rename File (SMBmv)
- Start Connection (SMBcon)
- End Connection (SMBtdis)
- Create Spool File (SMBsplclose)
- Get Machine Name (SMBgetmac)

This list is not exhaustive. The core list in the original protocol consisted of 37 commands. You can group the core commands into four types:

Session control messages   These commands start and end a redirector connection to the shared resource on the server.

File messages   These commands are used by the client to access files that reside on the server.

Printer messages   These commands are used to send data to a printer on a print server and receive status information about the printer and the data being held in the queue.

Message messages   These commands allow the sender and receiver to send messages back and forth.

As the protocol developed, commands were added that extended SMB's functionality. Commands such as Lock Then Read Data (SMBlockreadr), Write Then Unlock Data (SMBwriteunlock), Copy (SMBcopy), Open and X (SMBopenX), Tree Connect and X (SMBtconX), or Session Set Up and X (SMBsesssetup) can all be found in nearly every packet trace between two Windows-based computers.

The "and X" designation in an SMB command is a batching mechanism whereby multiple commands can be batched and sent over the line to the target computer and then processed asynchronously at the other end.

Configuring SMB

Because there are several versions of the SMB protocol, during the dialect negotiation of the TCP handshake, the client and the server agree on the version of the SMB protocol that they will use to pass information back and forth. Agreement on the dialect indicates which set of commands will be considered valid by both machines.

Because the SMB protocol is an application layer protocol, it can run over different transport and network layer protocols, including Network Extended Basic User Interface (NetBEUI), Internetwork Packet Exchange/Sequenced Packet Exchange (IPX/SPX), and TCP/IP.

The SMB security model has two levels: Share and User. The Share level model applies protection at the share on the resource that resides on the server. Each share can have a password, and a client needs only to present that password to the server to access all files under that share. Once a client is authenticated, all SMB commands are available for use between the client and the server. This was the default SMB dialect that was selected between Windows for Workgroups machines.

The User security model requires the user to log in to the server and be authenticated by the server. In addition, protection is applied to individual files in each share, and access is based on user rights configured for each file or folder. When the user is authenticated, the user is given a user ID (UID), which they must present on all subsequent accesses to the server. This model was first introduced in the LAN Manager 1 dialect and was available starting with Windows 95.

The Common Internet File System (CIFS)

CIFS is a public version of the SMB protocol that is essentially the NT LM 0.12 dialect with some modifications for easier use over the Internet. CIFS is the protocol used by Windows 2000. As you may have noticed, SMB did not contain any method for ensuring security in the packets as they are passed back and forth. CIFS has this capability—and more.

The CIFS protocol requires server authentication of users before file accesses are allowed. The server requires the client to provide a username and (usually) a password. (Actually, any method whereby a client provides proof of identity is acceptable to CIFS. Passwords are the most common form of accomplishing this goal.) How the user is authenticated is not a concern to the CIFS protocol. Hence, the Kerberos authentication protocol can be used in conjunction with the CIFS protocol to authenticate the client to the server.

In addition, messages passed between the client and server can be authenticated by computing a message authentication code (MAC) for each message and attaching it to the message. The MAC key is computed from the session key. The MAC can either sign and/or encrypt the message text plus a sequence number, which prevents replay attacks. What the CIFS calls the MAC is what Microsoft calls SMB signing.

Enabling SMB Signing

SMB signing places a digital security signature into each SMB message, which is then verified by both the client and the server to deter impersonation and man-in-the-middle attacks.

SMB signing will impose a 10 to 15 percent overhead hit on each server and client due to the additional processing required for each packet. Additional bandwidth is not required, however, to implement SMB signing.

SMB signing must be enabled on both the client and the server before it can be used. It is not turned on by default in Windows Server 2000; however, it is turned on by default in Windows Server 2003. It is very important to note that with SMB signing enabled, Windows 9 *x* clients will be unable to connect to Windows Server 2003 servers unless they have the Directory Services client installed.

To use SMB signing, you must enable it or require it on both the client and the server. If SMB signing is enabled on a server, clients that are enabled for SMB signing will use SMB signing when connecting to the server. If SMB signing is required on a server, a client will not be able to establish a session unless it is at least enabled for SMB signing. SMB signing is enabled in a Group Policy in the Security Options node under the Local Policies node (see Figure 4.16). The configuration options are available under the Domain Member, Microsoft network client, and Microsoft network server headings, and must be configured for all computer types for SMB signing to be used across the network.

Here is an explanation of what each policy setting does:

Digitally Sign Client Communication (Always) When this option is selected, the computer requires that SMB messages be digitally signed before accepting a network connection. Only do this in pure Windows 2000, Windows XP, and Windows Server 2003 environments, because other platforms do not work with this feature.

FIGURE 4.16 The SMB signing options under the Security Options node

Digitally Sign Client Communication (When Possible)   When enabled, this policy causes the client to perform SMB packet signing when communicating with a Windows 2000 or Windows Server 2003 server that is enabled or required to perform SMB packet signing.

Digitally Sign Server Communication (Always)   When this policy is enabled, you are requiring the Windows 2000 or Windows Server 2003 server to perform SMB packet signing. If the clients are not set to at least Digitally Sign Client Communication (When Possible), the server cannot communicate with the client.

Digitally Sign Server Communication (When Possible)   When this policy is enabled, the Windows 2000 or Windows Server 2003 server attempts to perform SMB signing when communicating to another Windows 2000 or Windows Server 2003 machine on the network. This policy is enabled by default on the Domain Controllers OU.

To enable SMB signing in Windows NT 4, you'll need to be running at least Service Pack 3 and then enter the following edits in the Registry:

```
HKLM\System\CCS\Services\LanManServer\Parameters
```

After navigating to the previous location in the Registry editor, choose Edit ➢ Add Value to open the Add Value dialog box, and then add the following two values:

Value name: `EnableSecuritySignature`
Data type: REG_DWORD
Value: 0 (disable), 1 (enable)
Enter a value of 1 for this Registry key.

Value name: `RequireSecuritySignature`
Data type: REG_DWORD
Value: 0 (disable), 1 (enable)
Enter a value of 1 for this Registry key.

You need to restart Windows after making these Registry entries before they will take effect. Obviously, you cannot enable both keys. If you want to require SMB signing, you need to use the `RequireSecuritySignature` Registry key. If you want SMB signing to be used when possible, use the other key.

To enable SMB signing on a Windows NT 4 workstation, open the Registry Editor and navigate to the following key:

```
HKLM\System\CCS\Services\Rdr\Parameters
```

Choose Edit ➢ Add Value and then enter one or the other value, depending on whether you want to merely enable SMB signing or require it:

Value name: `EnableSecuritySignature`
Data type: REG_DWORD
Value: 0 (disable), 1 (enable)
Enter a value of 1 for this Registry key.

Value name: `RequireSecuritySignature`
Data type: REG_DWORD
Value: 0 (disable), 1 (enable)
Enter a value of 1 for this Registry key.

You need to restart the Windows NT 4 workstation for these changes to take effect. If you are running a Windows NT 4 network and need to require SMB signing, first require signing on the servers and then reboot them. You then need to require signing on the workstations and reboot them as well.

To enable SMB signing on a Windows 98 client, open the Registry for the Windows 98 client, and then navigate to the following key:

`HKLM\System\CCS\Services\VxD\VNetsup`

Add the following two values to the key listed previously:

Value name: `EnableSecuritySignature`
Data type: REG_DWORD
Value: 0 (disable), 1 (enable)
Enter a value of 1 for this Registry key.

Value name: `RequireSecuritySignature`
Data type: REG_DWORD
Value: 0 (disable), 1 (enable)
Enter a value of 1 for this Registry key.

Just like Windows NT 4, you need to add both keys, but not enable both keys. After adding these items in the Registry, you need to reboot the Windows 98 client in order for the changes to take effect.

If you are running in a mixed environment, you may find that SMB signing doesn't work between Windows 2000 clients and Windows NT 4 servers. This is actually a problem with the Windows 2000 client and is fixed by installing the latest service pack. The error message is "Network name is no longer valid," which is a result of the initial attempt being made with an invalid password.

SMB signing is really a LAN-based security measure and should be employed only between Windows-based computers.

Network Analyzers

Network analyzers, protocol analyzers, and packet sniffers are names that pretty much mean the same thing. Each of these components captures packets off the network and stores them for view and interpretation. Microsoft has its own tool—Network Monitor—which comes in two versions: the version that ships with the Windows Server products and the version that ships with Systems Management Server (SMS). The main difference between the two versions is that the Windows version captures traffic only between the single computer and other computers on the network. The SMS version captures any and all packets that it can see on the network.

Microsoft's Network Monitor, the Windows version, can be installed through the Windows Components portion of the Add/Remove Programs applet in the Control Panel. The option to install Network Monitor Tools is under Management And Monitoring Tools. Expanding the Management And Monitoring Tools reveals the option to install Network Monitor Tools, as shown in Figure 4.17.

The Network Monitor allows you to capture, analyze, and troubleshoot packets to and from the particular computer where it is installed. To capture, analyze, and troubleshoot packets between other computers, you need to install the SMS version of Network Monitor.

FIGURE 4.17   Network Monitor Tools

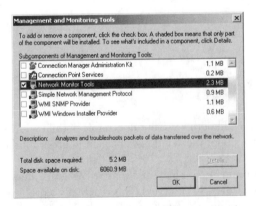

One of the major concerns with network analyzers is that a great deal of proprietary information is sent over the network, and this includes highly confidential information such as account names and passwords. The only person that should ever be running a network analyzer on the network should be a network administrator or server administrator. One of the nice features of the SMS Network Monitor is that you can use it to identify others on the network who are also using the SMS Network Monitor. You, as an administrator, can find potential malicious users by scanning for other Network Monitor users. However, the SMS Network Monitor cannot tell you if other types of network analyzers are being used on the network.

Network analyzers are usually passive devices or passive software on the network. This means that all they do is listen to the network traffic and capture it to local files or local memory. It is very hard to detect the user of a network analyzer, because it does not readily identify itself to the network. There are a few tools available on the Internet that help to identify network analyzers, but they are not always completely reliable and are not able to detect all potential network analyzers on the network. Many organizations reduce their exposure to network analyzers by using switched networks; they don't allow the switch ports to be changed to promiscuous mode. A switched network sends traffic only to the port where the target computer resides and does not send network traffic to other ports like a hub.

Summary

This chapter covered the important topics: the IPSec Protocol, SMB signing, and Network Monitor.

We spent a great deal of page space on IPSec: how to configure this service and how to manage it. You learned that IPSec is rather complicated in that the rules that govern how IPSec operates can be configured at a granular level and applied via Group Policies. You also learned that IPSec depends on a successful deployment of a public key infrastructure and that deployment of client certificates and their renewal is essential to a successful deployment of IPSec.

We also spent some time discussing the different authentication and encryption standards that are used by IPSec in Windows 2000 and Windows Server 2003. In addition, you learned some ideas about how to implement IPSec for web, database, and e-mail servers.

We finally ended the IPSec section by discussing troubleshooting tips and ideas to work with when taking the exam. One of the paramount ideas to keep in mind is that both client and server must trust the same CA, and successful certificate renewal is essential to an ongoing IPSec deployment.

You learned that SMB signing is really placing a digital signature in each packet to allow the receiver to verify that the sender is who they claim to be. This can be of great help in overcoming security threats and securing network traffic in the LAN and as well as in the WAN.

Finally, you learned that Network Monitor is a Microsoft network analyzer that can be used to capture, analyze, and troubleshoot network packets. Along with learning about network analyzers at a high level, you also learned how to detect others using network analyzers on your organizations network.

Exam Essentials

Understand the role of a certificate authority for IPSec. Having a trusted CA is essential to a successful deployment of IPSec.

Understand the difference between an authentication protocol and an encryption protocol. It will be easy to mix up the different protocols on the exam. Be sure you understand which protocols are involved in encryption and which are involved in authentication.

Understand how to configure IPSec using Group Policies. Because so much of an IPSec deployment is accomplished through Group Policies, it is important to understand how IPSec is deployed and then managed.

Understand how to fix problems when they occur. You will be presented with scenarios on the exam that will be problematic: a certificate isn't working, the wrong protocol was selected, and so on. Be sure you spend some time thinking about what could go wrong with IPSec and the basic steps you would take to fix the problem.

Review Questions

1. The architecture of SMB signing is which of the following?

   A. Client-server

   B. Peer-to-peer

   C. Request-response

   D. Offer-acceptance

2. The Common Internet File System (CIFS) contains which new features over traditional SMBs? (Choose all that apply.)

   A. Clients must connect using IPSec.

   B. Clients must be authenticated before using CIFS.

   C. A message authentication code can be used.

   D. Clients must connect to the CIFS using a secure messaging channel.

3. One of the goals of secure communication is to ensure that the sender of the message is the only one who could have sent the message. Which security goal does this represent?

   A. Antireplay

   B. Confidentiality

   C. Nonrepudiation

   D. Integrity

4. You are the system administrator for your Windows-based network. You have one Active Directory domain. Your domain controllers are in the default Domain Controllers OU. You have 50 Windows 98 workstations, 25 Windows Server 2003 member servers, and 200 Windows 2000 Professional workstations. The Windows 98 workstations are in the Research OU, and the Windows 2000 Professional workstations and Windows Server 2003 member servers are in the Admin OU. You need to require SMB signing for all computers on your network. What should you do? (Choose three answers; all three represent one part of one solution.)

   A. On the Windows 98 workstations, set the `EnableSecuritySignature` to one.

   B. On the Windows 2000 workstations, set the `RequireSecuritySignature` to one.

   C. In Active Directory, enable Digitally Sign Server Communication (Always) on the Domain Controllers OU.

   D. In Active Directory, enable Digitally Sign Server Communication (Always) on the domain object.

   E. In Active Directory, enable Digitally Sign Client Communication (Always) on the Domain Controllers OU.

   F. In Active Directory, enable Digitally Sign Client Communication (Always) on the Research OU.

   G. In Active Directory, enable Digitally Sign Server Communication (Always) on the Admin OU.

5. You are the system administrator of an Active Directory domain. You have 200 remote users who have Windows 2000 Professional installed on their laptops. You have another 200 users who have Windows XP Professional installed on their desktops in your network. Your remote users trust a third-party certificate authority, and your network users trust your internal Microsoft certificate authority. Your remote users need to trust the external CA in order to access secured databases shared by your company and three other partner companies. You need to enable SMB signing for all 400 users. What should you do first?

   A. Install a certificate on every remote client laptop. Have the client trust your internal CA.

   B. Use the Encapsulated Payload to transfer certificates between CAs.

   C. Use Active Directory to add a trusted root certificate from the external CA. Apply this to all machines on your internal network.

   D. Ensure that the security associations (SAs) are trusting both CAs.

6. When a packet has been altered by an attacker to look like the sender is someone other than the real sender, the attacker has engaged in which of the following?

   A. Eavesdropping

   B. Impersonation

   C. Man-in-the-middle attack

   D. Identity spoofing

7. Which of the following is responsible for key exchange between two computers during the session authentication negotiation?

   A. 3DES

   B. Diffie-Hellman

   C. Dynamic rekeying

   D. Authentication headers

8. Which of the following are considered hash algorithms? (Choose all that apply.)

   A. DES

   B. MD5

   C. Preshared keys

   D. Diffie-Hellman

   E. 3DES

   F. SHA

   G. ESP

9. Which of the following is the module responsible for enforcing IPSec rules against every packet?

    A. IPSec driver

    B. Certificate Authority Policy Module

    C. Security association

    D. Encapsulated Payload Protocol

10. You are the system administrator for an Active Directory domain. You have 4 Windows Server 2003 machines and 50 Windows XP Professional workstations. You want to ensure that the computers on your network use secure communications on your network. Which selections should you make? (Choose all that apply.)

    A. Client (Respond Only)

    B. Server (Request Security)

    C. Secure Server (Require Security)

    D. Encapsulated Payload Protocol

11. You are the system administrator for an Active Directory domain. You have 50 Windows 2000 Professional workstations in the Research OU. You have 4 domain controllers in the Domain Controllers OU. You also have 50 Windows 98 computers in the Admin OU. The Admin OU is a child OU of the Research OU. You have 20 Windows 2000 member servers. The member servers are members of the Marketing OU. You want to assign IPSec to each computer on the network with the least amount of administrative effort. What should you do? (Choose all that apply.)

    A. Assign the Client (Respond Only) setting to the Research OU.

    B. Block policy inheritance on the Admin OU.

    C. Assign Secure Server (Require Security) on the Domain Controllers OU and the Marketing OU.

    D. Create a policy to assign the correct Registry key on the Admin OU.

    E. Assign Secure Server (Require Security) on the Marketing OU.

12. You are the system administrator for a Windows Server 2003 Active Directory domain. You need to securely transfer files every day to a Windows Server 2003 file server on the Internet. You want to use IPSec to perform this task. What should you do?

    A. Use the Encapsulated Payload service.

    B. Use Authentication Headers.

    C. Use IPSec transport mode.

    D. Use IPSec tunnel mode.

13. When two computers use IPSec to secure their transmissions, how many IPSec rules need to be in place in order for the transmissions to be successful?

   A. One

   B. Two

   C. Three

   D. Four

14. You are the system administrator for an Active Directory domain. You have just implemented IPSec to secure internal data transmissions. However, two hours after you implement this policy, no one can communicate with anyone else. You suspect that your configurations are wrong, and you need to get communications going again as fast as possible. What action should you take?

   A. Unassign the policy settings in Active Directory.

   B. Select Restore Defaults and reapply the policy.

   C. Disable all enabled policy settings and reapply the policy.

   D. Use the `secedit` command.

15. You have four servers on the Internet to which you need to set up secure communications. You decide to use tunnel mode for IPSec to securely transmit data to these four servers. Each server is directly available on the Internet, and each server has a unique IP address. How many IPSec rules will you need to configure?

   A. One

   B. Four

   C. Eight

   D. Ten

16. Using the information in Question 15, how many tunnels can be active at any given time?

   A. One

   B. Four

   C. Eight

   D. Ten

17. You want to implement IPSec in the most secure fashion possible. Of the answers provided, which of the following choices should you select? (Choose three; each correct answer represents one part of the overall solution.)

   A. Encapsulated Payload

   B. Perfect forward secrecy

   C. Server (Request Security)

   D. Secure Server (Require Security)

18. You ping a Windows 2000 server that is configured for Server (Request Security). You receive the "Negotiating IP Security" message. What does this mean?

   A. The server responded to the `ping` command using secure data transmissions.

   B. The server did not respond to the `ping` command, because the Security Association was being established.

   C. The Security Association was not able to be established.

   D. You should use Authentication Headers and DES instead of the Encapsulated Payload and 3DES.

19. You are the system administrator for a Windows Server 2003 Active Directory domain. You have a member server, Server1, in the Research OU. Your domain is named Corp. You have configured IPSec policies in the following manner: Corp: Secure Server (Require Security); Local Policies of Server1: Server (Request Security). Unix-based users on your network are complaining that they cannot communicate with Server1. What should you do?

   A. Change the policy setting on the Corp domain object to Server (Request Security).

   B. Change the policy setting on the Research OU to Secure Server (Require Security).

   C. Create a new policy and configure it with Server (Request Security). Link the new policy to the domain object.

   D. Create a new policy and configure it with Client (Respond Only). Link the new policy to the domain object.

20. You need to allow IPSec traffic past your IP filter on your network. Which of the following should you do? (Choose all that apply.)

   A. Open port 53, inbound only.

   B. Open port 500, inbound only.

   C. Open port 500, inbound and outbound.

   D. Open port 53, inbound and outbound.

   E. Allow protocol ID 43.

   F. Allow protocol 50.

   G. Allow protocol 51.

Answers to Review Questions

1. C. The SMB architecture is a request-response architecture. The client sends requests to the server, and the server responds to those requests. For instance, when a client wants to perform a file move function, a request is sent to the server, and the server performs the function and then responds to the client.

2. B, C. One of the two main upgrades to SMB in CIFS is the ability to use a message authentication code (MAC) on each packet. This is what Microsoft calls SMB signing. Each packet can be digitally signed to deter impersonation and ensure confidentiality.

3. C. Nonrepudiation is the assurance that the person who sent the message is the only one who could have sent the message. Confidentiality is the assurance that only the sender and receiver of the message can actually read the message. Similar in concept is the notion of integrity, which ensures that the packet was not altered during transit. Antireplay means that the packet cannot be captured, modified, and then replayed with bogus information.

4. C, F, G. To require SMB signing in a mixed environment, you will need to use the `RequireSecuritySignature` on Windows NT and 9x machines in their Registry. Then, in Active Directory, you need to require SMB signing on all the domain controllers, member servers, and workstations. This is accomplished by creating a Group Policy on the correct objects and then applying it. The correct objects, in this instance, are the Domain Controllers and Admin OUs. Applying the policy at the domain level works, but is not the best answer, because a more granular, more specific correct answer was available.

5. C. You can use a Group Policy to add a trusted certificate authority to your local network. All you need is a root certificate from the CA to be used as a basis for trusting the CA. Then, when the remote users need to perform SMB signing, everyone can use the third-party CA as a common, trusted CA for the SMB digital signatures.

6. D. If the attacker had created new packets to look like they came from someone else when they really came from him, that is impersonation. Impersonation is a form of identity spoofing. Here, the attacker is changing who the sender is and is not altering the data. Hence, this is a more generalized form of identity spoofing.

7. B. The Diffie-Hellman algorithm provides a way for the two computers to send keying information to each other so that both can generate the keys of the other system and thereby engage in secure communications. The keys themselves are never passed over the line, just the keying information, and that information is hashed by Windows 2000 and Windows Server 2003 to ensure the information's integrity and confidentiality.

8. B, F. The purpose of this question is to ensure that you have a good understanding of which protocols and technologies are used for which purpose. In the answers to this question, we have inserted encryption and hash algorithms, authentication methods, and the DH key generation exchange method. It is easy to confuse DES with MD5, thinking that they are both encryption methods. To a point, perhaps they are, but when used in conjunction with the SA setup, DES is thought of as an encryption algorithm and MD5 as an algorithm. Because the question was about hash algorithms, the correct answers are MD5 and SHA.

9. A. The IPSec driver is responsible for rule enforcement in Windows 2000– and Windows Server 2003–based machines.

10. A, C. If you need to ensure that all computers on your network will use secure transmissions, A and C are the correct answers. If you need to provide secure transmission, but not require them, answers A and B would be correct.

11. A, B, C, D, E. Because the Windows 98 workstations are in a child OU, you need to block policy inheritance and then assign the correct Registry keys to the Windows 98 workstations via a Windows 98 Group Policy. All other answers are actions that you would need to take in order to implement IPSec in your environment.

12. D. The tunnel mode is designed to protect the packet as it flows over an untrusted network. The Internet is considered an untrusted network, so it is important to ensure that packet flow is encrypted to the destination you specify. The endpoint of the tunnel is really an IP address that is used to define the end of the tunnel. The packet may continue to travel on from there, but it will not be secure.

13. B. The number of rules depends on the type of traffic each rule is configured to secure. A rule is created for each direction of packet flow. Although you can have many active rules on the server, only one rule per server/client relationship can actually be used; hence, the answer is two—one rule for each direction.

14. B. If you want to return the IPSec rules and settings to default quickly, click the Restore Defaults button and then reapply the policy.

15. B. The answer depends on the type of data you want to secure. If you need to set up multiple tunnels, you need to configure multiple rules—one rule per tunnel—because each tunnel requires its own rule in the policy settings.

16. A. The answer depends on the resources of the server and the available bandwidth. Even though you can have multiple tunnels configured and created in Windows 2000, only one tunnel can be used at any given time.

17. A, B, D. The Encapsulated Payload is a higher, more secure method of encrypting the data than Authentication Headers. Perfect forward secrecy regenerates the master key during rekeying from which other keys are derived during secure transmissions, and Secure Server (Require Security) requires your servers to interoperate using only secure transmissions.

18. B. When you receive the response "Negotiating IP Security" after using the `ping` command, the client from whom the `ping` command was initiated is setting up the secure channel with the server. Once the SA is set up, the `ping` command will work.

19. A. IPSec policies set at the domain level override local policies of member servers. If you want to allow the Unix-based workstations to communicate with Server1, changing the policy on the domain object overrides the local policies of the server.

20. C, F, G. Protocols 50 and 51 should be allowed passage on your firewall. Port 500 should be opened for inbound and outbound traffic to allow the Internet Key Exchange protocol to work properly.

Chapter

5

Implementing Security for Wireless Networks

THE MICROSOFT EXAM OBJECTIVES COVERED IN THIS CHAPTER:

✓ **Plan and implement security for wireless networks.**

- Plan the authentication methods for a wireless network.
- Plan the encryption methods for a wireless network.
- Plan wireless access policies.
- Configure wireless encryption.
- Install and configure wireless support for client computers.

Almost every business and aspect of life will change in the near future as result of the drastic changes in Internet implementation and wireless device support. Sure, many things won't change because of the Internet and wireless technologies, but those things probably have not changed much in the last 50 years. Anything impacted by technology will be impacted by mobile solutions.

So why wireless? Well, first, dragging that really long Category 5 cable around can be a bit of a killjoy. Second, if businesses want to implement more technology connected to the Internet, Joe User cannot be running Category 5 cables around his house to support all his home devices. Nor can you expect to add more network cable for all business applications. At last count, there were six network drops running to one of our desks. Wireless connectivity just makes sense to provide a means for connecting all these devices, quickly, to the home network and the Internet. Wireless is convenient.

As wireless networks begin taking hold in business, you have a new problem—securing these networks. Just as your normal networks need to be secured, so do your wireless networks. Actually, your wireless networks need to be secured even more than your wired networks, because the wireless aspect often means that the network is not only available within the office, but often outside the office and even outside the building. Using a wireless network is much like having Ethernet ports on the outside of your office building. Anyone can bring a wireless device within the range of your network and start attacking it. Implementing security is extremely important if you want to properly protect your company network resources from intruders.

This chapter covers the important aspects of securing your wireless networks.

Configuring Public and Private Wireless LANs

Remember the days when people would come to a big budget meeting with their laptops and fight over the wall jacks so they could get on the network? Well, now you can easily deploy wireless to locations such as conference rooms and other common areas where workers gather to discuss their projects. You can also set up WLANs for your clients to use when they visit your place of business. *Wireless LANs (WLANs)* are wonderfully convenient and can really increase user productivity. This section explains how to set up such a network.

To set up a WLAN, you need hardware, software, and configuration settings such as

- A *wireless access point* (AP), sometimes referred to as a WAP

- A network connection and power for the AP

- Wireless Ethernet adapters or wireless network interface cards (NICs), usually in the form of a PCMCIA (PC Memory Card International Association) or PCCardProximity, meaning you have to be within range of the radio signals emitted by the AP

Configuring a Public Wireless LAN

The idea behind a public WLAN is that getting on the network should be easy, so let's go through the rudimentary steps of building a public WLAN now that you've looked at the necessary components. In Exercise 5.1, you'll configure a public wireless LAN for a Windows XP Professional client.

The *service set identifier (SSID)* is an alphanumeric string identifier that distinguishes one wireless LAN from another. It is similar to an address for the wireless network. For example, an SSID might be a simple string such as "CorpA", "CompanyB", or even "JoeSnuffy" that identifies an AP or a group of APs.

EXERCISE 5.1

Configuring a Public Wireless LAN with a Windows XP Professional Client

1. Connect the AP to the Ethernet network and plug in its power cable or use the inline power option for the AP if no power outlet is available. Turn on the AP if it has a power switch. Refer to the hardware vendor documentation if needed. This exercise cannot address each and every AP and wireless NIC, because so many are available.

2. Connect to the AP using the serial port or use either Telnet or the web browser after IP address assignment through DHCP. Each AP will have its own process. Refer to the hardware vendor documentation as needed.

3. Set the SSID to be used and configure the IP address of the AP as a static IP address. Refer to the hardware vendor documentation as needed.

4. Start up a client system and install the wireless NIC. Depending on the vendor and the version of the operating system, you may have to download the proper drivers for the wireless adapter.

5. In Control Panel (in Category view), click Network And Internet Connections and then click Network Connections.

6. Right-click the Wireless Network Connection and choose Properties from the shortcut menu to open the Wireless Network Connection Properties dialog box. Click the Wireless Networks tab.

7. Select the SSID in the Available Networks box and then click Configure. If the SSID is found, proceed to step 10.

8. If you don't find a network name (SSID) in the Available Networks box (because the AP is not broadcasting the SSID), click the Preferred Networks check box. If the SSID is there, select it, click Properties, and proceed to step 10.

EXERCISE 5.1 *(continued)*

---

9. If you don't find an SSID in the Preferred Networks box or in the Available Networks box, click Add to manually add the SSID information.

10. Update the SSID information in the Network Name (SSID) box.

At this point, the client and the AP should be able to communicate, and the client should also be able to talk to the rest of the public network.

This is normally all that is needed for a Windows XP Professional client. Setting up a Windows 2000 Professional client is similar. In Exercise 5.2, you'll configure a public WLAN with Windows 2000 Professional.

EXERCISE 5.2

Configuring a Public Wireless LAN with a Windows 2000 Professional Client

1. Connect the AP to the Ethernet network and plug in its power cable or use the inline power option for the AP if no power outlet is available. Turn on the AP if it has a power switch. Refer to the hardware vendor documentation if needed. This exercise cannot address each and every AP and wireless NIC, because so many are available.

2. Connect to the AP using the serial port or use either Telnet or the web browser after IP address assignment through DHCP. Each AP will have its own process. Refer to the hardware vendor documentation as needed.

3. Set the SSID to be used and configure the IP address of the AP as a static IP address. Refer to the hardware vendor documentation as needed.

4. Start up a client system and install the wireless NIC. Depending on the vendor and the version of the operating system, you may have to download the proper drivers for the wireless adapter.

5. In Control Panel, select Network, right-click the Wireless Network Connection, and choose Properties from the shortcut menu to open the Wireless Network Connection Properties dialog box.

6. In the General tab, click Configure to open the wireless NIC Properties dialog box.

7. Click the Settings tab, enter the SSID in the Wireless LAN Service Area box (this is for a 3Com wireless NIC), and click OK. Steps 6 and 7 may be a bit different for other wireless NICs.

At this point, the client and the AP should be able to communicate, and the client should also be able to talk to the rest of the public network.

Generally, if you know the SSID, you can get on the wireless network. This is true for almost all public WLANs, and it is also true for the majority of private WLANs. Using Dynamic Host

Configuration Protocol (DHCP) to provide the IP address and all the IP configuration information streamlines the process of adding new wireless clients and decreases the administration involved.

Configuring a Private Wireless LAN

The idea behind a private WLAN is that it is secured so that only authorized people with the appropriate credentials can get on the network. This section describes how to build a private WLAN.

As mentioned in the previous section, DHCP can reduce the administration required to configure and maintain a WLAN whether it is public or private. Configuring a private WLAN is much the same as configuring a public WLAN, except you need to take some additional steps.

Many private WLANs are misconfigured when it comes to security. Many companies use DHCP for their wireless networks, and they do not use WEP, MAC filtering, or 802.1x to increase the security levels. SOHO (small office, home office) networks are almost always wide open and are not configured securely. To make it even easier to join a wireless network, Windows XP Professional can detect the SSID broadcasts of APs and automatically set up the wireless connection configuration for you. Connecting to a wireless access point is looking rather easy now, right? Well, in many cases, it is extremely easy.

Figure 5.1 shows how most companies install an AP, directly connecting it to their company network. In this configuration, the wireless devices connect to the AP and gain access to the company network through the AP so that they are on the same network as the wired clients. This configuration is not a best practice; however, it is a good starting point for this chapter. In this configuration, all the company client systems are behind the firewall and protected from the Internet.

FIGURE 5.1   A basic wireless network

This configuration is easy for most administrators to support, especially with wireless devices that can receive the SSID information through broadcasts and also receive all their TCP/IP (Transmission Control Protocol/Internet Protocol) configuration information through DHCP servers on the local network. You will learn to love that Windows XP Professional is self-configuring in this sense; it is incredibly easy to get up and running. Windows 2000 Professional takes a little more work, but it is also easy to configure as a wireless client. In the configuration in Figure 5.1, all the company client systems are behind the firewall and protected from the Internet. In Exercise 5.3, you'll configure a private wireless LAN for a Windows XP Professional client, and in Exercise 5.4, you'll do the same using a Windows 2000 Professional client.

EXERCISE 5.3

Configuring a Private Wireless LAN with a Windows XP Professional Client

1. Connect the AP to the Ethernet network and plug in its power cable, or use the inline power option for the AP if no power outlet is available. Turn on the AP if it has a power switch. Refer to the hardware vendor documentation if needed. This exercise cannot address each and every AP and wireless NIC, because so many are available.

2. Connect to the AP using the serial port or use either Telnet or the web browser after IP address assignment through DHCP. Each AP has its own process. Refer to the hardware vendor documentation as needed.

3. Set the SSID to be used and configure the IP address of the AP as a static IP address. Refer to the hardware vendor documentation as needed.

4. Set the allowed MAC address range, set the WEP key, and configure 802.1x if available in the AP configuration tools. Refer to the hardware vendor documentation as needed.

5. Start up a client system and install the wireless NIC. Depending on the vendor and the version of the operating system, you may have to download the proper drivers for the wireless adapter.

6. In Control Panel (in Categories view), select Network And Internet Connections and then select Network Connections.

7. Right-click the Wireless Network Connection and choose Properties from the shortcut menu to open the Wireless Network Connection Properties dialog box. Click the Wireless Networks tab.

8. Use the Add button to manually add the SSID information in the Association tab. You need to do this because the AP is not broadcasting the SSID. Enable WEP and then click the Authentication tab.

9. In the Authentication tab, enter the 802.1x configuration information and then click OK.

At this point, the client and the AP should be able to communicate, and the client should also be able to talk to the rest of the public network.

Again, because Windows 2000 Professional is a bit different from Windows XP Professional, its steps are a little different and are outlined in Exercise 5.4.

EXERCISE 5.4

Configuring a Private Wireless LAN with a Windows 2000 Professional Client

1. Connect the AP to the Ethernet network and plug in its power cable, or use the inline power option for the AP if no power outlet is available. Turn on the AP if it has a power switch. Refer to the hardware vendor documentation if needed. This exercise cannot address each and every AP and wireless NIC because so many are available.

2. Connect to the AP using the serial port or use either Telnet or the web browser after IP address assignment through DHCP. Each AP has its own process. Refer to the hardware vendor documentation as needed.

3. Set the SSID to be used and configure the IP address of the AP as a static IP address. Refer to the hardware vendor documentation as needed.

4. Set the allowed MAC address range, set the WEP key, and configure 802.1x if available in the AP configuration tools. Refer to the hardware vendor documentation as needed.

5. Start up a client system and install the wireless NIC. Depending on the vendor and the version of the operating system, you may have to download the proper drivers for the wireless adapter.

6. In Control Panel, select Network, right-click Wireless Network Connection, and choose Properties from the shortcut menu to open the Wireless Network Connection Properties dialog box.

7. In the General tab, click the Configure button to open the Wireless NIC Properties dialog box.

8. Click the Settings tab and enter the SSID in the Wireless LAN Service Area.

9. Click the Advanced button and then click the Wireless Client tab. In the Operating Mode drop-down list box, select the proper level of WEP encryption and the proper key. These last few steps may be a bit different for other wireless NICs.

At this point, the client and the AP should be able to communicate, and the client should also be able to talk to the rest of the public network.

Exercises 5.1 through 5.4 may be a bit difficult to work through because of the unique tools and menus for all the APs and wireless NICs, but it's important to understand the process of setting up a wireless network. Now let's look at the differences between a public and a private WLAN when it comes to the security settings and configurations.

Configuring Windows CE as a Wireless Client

With the heavy emphasis on mobile devices, Windows CE has become important to the future of wireless and to the future of wireless security. Windows CE is widely used in a large number of handheld devices, including personal digital assistants (PDAs). Pocket PC standards usually specify a version of Windows CE for certain types of hardware. The current version of Windows CE is 4.2.

Windows CE 4.2 can participate in a company network using Ethernet adapters and it can also participate on the company wireless network. Because Windows CE 4.2 can be a wireless client, you need to know which technologies can be used to secure CE devices. Windows CE currently supports the following security measures for wireless access:

- 64- and 128-bit WEP, with the high encryption pack installed
- MAC address filtering
- *VPN (virtual private network)* clients
- Personal firewalls
- 802.1x using Cisco components

Again, you must deal with the same limitations when it comes to wireless security and Windows CE devices. You can implement the same security components as you implement on Windows XP Professional clients, with the exception of 802.1x, which is available only through vendor-specific solutions. Obviously, you should use 802.1x where possible.

 At this time, Windows CE does not support mutual authentication for wireless connectivity. According to the latest information, Windows CE .NET will not be supported for the newer releases in the near future.

Windows CE can use different authentication methods that can be plugged in to 802.1x through the EAP (Extensible Authentication Protocol) "extensible" capabilities, which allow some choices for the authentication methods. Vendor-specific solutions at this time include the ability to support usernames and passwords, certificates and certificates on smart cards, and even fingerprints. The EAP-MD5 supports usernames and passwords, and the EAP-TLS (Extensible Authentication Protocol-Transport Layer Security) supports certificate-based authentication. Again, 802.1x is vendor-specific, with Cisco currently taking much of the initiative in this area.

Pocket PCs are beginning to take hold in the market today. Not only can you purchase a Pocket PC and then add PC cards such as a wireless adapter, but you can purchase cellular telephones combined with the Pocket PC operating system all in one device. Connecting to wireless networks has become extremely easy when using a Pocket PC and a wireless card, and even easier when using a Pocket PC, Phone Edition because it has a built-in wireless modem and is not restricted to areas enabled by wireless access points.

Wireless Components

As far as hardware is concerned, a WLAN consists of two components: APs and wireless NICs. The AP is an important piece of equipment for a WLAN. After all, it is your main radio transmitter and receiver for the network and its devices. The decision about which technology to use and how to place the APs is also important. You need to give strong consideration to the type of AP that you purchase for your network. Some are really better than others. Look for the following key features:

- Support for *802.11a* or 802.11g, as well as *802.11b* for easy upgrades.
- Support for multiple radio cards. This allows you to have one 802.11b card and one 802.11a card so that the device can support two different network architectures with a single AP.
- Support for external antennas using *RP-TNC* connections. This allows the AP to be well hidden for cosmetic reasons and expose just the antenna.

Reverse polarity threaded naval connectors (RP-TNCs) are the standard connections used for external antennas for wireless access points.

- Support for inline power. This allows the AP to draw its power through the Ethernet cable and makes it much easier to deploy APs where they are needed, such as in drop-down ceilings, without separate power connections.
- Support for multiple SSIDs.
- Support for 802.1x authentication.
- Support for *WPA (Wi-Fi Protected Access)*.
- Support for *RADIUS (Remote Authentication Dial-In User Service)*.

Wireless NICs are supposed to be fully compatible with the various brands of APs. However, in practice, we have found this is not true. We highly encourage you to purchase APs and wireless NICs from the same vendor to avoid any potential compatibility problems. The key will be mostly how the NICs interact with the APs installed in the organization. A few brands let you install an external antenna to supplement the antenna built in to the PCMCIA card to help extend its range.

Choosing between 802.11a, 802.11b, and 802.11g is difficult for many organizations. The 802.11a and 802.11g standards are still fairly new, and equipment can be a good bit more expensive than 802.11b equipment. Equipment based on 802.11a is even more expensive, though, because the range is significantly smaller and requires more equipment for the same coverage areas.

Notice in Figure 5.2 that 802.11a has significantly higher bandwidth, but that bandwidth decreases dramatically with distance from the AP. Equipment based on the 802.11b standard requires fewer APs; however, it does not provide the high bandwidth that many of today's applications need. 802.11g is a good compromise for many organizations. 802.11g bandwidth can be as high as 54 Mbps, like 802.11a. However, because 802.11g uses the same 2.4GHz spectrum as 802.11b, it is capable of much longer distances for connections. Also, 802.11g is backward compatible with 802.11b in almost all cases.

FIGURE 5.2   Comparing 802.11a and 802.11b

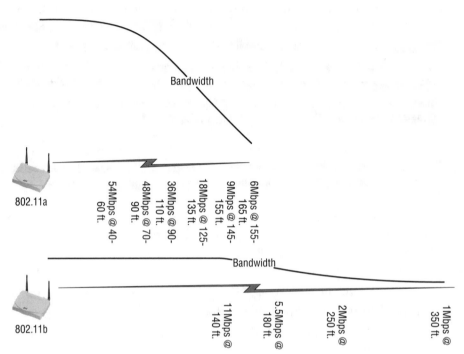

So, you plug in the AP, hook it up to the network, install your wireless cards, and away you go? Well, close. You need a little information about the network first. You need to answer some questions:

- Does the wireless network support DHCP, or do you need to get a static address for your card?
- What is the SSID for the AP?
- Are you using *Wired Equivalent Privacy (WEP)*, and what level of encryption?
- Are you using *MAC (Media Access Control) filtering*?
- Do you use 802.1*x* security?
- Have you implemented WPA?

The answers to these questions depend on whether this WLAN is public or private. A public wireless network is set up without any regard to security. It is built to allow anyone to use it, but usually it is built by a business so that their customers can use it. For example, Millennium Trenz Wireless, a business in Denver, Colorado, offers free 802.11b access, but it is intended for customers who come in to purchase wireless devices. You can find information about Millennium Trenz Wireless at www.wi-fihotspotlist.com, along with many other business and government entities that offer 802.11b access to the general public. A private wireless network is closed to the public and is intended for the private use of an individual or group of people defined by the owner of the AP.

> ### ⊕ Real World Scenario
>
> **Extending the Capabilities of Wireless**
>
> Let's say you want to connect two buildings that are about 700 feet apart via a WAN link. You can't afford a dedicated T1 between the buildings, you can't run fiber-optic cable between the buildings because of the costs of protecting it, and there is property between the two buildings that your company doesn't own.
>
> By purchasing and deploying two wireless access points with RP-TNC for external antennas and connecting external directional antennas, it is easy to go beyond normal 802.11b distances and still get better bandwidth than a T1 link. The best part of the solution is that no monthly fees are involved.

Configuring Secure Wireless Network Settings

As previously discussed, you need to answer the following questions before you can add clients to an existing WLAN:

- Does the wireless network support DHCP, or do you need a static address for your card?
- What is the SSID for the AP?
- Are you using WEP, and what level of encryption?
- Have you implemented WPA?
- Are you using MAC filtering?
- Do you use 802.1x security?

The answers to these six questions are the basis for controlling access to the wireless network and the ability to control whether others can listen in on your radio traffic. Another way to put it is that the answers to these six questions are the basis on which to implement security for your wireless network. Securing wireless networks involves a great deal of effort.

Dynamic Host Configuration Protocol (DHCP)

Implementing DHCP for the wireless network is a good plan if the goal is to reduce administration. However, it is not a good plan if security is more important. Giving intruders a working IP address is like giving them a hall pass to roam around the network. With this level of access, intruders can probe the many resources on the network to identify targets for further intrusion. An anonymous user attached directly to your network can cause incredible amounts of damage from the information they gather.

It's a tradeoff between reduced administration and security issues. This is not a fun decision to make. Last year, reduced administration would have won, but in today's computing environment, security has to come out on top.

Using static IP configurations for wireless devices eliminates the DHCP issues. However, this also means that you have to either talk the users through this configuration or do it yourself, plus you have to manage the list of IP addresses that are being used and who has them. In either case, the more you handle such tasks manually, the greater the chance that the settings will be entered incorrectly, and the more time you have to spend troubleshooting the configuration.

Another option provides a little administrative relief and also provides security to a degree: Use a scope of addresses that are all set up with reservations. Using DHCP to provide addresses to certain MAC addresses as provided in the DHCP request can be both secure and helpful to administrators. First, with DHCP, you can change configuration information from the DHCP server without touching the client systems. This is, of course, a very good thing. Second, with DHCP options such as DNS (Domain Name Service), WINS (Windows Internet Naming Service), domain names, and default gateways, you can eliminate the problems of users fat-fingering the information in their configurations. At the same time, you can stop potential intruders from getting an address and configuration options from your DHCP servers.

Without valid IP address information, an intruder really can't cause too many problems. However, if an intruder is in proximity, they can still attack your AP, consume bandwidth with their attacks, and listen in on your radio traffic to get the information they need to potentially connect to your AP. The best you can really do when it comes to IP configuration information is make it a bit harder on the potential intruders by using either statically assigned IP addresses or DHCP reservations.

Let's look at some other configuration options that can help secure your wireless network.

Service Set Identifier (SSID)

The SSID is really just a network name. In many APs and wireless NIC configurations, it is even referred to as a network name. All that you're doing with SSIDs is providing a unique name for your wireless network to distinguish it from other wireless networks. The SSID is extremely important for connecting to a wireless network. The main problem with SSIDs, though, is that few administrators understand the security issues around wireless, and they do not know that the standard SSID for each vendor is part of the default configuration for each AP. The following SSIDs are implemented right out of the box:

- 3Com uses "101".

- Addtron uses "WLAN".

- Cisco uses "tsunami".

- Compaq uses "Compaq".

- Intel uses "intel".

- Linksys uses "linksys" and "default".

- Lucent uses "RoamAbout Default Network Name".

Administrators who do change the defaults often choose names that are easy to remember such as the name of their company or terms such as "wireless," "default," and "WAP." It is highly recommended that you change all APs from their default SSIDs as well as change default administrative passwords to settings that are not easy to guess or successfully used for brute force attacks.

SSIDs can be case-sensitive. Be sure to consult your manufacturer's documentation for more information.

Figure 5.3 shows an example of how the wireless card configuration might look when a wireless network has multiple APs.

In Figure 5.3, multiple SSIDs are configured, with a priority given to the 3449 SSID. In this example, SSID 3449 is the preferred AP, and 3350 is next on the list.

Generally, the SSID is used to segment the wireless network devices into networks of one or more APs. A large organization might have APs in the marketing area with one SSID, and all the marketing laptops are set up to use that SSID. The research engineers might also have some APs in their area of the building, and they are all set up with a different SSID. Research engineers use only their APs, and the marketing team uses only their APs. This is one way for the client systems to handle overlapping coverage areas when multiple APs provide service.

Figure 5.4 shows an example in which two APs overlap. If a user brings their computer from their office to the conference room in the middle, they can connect to either AP. Setting the preference as shown in Figure 5.3 allows the system to remain configured to its preferred AP and lets it switch over to its secondary AP if it is out of range of the preferred AP.

FIGURE 5.3   Configuring the SSID

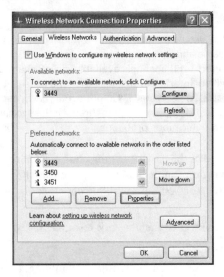

FIGURE 5.4   A sample office layout

Overlap is important to a wireless network because you want higher bandwidth. Walls and other factors such as interference from devices such as microwave ovens and 2.4GHz wireless phones can reduce the broadcast distances and make them much shorter than those specified.

Overlap of wireless zones can also be a problem with wireless networks, because limited frequencies are available and overlap can cause interference with devices. In 802.11b, of the 11 (numbered 1–11) channels available, only 3 channels are within the frequency that will not interfere with each other and cause interference when their zones overlap; channels 1, 6, and 11 do not overlap with each other. This means that even in the best design, more than three wireless zones cannot overlap without causing communications problems.

Now, so far in this chapter, you have looked at the basics of connecting a client to a wireless access point, and you have seen how a connection can be made to a standard AP using a standard wireless NIC in Windows XP Professional or Windows 2000 Professional by setting the SSID. The primary security issues are

- Controlling who can access the APs to connect to the network resources
- Preventing others from listening in on your radio traffic

As Figure 5.4 clearly shows, signals do not always remain within the building. Many times, radio signals cover areas outside the building. This excess coverage is much like putting network jacks on the outside of the building. Most everyone would agree that this is a bad idea. So how do you remove these wireless jacks? You use SSIDs, WEP, 802.1*x*, and VPNs, which are all covered in the rest of this chapter.

SSID Security Concerns

You can implement network access control using an SSID associated with an AP or with a group of APs. The SSID provides a mechanism to segment a wireless network into multiple networks serviced by one or more APs. Every AP is configured with an SSID for a specific wireless network. To access the network, client computers must be configured with the correct SSID. An office or a building might be segmented into multiple networks by floor or department. Normally, you can configure a client computer with multiple SSIDs for users who require access to the network from a variety of different locations. Look back at Figure 5.3 for an example.

Because a client computer must present the correct SSID to access the AP, the SSID acts as a simple password, and it provides a measure of security. Although this security is fairly basic, you can configure the normal user's computer on the wireless network with the appropriate SSID for the department or group within the company, and you can segment their network traffic away from other APs that have different SSIDs. For example, if accounting has APs in their area and doesn't want everyone in the company using their APs, they can create an SSID for the accounting team APs. Anyone else in the company who doesn't have this SSID configured would be unable to connect to their APs. SSIDs can also be controlled through GPOs when using Windows Server 2003. This capability does not exist with Windows 2000 Active Directory; however, it does exist with Windows Server 2003 and Windows XP Professional.

You can configure any GPO at any level of the Active Directory architecture to provide connection order preferences and to provide 802.1*x* authentication options to wireless network clients. Using the Wireless Network (IEEE 802.11) Policies GPO configuration, as shown in Figure 5.5, you can define which wireless network users should attach to which wireless network access points in which order to help distribute the network load.

However, this minimal security is easily bypassed and compromised, primarily as a result of the improper configuration of the AP itself. If the AP is configured to broadcast its SSID, it can be picked up off the radio waves fairly easily. When this broadcast feature is enabled, any client computer that is not configured with a specific SSID is allowed to receive the SSID and access the AP. Windows XP Professional is really good at sniffing out these broadcast SSIDs in order to configure its wireless network settings automatically and make it easy for the user to connect to unsecured wireless networks. With the latest updates, Windows XP can even identify which networks that it has found are secure and offers you the ability to input the key to quickly connect. Applications such as NetStumbler and AirMagnet can also sniff out these SSIDs, even if the AP isn't broadcasting them.

SSID broadcasting is usually configured in the AP by changing the *beacon* settings. This beacon broadcasts information to the wireless network—including the SSID.

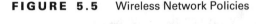

FIGURE 5.5   Wireless Network Policies

The default configuration of most APs enables broadcasting of the SSID on the channel being used by the AP. Obviously, if you shout out your configuration information, your network is not very secure. So here is the first area in which you can tighten up security. Most vendors' APs can turn off this broadcasting. You would be negligent if you didn't at least do that much.

Okay, so you turn off the broadcasting of the SSID at the AP, but that doesn't eliminate the problem. After all, a hacker can use an 802.11 analyzer to sniff the radio packets. Any time a system associates or reassociates with the AP, the SSID is passed in the clear. Even if the broadcasting is turned off, the SSID can be found out easily enough. To top it off, you know that your network users do really odd things such as share SSIDs with their friends so they can also use the wireless network.

Association in wireless networks is the process of the wireless NIC getting the data rates and other bits of info from the AP as it connects to it. Once the association is complete, the client and the AP can send data back and forth.

Protecting the SSID really isn't possible. All it really does is keep authorized users from accessing the wrong APs. When it comes to keeping out knowledgeable intruders, the SSID is pretty much worthless.

Configuring Wireless Encryption Levels with WEP

You can use WEP to improve the security of your wireless networks. The idea behind WEP is to make wireless traffic as secure as traffic traveling a wired network. WEP encrypts the body of each wireless frame. As you have learned, encryption is a good thing because it keeps data and communications private. E-mail, instant messaging, usernames, passwords, and other extremely important information should be encrypted if it contains proprietary data. This is even more important with wireless networks that are accessible from outside the office because of their broadcast range.

The Basics of WEP

The concept is simple. If WEP is activated at both the AP and the client, the wireless NIC encrypts the data payload and the CRC (cyclic redundancy check) of each and every frame sent to the AP using RC4 ciphers. All data between the AP and the wireless NIC is protected. The seed used to create the RC4 ciphers is a combination of the WEP base key and the *initialization vector (IV)* to create a 64-bit or 128-bit encryption key. The data sent between the AP and the client includes the IV along with the encrypted payloads. The IV just happens to be transmitted in the clear. "Transmitted in the clear" is a phrase that makes most security guys shudder, and for good reason. Anyone listening in on the traffic can read the IV in their packet sniffer. The IV is used on the receiving end along with the base key to decrypt the payload.

The transmission is encrypted with the IV combined with the WEP base key, which is stored in the configuration information for the NIC and the AP. The receiving side then decrypts the data using the IV that it receives as part of the transmission and combines it with the WEP base key that is part of its configuration information. Assuming that the WEP base keys are the same on both ends, the data will be successfully decrypted. It is a little more complex than this quick explanation, but there isn't any real value in going deep into the hows and whys of WEP encryption. The basics will do here.

In many access points, WEP is optional. Even if WEP is enabled and the encryption is turned on, it is not enforced by the AP. A client without encryption can still access that base station if they have the proper SSID.

You can typically configure WEP in three modes:

- No encryption
- 40-bit encryption
- 104-bit encryption

There is some confusion with the number of bits, so let's take a second to straighten that out. The IV is 24 bits. The IV is combined with the 40-bit key to create a total of 64 bits for use in encrypting and decrypting. In the 104-bit mode, the 24 bits for the IV are added to get 128 bits. Thus, the total encryption is 64 or 128 bits. The standards call for a maximum of 64 bits; however, many manufacturers have extended the encryption to 128 bits.

Almost every AP has WEP disabled by default. While WEP has serious flaws, it is better than implementing no security for your wireless network. WEP will keep many curious people out of your wireless network. Going from 64-bit encryption to 128-bit encryption does not help with the known problems of WEP. A 128-bit encryption can be broken almost as easily as a 64-bit encryption. Fully protecting the wireless network will take much more than implementing WEP.

The steps for configuring WEP are rather basic, as you'll see in Exercise 5.5.

EXERCISE 5.5

Configuring WEP

1. Configure and enable WEP and the AP using the tools and processes described in the vendor's hardware guide.

2. In Control Panel (in Categories view), select Network And Internet Connections and then select Network Connections.

3. Right-click Wireless Network Connection and choose Properties from the shortcut menu to open the Wireless Network Connection Properties dialog box. Click the Wireless Networks tab.

4. Select the SSID (Network Name) in the Available Networks box and then click the Configure button to open the Wireless Network Properties dialog box. Click the Data Encryption (WEP Enabled) check box to enable WEP.

5. In the Network Key box, type the key from the AP and confirm it if necessary. Click OK twice to close the open dialog boxes.

6. Restart the AP.

At this point, the client and the AP should be able to communicate, and the client should also be able to talk to the rest of the public network.

Enabling WEP

What is really unsettling is that few companies turn on WEP for their access points. This can be the case for several reasons:

- It is not easy to change the default configurations on most APs.

- Many administrators deploy APs for evaluation and forget to secure them once they decide that wireless is making life easy for the company employees.

- Some administrators are just plain overworked and can't take the time to change the default configuration of the APs that they deploy and all the client configurations.

Figure 5.6 shows the WEP base key that will be used along with the IV to encrypt the payload. In the Network Key box, you can see the 13 characters of the WEP key used for this client to connect to the AP using SSID 3449. Notice that the Data Encryption check box is checked, which means that WEP is enabled. The Network Authentication (Shared Mode) check box is also checked. Again, keeping it basic, you provide another means of authenticating the client to the AP by marking this check box. Using the WEP key, much like using the SSID as a password of sorts, you can prevent clients from attaching to your wireless network unless they have the correct key. Not only is the key used to encrypt the payload of each frame, but it is used to authenticate client and AP to each other.

FIGURE 5.6   Enabling WEP

The basis of all the issues with WEP is the IV. In most WEP implementations, the base key is static, meaning that it does not change from frame to frame. The base key is the shared secret that you enter in the APs and in the wireless NIC configuration settings as the WEP key. Even with the IV being rotated, the IV will be repeated fairly often over a day or two because the IV is only 24 bits. A hacker who captures enough packets with the same IV (remember, it's in the clear) can decrypt the base key. Once the base key is decrypted, the encryption itself is worthless. With the base key in the possession of an intruder or somebody trying to listen in, each and every frame traveling on the radio signal can be easily decrypted, because the IV is traveling in the clear and those are the only two pieces used to build the encryption keys.

This is not saying that the RC4 algorithms are defective. In fact, the RC4 ciphers are strong and reliable. WPA also uses RC4. It is a weakness in the implementation of WEP with the IV being in the clear that makes it a poor implementation. If the encryption is based on the combination of the IV and the base key and the IV is a problem, the only way to really address the problem is to rotate the base key using some automated method or to change it manually on a regular basis. Compounding the difficulty is that wireless data is easy to capture compared to data transmitted over wired net-works. You don't even have to be in the building to get to it in most cases.

Let us add to your woes. If a client system is stolen or lost, standard security practices require that you rekey each and every system in your wireless network. You can't afford the risk of somebody getting the WEP key from the lost or stolen system. Because 802.11 standards do not specify tools or processes for mass updates, it all has to be done manually.

Okay, so WEP is broken too. Great! So why in the world would you want to even go through the trouble of using WEP? The answer is simply that WEP is better than not doing anything at all. At least you can make your intruders work for it. You can only hope that they find other targets that are easier to penetrate and leave you alone.

If you have been keeping up with security bulletins—some of the driest reading in the known world— either you have heard of the problems with WEP, or you have fallen asleep at your desk more than you care to admit. WEP has flaws. WEP has serious flaws. WEP has easily exploitable, serious flaws. WEP—meant to be equivalent to a wired network for security—isn't.

Beginning September 2003, the Wi-Fi Alliance no longer certifies any WEP installations as secure because of the many problems existing with the implementation of WEP.

Wi-Fi Protected Access (WPA)

WPA replaces WEP. The two wireless encryption methods do not work together. You can have one or the other, but you cannot have both. Well, that is not completely correct. The two standards can coexist on different equipment in the same network. For example, you may be in the process of migrating from WEP to WPA and will have two access points (one for WEP and one for WPA) to support the clients while they are being converted from WEP to WPA. However, you cannot configure an access point to support both WEP and WPA.

WPA is a subset of 802.11i and first started appearing in 2003. WPA is meant to replace WEP by fixing all of the problems found in WEP to date. So far, in a limited number of implementations, WPA has not been broken. Even with the strength of WPA, WPA version 2 is expected in late 2004, eventually to be followed by the complete implementation of 802.11i.

There are two types of implementations for WPA: Enterprise mode and Pre-Shared Key (PSK) mode. These two types of implementations allow WPA to be scaled from the home and small office all the way up to the larger enterprises that use wireless technologies. The requirements for Enterprise mode differ a great deal from the requirements for the PSK mode:

- Enterprise mode

    - Authentication Server: Required for verification of the user account and password.

    - RADIUS: Required to protect the logon process using the RADIUS protocol methods.

    - Centralized user management: Required to provide a central point for adding new users, changing current user access, and deleting uses as they leave the organization.

- Pre-Shared Key mode

    - Does not require an authentication server.

    - Does not require RADIUS.

    - Requires a strong "shared secret" key that is used for authentication of devices but is not used for encryption.

Enterprise mode is more secure and can be scaled out to support a large number of wireless users. The key to the Enterprise mode is that with RADIUS providing security for the usernames and passwords submitted during network logon and Active Directory providing support for the accounts database, new access points and users can be added to the environment quickly. However, this does not mean that the PSK mode is not also extremely strong and reliable.

The PSK mode option is still very strong and very reliable even though it does not require an authentication server (Active Directory) and it does not require RADIUS. The shared secret passphrase is used to authenticate the client and the wireless access point. The shared secret passphrase—like the shared secret often used in RADIUS implementations—can be extremely complex and long, so it is extremely hard to break if it can be broken at all. The only real problem regarding using the shared secret is that there is no automated way to update all access points and wireless clients with new shared secrets. Each device needs to be updated individually. This amount of work can be troublesome depending on the size of the wireless network and the availability of the users.

Configuring the wireless client is almost exactly like configuring the WEP-enabled wireless network client, except when selecting the mode and Data Encryption. When prompted for the network key, you should enter the shared secret passphrase. While the passphrase is not the same thing as a network key, it serves the same function from the wireless client perspective when it comes to authenticating to the wireless access point. You should also select WPA-PSK (WPA for Pre-Shared Key mode) and WPA-TKIP (WPA for Temporal Key Integrity Protocol) for the Data Encryption option.

MAC Filtering

Yes, a *Media Access Control (MAC)* address is not exactly friendly and easy to use. Anyone who has done MAC filtering with other devices knows how difficult it is to configure. Just entering the MAC—12 hexadecimal numbers—can be a pain all its own. It is easy to read the wrong number or mistype it.

A MAC address is unique to the network device. At least it is supposed to be unique. Assuming that it is unique and that you can identify a single network device from its MAC address, this may have some potential for security. If you can somehow identify each system by its MAC address and then grant it access or deny it access based on a list of those MAC addresses, you are in business.

But can you actually do this? The answer is, of course. Why else would it be here in the book?

You can find the MAC address of your wireless network cards by entering IPConfig/all at a command prompt in Windows 2000 or Windows XP. Also, many NICs print the MAC address on the outside of the network card.

To administer the AP, you can use Telnet over IP, a direct serial connection, or a web browser, and you can dig around in the AP configuration until you find MAC filtering. It is as simple as adding the MAC addresses that you are willing to allow on your wireless network. In Figure 5.7, you can see how a 3Com AP can be managed using a web browser to make changes to the security. It is as simple as clicking the View/Add/Delete button next to Ranges Of Allowed Wireless Clients and adding the MAC addresses of the wireless NICs that you want to allow on your network. Anyone trying to gain access to the network will be denied unless they have a NIC with an appropriate MAC address.

Clicking the View/Add/Delete button next to Disallowed Wireless Clients lets you manage a list of MAC addresses not allowed on the network. Because there is likely some confusion, let's look at why there is a list to allow and a list to disallow. Assuming that you really want to know, think of it this way. In the list to allow access, you can enter a range of MAC addresses. Entering a range of addresses makes much more sense than adding many MAC addresses to the list one at a time, right? Well, if you do that, and an employee quits or is about to be terminated because of some fishy things they are doing, you can take action right away and place them on the disallow list, which removes their access.

FIGURE 5.7 Configuring MAC filtering

You can use SSIDs to identify APs, and you can use MAC addresses to identify client network cards. Combining the two can definitely help secure the wireless network from unauthorized users. Two pieces working together can definitely be better than one.

But are you ready for the bad news? MAC addresses are fairly easy to spoof. Some Unix and Windows applications allow the user to spoof a MAC address. With a little monitoring of the network, valid MAC addresses can be found, and these addresses can be used to get past the MAC filtering that is in place. Sometimes it just seems that you can't win when it comes to wireless security. Despite the ability to spoof MAC addresses, you should still filter on them if it is possible. Again, you don't want to make it easy for intruders. If you make it hard enough, they might go on to other more inviting targets.

MAC address filtering (along with SSIDs) provides improved security. Combine the two with WEP and some security around IP addressing, and you are actually getting a fairly secure environment. The biggest problem with using MAC filtering, though, is the administration involved. With large networks, keeping track of each adapter's MAC address and the owner of each card can be difficult. Using MAC filters is best suited to small networks for which the MAC address list can be efficiently managed. Each AP must be manually programmed with a list of MAC addresses, and the list must be kept current. Even with tools from the manufacturer that let you update multiple APs simultaneously, this can be cumbersome. Administrative overhead limits the scalability of MAC filtering just as it limits changing WEP keys regularly, and it limits the ability to control IP configurations. Administration is a major impediment.

Configuring Wireless Encryption Levels Using 802.1*x*

The IEEE (Institute of Electrical and Electronics Engineers) 802.1*x* standard is the next big step in wireless security. This standard manages and controls access to the wireless network using *Extensible Authentication Protocol Over LANs (EAPOL)* in combination with *Protected Extensible Authentication Protocol (PEAP)*, *Extensible Authentication Protocol-Transport Layer Security (EAP-TLS)*, Kerberos, or Message Digest 5 (MD5). The 802.1*x* standard is not just for wireless implementations; it can also be used for LAN-based devices.

Windows XP Professional is the only client that fully supports 802.1*x*. Windows 2000 Professional cannot use the features at this time, and only the very latest version of Windows CE (version 4.2) supports 802.1*x*; previous versions depend on certain vendor implementations through the vendor's drivers and other tools.

The 802.1*x* standard is a great step forward for security. However, setting it up requires some extensive resources and a private key infrastructure (PKI) to provide the certificates. The necessary resources include the following:

- Wireless clients such as Windows XP Professional that support 802.1*x*
- Active Directory running on Windows 2000 Server, SP3
- A *certificate authority*
- A remote access policy for wireless clients
- RADIUS servers

The IEEE is an international electrical standards organization.

In Figure 5.8, you can see the additional infrastructure needed to make all this work. DC1 and DC2 are the Active Directory domain controllers (you want at least two for redundancy), IAS1 and IAS2 are the *Internet Authentication Servers* (again, two for redundancy) that will be used for RADIUS, and CA is the certificate authority.

The main goal of 802.1*x* is to securely authenticate clients associating with APs and to exchange encryption keys. The process is somewhat confusing, but it can be clarified a bit. See Figure 5.8 for the visual of the process; the steps are outlined here.

1. The AP sees that a client exists on the network and initiates contact. Access is blocked by the AP until authentication is completed by the client. If authentication fails, no data is ever forwarded onto the wired network.

2. The AP sends an EAPOL-encapsulated EAP Request-ID to the client.

3. The client sends an EAPOL-encapsulated EAP Response-ID message that contains the user's identification information to the AP.

4. The AP then forwards this EAP Response-ID by encapsulating it in a RADIUS access request packet and sending it to a RADIUS server. This could be either IAS1 or IAS2.

5. The RADIUS server responds with an EAP-Request-ID, encapsulated in a RADIUS packet, that contains a password challenge for the client, and it is forwarded by the AP to the client after the AP encapsulates it using EAPOL.

6. The client responds to the challenge with EAPOL-encapsulated response information that is sent to the AP and then forwarded to the RADIUS server in an encapsulated RADIUS packet.

7. The RADIUS server responds with a RADIUS-encapsulated EAP success message to the AP. The AP then forwards this EAP success message to the client encapsulated with EAPOL.

FIGURE 5.8 Authentication for 802.1x

Once all these steps have taken place, the client is considered properly authenticated and can start transmitting data on the wireless network to the wired network. In this exchange, all traffic between the client and the AP is encapsulated using EAPOL. All traffic between the AP and the IAS (RADIUS) servers is encapsulated using RADIUS.

Now that you understand the architecture of it at a high level, let's look at the client configuration. Figure 5.9 shows how to enable 802.1x access control for a wireless client. You need to enable it, and then you need to set the EAP type. Normally, this is set to use a certificate in the Registry or a certificate on a smart card.

When a Windows XP Professional client starts, it broadcasts three EAP messages in an attempt to prompt the AP to start the process discussed previously and illustrated in Figure 5.8. Remember, the AP needs to see the client on the network to start the process. If the AP does not send the request, the client will not attempt to connect via 802.1x authentication and will send normal wireless data to the AP. If the AP, however, does send the request, the client will respond and start the 802.1x authentication process.

If the Enable IEEE 802.1x Authentication For This Network check box is checked and the AP is not set to use 802.1x or does not support it, the client will not be prevented from properly accessing the AP and participating in the wireless network. If the Enable IEEE 802.1x Authentication For This Network Enable check box is cleared and the AP is enforcing 802.1x authentication, the client will not connect.

In the EAP Type drop-down box list box shown in Figure 5.9, the Protected EAP (PEAP) option will be available, along with the Smart Card Or Other Certificate option after you apply SP1. Prior to SP1, the default types available include MD-5 Challenge and Smart Card Or Other Certificate.

FIGURE 5.9   Configuring an EAP type

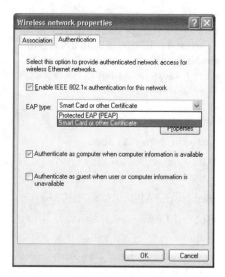

EAP Authentication Methods

Windows XP Professional, prior to SP1, supports EAP-TLS and EAP-MD5 authentication methods. MD5 is not recommended, because it is not a mutual authentication method and it is susceptible to offline dictionary attacks. TLS utilizes certificates stored either in the Registry or on smart cards and can provide mutual authentication as well as an encrypted means of transferring keys.

EAP-TLS is the default EAP type. TLS is intended for wired networks, but can also be used in wireless environments. Using TLS requires that both the RADIUS server and the client have certificates and that both devices have the certificates residing within a trusted CA. In order for the client to get a certificate for use with wireless access, though, it must first have wired access to the CA to make the request and then apply the certificate. This is a problem in that each wireless client must also be a wired client before it can then become a wireless client. It just doesn't make sense on the surface of it. Administrative overhead for TLS can be a bit high.

Windows XP Professional with SP1 provides support for PEAP. Using PEAP, the initial communications are encrypted with TLS. Because TLS encrypts the data flow, password-based authentication protocols such as *Microsoft Challenge-Handshake Authentication Protocol version 2 (MS-CHAP v2)* can be used securely. MS-CHAP v2 is not susceptible to offline dictionary attacks if it is being passed within a TLS channel. One huge benefit of this solution is that user and computer certificates are not required; only the RADIUS servers require certificates for a fully secured association and authentication process for wireless users.

PEAP with MS-CHAP v2 deserves more attention than we can give it here, but it is important to know how it works in comparison to the previous 802.1x authentication process illustrated in Figure 5.8. PEAP authentication takes place in two parts. In the first part, the client and the AP create the TLS channel. In the second part, the client authenticates using MS-CHAP v2.

 MS-CHAP v2 is a password-based challenge-and-response authentication protocol that uses Message Digest 4 (MD4) and Data Encryption Standard (DES) ciphers to encrypt messages and responses. Although MS-CHAP v2 is susceptible to offline dictionary attacks to break the encryption and find the passwords, adding TLS in PEAP provides strong security.

Creating the TLS channel involves the following steps:

1. The AP sends an EAP Request-ID message to the wireless client.
2. The wireless client responds with an EAP Response-ID message that contains the ID of the client.
3. The EAP Response-ID message is forwarded by the AP to the RADIUS server.
4. The RADIUS server sends an EAP Request/Start PEAP message to the client through the AP.
5. The client and the RADIUS server send TLS messages back and forth to establish the cipher for the TLS channel, and then the RADIUS server sends a certificate to the client for authentication.

Once the TLS channel is in place, the second part of the process begins. It includes the following steps to establish authentication using MS-CHAP v2:

1. The RADIUS server sends an EAP Request-ID

2. The client responds with an EAP Response-ID that contains the client ID.

3. The RADIUS server sends an EAP Request/EAP MS-CHAP-v2 challenge that contains a challenge string to the client for authentication.

4. The client responds with an EAP Response/EAP MS-CHAP-v2 response that contains the response to the RADIUS server challenge. It also issues a challenge string for the RADIUS server to establish mutual authentication.

5. The RADIUS server sends an EAP Request/EAP MS-CHAP-v2 Success message, which tells the client that its response was accepted. It also sends a response to the client challenge sent in step 4 to authenticate itself to the client.

6. The client sends an EAP Response/EAP MS-CHAP-v2 Ack message to the RADIUS server to verify that its response was accepted.

7. The RADIUS server sends an EAP Success message. This ends the mutual authentication process using MS-CHAP v2.

At the end of this mutual authentication exchange, the wireless client has provided proof of knowledge of the correct password (the response to the RADIUS server challenge string), and the RADIUS server has provided proof of knowledge of the correct password (the response to the wireless client challenge string). The entire exchange is encrypted through the TLS channel created in PEAP in the first part of the process.

The real benefit to PEAP with MS-CHAP v2 is that passwords are used, not certificates. In the release of Windows .NET Server, the IAS (RADIUS) implementation requires using a certificate for it, but not for the clients. This is important because it considerably reduces the overhead of the solution. Instead of having to implement a full PKI solution to support wireless client security, you can purchase a single certificate from a commercial certificate authority.

Problems and Attacks Specific to Wireless Networks

Now that your head is spinning from trying to figure out how wireless communications can be secured, it is time to apply some of this newly gained knowledge. First, let's identify some of the common problems and the common attacks. Although you've probably heard of most of them, this is still the perfect time to review them.

Rogue APs

The word *rogue* fits well here because it really does describe this problem of unsanctioned or unauthorized activity. Your users are supposed to come to you in the IT department to install things like APs for their use. However, sometimes your security department does not approve the installation. So what do your users do? Do they just gladly accept that security denied their request? Of course not. They read the manual and do it themselves. They participate in rogue activities and go to great lengths to hide their work. In some instances, APs have been found locked up in wooden file cabinets where employees have drilled holes to run the power and network cables inside the cabinet.

Being busy people and bucking the system at the same time, they do the minimum to get it to work and do not seek advice from the IT staff about the proper way to do it because they are trying to keep it a secret. They aren't being malicious; they just want the benefit of using all those cool wireless toys, such as their pocket PCs and laptops, without hassling with wires and cradles and all that stuff. Gee, go figure—they want to be productive!

You all know that it happens, but how do you stop it? Well, you take advantage of the tools in your bag of tricks. You install NetStumbler, AiroPeek, AirSnort, or some of your other wireless tools that will find those rogue signals. You walk around the building with your laptop hooked up with a wireless card and run the applications looking for unauthorized radio signals. Your goal is simple: Find the unauthorized APs and then take action to either get rid of them or secure them properly.

War Driving

Test

No, it is not a conspiracy to rid the world of Wi-Fi. War driving is not against the law. *War driving* is the act of looking for and logging active wireless access points. In most cases, it has become a really sophisticated process using a laptop, a wireless NIC, some good software, and even a global positioning system (GPS) to provide exact coordinates for logging the find. A war driver can simply hook up their laptop, start up their software, and drive around the neighborhood or the business park while the software automatically logs the location and type of device using its wireless card and the attached GPS.

So why is this bad? Well, if you screwed up your implementation of wireless access, you might be found by a war driver. Worse yet, this war driver might be one of the many out there who participate in war-driving sites and then might upload your information to the Internet. There, on the Internet, all the information needed to come and attack your network will be made available. It is clear how bad this can be.

How do you stop it? Basically, you stop it the same way you stop rogue access points. You war-drive your own buildings using the same software and tools that the culprits use, and if you find anything, you fix it right away.

War Chalking

Test

War chalking is much like war driving. What is done with war chalking, though, is that somebody actually gets out of the car and puts a special symbol on your sidewalk, driveway, garage, or the middle of the street indicating that an unsecured wireless network is nearby. War chalking gets its name from two sources. First is the practice of war dialing, in which a user uses a modem and dials all the numbers that it can find in the area to look for a modem that answers. Once a modem is found, the user can then start attacking it and attempt to break into the system. Second is the practice during the Depression when hungry and homeless people put chalk marks on homes to indicate to each other which ones were friendly and might give them a meal or a place to stay for a night.

What is most interesting about war chalking is that many of the chalk marks that people see on their buildings at work or on their driveway are readily dismissed as kids playing. Bcause the chalk is not permanent, they really don't pay too much attention to it.

How do you avoid being war chalked? Again, you check out your networks and secure them, so even if you are chalked, hopefully it will be with a symbol showing that you are secured.

Radio Interference

Remember, 802.11 traffic utilizes unlicensed radio frequencies. Did you know that the 2.4GHz phone that you just bought might interfere? How about that microwave oven right down the hall? It's really odd how many electronic devices use the same unlicensed frequency that your wireless networks also use. So, if you can interfere with your network without even trying, can it be done on purpose? Absolutely!

Only 11 channels are available to you in 802.11b and 802.11g. Of those 11 channels, only three provide non-overlapping traffic between the other eight channels. Most wireless administrators are aware of this, so they generally choose one of those three. It makes perfect sense. Knowing that almost all wireless networks will be using one of three different channels, just how hard could it be to set up a transmitter that sends traffic on all three channels at the same time and then provide enough power to totally drown out and overpower all devices trying to use those bands? In practice, it is easy, and this is scary. Imagine the number of ways that a malicious user can attack an entire building of wireless networks from the parking lot and cause all work to come to a grinding halt.

The real problem is that there are no known defenses against this type of attack. Because the frequency is unlicensed, you can't go to the FCC unless the user is exceeding the FCC power restrictions of one watt. To be honest, there are very few reports of this happening, but you do need to be aware that it's a possibility. Maybe, when you design a new building for construction, you might put in thicker exterior walls to defend yourselves from this kind of activity.

WEP Attacks

As you saw earlier, WEP is not fully secure. However, as discussed earlier in this chapter, you should use it in combination with other measures to help secure your network.

Using an application such as NetStumbler or AirSnort, an intruder can capture the packets over time and then use tools to break the encryption key to find the base key for WEP. It really doesn't take too much effort for a high-end PC to break the encryption, and on a busy network, less than a day's worth of packets are all that are needed.

So how do you stop it? Well, you need to set some monitoring of your own. One way to beat those trying to break in is to do your best to secure your wireless network and then use AirSnort or some other tool to watch the network. Monitoring your traffic can help you identify when the traffic is higher than established baselines and let you know that something fishy might be going on. Of course, even then, it might not be enough, so what are the next steps? On to the next section for the answer.

The Next Steps

Now that you've learned more about wireless networking, you can see some of the challenges in deploying it and the challenges in securing it. Going all the way back to Figure 5.1, you can see that this typical wireless network implementation is probably much more typical than you hoped. You can take your simple network and make one quick and easy change.

Simply move your AP to the DMZ (de-militarized zone), or if you have only a single firewall, put the AP on the outside of it, as shown in Figure 5.10. Now, even if intruders defeat the security of the AP device, they still have to defeat the firewall to get access to the inside of your network and have access to your resources. That seems like a simple solution; however, it does present some challenges.

One of the biggest challenges that you will face with the AP outside the firewall is figuring out what ports you need to open and then doing it without compromising the security of your firewall. This is why you may end up with a DMZ implementation as the preferred solution. At least your external firewall will provide greater security for those attackers not in your general area of the AP.

FIGURE 5.10   Moving the AP

Let's not forget about one key piece of security here: If your wireless clients are not protected by the firewall, as shown in Figure 5.1, you need to provide personal firewalls for them. You can't have your client systems susceptible to attacks from the Internet, and you need to take measures to protect their local data as well as the applications they use. A personal firewall might be one of the best ways to do that.

Implementing VPNs to Protect Wireless Networks

The more companies started looking at the option of moving the AP outside the firewall, the more they started to think that it really looks like any other implementation in which clients are outside the firewall. Consider the example of the user at home coming in via DSL (digital subscriber line) or cable modem. How are you, as an organization, currently providing the applications that they need and access to the data that they need to do their jobs from home? Well, if you can properly provide secure access for them, why not your wireless users outside the firewall too?

If you use VPNs to secure all traffic from your clients on the Internet through the firewall and into your organization's network, you should be able to use them for the wireless side too. Figure 5.11 shows the remote user coming in via the Internet. You have been using VPNs for these types of users for a couple of years now and have not had any problems with security with a proper VPN implementation. If you take that same VPN technology and use it for wireless access, you will have high levels of security for your wireless traffic. The wireless traffic will be secure, and you don't have to worry about having to punch additional holes through your firewall.

FIGURE 5.11   Using VPNs

VPN technology has many advantages, including the following:

- It is pre-existing on most enterprise networks.
- It is scalable.
- The administration is already in place, and the additional number of users in most cases will not adversely impact the environment.
- Wireless traffic cannot enter the private network until VPN authentication takes place.
- WEP implementations and MAC filtering are not as important because of the strong security found in the VPN implementation.
- Users will have a consistent process for connecting to the network, whether at home using VPNs, while traveling and using remote Internet connections, or while using wireless access in the office.

The VPN solution for wireless network access may actually meet all the needs of the organization for security and still provide the convenience of wireless access.

Combining VPN and 802.1x

You have seen that a VPN for wireless clients is a great way to really secure the traffic. You have also seen that 802.1x with the newer PEAP implementation can also secure your wireless network. Although many see these as competing technologies, you need to step back and look at them for what they really are: highly complementary technologies that can be used together in many cases.

First, using 802.1x allows you to use a RADIUS server inside your network to provide authentication for your clients. You can combine this capability with certificates to fully encapsulate and encrypt the authorization traffic. However, even if you use authentication methods such as EAP-TLS and PEAP, you are not properly covering the traffic from end to end. You need to secure the traffic all the way from the wireless client and into the network so that it is not susceptible to attacks from outsiders. The 802.1x solution encrypts traffic only from the wireless client to the AP. If the AP is outside the network, you are not protecting the traffic from the AP to inside the network. You have a gap that needs to be covered.

Second, you have seen that using VPNs to provide access to most enterprise networks is a fairly common solution. Accessing data and applications inside the network from the Internet requires the client to establish a VPN to the network. A VPN connection ensures data security all the way from the client end to the VPN server itself, inside the network.

If you combine the security of 802.1x, which protects the wireless side and provides extremely secure authentication using RADIUS, with the high levels of security provided by a VPN solution, you can see how they work together and provide secure access to clients accessing the company network from the Internet from public places and homes and from the wireless network. A couple of layers of security can really make the difference.

Wireless Security Moving Forward

Okay, you use 802.1x and VPNs. You also use WEP and MAC filtering and change your SSID to a difficult-to-guess string, and you turn off broadcasting of your SSID. You provide limited access to TCP/IP addresses for your wireless networks, and after all that, you have a rather nice, secure wireless implementation.

However, combining all these will only work if you have Windows XP Professional wireless clients. Windows 2000 Professional clients can still take advantage of many of the security provisions as discussed in this chapter; however, Windows 2000 Professional clients do not currently support 802.1*x*.

Wireless security is important, but it really isn't being implemented properly. Reports from war drivers still show that about 50 to 60 percent of wireless networks are implemented without changing SSIDs and without using WEP. Wireless security can be broken down into four basic levels of security:

No security   A wide open network without WEP, using the default SSID, and probably even broadcasting its SSID

Basic security   A network utilizing at least 40-bit WEP and renaming its default SSID and turning off broadcasting

Enhanced security   A network utilizing mutual authentication and 802.1*x*, along with implementing WEP or WPA, turning off the SSID broadcasts, and changing the SSID to a difficult-to-guess string

VPN security   Utilizing VPN connectivity to secure wireless clients and combining it with enhanced security

It would be nice to see more of the enhanced level and to see more implementations utilizing VPNs. You really need to take wireless security seriously, because it is absolutely one of the weakest entry points to your network resources.

Summary

This chapter covered wireless networking and how to secure a wireless network. We discussed some common configuration problems and described several ways to improve the security of an organization's network by making configuration changes.

In particular, we described how to configure wireless networks—including private and public networks—and how to configure encryption levels for wireless networks, including WEP, WPA, and 802.1*x*. We also discussed how to configure different client operating systems, including Windows 2000 Professional, Windows XP Professional, and Windows CE.

Finally, we finished with a discussion on how to protect networks from attacks specific to wireless networks, including the utilization of VPNs to improve security for wireless networking.

Exam Essentials

Be able to configure a public wireless network.   Make sure you understand the significance of the SSID and how and when to change the SSID to segment networks. In addition, understand how to configure Windows XP Professional and Windows 2000 Professional, and understand the major features of Windows CE.

Be able to configure a private wireless network.   Make sure that you understand how private wireless networks operate and know how to implement security measures for a private wireless network, including

- Implementing MAC filtering
- SSID broadcast issues and how to fix them
- DHCP issues

Be able to configure wireless encryption levels.   Make sure you can do the following:

- Enable and configure WEP.
- Enable and configure WPA.
- Enable and configure 802.1x.
- Implement VPNs for wireless.

Review Questions

1. Your company has two groups that want to use wireless networks. Accounting is willing to fund their own hardware purchases to pay for the wireless network that will cover their part of the building, but they do not want any other groups using their hardware and reducing the performance for their users. Based on some testing, you will need to install two new APs to provide proper coverage for the accounting area. How should you configure their wireless hardware?

    A. Create a unique SSID for each of the APs and then configure the clients so that they have the SSID of the AP closest to their office.

    B. Create a new SSID, configure it for both APs, and then configure the accounting clients so that they have the SSID that goes to both APs.

    C. Create a unique SSID for each of the APs, then create a third SSID for the clients, and configure the clients to use both the SSID for the clients and the SSID of the AP closest to their office.

    D. Use the default SSID for the equipment so that accounting can get on the network easily. Make the other group change their SSID so that they don't interfere with the accounting network.

2. Your company has only five wireless clients that access the wireless network set up in the conference room. Recently, you were reviewing the configuration of the AP and noticed that it had eight wireless clients attached to it that were active. You verified that the five normal wireless clients were being used in the conference room, but you could not find any others. You are sure that they are not authorized, and you want to kick them off and prevent them from ever connecting to your network again. How should you configure the AP without reconfiguring the client systems so that only the five approved users will be able to access the AP and the intruders will not be able to connect?

    A. Implement WEP on the AP.

    B. Implement 802.1x for the wireless network.

    C. Implement MAC filtering and allow only the MAC addresses of the five client systems that are approved.

    D. Implement MAC filtering and deny the MAC addresses of the intruders.

3. Your company has entered into a strategic partnership with another company. The other company often sends representatives to your office, and they need access to the Internet to get their e-mail and to browse the Internet as part of their research. They do not need access to the internal network. These visitors all use Windows XP Professional clients, and they use a wireless network in their office. Your boss has told you to provide this access to them using an AP that their company has sent to him. He wants the AP installed so that their users cannot access any of the internal company network resources, and he says that they do not want the AP security changed in any way from its current configuration. You set up a meeting with everyone involved, including your network architecture guys and the firewall team. They propose the following options. Which is the best option?

   A. Install the AP on a separate network in the company and configure a router to allow only HTTP (Hypertext Transfer Protocol) and SMTP (Simple Mail Transfer Protocol) traffic out of the wireless network.

   B. Install the AP on a separate network in the company and configure a router with VPN from the wireless network to a VPN device at the other company's network.

   C. Install the AP in a DMZ off the company firewall and configure the firewall to allow AP traffic to go to and from the Internet—not into the company network.

   D. Install the AP outside the firewall and purchase IP addresses from the ISP to support all wireless users.

4. Which of the following are valid 802.11 specifications for wireless networks commonly in use? (Choose all that apply.)

   A. 802.11a

   B. 802.11b

   C. 802.11c

   D. 802.11t

5. Many APs provide support for inline power. What does inline power actually provide?

   A. Power for the AP by drawing on the power through Ethernet cables

   B. A battery backup for the AP

   C. Support for changing out the radio card in an AP

   D. Additional power for external antennas

6. Internet Authentication Service (IAS) is required in Windows 2000 Server architecture to support 802.1x implementations. What other acronym is considered the same thing as IAS?

   A. ISA (Internet Security and Accelerator)

   B. AD (Active Directory)

   C. MS-CHAP v2 (Microsoft Challenge Handshake Authentication Protocol version 2)

   D. RADIUS (Remote Authentication Dial-In User Service)

7. A good friend of yours comes to visit you at your office, and he pulls out his laptop to show you pictures of his new office. Once he powers up his laptop, he gets a notification balloon in the lower-right corner saying that it found a wireless network. He shows you the notification balloon, and you recognize the SSID as the one for the AP you installed yesterday. After he leaves, you want to fix this so it doesn't happen again. What should you do?

   A. Change the default password on your AP.

   B. Change the AP from DHCP to a static IP.

   C. Change the SSID from the default to a new value.

   D. Turn off broadcasting for the SSID.

8. Your company will be buying three different APs in the near future, and their coverage areas will overlap once they are set up in the building. What channels should the APs be set on so that they will not interfere with one another?

   A. All three APs should be set up on channel 1.

   B. The APs should be set up so that one uses channel 1, one uses channel 2, and one uses channel 3.

   C. The APs should be set up so that one uses channel 9, one uses channel 10, and one uses channel 11.

   D. The APs should be set up so that one uses channel 1, one uses channel 6, and one uses channel 11.

9. You come into work after being on vacation and find that one of your co-workers has installed all the APs for the new 802.11b wireless network. He is just getting around to testing them and has found that one AP seems to have problems maintaining connectivity with clients, intermittently. This AP is installed in the conference room. Which device is most likely causing interference?

   A. The copier machine 30 feet and 2 walls away

   B. The conference room projector about 10 feet away

   C. The TV and VCR in the conference room about 5 feet away

   D. The microwave oven about 10 feet away on the other side of the wall

10. Which of the following are needed to install a wireless network? (Choose all that apply.)

   A. A wireless access point

   B. Wireless network cards for client systems

   C. Appropriate TCP/IP addresses for the network

   D. The DNS name of the wireless access point

11. You have decided to implement MAC filtering on your AP. How do you find the MAC addresses of the wireless NICs for your network? (Choose all that apply.)

    A. Run `IPConfig /all` from the command prompt.

    B. Copy the MAC address from the outside of the network adapter.

    C. Run `MACID` from the command prompt.

    D. Use the IP address if it is a static IP address instead.

12. Which of the following security measures requires getting a certificate?

    A. MAC filtering

    B. WEP encryption

    C. 802.1x

    D. All of the above

13. Which 802.11 standard provides for the widest coverage, meaning the signal travels farther than the others?

    A. 802.11a

    B. 802.11b

    C. 802.1x

    D. They are all the same.

14. Your supervisor asks you to set up his laptop with wireless connectivity. The company standard is to use 802.1x. His laptop runs Windows 2000 Professional. What do you need to do to make it work?

    A. Install the high encryption pack from Microsoft's download site.

    B. Upgrade his laptop to Windows XP Professional first because Windows 2000 Professional does not support 802.1x.

    C. Buy a wireless NIC that supports 128-bit encryption.

    D. Select 128-bit Shared Key Algorithm for the Encryption Algorithm option.

15. You need to set up a conference room for wireless access. It is your first wireless project for the company, so there is no existing equipment. Your supervisor says that high bandwidth is important for wireless users in the conference room. Which 802.11 standard should you implement for the equipment?

    A. 802.11a

    B. 802.11b

    C. 802.1x

    D. They all have the same bandwidth.

16. You replace all company 802.11b equipment with 802.11a equipment. When replacing the APs, you put 802.11a APs in exactly the same places where the 802.11b APs were installed. Users report that they are finding a large number of areas in the office where wireless access is not working. What is the most likely cause of this problem?

    A. 802.11a APs do not cover the same amount of area as 802.11b APs, so more APs will need to be added to cover the dead zones.

    B. 802.11a APs must be overlapping and interfering with each other. The overlaps are causing dead zones.

    C. 802.1x authentication must have been configured, but not all APs are configured properly.

    D. 802.11a is more susceptible to fluorescent lights than 802.11b. Light filters are needed so that 802.11a can provide the same coverage area.

17. Your company uses 802.11b for wireless access. You accidentally break your wireless NIC. You buy another wireless NIC of the exact same brand, but it will not connect to the network. You know that your company uses WEP, so you make a quick call to the help desk. When talking to the help desk, you tell them that your computer somehow lost its configuration information. The help desk walks you through entering the custom SSID and enabling WEP. You still are not able to connect. What is the most likely cause of the problem?

    A. Your new NIC must be an 802.11a NIC.

    B. You are out of range of an AP.

    C. DHCP is not working.

    D. MAC filtering needs to be reconfigured on the APs.

18. Your company uses 802.11b for wireless access. Your company uses a mix of Windows 2000 Professional and Windows XP Professional wireless client computers. You have set up and configured DHCP for wireless clients. You review the DHCP logs and see that an unauthorized user is gaining access to the network. You do not want to set up WEP or WPA. What other methods can you use to secure your wireless network? (Choose all that apply.)

    A. Set up MAC filtering on the APs.

    B. Set reservations in DHCP for all authorized MAC addresses and remove all other addresses from the DHCP scope.

    C. Configure a custom SSID.

    D. Implement 802.1x.

19. Your company uses 802.11b for wireless access. Your company executives request information about possibly upgrading the network for higher bandwidth. The stated goals are to provide higher bandwidth than possible with 802.11b without increasing the number of wireless access points. What is the best solution?

    A. Implement 802.11g wireless access points and upgrade all wireless clients with 802.11g adapters.

    B. Implement 802.11a wireless access points and upgrade all wireless clients with 802.11a adapters.

    C. Upgrade all 802.11b devices to full-duplex–capable devices.

    D. Implement 802.1x on all wireless access points and all wireless clients.

20. Your company uses 802.11b for wireless access. You configure several new laptop computers to join the wireless network in the accounting area. All users in the accounting area are reporting very poor wireless performance since the new laptops were deployed. What can you do to improve the wireless performance?

    A. Upgrade all of the new accounting wireless clients with 802.11a adapters.

    B. Set up MAC filtering on the AP in accounting so that only accounting wireless clients can use the AP.

    C. Add a new AP in the area with a new SSID. Configure the new laptops to use the new AP.

    D. Add a new AP in the area with a new SSID. Configure all of the wireless clients in the accounting area to use the new AP.

Answers to Review Questions

1. B. This solution allows accounting clients to roam and connect to the closest AP for best performance.

2. C. Implementing MAC filtering will not affect the five approved users, because the filter is implemented on the AP and does not require configuration changes for the clients. Also, setting up the filter to allow only the five MACs will prevent any and all other MACs from connecting.

3. C. This option is the easiest, least expensive, and most secure solution to provide Internet access to the visitors.

4. A, B. The 802.11a standard is the 54MB implementation that is designed to operate in the 5GHz frequency range. 802.11b is the 11MB solution that is designed to operate in the 2.4GHz frequency range.

5. A. A is the proper description for inline power.

6. D. IAS is Microsoft's implementation of RADIUS in Windows 2000 Server.

7. D. Broadcasting the SSID causes the behavior described in the question.

8. D. Only three channels do not overlap and interfere with one another: channels 1, 6, and 11.

9. D. Microwave ovens use the same 2.4GHz frequency used by 802.11b and 802.11g devices and can cause interference when they are running.

10. A, B, C. The DNS name associated with an AP is not required to install and configure a wireless network.

11. A, B. The `IPConfig /all` command displays the MAC address of all installed network adapters in a computer; it is standard practice to print the MAC address on the outside of the NIC. There is no such command as `MACID`, and IP addresses will not work for MAC filtering.

12. C. Of these options, only 802.1x requires using certificates.

13. B. The 802.11b standard covers a much larger area than 802.11a, and 802.1x is not a transmission standard—it is an authentication standard for wireless.

14. B. Windows 2000 Professional does not support 802.1x.

15. A. The 802.11a standard has much higher transmission rates than 802.11b, and 802.1x is not a transmission standard.

16. A. The 802.11a standard has much lower range than 802.11b. Using 802.11a requires the installation of more APs to cover the same amount of area.

17. D. The help desk would not have asked for MAC information because you never told them it was a new wireless NIC.

18. A, B, C. 802.1x cannot be used for Windows 2000 client computers.

19. A. 802.11g has the same distance capabilities as 802.11b and does not require additional WAPs. 802.11a requires additional WAPs.

20. C. The new wireless clients and the old wireless clients all in the same area must be broken into groups so they do not all use the same AP.

Chapter

6

Deploying, Managing, and Configuring SSL Certificates

THE MICROSOFT EXAM OBJECTIVES COVERED IN THIS CHAPTER:

✓ **Deploy, manage, and configure SSL certificates, including uses for HTTPS, LDAPS, and wireless networks. Considerations include renewing certificates and obtaining self-issued certificates instead of publicly issued certificates.**

- Obtain self-issued certificates and publicly issued certificates.

- Install certificates for SSL.

- Renew certificates.

- Configure SSL to secure communications channels. Communications channels include client computer to web server, web server to SQL Server computer, client computer to Active Directory domain controller, and e-mail server to client computer.

Data needs to be secured in several places on the network:

- Databases
- File shares
- Websites
- Client computer hard drives
- Other areas such as public folders on Exchange servers

However, all these places are basically physical locations where data is stored. If you focus on these areas alone, you miss a large vulnerability—the transmission media. When you use the Internet—or even an intranet in many organizations—the traffic from your client system to the web server can go through several servers or routers before it is received. All sorts of confidential information passes through these systems, including passwords, company private documents, personal identification numbers (PINs), credit card numbers, online purchase orders, electronic invoices, and other personal and company information.

In between the client and server are many other systems that also might be monitoring the traffic and actively capturing the data so it can be used later to break into systems or to steal your personal identity and your company network credentials. This traffic needs to be secured so that information cannot be stolen from the packets traveling across the network.

In Chapter 5, "Implementing Security for Wireless Networks," you saw how to secure wireless networks. In Chapter 4, "Configuring IPSec and SMB Signing," you saw how to use IPSec and SMB signing to secure communications. In this chapter, you will use the *Secure Socket Layer (SSL)* protocol to secure transmissions to and from the Internet, as well as internally on an intranet. Initially, SSL was developed to secure web traffic; however, SSL has been adapted to securing other protocols.

This chapter looks at using SSL to

- Secure Internet traffic from the client system to the web server.
- Secure traffic from the web server to the SQL server.
- Secure traffic from a client system to Active Directory domain controllers.
- Secure e-mail traffic from the e-mail server to the client system.

This chapter describes how to get a certificate, install a certificate, and renew a certificate. It also covers how to implement SSL for these different processes. Because knowing how to configure SSL is critical, this chapter includes a number of hands-on exercises.

An SSL Primer

Before you look at how to implement SSL, you need to understand some basics. Once you understand how SSL works, it is much easier to understand how to deploy and support SSL implementations.

SSL provides two main services: (*authentication* and *encryption*.) When a client system and a server communicate using SSL, the client system can verify the identity of the server from the certificate installed on the server; this is authentication. Once the client system has verified that the server is who it says, the client system can establish a secure tunnel in which all data traveling through this tunnel is encrypted. Once the server has properly installed its certificate, the process follows the steps, which are shown in Figure 6.1 and detailed following that figure.

1. The client system initiates SSL and sends its capability information to the server, including the SSL versions, cipher suites, and compression methods that it supports.

2. The server responds by sending its digital certificate to the client; the digital certificate contains information about the server such as its DNS (Domain Name Service) name, the public encryption key, the cipher suite, and the compression method that it has selected for the session.

(*Public key cryptography* is the technique that uses a pair of *asymmetric keys* for encryption and decryption.) Each pair of keys consists of a *public key*, which is widely distributed and should be made available to anyone who needs the key, and a *private key*, which is always kept secret. (Data that is encrypted with the public key of the pair can only be decrypted using the private key, and conversely, data that is encrypted with the private key can only be decrypted by using the public key.)

FIGURE 6.1   The SSL process

3. The client verifies that the certificate is valid and that the certificate authority (CA) is in the list of trusted CAs. The client also checks the expiration date to make sure that the server certificate is still valid. All this proves the identity of the server to the client.

4. The client generates and sends a master secret (master key) to the server that is encrypted using the server's public key.

5. The server decrypts the master secret using its private key and then uses the master secret to generate encryption keys for bulk data encryption and for message authentication. The client generates the same keys, because it has the same master secret and is using the same algorithm as specified in Step 2.

6. The server sends a verification message to the client, and the handshake process is completed.

7. The tunnel is now established, and data can flow through it.

SSL provides the ability to encrypt all types of traffic as previously discussed and also provides message integrity because the data traveling through the encrypted tunnel cannot be altered in route. Message integrity is guaranteed through the use of the message authentication code inserted in the data between the two systems using SSL. The message authentication code provides protection against message alterations by using a digest. If a message is altered during transport between the systems, the digest will not be the right one for the message, and the altered information will not be accepted. If enough altered messages are received, the two systems will stop communicating.

SSL also provides the ability to prevent replays. In a *replay,* a potential intruder captures all the data in a session and then later resends the messages to the server or to the client to try to trick one of them into responding. SSL provides protection against replay attacks by using sequence numbers in both directions of the session. Any attempts to send packets at a later time with incorrect sequence numbers will result in the packets being disregarded.

When SSL is installed, many resources are accessed using a different port. Most system administrators know that by default, HTTP uses port 80 and HTTPS (SSL secured) uses port 443. Table 6.1 lists some of the common port assignments for the protocols discussed in this chapter.

TABLE 6.1   (SSL Port Assignments)

Protocol	Standard Port	SSL Secure Port
HTML	80	443
IMAP	143	993
LDAP	389	636
POP3	110	995
SMTP	25	465

Now that you've seen the basics of how SSL works, let's look at how to obtain certificates from both public certificate authorities and private certificate authorities, how to install certificates to support SSL, and how to renew certificates.

Obtaining Public and Private Certificates

Certificates are the basis of the security mechanisms discussed in this chapter. In order for SSL to work properly, both computers must trust the certificate used. These certificates can be obtained from *public certificate authorities* and *private certificate authorities*. The general rule as to whether you use a public CA or a private CA is whether you will use the certificate externally or internally. If it is used internally, you can still choose to use a public CA rather than create your own *public key infrastructure (PKI)* to support certificate use. External use is the main reason for using public CAs. Because the better public CAs have their information preinstalled on most current operating systems, the users of the secure links do not have to do anything special to start using them. With private CAs, you need to install the certificates for the CA in the trusts lists of the client systems that will be using the certificates. This can be difficult and time-consuming, not to mention politically difficult if some clients refuse to make the necessary configuration changes. So to avoid the additional work, you should use public CAs much of the time.

Obtaining Public Certificates

You obtain a public certificate from a public certificate authority. A certificate authority (CA) is a service that generates and maintains information about certificates. Some well-known certificate authorities include Baltimore, Comodo, Entrust, GeoTrust, Thawte, Valicert, and VeriSign. There are many others, but these are some of the best known. These CAs are public CAs because they interact with the general public. Basically, any company can get a certificate from one of these public CAs. The CA acts much like a driver's license office or a passport office. Before they can issue identification, they need proof of identity. Once you prove that you are a legal representative of a company, you can get a certificate. This certificate will include the following:

- Your organization name
- Additional information such as your physical address
- A unique serial number
- Your public key
- The expiration date of the public key
- The CA's digital signature showing that they issued it

Normally, the process of obtaining a certificate from a public CA takes a few days for the first certificate. Once you have established the relationship with the CA, you can normally purchase new certificates online and receive them immediately. First, you must submit some of the following documentation as proof of company identity. (Not all this information is needed; this is just an example of items that might be requested.)

- Business license
- Dun & Bradstreet number
- Articles of incorporation
- Trade name registration
- Proof of ownership of the domain name
- Names of corporate officers
- Full company name, address, and phone number
- Technical contact information
- Billing contact information

Second, you must provide proof of domain name ownership or of the authorization from the owner to purchase the certificate on their behalf. Generally, this step requires choosing the common name that will be used for the certificate. The common name is the fully qualified domain name of the server on which the certificate will be installed, for example, www.companyname.com. It is important that this common name be acceptable before the certificate is purchased because changing the common name requires purchasing a new certificate. Ownership of the domain name is usually proven by faxing or mailing documentation on company letterhead, stating ownership, and also faxing or mailing documentation showing legal ownership of the name.

The third step is to generate a *Certificate Signing Request (CSR)*. The process of generating the CSR depends on the operating system of the server. We'll describe this process in detail shortly. The CSR process will ask you for the following information:

Common name   This is the same as the URL or fully qualified domain name for the server, such as www.companyname.com.

Organization or company   This is the registered trade name or the corporate name of the company purchasing the certificate. You should use the full name and not any abbreviations.

Organizational unit   This is an optional field that might be used to show which department or division in the company is purchasing the certificate, or it might be used if there is a Doing Business As (DBA) name. This field does not need to be filled out.

City/Locality   This field is used to show where the company is physically located. If this is a division or a department of the company, it is generally expected that you enter the local office location in this field.

State/Province   U.S. and Canadian organizations must enter this information. Organizations outside the United States and Canada can skip this field as long as they enter a city/locality.

Country   This is the two-character country code. For example, the United States is US, and Japan is JP.

The fourth step is to generate the certificate request. The information is dumped into a text file, so you will need to cut the information out of the text file and insert it in the enrollment form for the CA. The CSR information will look something like that in Figure 6.2.

FIGURE 6.2   CSR information

After the certificate request is generated and entered into the online template, the fifth step is to complete the rest of the CSR form and submit it. Part of the application may require entering a challenge phrase. This is the same thing as a password. Make sure you remember this phrase or document it in a secure place because it will be needed to renew or revoke the certificate, and the account and passphrase will make it easier to obtain certificates in the future.

The CSR password created during the process should be eight characters or fewer and should not use these special characters: ~ ! @ # $ % ^ & * ( ) _ { } | : " < > ? / \.

Generally, you need to provide payment during the application using a credit card, a purchase order, a bank draft, or a wire transfer. Once the payment has been properly received by the CA along with all the requested information, you will have to wait for the application to be completed by the CA. If there any problems, they will contact one of the individuals set up as contacts for the company to request clarification or more information. If everything goes as planned, you will receive your approval, and the certificate will be e-mailed to the technical contact. Once a certificate is received, you can install it on the server.

Backing up the certificate is a good idea. You can copy it to a floppy disk and then properly secure that disk in a safe location or in some other properly locked area.

Now that we've gone over the process at a high level, let's look at the individual steps. In Exercise 6.1, you'll obtain a certificate from a public CA.

At this point, you have obtained the certificate. It resides within the .cer file. However, just having the certificate doesn't really do much for you. The next step is to install the certificate.

EXERCISE 6.1

Obtaining a Public Certificate

For this exercise, you will obtain a certificate from a public certificate authority for a web server running IIS 5. These are the steps for Comodo's InstantSSL. If you really want to purchase a certificate for SSL, go to the website of the CA that you want to use. For this exercise, we went to www.instantssl.com and then selected the InstantSSL Certificate without any upgrades for express credentials. This CA covers 99 percent of the existing browser market.

1. Provide your CSR. To get the CSR, you need to generate it on the web server. So, on your web server, run the IIS MMC snap-in.

2. In Windows Server 2003, choose Start ➢ Administrative Tools ➢ Internet Information Services (IIS) Manager to start the console. The process is very similar for Windows 2000.

3. Expand the Server node, if necessary, and expand the Web Sites node. Right-click the website where you want to install the certificate and then choose Properties from the shortcut menu to open the Properties dialog box for the website.

4. Click the Directory Security tab, and then click the Server Certificate button in the Secure Communications section of the Properties page to initiate the wizard.

5. At the Welcome screen, click Next.

6. Select Create A New Certificate and then click Next.

7. Verify that the Prepare The Request Now, But Send It Later radio button is selected. If it isn't, select it and click Next.

8. On the next screen, enter the name of the site. This name is just to make it easier for you to refer to later when applying the certificate. Also select the bit length for the CSR. The higher the bit length, the more secure the protection. A bit length of 512 will result in only a 40-bit SSL certificate. Most commercial CAs recommend 1024 bits for the CSR so that you can get the full 128-bit certificate. Higher bit lengths can cause performance problems, so don't get too carried away. Click Next.

9. On the next screen, enter the organization and the organizational unit. Normally, the organization will be the company name, and the organizational unit will be the department or division. Click Next.

10. On the next screen, enter the common name of the organization. This will be the fully qualified domain name for the server as it will be accessed from the Internet. Click Next.

11. On the next screen, enter the country/region, state/province, and city/locality information as discussed earlier in this chapter. Click Next.

12. Now you need to specify a filename and location for the CSR. This will be a text file, and you will use a text editor to open it later. Remember the name and location of the file. Click Next to open the Summary screen.

13. Verify that all the information is correct. If anything is wrong, click the Back button and fix the problem. Otherwise, click Next and then click Finish.

14. Click OK to close the Properties dialog box for your website.

15. Find the file that you saved in Step 12, and open it using Notepad or some other text editor. Copy the entire file, including the dashes, in the Begin New Certificate Request and the End New Certificate Request lines in the template for the CA. (See Figure 6.2 earlier in this chapter.)

16. Select the software used to generate the CSR and item 2 on the screen shown in the following graphic. Use the drop-down box in Step 2 and select Microsoft IIS 5.*x* And Later.

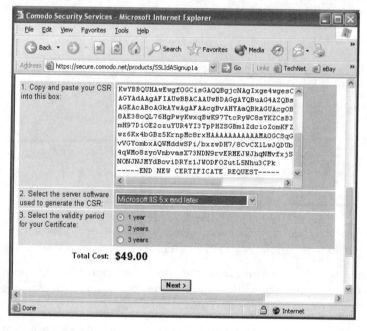

17. Select the length of the certificate and item 3 on the screen. Click Next in the browser to open the Company Details screen.

EXERCISE 6.1 *(continued)*

18. Fill in all the company information as seen in the following screen. On this same screen, complete the blanks for the Administrative, Billing, and the Organizational Contact information. Enter the account name and password so you will not have to enter this information again in the future. Click the Submit Details & Proceed To Payment button.

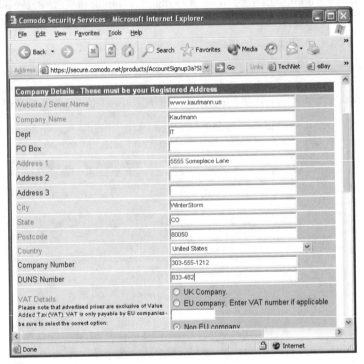

19. Normally, payment will be via credit card or purchase order. Once payment information is submitted, finish the request. For many CAs, processing the request takes a few days.

20. Once your request has been processed, the technical contact should receive an e-mail from the CA. Some CAs will send it to you on floppy disk using FedEx or some other delivery service that requires a signature receipt.

21. Cut and paste the certificate information out of the e-mail and create a file with the .cer extension using this information as the content, or use the text file on the floppy disk sent by the CA. Include the dashes and the Begin Certificate and the End Certificate in creating the file.

> ### ⊕ Real World Scenario
>
> #### Using Multiple DNS Names
>
> Let's say you are the network administrator for a company that uses Outlook Web Access so that many people can access their e-mail from outside the office without having to install Outlook or configure Outlook Express.
>
> The problem is that you have heard that many people in the company have been told to use https://owa.*companyname*.com/exchange to access their e-mail, and others have been told to use https://email.*companyname*.com/exchange. Because the certificate was purchased for the email.*companyname*.com common name, the owa.*companyname*.com DNS name causes a security alert to appear for the users who try to use the owa.*companyname*.com address saying, "The name on the security certificate does not match the name of the site." This situation is causing excessive calls to the help desk employees, and they are not able to keep up with them.
>
> The key here is that the name has to be email.*companyname*.com for the certificate, because that is what was purchased. Because many users think they need to use https://owa.*companyname*.com/ exchange, rather than redirecting the request through DNS, the requests can be properly redirected through a web page. Create another website for the owa.*companyname*.com/exchange address and secure it properly with SSL by purchasing another certificate using owa.*companyname*.com as the common name. Then create a web page on https://owa.*companyname*.com/exchange that redirects all requests to https://email.*companyname*.com/exchange. This way, all requests—whether to https:// owa.*companyname*.com/exchange or to the proper address of https://email.*companyname*.com/ exchange—will end up at the right location and will be able to use the certificate without getting any error messages.

Installing an SSL Certificate

In Exercise 6.2, you will install an SSL certificate on an IIS 6 web server. The process for IIS 5 on Windows 2000 is very similar. At this point, the IIS administrator can start utilizing SSL to encrypt connections for the server. We will describe how to do this later in the chapter, after installing the certificate.

EXERCISE 6.2

Installing an SSL Certificate

For this exercise, you will use the certificate obtained in Exercise 6.1 and install it on an IIS 6 server.

1. On your web server, run the IIS MMC snap-in. Choose Start ➤ Administrative Tools ➤ Internet Information Services (IIS) Manager to start the console.

2. Expand the Server node, if necessary, and expand the Web Sites node. Right-click the website where you want to install the certificate and then choose Properties from the shortcut menu to open the Properties dialog box for your website.

EXERCISE 6.2 *(continued)*

3. Click the Directory Security tab and then click the Server Certificate button in the Secure Communications section to start the wizard.

4. At the Welcome screen, click Next at the first page of the wizard.

5. Select Process The Pending Request and install the certificate. Click Next.

6. Navigate to the .cer file, either on a floppy disk or some other storage medium, and click Next once it has been found using the Browse button.

7. Confirm the SSL port for the site is 443. Click Next.

8. The summary screen provides some details such as the name of the file, the common name of the server, the CA that issued it, the expiration date, and the certificate's intended use. It also includes other identifying information. Verify that the information is correct, click Next, and then click Finish to install the SSL certificate. Close all open property pages and the Internet Information Services (IIS) Manager snap-in.

Renewing a Public CA Certificate

When you purchase a certificate, it has an expiration date. Normally, two years is considered the normal timeframe for a certificate; however, it can be more or less. The certificate you obtained in Exercise 6.1 is a one-year certificate. It will expire. Your options, when it expires, are to either remove it or renew it. Removing it is a valid option; however, it is probably a bit quicker to renew an existing certificate. In Exercise 6.3, you'll renew a certificate.

EXERCISE 6.3

Renewing a Certificate

For this exercise, you will use the certificate obtained in Exercise 6.1 and installed for use by IIS 6 in Exercise 6.2.

1. On your web server, run the IIS MMC snap-in. Choose Start ➢ Administrative Tools ➢ Internet Information Services (IIS) Manager to start the console.

2. Expand the Server node, if necessary, and expand the Web Sites node. Right-click the website on which you want to renew the certificate and then choose Properties from the shortcut menu to open the Properties dialog box for the website.

3. Click the Directory Security tab and then click the Server Certificate button in the Secure Communications section to start the IIS Certificate Wizard. (Clicking View Certificate at this point will allow you to see when the certificate is to expire and will also tell you which CA provided it.)

4. At the Welcome screen, click Next to open the Modify The Current Certificate Assignment screen:

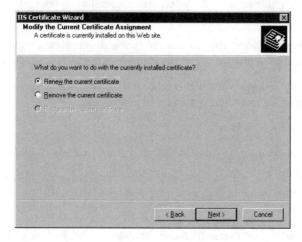

5. Select Renew The Current Certificate and then click Next.

6. Verify that the Prepare The Request Now, But Send It Later button is selected. If it isn't, select it and then click.

7. Select a filename and a location for the CSR. This will be a text file; you will use a text editor to open it later. Remember the name and location of the file. Click Next to open the Summary screen.

8. Verify that all the information is correct. If anything is wrong, click the Back button and fix the problem. Otherwise, click Next and then click Finish.

9. At this point, you need to go to the website of the CA and follow their procedures for renewing the certificate. The process is similar to that of creation, except this time you will use the account and passphrase from Exercise 6.1 to renew the existing certificate. You will not have to re-enter all the information for all CAs; however, some will require that you enter the information for many of the fields again as a means of proving identity.

10. Select the renewal length and then proceed to the payment screen.

11. Make the appropriate payment arrangements and submit the request to renew the certificate.

12. The CA will distribute the renewal key in the same way it distributed the original key.

13. Upon receipt of the key, cut and paste the certificate information out of the e-mail and create a file with the .cer extension using this information as the content, or use the text file on the floppy disk sent by the CA. Include the dashes and the Begin Certificate and the End Certificate in creating the file.

EXERCISE 6.3 *(continued)*

14. On your web server, run the Internet Information Services (IIS) Manager MMC snap-in.

15. Choose Start ➢ Administrative Tools ➢ Internet Information Services (IIS) Manager to start the console.

16. Right-click the website on which you want to renew the certificate and then choose Properties from the shortcut menu to open the Properties dialog box for the website.

17. Click the Directory Security tab and then click the Server Certificate button in the Secure Communications section to start the IIS Certificate Wizard.

18. At the Welcome screen, click Next.

19. Select Process The Pending Request And Install The Certificate. Click Next.

20. Navigate to the .cer file, either on a floppy disk or some other storage medium, using the Browse button. Click Next once the file has been found using the Browse button.

21. The summary screen provides some details such as the name of the file, the common name of the server, the CA that issued it, the expiration date, and the certificate's intended use. It also includes other identifying information. Click Next and then click Finish to renew the certificate.

Renewing an SSL certificate is much like the process of obtaining an SSL certificate. It is a bit quicker, though, because the information has already been accepted and processed by the public certificate authority.

Obtaining and Renewing a Private Certificate

To get a private certificate, you need an existing PKI implemented. Of course, you can always install one when it is needed, but doing so usually requires some significant planning. If the PKI is not rolled out properly, you might need to tear it down and rebuild it completely, which would make all the certificates that it had previously issued completely worthless. Installing a CA is described in Chapter 9, "Installing, Configuring, and Managing Certificate Authorities."

The process is similar to obtaining a public certificate; however, you can obtain a private certificate much more quickly and without all the painful paperwork.

The exercises in this chapter assume that you have Certificate Services installed on a Windows Server 2003 server computer. If you don't, see Chapter 9 for details about how to install Certificate Services.

In Exercise 6.4, you'll obtain a private certificate using the web interface.

Obtaining a Private Certificate Using the Web Interface

For this exercise, you will obtain a certificate from the Microsoft Certificate Authority residing on your internal network on a Windows Server 2003 server. You can obtain private certificates in two ways: by using the web interface for the private CA, as shown in this exercise, and by sending the request directly to the CA online, as shown in Exercise 6.5. The process is very similar for Windows 2000.

1. On your web server running Windows Server 2003, run the Internet Information Services (IIS) Manager MMC snap-in. Choose Start ➢ Administrative Tools ➢ Internet Information Services (IIS) Manager to start the console.

2. Expand the Server node, if necessary, and expand the Web Sites node. Right-click the website on which you want to install the certificate and choose Properties from the shortcut menu to open the Properties dialog box for the website.

3. Click the Directory Security tab and then click the Server Certificate button in the Secure Communications section to start the IIS Certificate Wizard.

4. At the Welcome screen, click Next.

5. Select Create A New Certificate. Click Next.

6. Verify that the Prepare The Request Now, But Send It Later button is selected. If it isn't, select it and then click Next.

7. On the next screen, enter the name of the site. This name is just to make it easier for you to refer to later. Also select the bit length for the CSR. The higher the bit length, the more secure the protection. Microsoft's CA supports from 384 to 1024 bits for the CSR. A bit length of 1024 is the recommended value. Click Next.

8. On the next screen, enter the organization and the organizational unit. Normally, the organization will be the company name and the organizational unit will be the department or division. Click Next.

9. On the next screen, enter the common name. This will be the fully qualified domain name for the server as it will be accessed from the network. Click Next.

10. On the next screen, enter the county/region, state/province, and city/locality information as discussed earlier in this chapter. Click Next.

11. Specify a filename and location for the CSR. This will be a text file; you will use a text editor to open it later. Remember the name and location of the file. Click Next to open the Summary screen.

12. Verify that all the information is correct. If anything is wrong, click the Back button and fix the problem. Otherwise, click Next and then click Finish.

13. Click OK to close the Properties dialog box.

14. Find the file that you saved and open it using Notepad or some other text editor. Copy the entire file—including the dashes—in the Begin New Certificate Request and the End New Certificate Request lines into the template for the CA.

15. Open Internet Explorer and enter the URL for the certificate server, `http://servername/ certsrv`, as shown here:

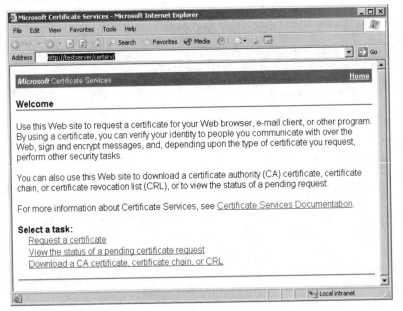

16. On the opening screen of the certificate server, click the Request A Certificate link.

17. Click the Advanced Certificate Request link.

EXERCISE 6.4 *(continued)*

18. Click the Submit A Certificate Request Using a Base-64-Encoded CMC Or PKCS #10 File, Or Submit A Renewal Request Using A Base-64-Encoded PKCS #7 File link.

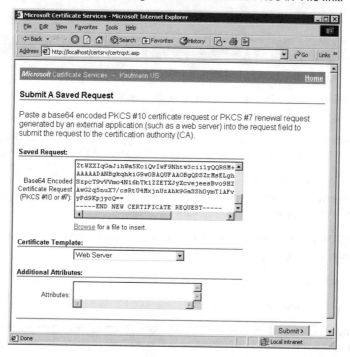

19. Insert the CSR, and in the Certificate Template drop-down list box, select Web Server. Click Submit to open the Certificate Issued screen.

20. To download the certificate, click the Download CA Certificate link.

Clicking the Download CA Certificate link downloads the `.cer` file and saves it to your disk. Make sure that this file is saved to a secure area. Refer to Exercise 6.2 for details about how to install the SSL certificate. The process is exactly the same once the certificate has been received and is available to install on the web server. In Exercise 6.5, you'll obtain a private certificate using an online CA.

EXERCISE 6.5

Obtaining a Private Certificate Using an Online CA

For this exercise, you will obtain a certificate from the Microsoft Certificate Authority residing on your internal network running Windows Server 2003.

1. On your web server running Windows Server 2003, run the IIS MMC snap-in. Choose Start ➤ Administrative Tools ➤ Internet Information Services (IIS) Manager to start the console.

2. Expand the Server node, if necessary, and expand the Web Sites node. Right-click the web-site on which you want to install the certificate and then choose Properties from the short-cut menu to open the Properties dialog box for the website.

3. Click the Directory Security tab and then click the Server Certificate button in the Secure Communications section to start the IIS Certificate Wizard.

4. At the Welcome screen, click Next.

5. Select Create A New Certificate. Click Next.

6. Select the Send The Request Immediately To An Online Certificate Authority radio button and click Next.

7. In the Name field, enter the name of the site. This name is just to make it easier for you to refer to later. Also select the bit length for the CSR. The higher the bit length, the more secure the protection. Microsoft recommends 1024 bits for the CSR. Click Next.

8. Enter the organization and the organizational unit. Normally, the organization will be the company name, and the organizational unit will be the department or division. Click Next.

9. In the Common Name field, enter the common name. This will be the fully qualified domain name for the server as it will be accessed from the Internet. Click Next.

10. Enter the county/region, state/province, and city/locality information as discussed earlier in this chapter. Click Next.

11. From the drop-down list box, select the name of the certificate server on the network and click Next to open the Summary screen.

12. Verify that everything is entered properly, click Next, and then click Finish.

At this point, the server generated the request, received the certificate, and installed it all at the same time. Using the online CA really saves many steps and completely eliminates the process of cutting and pasting the CSR.

Renewing Private Issued Certificates

Renewing certificates with a private CA is easier than renewing public certificates. To renew private certificates, though, you must first install the Certificates MMC snap-in. In Exercise 6.6, you'll install the Certificates snap-in.

EXERCISE 6.6

Installing the Certificates Snap-In

This exercise will create an MMC console to manage certificates.

1. Choose Start ➤ Run to open the Run dialog box.

2. In the Open box, enter MMC and press Enter to open the MMC console.

3. Choose File ➤ Add/Remove Snap-in to open the Add/Remove Snap-in window.

4. In the Add/Remove Snap-in window, click Add down at the bottom.

5. In the list of snap-ins, select Certificates and then click Add.

6. Because, in this chapter, the certificates are to be used for SSL, click the Computer Account button and then click Finish.

7. Click Close to close the list of snap-ins.

8. Click OK to close the Add/Remove Snap-in window.

9. Choose File ➤ Save As to open the Save As dialog box.

10. Enter the location and the filename for this MMC. We recommend saving the MMC either to the Desktop or to the Administrative Tools group.

Now that you have an MMC console with the Certificates snap-in, you're ready for the next step. In Exercise 6.7, you'll renew a private certificate.

EXERCISE 6.7

Renewing a Private Certificate

This exercise walks you through the steps of renewing a private certificate.

1. Start the Certificates MMC.

2. Right-click Certificates in the MMC and choose Connect To Another Computer from the shortcut menu. Connect to the computer on which you installed the SSL certificate.

3. In the console tree, expand Personal and then click Certificates to display the installed certificates.

4. In the pane on the right, select the certificate that you want to renew.

5. Choose Action ➤ All Tasks ➤ Renew Certificate With Same Key to start the Certificate Renewal Wizard. Renew Certificate With New Key is actually recommended in most cases. After using the same key for a long time, it is a good idea to get a new key to reduce the risk of compromise. Both the Same Key and New Key renewal options are processed the exact same way.

6. Click Next on the Welcome page for the wizard.

7. Select the appropriate certificate type if it is not already selected and click Next to open the Certificate Friendly Name And Description screen.

8. Enter a friendly name and some description so that you can refer to the certificate better within the MMC console.

9. Click Next and then click Finish.

Configuring SSL to Secure Communications Channels

So far in this chapter, we've discussed how to get certificates from both public and private certificate authorities, and we've looked at the basics of how to install a certificate on a web server and how to renew a certificate. It is time to fill in the blanks a little in this section of the chapter. Although we may have shown how to install the SSL certificate on the web server, we never really explained how to use it. This section explains how to use the certificate for a web server and also explains how to use certificates for traffic between the web server and the SQL server, between client systems and Active Directory domain controllers, and between client systems and e-mail servers.

Using SSL to Secure a Client Machine to Web Server Traffic

As you saw in the previous exercises, installing SSL on IIS 6.0 is really not difficult. Refer to Exercise 6.2 for the details. After a little practice, obtaining and installing the SSL certificate are both fairly straightforward processes.

SSL on IIS 6 can provide an extremely secure platform for secure commerce or for applications that use highly confidential information. The client system and the secure web server can transfer information back and forth in an encrypted form that is extremely difficult to decrypt unless you have the proper keys. Usually, you use SSL to protect your customers and their data while it travels the Internet and to protect your business interests.

Now that you have installed the SSL certificate on your web server, how do you use it? Well, that's the easy part. After completing Exercises 6.1 and 6.2, you have a secured web server. Before installing SSL, you should have done some testing to make sure that your IIS 6 server worked properly. If you did that, you might have created a test page and then verified that it worked by using a web browser on your network. Entering the address of your server as `http://testserver` and then pressing Enter sets the page up as the default page, as shown in Figure 6.3.

Okay, this page is pretty bare, but it is being used here only to illustrate the difference between a standard web page and an SSL-secured web page. After you install your certificate, SSL is available. So, simply changing the address in the browser to `https://testserver` will give you a page that looks like the one in Figure 6.4.

Notice that using `https://` instead of `http://` provides the cue from the browser to the web server that you want your page encrypted. You can see that it is properly encrypted by checking for the Lock icon in the Status Bar in Internet Explorer. You can double-click the lock to display the certificate itself, and you can see which CA issued the certificate, the valid dates for the certificate, and many other details.

There is a problem with this default IIS configuration, though. The browser can access the page regardless of whether it is using SSL. For secure websites, you really should force the browser to connect only using SSL. You can force this behavior by making a configuration change in IIS, which is what you'll do in Exercise 6.8.

FIGURE 6.3   A standard web page

FIGURE 6.4   An SSL web page

EXERCISE 6.8

Enforcing SSL on IIS 6

In this exercise, you will configure IIS 6 so that any browser connections to the website on which the SSL certificate has been installed must use SSL.

1. On your web server, run the IIS MMC snap-in. Choose Start ➢ Administrative Tools ➢ Internet Information Services (IIS) Manager to start the console.

2. Right-click the website on which you want to install the certificate and choose Properties from the shortcut menu to open the Properties dialog box for the website.

3. Click the Directory Security tab, and then click the Edit button in the Secure Communications section to open the Secure Communications dialog box.

4. Click the Require Secure Channel (SSL) check box, as shown here, and then click the Require 128-Bit Encryption check box if you want to enforce 128-bit encryption. Then click OK in all the boxes until the Properties page is closed.

Making this change in Exercise 6.8 will not impact the use of the `https://` address. However, if you now type **http://testserver** in your web browser, you will not get the test page. Instead, you will receive an HTTP 403.4 error page that says that this page is only accessible using SSL and that you need to use `https://` to access it, as shown in Figure 6.5.

FIGURE 6.5 The HTTP 403.4 error page

With SSL enforced on your sites, you can rest assured that your customers and their data as well as your business are secure from prying eyes. SSL encryption of 128 bits is strong and will do a great job of encrypting the traffic between a web client and an IIS 5 or IIS 6 server with SSL configured properly. All traffic from the browser to the web server will now use port 443—the default port for HTTPS traffic—instead of port 80, the default port for HTTP traffic.

Using SSL to Secure Web Server to SQL Server Traffic

The ability to use SSL to secure SQL is new to SQL Server 2000. Installing and properly configuring it can be a problem because there are no wizards for this process, and there is no way to identify which connections are encrypted. So this erodes some of the comfort level associated with using SSL and SQL. To verify that SSL is properly working after the installation and configuration, you might need to use a packet sniffer of some kind to capture some transactions and then look at them.

The process involves some high-level steps with lots of little steps in between. Let's start with the high-level steps:

1. Install a certificate on your SQL server.

2. Configure encryption for either every SQL client attaching to the server or for the client so that uses encryption when it connects to any SQL server.

3. Test.

Now, Steps 1 and 2 are much more in depth than just a couple of lines. You may need a SQL database administrator to assist you with getting this to work in a lab or production environment.

Installing a Certificate on a SQL Server

To install the certificate on the SQL server, you need to use the Certificate MMC snap-in that you used earlier in this chapter to renew certificates. On the SQL server itself, install the MMC snap-in as you did in Exercise 6.6. You will use the snap-in to manage certificates for the computer account. Once the Certificate MMC is ready, open it and verify that you are connected to your computer (the SQL server). You are now ready for Exercise 6.9.

This process cannot be used for a SQL cluster, and it's only supported for SQL Server 2000.

EXERCISE 6.9

Installing a Certificate on a SQL Server

You will install a certificate on a SQL Server 2000 server in this exercise to support encryption of SQL data between a web server and the SQL server. The process is the same whether SQL is installed on Windows 2000 or Windows Server 2003.

1. Open the Certificate MMC.

2. Right-click the Personal folder and choose All Tasks ➢ Request New Certificate to start the Certificate Wizard.

3. Once the Certificate Wizard opens, click Next and verify that the Certificate Type Of Computer is selected. Click Next.

4. In the Friendly Name box and the Description, fill in information to make it easy to remember what the certificate is being used for once it is properly installed. Click Next to open the Summary screen.

5. Verify the information and click Finish.

6. Restart the MSSQLServer (SQL Server) service, click the Force Protocol Encryption check box, and then click OK if you want all SQL connections to the SQL Server server encrypted. If you want only the IIS server to connect using encryption, skip this step.

Notice that there is nothing really special about this certificate that distinguishes it from any other computer certificate. This same process can be used on any computer to install a computer certificate for a variety of uses. The real key to this exercise is Step 6, in which the Force Protocol Encryption option is enabled. This option forces the traffic to the SQL server to be encrypted; if it is not encrypted, the request will fail. You can choose to encrypt only the web server connections and unencrpyt all other SQL connections. To encrypt only the IIS server connections, you need to configure the encryption for a specific client. If you want all connections to the SQL server encrypted, skip configuring encryption for a specific client and go right into testing.

Configuring Encryption for a Specific Client

Okay, the SQL server is ready. Now you can configure the IIS server to use encryption when connecting to the SQL server. In order for the client computer (the IIS server) to initiate the SSL encryption with the server computer (the SQL 2000 server), it must trust the SQL server's certificate. To trust the SQL server's certificate, the CA must be on the Trusted Root Certification Authorities list on the IIS server. In Exercise 6.10, you'll add a CA to the Trusted Root Certification Authorities list.

EXERCISE 6.10

Adding a CA to the Trusted Root Certification Authorities List

In this exercise, you'll use the Certificates MMC snap-in to export the SQL server's certificate Trusted Root Certificate Authority and then import this information into the IIS server.

1. Using the MMC console created on the SQL server in Exercise 6.9, open the Certificate snap-in.

2. Select the `Personal` folder to expose the certificates.

3. Right-click the certificate name and choose Open from the shortcut menu to open the dialog box.

4. Click the Certification Path tab. Note the name at the highest level of the path. This is the root CA. Click OK.

5. In the Certificate MMC, double-click the `Trusted Root Certification Authorities` folder to expand it, and then click Certificates.

6. In the right pane, scroll down the list of CAs until you find the one that was at the top of the Certification Path in Step 4.

7. Right-click the CA and choose All Tasks ➢ Export to start the Certification Export Wizard.

8. At the Welcome screen, click Next.

9. The DER Encoded Binary X.509 (.CER) option is selected by default. Click Next.

10. Enter the filename and location. It's a good idea to put this on a common file server, because this location will later be used by the IIS server. Click Next to open the Summary screen.

11. Click Finish to complete the export process. Click OK when the confirmation message appears.

EXERCISE 6.10 *(continued)*

12. On the IIS server, create an MMC console with the Certificates snap-in as you did in Exercise 6.6. Open the Certificates snap-in when completed.

13. Right-click the `Trusted Root Certification Authorities` folder and choose All Tasks ➤ Import.

14. Click the Browse button to find the file or manually enter the location of the exported `.cer` file created in Step 10. Click Next.

15. Verify that the Place All Certificates In The Following Store radio button is selected and click Next.

16. Click Finish to complete the import process.

Now that the IIS server trusts the SQL server's certificate, it can establish an SSL connection to it. To complete the process for setting up the IIS server encrypted connection, you must use the SQL Server Client Network Utility. In this tool, enable the Force Protocol Encryption option, which will require all SQL traffic from the IIS server to the SQL server to be encrypted.

> Encryption can be enforced either at the client or at the SQL server. Trying to enforce encryption at both ends will cause it to fail.

Testing the Connection Encryption

Because you are not using a web browser to pass the SQL data and requests, you can't look for that little Lock icon in the web browser to confirm that security is working. To test the IIS server connection, you can use either the Query Analyzer tool or an ODBC (Open Database Connectivity) application. To use an ODBC application, you must change the connection string.

To use the Query Analyzer, you connect to the SQL server and run a simple query against it. If the Force Protocol Encryption option is properly set up, the SQL requests and responses will be encrypted. You can verify this using the Microsoft Network Monitor on either the IIS server or the SQL server. You can also verify this by using any other packet sniffer to monitor the traffic between the two systems.

To use an ODBC application, you need to modify the connection strings. Once the connection strings are modified, you can then test the connection by using Microsoft Network Monitor on either system or by using a packet sniffer to verify that the data is encrypted.

For ODBC, modify the connection string so that it looks like this:

```
Driver=SQLServer;Server=ServerNameHere;UID=UserIdHere;PWD=PasswordHere;
➥Network=DBNETLIB.DLL;Encrypt=YES
```

This enables encryption from the client system for ODBC.

For OLEDB, you need to modify the configuration so that it looks like this:

```
Provider=SQLOLEDB.1;Integrated Security=SSPI;Persist Security Info=
➥False;Initial Catalog=dbNameHere;Data Source=ServerNameHere;Use Encryption
➥for Data=True
```

One of the main problems with encrypting the SQL communications between systems is not being absolutely sure that they are encrypted and that you did it right. The only way to tell for sure is to use some kind of packet analyzer or sniffer and look at the packets. This can be a pain for many people, but it's a good idea to become familiar with these tools for security purposes.

Using SSL to Secure Client Machine to Active Directory Domain Controller Traffic

One of the big concerns with Windows NT, Windows 2000, and Windows Server 2003 is the way that hackers can capture packets during the logon process and then use brute force to get the usernames and passwords for user accounts. In security, it's important that you not give information to potential intruders. This information can easily be used against your systems. For example, to log in to the network, you need a user name and its associated password. With Active Directory and the *Lightweight Directory Access Protocol (LDAP)* used in Windows 2000 and Windows Server 2003, it can be fairly easy to get user information. So this section will address what you need to do to secure LDAP traffic between the client systems and the Active Directory domain controllers in the network using SSL. Once SSL is configured, this traffic can be encrypted and properly protected.

Configuring SSL for Active Directory Domain Controllers

To install SSL for protecting LDAP requires installing certificates on all the Active Directory domain controllers. You must take a few steps make it all happen:

1. Install an Enterprise Certificate Authority on one of the Windows Server 2003 domain controllers.

2. Configure Group Policy Objects for the Domain Controllers Organizational Unit to automatically receive certificates.

3. Configure the client systems.

Installing an Enterprise Certificate Authority is discussed in Chapter 9, so we won't cover that information here. Once the CA is installed, though, you need to set up the rest of the domain controllers. Exercise 6.11 walks you through this configuration.

Testing SSL for Active Directory Domain Controllers

You can test for SSL security over LDAP by using the Address Book. Because the certificates were installed using the Domain Controller organizational unit GPO, all domain controllers will automatically install a certificate. Once the certificates are installed, the domain controllers will communicate over port 389 for standard LDAP or port 636 for SSL-encrypted LDAP.

EXERCISE 6.11

Configuring GPO for Automated Certificate Distribution for Domain Controllers

In this exercise, you will set up the Group Policy Object (GPO) for the Domain Controllers organizational unit to distribute certificates to the domain controllers.

1. On an Active Directory domain controller, open the Active Directory Users And Computers MMC snap-in by choosing Start ➤ Administrative Tools ➤ Active Directory Users And Computers.

2. Right-click Domain Controllers and choose Properties from the shortcut menu to open the Default Domain Controller policy. Click the Group Policy tab and then click Edit to open the default GPO.

3. Choose Computer Configuration ➤ Windows Settings ➤ Security Settings ➤ Public Key Policies to expand the policy.

4. Right-click Automatic Certificate Request Settings (as shown in the following graphic) and choose New ➤ Automatic Certificate Request Wizard to start the Automatic Certificate Request Wizard.

5. At the Welcome screen, click Next to open the Certificate Template screen.

6. Select Domain Controller and then click Next.

7. Verify that the certificate authority is selected. Click Next and then click Finish to complete the wizard.

The Address Book is the default search client for Windows 2000 and Internet Explorer (IE) 5 and later. It uses LDAP to connect to a domain controller, and it can be configured to use secure LDAP. This process will work with Windows 2000 running IE 5 or later. In Exercise 6.12, you'll test SSL-secured LDAP to Active Directory.

Windows 95 and Windows 98 clients with IE 5 are considered down-level clients and will not function like Windows 2000, Windows XP Professional, and Windows Server 2003. See q238007 for instructions for down-level clients.

EXERCISE 6.12

Testing SSL-Secured LDAP to Active Directory

In this exercise, you'll test the connection between a Windows 2000 client and a Windows Server 2003 Active Directory domain controller.

1. Choose Start ➢ Search ➢ For People.

2. In the Look In drop-down list box, select Active Directory.

3. Right-click Active Directory (while this may look odd, it will work) and choose Properties from the shortcut menu to open the Active Directory Properties dialog box:

4. In the Server Name box, enter the domain controller's server name. This must be the fully qualified domain name such as *servername.domainname*.com.

5. Leave the account name and password fields alone, unless you have set up special security on searching Active Directory. If Active Directory is set up so that only certain users or accounts have access, enter a username and password. Make sure to enter the username with the NetBIOS name of the domain such as *domainname\username*.

6. Click the Advanced tab.

7. In the Directory Service (LDAP) box, enter **636** (the secure LDAP port number).

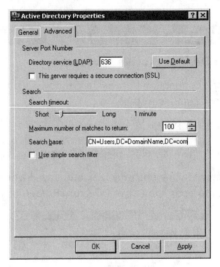

8. In the Search Base box, enter the Active Directory container to be used, such as CN=Users,DC=domainname,DC=com, and click OK.

9. In the Name box of the Find People dialog box, enter a username such as Administrator.

Assuming that everything worked correctly, Step 9 will provide the results of the search you requested, using port 636.

Using SSL to Secure Client Machine to E-Mail Server Traffic

Exchange 2000 and Exchange Server 2003 use *Transport Layer Security (TLS)* protocol, which is a protocol based on SSL that is completely compatible with SSL. Enabling TLS in Exchange 2000 or Exchange Server 2003 is the same thing as implementing SSL. When discussing SSL and Exchange, the terms can be used interchangeably. For the sake of consistency, we will use SSL in this section, although we may use TLS along with it to remind you that they are one and the same thing in the discussions about SMTP (Simple Mail Transport Protocol) and the encryption of SMTP traffic.

Securing e-mail through Exchange can be complicated. You need to secure the download of e-mail from the server to the client system, and you also need to secure the uploaded e-mail from the client system to the server. Think of e-mail as two completely different and distinct processes; one is receiving e-mail from the server and getting it to the client system, and the other is sending e-mail from the client system through the server to its final destination.

To send e-mail from the client system through the server and out to its final destination, you can use three methods:

MAPI   Microsoft's Messaging Application Programming Interface will get e-mail to and from client systems within the Exchange environment, but to send e-mail outside the company, you need to use SMTP.

SMTP   Simple Mail Transport Protocol is the standard for e-mail between mail servers on the Internet. All standard Internet e-mail traffic between e-mail servers uses SMTP, whether it is on the sending side or the receiving side.

OWA   Outlook Web Access is a web-based e-mail client that allows the user to send and receive e-mail using the Exchange server from a web browser without needing any other e-mail client software installed on it.

MAPI is primarily used with the Outlook client or one of the older mail clients such as the Exchange clients that shipped with previous versions of Exchange. MAPI is not an Internet protocol in that you will probably never send MAPI messages from one system on the Internet to another, except through VPN (virtual private network) tunnels or through the new technology called RPC over HTTP, which is available only with Outlook 2003 and Exchange Server 2003.

The main problem with securing SMTP is that the systems on the other side (the ones receiving your mail and sending mail to you) all expect SMTP traffic to be sent and received using the standard process over the standard port—port 25—which does not include SSL encryption. We will look at securing SMTP using SSL and show how to do it while still being able to send and receive e-mail to and from the rest of the world on the Internet. OWA is also covered in this chapter.

To receive e-mail from the server to the client, you use MAPI, OWA, and the following two methods:

IMAP4   Internet Messaging Access Protocol version 4 is one of two common Internet standards for pulling e-mail from an e-mail server down to a client machine where it can be read and archived.

POP3   Post Office Protocol version 3 is the other of the two common Internet standards for pulling e-mail from an e-mail server down to a client machine where it can be read and archived.

Again, MAPI is primarily used with the Outlook client or one of the older mail clients such as the Exchange clients that shipped with previous versions of Exchange Server. MAPI is not an Internet protocol in that you will probably never send MAPI messages from one system on the Internet to another. IMAP4 and POP3 are both protocols used to pull e-mail off of the e-mail server and bring it down to the client system where it can be read using a client application that supports these particular protocols.

What is important to remember with IMAP4 and POP3 is that the client application that uses either of these protocols must also use SMTP in order to send new e-mail out to or to respond to previously received e-mail. OWA is the web client that allows you to connect to the Exchange server and access your e-mail through a web browser. It is a nice, lightweight client that uses HTTP for reading and sending e-mail. You do not use SSL with MAPI, so we will not discuss it here. However, you can use SSL with IMAP4, POP3, and OWA, so we will describe the process to secure each of these methods. Figure 6.6 shows and explains the various Internet e-mail methods.

On Exchange, several *virtual servers* are used to process messages. Exchange can have multiple virtual servers supporting multiple instances of each protocol as needed. In Figure 6.6, you can see that the Exchange 2000 server on the right has a default SMTP virtual server and a secured SMTP virtual server. Each of these secured virtual servers will be discussed in more detail in this chapter. However, you might want to mark the page for Figure 6.6 so that you can look back on occasion when we discuss each of the protocols and how to secure them. The ultimate goal is that your environment will look like Figure 6.6, in which your Exchange server is able to communicate with external e-mail servers of all types using standard SMTP on port 25, yet is also able to communicate with external e-mail clients that are accessing their e-mail on the Exchange server using IMAP4 and POP3 clients with SMTP through encrypted connections using port 465. In some cases, you may also choose to enable SSL for SMTP transmitted between your Exchange environment and the e-mail system of your partners.

FIGURE 6.6 Internet e-mail methods

Securing SMTP

As discussed earlier, securing SMTP can be problematic. You need to protect your SMTP server from being used as a relay for spammers on the Internet. Therefore, you need to set up SMTP authentication for who can send e-mail and allow others to send you e-mail as anonymous users. When configuring SMTP security, the default SMTP virtual server should be used as your Internet mail connector from the Exchange server to and from the rest of the Internet. This SMTP virtual server connects to remote Internet domains to deliver and receive messages to and from external organizations. This becomes a problem because you don't want others on the Internet to be able to see the e-mail being downloaded from the Exchange server by client systems on the Internet. To protect against that, you need to configure authentication and set up encryption for your POP3 and IMAP4 clients. This problem becomes even bigger though, if you configure your existing SMTP virtual server to use SSL. If you make this change, the inbound sessions from SMTP servers outside your location will be affected, and they will not be able to send you e-mail. You need to properly secure SMTP in order to support IMAP4 and POP3 clients, too. To secure SMTP client access and avoid open relays that can be abused, you must first create a new SMTP virtual server to use with inbound client connections.

In Exercise 6.13, you'll go through the steps to properly secure SMTP using SSL.

EXERCISE 6.13

Creating a Dedicated SMTP Virtual Server

In this exercise, you will create a new virtual server on your Exchange server to be used for dedicated external IMAP4 and POP3 clients. You will use this virtual server in the next exercise and implement SSL encryption.

1. On the Exchange server, or on a system with the proper Exchange client tools, choose Start ➤ Programs ➤ Microsoft Exchange ➤ System Manager to open the System Manager.

2. Expand the Servers object, select the server to be used if you have more than one, expand Protocols, and then expand SMTP as shown here:

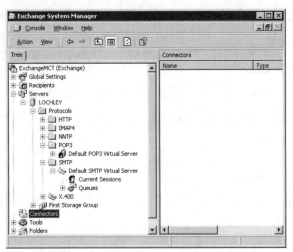

EXERCISE 6.13 *(continued)*

3. Right-click the SMTP folder and choose New ➤ SMTP Virtual Server.

4. Enter a name for this virtual server—something like Secure Server—and then click Next.

5. Select the IP address to use and click Finish. A dedicated IP address is recommended for this virtual server that is different from the one used for the default SMTP virtual server.

Now that you have an SMTP virtual server on the Exchange server, you can start configuring it. The nice thing about having these two SMTP virtual servers—the default and the new one—is that all normal e-mail can still continue processing. You have not changed that in any way. However, it is a good idea to test SMTP before continuing by sending and receiving a few e-mails between your Exchange environment and Hotmail. The next step, after you test the current configuration, is to install SSL. In Exercise 6.14, you will secure SMTP on Exchange 2000 Server.

For the purpose of the following exercise—and several others in this chapter and other chapters—you will use a private certificate from an internal CA. Generally, you will want to use a certificate from a public CA for external resources such as the Exchange server so that all external clients will automatically have the appropriate entries in their Trusted Root Certification Authorities list.

EXERCISE 6.14

Securing SMTP on Exchange 2000 Server

In this exercise, you will install and configure SSL on the SMTP virtual server created in Exercise 6.13.

1. Choose Start ➤ Programs ➤ Microsoft Exchange ➤ System Manager to open the System Manager.

2. Expand the Servers object, select the server to be used if you have more than one, expand Protocols, and expand SMTP.

3. Right-click Secure Server (your new virtual SMTP server) and choose Properties.

4. Click the Access Tab and then click Certificate in the Secure Communications section to start the Certificate Wizard.

5. At the Welcome screen, click Next to start the wizard and verify that the Create A New Certificate radio button is selected. Click Next.

6. Click the Send The Request Immediately To An Online Certificate Authority radio button and then click Next.

7. Enter the name of the certificate and set the bit length. The preference is 1024 bits. Click Next.

8. Enter the organization and the organizational unit. Normally, the organization will be the company name, and the organizational unit will be the department or division. Click Next.

9. Enter the common name. This will be the fully qualified domain name for the server as it will be accessed from the Internet. Click Next.

10. Enter the county/region, state/province, and city/locality information as discussed earlier in this chapter. Click Next.

11. In the drop-down list box, select the certificate server to be used. Click Next to open the Summary screen.

12. Verify that the information is correct, click Next, and then click Finish to complete acquisition of the certificate for the SMTP virtual server.

13. Click the Communications button on the Access tab in the Secure Communications section to open the dialog box.

14. Check the Require Secure Channel check box and the Require 128-Bit Encryption check box, and then click OK.

15. Stop and restart the Secure Server SMTP Virtual Server.

Configuring SMTP with SSL is only part of the solution. As previously stated, SMTP is the sending side of the e-mail client. Now you need to address the receiving side of the e-mail client.

Securing IMAP4

Many companies set up IMAP4 for their external e-mail users who want to use Outlook or Outlook Express from home to read and respond to their e-mail. Using IMAP4, you don't have to worry about users dumping their entire e-mail from the e-mail server to their local client, which can happen with POP3 if it isn't set up correctly. IMAP4 is a good protocol to use externally, because it will not remove e-mail from the server except when it is normally deleted from the server.

The main problem with using IMAP4 to download e-mail to an external e-mail client is that the messages travel in the clear. This means that the e-mail and all its contents—including attachments—can be captured off the Internet and viewed by a potential hacker. To prevent this, you need to use SSL to secure IMAP4. Exercise 6.15 walks you through the process of securing IMAP4 on the Exchange e-mail server.

In many of these exercises, you have been creating new certificates. In reality, you can use the Assign An Existing Certificate radio button and then select one of the certificates that you have already acquired and use it to secure the virtual server. We recommend using a new certificate for each virtual server, because each service is not dependent on the same certificate in the event that the certificate is compromised.

EXERCISE 6.15

Securing IMAP4 on Exchange

In this exercise, you will install the certificate for IMAP4 and configure Exchange Server to support secure IMAP4 connections from external clients.

1. On the Exchange server, or a system with the proper Exchange client tools, choose Start ➢ Programs ➢ Microsoft Exchange ➢ System Manager to open the System Manager.

2. Expand the Servers object, select the server to be used if you have more than one, expand Protocols, and expand IMAP4.

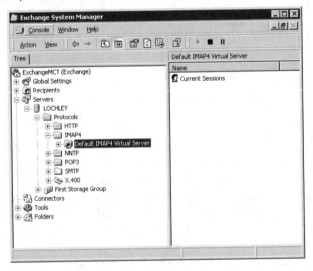

3. Right-click Default IMAP4 Virtual Server and choose Properties from the shortcut menu to open the Properties dialog box.

4. Click the Access tab and then click the Certificate button in the Secure Communications section to start the Certificate Wizard that you have used several times in this chapter already. Click Next.

5. Verify that the Create A New Certificate radio button is selected and then click Next.

6. Click the Send The Request Immediately To An Online Certificate Authority radio button and then click Next.

7. Enter the name of the certificate and set the bit length. The preference is 1024 bits. Click Next.

8. Enter the organization and the organizational unit. Normally, the organization will be the company name, and the organizational unit will be the department or division. Click Next.

9. Enter the common name. This will be the fully qualified domain name for the server as it will be accessed from the Internet. Click Next.

10. Enter the county/region, state/province, and city/locality information as discussed earlier in this chapter. Click Next.

11. In the drop-down list box, select the certificate server to be used and then click Next to open the Summary screen.

12. Verify the information, click Next, and then click Finish to complete acquisition of the certificate for the IMAP4 virtual server.

13. On the Access tab, click the Communication button in the Secure Communications section to open the Security dialog box.

14. Check the Require Secure Channel check box and the Require 128-Bit Encryption check box to use the most secure setting and then click OK.

15. Click the General tab and verify that the IP address is the same one that you used in Exercise 6.13 for the new virtual SMTP server. If it isn't, select the proper IP address from the drop-down list box and then click OK.

16. Stop and Restart the IMAP4 virtual server to make the setting take effect.

Configuring IMAP4 for the Exchange server is now complete. We will test this, along with the SMTP and POP3 configurations shortly. With IMAP4 and SMTP properly secured, you can now safely connect client e-mail applications from the Internet and not have to worry about anyone capturing your e-mail and reading it. Next, let's look at how to secure POP3 using SSL.

Securing POP3

Many companies set up POP3 for their external e-mail users who want to use Outlook or Outlook Express from home to read and respond to their e-mail. Using POP3, though, you need to be careful in configuring the e-mail client so that it does not download all of your e-mail from the e-mail server. If you are not careful, the next time the user is in the office, they will find an empty e-mail box and may then ask for it to be restored from tape.

Just like IMAP4, the main problem with using POP3 to download e-mail to an external e-mail client is that the messages travel in the clear. This means that the e-mail and all its contents—including attachments—can be captured off the Internet and viewed by a potential hacker. To prevent this, you need to use SSL to secure POP3 from these unintended viewers. Exercise 6.16 walks you through the process of securing POP3 on the Exchange 2000 e-mail server.

EXERCISE 6.16

Securing POP3 on Exchange 2000 Server

In this exercise, you will install the certificate for POP3 and configure the Exchange server to support secure POP3 connections from external clients.

1. On the Exchange server, or on a system with the proper Exchange client tools, choose Start ➢ Programs ➢ Microsoft Exchange ➢ System Manager to open the System Manager.

2. Expand the Servers object, select the server to be used if you have more than one, expand Protocols, and then expand POP3.

3. Right-click Default POP3 Virtual Server and choose Properties from the shortcut menu to open the Properties dialog box.

4. Click the Access tab and then click the Certificate button in the Secure Communications section to start the Certificate Wizard that you have used several times in this chapter already. Click Next.

5. Verify that the Create A New Certificate radio button is selected and then click Next.

6. Click the Send The Request Immediately To An Online Certificate Authority radio button and then click Next.

7. Enter the name of the certificate and set the bit length. The preference is 1024 bits. Click Next.

8. Enter the organization and the organizational unit. Normally, the organization will be the company name, and the organizational unit will be the department or division. Click Next.

9. Enter the common name. This will be the fully qualified domain name for the server as it will be accessed from the Internet. Click Next.

10. Enter the county/region, state/province, and city/locality information as discussed earlier in this chapter. Click Next.

11. In the drop-down list box, select the certificate server to be used and then click Next to open the Summary screen.

12. Verify the information as correct, click Next, and then click Finish to complete acquisition of the certificate for the POP3 virtual server.

13. On the Access tab, click the Communication button in the Secure Communications section to open the Security dialog box.

14. Check the Require Secure Channel check box and the Require 128-Bit Encryption check box to use the most secure setting and then click OK.

EXERCISE 6.16 *(continued)*

15. Click the General tab and verify that the IP address is the same one that you used in Exercise 6.13 for the new virtual SMTP server. If it isn't, select the proper IP address from the drop-down list box and then click OK.

16. Stop and restart the POP3 virtual server to make the setting take effect.

At this point, configuring POP3 for the Exchange server is now complete. You'll test this—along with the SMTP and IMAP4 configurations—right now. With IMAP4, POP3, and SMTP properly secured, you can now safely connect client e-mail applications from the Internet using either of the two protocols for reading e-mail and SMTP to send e-mail and not have to worry about anyone capturing your e-mail and reading it.

Setting Up and Testing Secured IMAP4, POP3, and SMTP with Outlook Express

Going through all of these options and configurations can be tiresome, but now you can actually see them all work. So dive right in with Exercise 6.17 and set up Outlook Express to test your configurations.

 To test IMAP and POP3, you will have to create the account for one, delete it, and create the account again using the other.

EXERCISE 6.17

Testing Secure E-Mail with Outlook Express

In this exercise, you will set up Outlook Express to connect to the Exchange server using the new secured virtual SMTP server and the secured IMAP4 and POP3 virtual servers.

1. Choose Start ➢ Programs ➢ Outlook Express to start Outlook Express.

2. Choose Tools ➢ Accounts to open the Internet Accounts dialog box.

3. Choose Add ➢ Mail to start the Internet Connection Wizard.

4. In the Display Name box, enter your display name, which is generally your full name, and then click Next to open the Internet E-Mail Address screen.

5. In the E-Mail Address box, enter the e-mail address that you want others to use to send you e-mail. This is the address that will be in your e-mails sent out to the Internet that others will use for their reply e-mails. Click Next to open the E-Mail Server Names screen.

6. From the My Incoming Mail Server Is A drop-down list box, select IMAP or POP3, depending on which one you want to test. In the Incoming Mail (POP3, IMAP, or HTTP) Server box,
enter the IP address of the virtual IMAP4/POP3 server, which should be the same as the
secured SMTP virtual server IP address used in Exercise 6.13. In the Outgoing Mail (SMTP)
Server box, enter the same IP address as for the incoming mail server. Click Next to open
the Internet Mail Logon screen.

7. Enter the account name and password for the e-mail box that you want to access using
Outlook Express. Check the Remember Password box, unless you want to enter your password every time you access Outlook Express. Click Next and then click Finish.

8. In the Internet Accounts dialog box, click the Mail tab, click the account with the IP address
of your secure SMTP virtual server, and then click Properties to open the Properties dialog
box for that IP address.

9. Click the Servers tab.

10. Check the My Server Requires Authentication check box and then click Settings to open the
dialog box.

11. Verify that the Use Same Settings as the incoming mail server radio button is selected and
then click OK.

12. Back in the Properties dialog box, click the Advanced tab. You use the options on this tab to set up Outlook Express to use the secure virtual servers. Make sure the This Server Requires A Secure Connection (SSL) box is checked for both the Outgoing Mail (SMTP) and the Incoming Mail (IMAP), as shown in the following graphic. (IMAP4 is on the left, and POP3 is on the right.)

13. Click OK to close the Properties dialog box and then click Close to close the dialog box.

14. In the Would You Like To Download Folders From The Mail Server You Added dialog box, click Yes.

15. After the folders download, which should take only a minute or less, click OK. If you chose POP3, you can skip this step.

16. In Outlook Express, find the new mail account on the left and expand it, if necessary. Click the Inbox, and you should see it start to fill with any messages that might be on the Exchange server for the mailbox used. Using a packet sniffer such as Microsoft Network Monitor, you can verify that these messages are being downloaded securely.

17. To test the ability to send using the secure SMTP virtual server, click Create Mail and create a test message. Again, you can test whether it is sent encrypted by using a packet sniffer.

18. For POP3 accounts, you probably want to check the Leave A Copy Of Messages On Server box. If you do not check this box, Outlook Express downloads all the e-mail from your Exchange mailbox and removes the e-mail from the server. The e-mail box on the server will be empty if you do not check this box.

At this point, you can be confident that external e-mail users can connect to the secure virtual servers on the Exchange server for safe e-mail. With SSL encryption between the e-mail client and the e-mail server, nobody will be able to read the messages going back and forth between these two systems. However, you need to remember that if the e-mail is going out to another e-mail server on the Internet for its final destination, it will eventually end up going out in the clear and can be read out on the Internet as it travels from the Exchange server to other e-mail servers.

Securing Outlook Web Access

Securing Outlook Web Access (OWA) should be easy for you now. After all, if you think about it, OWA is just another IIS server. You need to take the same steps for OWA as you would for any other web server:

1. Obtain a public certificate as you did in Exercise 6.1. You use a public certificate because you want your certificate on as many Trusted Root Certification Authority lists as possible.

2. Install the certificate for IIS on the Exchange server that you will be using for OWA from the Internet, as you did in Exercise 6.2, and then get ready to configure it.

3. Configure SSL for IIS on the Exchange server. This step will be similar to Exercise 6.8. However, the big difference is that you can set up the web server to encrypt only the OWA directory, and not use encryption for any other web pages that may be on the server.

4. Test the configuration.

 Real World Scenario

Secure E-Mail Required

Let's say you are the network administrator for a large banking organization with branches around the United States and that you use Exchange Server for your e-mail system.

You just acquired another bank. As part of this acquisition, you need to provide e-mail accounts for the new users at the new bank without installing an e-mail server at their location. The e-mail must be accessible from their location, and it must be secured using SSL. You do not have people to send to the bank to set up the client computers.

You could use the processes discussed in this section of the chapter to configure secure SMTP and secure IMAP4 to your Exchange environment. You could then set up all the users on your current e-mail system and give them all directions on how to set up Outlook Express. However, a quicker solution is to have them use OWA and their web browsers as an e-mail client and secure OWA using SSL.

What makes configuring OWA different from configuring any other web server is that you may not have any other sites or directories on the IIS server on the Exchange server that need encryption. In Exercise 6.18, you'll secure OWA.

EXERCISE 6.18

Securing OWA

In this exercise, you will set up OWA so that any connections to it will be encrypted using SSL. This exercise assumes that you have already obtained and installed a certificate for IIS on the Exchange server. If you want, you can do this exercise using a private CA and a private certificate.

1. On your web server, run the Internet Services Manager MMC snap-in. Choose Start ➢ Administrative Tools ➢ Internet Information Services (IIS) Manager to start the console.

2. Double-click Default Web Site to expand it.

3. Right-click the directory—Exchange—as shown here and choose Properties from the short-cut menu to open the Properties dialog box.

4. Click the Directory Security tab and then click the Edit button in the Secure Communications section to open the Secure Communications dialog box.

5. Click the Require Secure Channel (SSL) check box and then click the Require 128-Bit Encryption check box if you want to enforce 128-bit encryption.

6. Click OK to close the Secure Communications dialog box and then click OK again to close the Properties dialog box.

To test the configuration, open Internet Explorer and go to https://*servername*/exchange. The web browser requests a logon if you are not already logged on to the network. If you are already logged on to the network, the web browser takes you directly to your e-mail box. Verify that you can see the SSL lock at the bottom of Internet Explorer, and consider the implementation another success.

Configuring OWA using SSL is extremely popular. The employees of companies around the world all love the ability to access their e-mail without having to worry about configuring an e-mail client. With SSL, not only is OWA easy to access and use, but it is also secure.

Summary

In this chapter, you learned about Secure Socket Layer (SSL) protocol. We covered the basics of how SSL works to encrypt traffic as well as how to do the following:

- Obtain certificates from public and private certificate authorities

- Renew certificates from public and private certificate authorities

- Install and configure certificates on the following:

  - IIS 5 and IIS 6

  - Exchange 2000 Server and Exchange Server 2003

  - SQL 2000 Server

- Use SSL to encrypt and secure network traffic for the following:
  - Client to an IIS server
  - Client to Active Directory domain controllers
  - IIS to SQL 2000 Server
  - Client to Exchange server

The exercises in this chapter provide step-by-step instructions for performing all these tasks. Although you may have understood that SSL is often used for web traffic, you can also use it in a number of ways to secure many types of traffic. Using SSL to properly secure your network is effective, and it meets almost all business needs for security when working with the Internet.

Exam Essentials

Deploy and manage public and private certificates.   Make sure you understand the difference between public and private certificates and when it is appropriate to use each type. Understand how to generate a CSR for all the different servers discussed in this chapter and understand how to renew certificates.

Configure SSL to secure communications channels.   You should fully understand how to use SSL to secure network traffic by enforcing its use and not allowing unsecured traffic. Understand how to use SSL to secure the traffic between client systems and IIS, Active Directory domain controllers, and Exchange servers. Also understand how to secure traffic between an IIS server and a SQL 2000 server.

Review Questions

1. Your company is about to bring two web servers—both running IIS—back in-house from a hosting facility. One server contains all your public company information. Customers can connect to it and learn about the company and its products. Clients can use the other server to purchase your products online and have them directly shipped using an e-business application developed in-house. This server uses SSL to encrypt all the customer-entered data that is sent to the server to process the order. Which ports need to be opened on your firewall to support these two servers? (Choose all that apply.)

   A. 110

   B. 143

   C. 80

   D. 443

2. You are the administrator of your IIS web servers in your company. You have set up SSL to protect Outlook Web Access (OWA). Your boss is concerned that somebody could be capturing all his sessions, even though it is encrypted, and then using it to try to break into the OWA server and read his e-mail. What will you explain to him to make him feel more comfortable with the technology and its ability to defend against this kind of attack?

   A. SSL provides message integrity checks and will break off communications with a system if the integrity checks fail.

   B. SSL provides the ability to prevent replay attacks by using sequence numbers in each direction of the session.

   C. SSL uses different port numbers for SSL-protected services than for standard services.

   D. The attacker would have to know the port number used for the Outlook Web Access server and would have a difficult time guessing it.

3. Your company needs certificates for deployments of SSL within the company. At no time will users outside the company be accessing these protected resources. Your supervisor is concerned about the high cost of purchasing certificates. What can you tell your supervisor?

   A. Using a private certificate authority—a service that can be installed on Windows 2000 and Windows Server 2003 servers without any additional charge—would not require spending money for each certificate used within the company.

   B. Public certificates may be expensive, but they are the only certificates that can be used to secure network traffic using SSL.

   C. SSL does not require that certificates be installed.

   D. Private certificates may be cheap, but they are not secure.

4. You purchased and installed a public certificate on your IIS web server used for Outlook Web Access (OWA) from the Internet. It has been working fine for several months. Now your supervisor wants to change the name of the server in DNS. Which of the following do you tell him?

   A. You need to shut down the server and restart it to change the server name in DNS; however, this does not affect the users in any way other than the outage time.

   B. You can't do it. Once a certificate is added, it cannot be removed, and the name cannot be changed.

   C. You can do it, but it means purchasing another certificate because the old certificate will generate error messages if it is used with a different name.

   D. You can't do it. To change the name of the server, you would have to rebuild the server completely.

5. You recently purchased a certificate. During the CSR generation, you entered the common name as email.*companyname*.com for the Outlook Web Access (OWA) server that is accessed by company users from the Internet. You found out after the server was deployed that the DNS administrator also created a record so that owa.*companyname*.com also directs users to the same server. Many users use the email.*companyname*.com address, and many others use the owa.*companyname*.com web address. You heard that users trying to use owa.*companyname*.com always get the "The name on the security certificate does not match the name of the site" error message. What can you do to prevent this error message from appearing?

   A. Obtain another certificate with owa.*companyname*.com and replace the email.*companyname*.com certificate with the new one.

   B. Create another site for https://owa.*companyname*.com that has a valid certificate with its common name and a web page to redirect all requests to the proper address.

   C. Renew the email.*companyname*.com certificate and change its name at the same time. This renewed certificate will then support both common names.

   D. Send everyone instructions about how to update their Trusted Root Certification Authority list so that it does not generate the error message.

6. You recently installed a certificate for SSL on your IIS web server named Server1, but you are not sure if it is working correctly. What is the easiest way to verify that SSL is working?

   A. Using Internet Explorer, connect to https://server1 and check the Status Bar to see if the lock appears.

   B. Using Internet Explorer, connect to http://server1 and check the Status Bar to see if the lock appears.

   C. Install the Certificates snap-in in the MMC and open the certificate to make sure that it has not expired.

   D. Install the Certificates snap-in in the MMC and open the certificate to verify that it is for a web server.

7. You are trying to get a certificate from a public certificate authority. You generate the CSR and paste it into the proper part of the template. When you submit the CSR, though, you receive an error message that the CSR is not compatible with a 128-bit certificate. What might be wrong?

A. The common name is not the same as the DNS site name for the server on which you will install the certificate.

B. The company name is not spelled correctly in the CSR.

C. You did not copy the header and footer of the CSR into the template.

D. If the CSR is generated using 512 bits, it isn't sufficient for 128-bit certificates. It must be at least 1024 bits.

8. When you test your installation of SSL on an IIS server named Server1, you notice that the web server responds to both `http://server1` and `https://server1`. What steps do you need to take to ensure that the web server responds only to `https://server1`?

A. Using the Internet Services Manager snap-in, open the Properties dialog box for the virtual server. In the Directory Security tab, click the Edit button to open the Secure Communications dialog box and verify that Enable Client Certificate Mapping is checked.

B. Using the Internet Services Manager snap-in, open the Properties dialog box for the virtual server. In the Directory Security tab, click the Edit button to open the Secure Communications dialog box and verify that Require Secure Channel (SSL) is checked.

C. Using the Internet Services Manager snap-in, open the Properties dialog box for the virtual server. In the Directory Security tab, click the Edit button to open the Secure Communications dialog box and verify that Enable Certificate Trust List is checked.

D. Using the Internet Services Manager snap-in, open the Properties dialog box for the virtual server. In the Directory Security tab, click the View Certificate button to open the Secure Communications dialog box and verify that the certificate is not expired.

9. You implemented SSL for securing IMAP4 access to the Exchange server in your company. You also set up SMTP for secure access. When configuring Outlook Express, you select the This Server Requires A Secure Connection (SSL) check box. You notice that the IMAP4 configuration is set to use port 993, so you change it to 995. When you test the Outlook Express configuration, it fails. What is the most likely reason for the failure?

A. IMAP4 uses port 143, and it does not work properly using anything else.

B. Secure IMAP4 uses port 143. Port 995 is for secure POP3, so it should be changed to 143.

C. The correct port for secure IMAP4 is 993, so it needs to be changed from 995 back to 993.

D. The Exchange server is configured incorrectly.

10. You recently set up a client system to use Outlook Express for secure access to Exchange with POP3 and SMTP both secured with SSL. You tested it, and everything seemed to be working fine as it downloads e-mail from the server and sends e-mail. The next day, a user calls to complain that all his e-mail in Outlook is missing and that he needs it restored. What is the most likely cause of the user's missing e-mail?

   A. Outlook Express was configured with IMAP4, which removes e-mail from the Exchange server.

   B. Outlook Express was not configured to use secure POP3. Standard POP3 removes all the e-mail from the Exchange server.

   C. Outlook Express was not configured to leave a copy of the e-mail on the Exchange server, and all the e-mail was downloaded to Outlook Express.

   D. The user deleted his e-mail accidentally and just didn't realize it.

11. You are trying to configure IIS to use a certificate for SSL. When you open the Properties dialog box for the website and click the Directory Security tab, you see that the Edit key is grayed out in the Secure Communications section. What is the most likely reason that it is grayed out?

   A. A certificate has not yet been installed on the IIS server.

   B. The certificate is expired.

   C. The certificate is from an untrusted certificate authority.

   D. The certificate is 40 bits, and only 128-bit certificates can be edited.

12. Your company has been using an IIS web server so that some customers can place orders from the Internet. Recently, a few customers have complained that the web traffic to this server is not secured because SSL is not being used for this server. You have never used SSL for web servers in your company before. You configure SSL and test it internally. It works fine. Now, customers are complaining that they are unable to access the server at all, even using SSL. What is the most likely reason for the web server to fail for external users?

   A. The certificate authority is not trusted by most web browsers.

   B. The certificate authority has not yet configured the certificate to make it available; they must be waiting for payment to clear before allowing it to be used.

   C. The common name was not correctly entered when the CSR was generated.

   D. The firewall between the IIS server and the Internet is not allowing port 443 traffic to the IIS server.

13. You recently configured Active Directory domain controllers to use SSL. When testing the configuration, you received the "The specified directory service could not be reached" error message. You start troubleshooting. You open Address Book, right-click Active Directory in the Look In box, and choose Properties from the shortcut menu to open the Properties dialog box. You notice in the Advanced tab that the Directory Server (LDAP) is set for port 366. You are certain that this is wrong and is the cause of the problem. How can you verify that you are correct?

   A. Change the port to 636 and make sure that the This Server Requires A Secure Connection (SSL) check box is selected. Then retry the search.

   B. Change the port to 3268 and make sure that the This Server Requires A Secure Connection (SSL) check box is selected. Then retry the search.

   C. Change the port to 389 and make sure that the This Server Requires A Secure Connection (SSL) check box is selected. Then retry the search.

   D. Change it to 993 and make sure that the This Server Requires a Secure Connection (SSL) check box is selected. Then retry the search.

14. A team member was recently trying to configure SSL on a SQL 2000 server so that it could use a secured communication channel to pass information back and forth from an IIS server. He was unable to get it working. He described his steps to you and said that he used the IIS server on the SQL server to get the certificate installed. You are sure this is not the proper method. What do you tell him to do?

   A. Install the Certificates snap-in in an MMC and use it to request a new certificate. Use a computer certificate, not a SQL certificate.

   B. Install the Certificates snap-in in an MMC and use it to request a new certificate. Use a service account certificate, not a web certificate. Configure it for the SQL service account.

   C. Install the Certificates snap-in in an MMC and use it to request a new certificate. Use an EFS certificate, not a web certificate.

   D. Install the Certificates snap-in in an MMC and use it to request a new certificate. Use a computer certificate, not a web certificate.

15. One of the members of your team installed a computer certificate on a SQL 2000 server as part of the process for configuring secure communications between the SQL 2000 server and an IIS server. He tells you that he set up the SQL 2000 server with the Force Protocol Encryption option and that he then set up the IIS server with the SQL 2000 client software to also use the Force Protocol Encryption option. He can't get the IIS server to talk to the SQL 2000 server using encrypted channels. What should you tell him?

   A. Force Protocol Encryption can be used only from the SQL 2000 server side, not the client side.

   B. Force Protocol Encryption can be used only from the client side (IIS server in this case) and cannot be used from the SQL 2000 server side.

   C. Force Protocol Encryption cannot be set up on both the SQL 2000 server and the client (IIS server) at the same time. Choose one or the other, but not both.

   D. Using a computer certificate and then setting up the Force Protocol Encryption option are not required. The systems automatically encrypt communications based on how the web application is coded.

16. SSL can be used on commercial sites to do which of the following? (Choose all that apply.)

  A. Encrypt the web traffic.

  B. Authenticate the web server to the client.

  C. Prevent replay attacks on the web server.

  D. Prevent port scanning.

17. You have employees in your company who want to access e-mail from home. Your supervisor has asked for the best solution to provide them with secure access without having to spend much money or take much administrative effort. What would you recommend to your supervisor?

  A. Configure SMTP and POP3 using SSL for external access.

  B. Configure SMTP and IMAP4 using SSL for external access.

  C. Configure the e-mail server to send copies of all e-mail to employees' homes as well as to work e-mail addresses.

  D. Configure OWA with SSL for external access.

18. You configured an internal website for payroll reporting. Accounting wants the site secured so that private company data about pay rates does not get out to the employees. Accounting intends to use the site internally only. They want to minimize costs. What should you do?

  A. Use a private certificate authority to get a certificate and configure the website using SSL.

  B. Use a public certificate authority to get a certificate and configure the website using SSL.

  C. Move the web server onto the accounting network segment. Set up a firewall to filter HTTP between accounting and the rest of the network.

  D. Move the web server into a secured room behind a firewall. Configure a firewall to allow only accounting IP addresses to access the web server.

19. A co-worker configured a web server with SSL about two years ago using a private certificate authority. You have been told that the certificate will expire in a couple of days. What should you do?

  A. Use the Web Enrollment pages on the private certificate authority to request a new certificate before the old one expires.

  B. Renew the certificate on the web server using the Certificates MMC snap-in.

  C. Wait for the certificate to expire and then get another one from the private certificate authority.

  D. Use the Web Enrollment pages on the private certificate authority to revoke the old certificate and get a new certificate.

20. Your co-worker implemented SSL for the SMTP service on the company e-mail server. Users report that they are no longer receiving e-mail. What is the most likely cause?

  A. Your co-worker did not create a new SMTP virtual server for the SSL implementation.

  B. Your co-worker forgot to use SSL on POP3 or IMAP 4 along with SMTP.

  C. Your co-worker didn't update the DNS server settings on the e-mail server.

  D. Your co-worker failed to reboot the e-mail server after making the changes.

Answers to Review Questions

1. C, D. HTTP uses port 80 for standard web traffic, and HTTPS uses port 443 for SSL protocol secured traffic.

2. B. The attack discussed is called a replay attack. SSL provides protection against replay attacks by inserting sequence numbers in the packets.

3. A. Private certificates for internal use are feasible and can be deployed effectively in the organization.

4. C. A certificate requires that the proper name be entered when generating the CSR; to change the name would mean generating a new CSR with the new name and obtaining a new certificate based on the new CSR.

5. B. If the page on `https://owa.companyname.com` redirects users to `https://email.companyname.com`, this error message will not be generated.

6. A. When using the `https://` address type, the lock icon appears in the Internet Explorer Status Bar if the connection is made using SSL.

7. D. A bit length of 512 for the CSR is only enough to generate a 40-bit certificate.

8. B. If Require Secure Channel (SSL) is not checked, IIS accepts both secure and unsecure access to web pages.

9. C. SSL-enabled IMAP4 uses port 993. SSL-enabled POP3 uses port 995.

10. C. If you do not select the Leave A Copy Of Messages On Server check box, Outlook Express downloads all the mail from the Exchange 2000 server, and the e-mail box on Exchange 2000 will be empty the next time it is accessed using another e-mail client.

11. A. Once the certificate is installed, the Edit button will be accessible.

12. D. To access the server using HTTPS, the firewall must allow traffic using port 443 to the IIS server.

13. A. LDAP secured with SSL uses port 636.

14. D. The SQL 2000 server needs a standard computer certificate in order to configure communications channels to use SSL.

15. C. Trying to use the Force Protocol Encryption for both the client and the server will cause the communications to fail between the systems.

16. A, B, C. SSL can be used for more than just encrypting the web traffic. It also prevents replays through the MIC and authenticates the server to the client system.

17. D. OWA is easy to configure with SSL to secure it. As an administrator, you would never have to support external e-mail clients because all users will use their web browser to access e-mail.

18. A. Private certificates are easy to configure and do not cost as much as the other solutions.

19. B. You can use the Certificates MMC snap-in to renew certificates as well as to request them.

20. A. If the only SMTP virtual server for the company is configured to use SSL, nobody on the Internet will be able to send e-mail to the server because they are not sending encrypted e-mail to the company.

Chapter

7

Configuring, Managing, and Troubleshooting Authentication

THE MICROSOFT EXAM OBJECTIVES COVERED IN THIS CHAPTER:

✓ **Configure security for remote access users.**

- Configure authentication for secure remote access. Authentication types include PAP, CHAP, MS-CHAP, MS-CHAPv2, EAP-MD5, EAP-TLS, and multifactor authentication with smart cards and EAP.

✓ **Plan and configure authentication.**

- Plan, configure, and troubleshoot trust relationships.
- Plan and configure authentication protocols.
- Plan and configure multifactor authentication.
- Plan and configure authentication for web users.
- Plan and configure delegated authentication.

Authentication, to provide a loose definition, is the process of verifying the identity of a person. Of course, this is incredibly important; otherwise, anyone could log on to your networks and cause all sorts of problems. In Windows 2000 and Windows Server 2003, a network user must be authenticated to an account before gaining access to any of the network resources. One of your goals is to make the authentication process secure while still meeting the business goals of the organization.

You use authentication in your daily life, so of course, you will also use it in your electronic life. For example, you use your driver's license (a commonly accepted form of authentication) to prove your identity when checking in at the airport, picking up a rental car, and writing checks, as well as when processing other financial transactions. You use looser forms of authentication, too. A great example of that is facial recognition. If somebody appears on your doorstep, and you recognize them as a relative, you'll probably let them in. When you walk into your office, you may have electronic keycards, but people recognize you walking down the hall and going to your cube or office. If you don't belong, you'll be identified as an intruder, and you'll be questioned and potentially even apprehended by internal security personnel.

But facial recognition is not a reliable authentication method for larger organizations, and it can really cause problems for new employees, so many organizations have implemented stronger authentication methods for access to their organizations such as private identification badges. When it comes to crossing international borders, even stronger authentication methods are required; most countries use passports issued by the country where the traveler is a citizen. Travel passports are very secure documents and are extremely difficult to forge, so they are generally accepted when traveling as a valid form of authentication of identity. Well, in the electronic world, you also need to use defined protocols to authenticate your network users and gain some confidence that they are who they say they are. Some of these protocols are stronger than others.

This chapter looks at the authentication protocols used for wired network authentication, web server authentication, and Routing and Remote Access Service (RRAS) authentication. For each of these types, we will discuss how to implement the protocols, and we will point out security problems as well as provide some troubleshooting tips as appropriate.

Configuring and Troubleshooting Authentication

This first section is focused on local area network (LAN) *authentication* protocols, as opposed to Internet and RRAS, which are covered later in this chapter. Although much of the information here also applies to web and RRAS users in Windows, this is probably the best place to start.

The LAN Authentication Protocols

Two authentication protocols are used in a LAN environment:

NT LAN Manager (NTLM)   This is the default protocol used in Windows NT 4 and earlier.

Kerberos v5   First introduced in Windows 2000, Kerberos v5 is used with Windows XP Professional and Windows Server 2003.

NT LAN Manager (NTLM)

NTLM is used by down-level operating systems such as Windows 95, Windows 98, and Windows NT 4. NTLM is also used by Windows 2000, Windows Server 2003, and Windows XP Professional when logging in to a Windows NT 4 domain and when logging in to the local computer accounts database (not Active Directory domains). There are three versions of NTLM:

LAN Manager (LM)   This form of NTLM is available in Windows 2000, Windows Server 2003, and Windows XP Professional so that computers running these operating systems can connect to file share points on computers running Windows 95 or Windows 98. This form of NTLM is the least secure of the three versions.

NTLM version 1   This is a more secure form of NTLM than LM. This version is available for connections to servers in a Windows NT domain that has at least one domain controller running Windows NT 4 SP3 or earlier. While it is an improvement over LM, it is still extremely susceptible to password attacks.

NTLM version 2   This is the most secure form of NTLM authentication that is supported. It is used when computers need to connect to servers in a Windows NT 4 domain in which the domain controllers are all running SP4 or later or when a Windows NT 4 server running SP4 is a member server in a Windows Active Directory domain. Windows 95 and Windows 98 can also use this version of NTLM if they have installed the Directory Services client.

By default, all three versions of NTLM are available in an Active Directory domain so that down-level clients can continue to function. It is very important that you consider the capabilities of older client operating systems before disabling any of the levels of NTLM on the network. If down-level computers can all support NTLM version 2, you can disable the LAN Manager Authentication Level security option in the Local Policy or using Group Policy Objects. The standard steps to authenticate when logging on are as follows:

1. In Windows 2000, Windows Server 2003, or Windows XP Professional, press Ctrl+Alt+Del, and Winlogon uses the *GINA (Graphical Identification and Authentication) dynamic-link library* to display the logon dialog box.

2. After the user enters their username and password, Winlogon sends the logon information to the *LSA (Local Security Authority)* for processing.

3. The LSA uses the local computer *SAM (System Account Manager)* database if the account and target name identify it as a local computer account and not as an Active Directory domain. The LSA uses the Net Logon service to query the domain SAM on a domain controller if the target account is an Active Directory domain account.

4. Once the logon information is identified as correct, the SAM sends an acceptance message to the LSA. This acceptance message contains the user account SID (security identifier) and the SIDs of all groups associated with the account. The LSA creates an access token using this information.

5. Winlogon then starts up the user interface and attaches the token to all current processes and all new processes except those created using Runas to run them under a separate security context.

This same process is valid whether using LM, NTLM version 1, or NTLM version 2. In the event there is no domain, NTLM can also be used for any peer-to-peer networking authentication needs.

In Exercise 7.1, you will disable LM and NTLM version 1.

EXERCISE 7.1

Disabling LM and NTLM version 1

In this exercise, you will disable LM and NTLM version 1 so that any clients attempting to use these authentication protocols will be ignored:

1. Choose Start ➢ Administrative Tools ➢ Active Directory Users And Computers.

2. If necessary, expand the MMC (Microsoft Management Console), right-click the domain name, choose Properties from the shortcut menu to open the Properties dialog box for the domain, and then click the Group Policy tab.

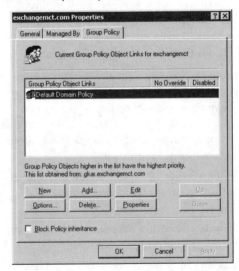

3. Select Default Domain Policy and then click Edit to open the Group Policy window. (You can also do this by creating a new policy, but because you would intend that this be done for all systems and as a permanent setting, it makes sense to edit the Default Domain Policy and use it.) Note that if you have Microsoft Group Policy Management installed, you need to click Open, navigate to and highlight the Default Domain Policy, and open it by right-clicking it and selecting Edit.

4. Expand Computer Configuration, expand Windows Settings, expand Security Settings, expand Local Policies, and then expand Security Options.

5. Double-click LAN Manager Authentication Level to open the Security Policy Settings dialog box.

6. Select the Define This Policy Setting check box and in the drop-down list box, choose Send NTLM Version 2 Response Only\Refuse LM And NTLM.

7. Click OK to close the Security Policy Settings dialog box, close the Group Policy window, and then click OK to close the Properties dialog box for the domain.

WARNING

If you are working on a live network, go back now and undo this exercise. It is highly possible that you could interfere with your down-level clients, and they might not be able to log on. The options available for NTLM are discussed in the "Configuring Authentication Protocols to Support Mixed Windows Client-Computer Environments" section later in this chapter. There are many options when it comes to securing the use of NTLM on the network, and there are many issues with LM and NTLM version 1 being disabled. It may not be appropriate for your public network.

✳The Kerberos Protocol

Kerberos is used by Windows 2000, Windows Server 2003, and Windows XP Professional when logging in to an Active Directory domain. Kerberos is not a new technology; it has been around for many years in the Unix world. What Microsoft has done is use a well-proven authentication protocol for improved security and to provide increased interoperability with Unix systems.

The Kerberos protocol provides mutual authentication between a client (which can be a user or a computer) and a server, meaning that not only does the client authenticate against the server, but the server authenticates itself against the client. With mutual authentication, each system can verify the identity of the other. Kerberos is extremely efficient for authenticating clients and has been proven in large network environments. Kerberos was designed and is implemented with the idea that all initial transactions between the clients and the servers occur in a semi-hostile environment, that is, on a network where potential intruders and hackers live and can try to appear to be either a client computer or a server on the network and capture and possibly even alter communications. Kerberos is designed to provide protection with secured authentication processes.

To provide security for the authentication process, Kerberos uses secret key encryption for authentication traffic from the client. The same secret key is also used on the server to decrypt the authentication traffic. The Kerberos *Key Distribution Center (KDC)* handles the decryption and is run on every domain controller as part of the Active Directory domain. As part of the security of Kerberos, an *authenticator* is used with the encrypted logon information. The authenticator contains information such as a time stamp that is used to prevent replays. As the logon information is received and accepted by the server, a new authenticator is inserted into the KDC response as part of the confirmation process. The KDC issues a *ticket-granting ticket (TGT)*, which is then used by the client computer's LSA to get service tickets for other systems that it needs to access.

One of the benefits of Kerberos is that it does not require constant reauthentication by the client in order to access other resources on the network. The client system can use its TGT to request access to other resources. The process of authentication using Kerberos involves the following steps:

1. After starting up Windows 2000, Windows Server 2003, or Windows XP Professional, press Ctrl+Alt+Del, and Winlogon will use the GINA to display the logon dialog box.

2. After the user enters their username and password, Winlogon sends the logon information to the LSA for processing.

3. The LSA passes the logon request to Kerberos. The client sends its logon information and an encrypted time stamp to the KDC as part of the authentication request. The TGT is requested in this step.

4. Using the secret key, the KDC decrypts the logon information and the time stamp and issues a TGT. This TGT contains a session key, the account name of the authenticated user, and the maximum lifetime of the ticket. Other information is also sent. The KDC then encrypts the response using the client key and is sent to the client. Included in the response is the TGT, which includes the SID for the user account and SIDs for any global and universal groups associated with the account.

The SIDs are provided to the LSA so they can be included in the *access token*. The maximum lifetime of the ticket is defined by the domain policy. The client will request new tickets if any tickets expire during an active network session.

5. Once the TGT is obtained, the client uses it to request a service ticket from Kerberos services on the domain controller. The ticket-granting service issues a service ticket. Service tickets are encrypted using the server's secret key. In addition, the SIDs for the account and its associated groups are copied from the TGT to all service tickets issued by the Kerberos service.

6. The client uses the service ticket to access the network services, and the ticket provides identification for the user and all the SID information for permissions.

Tickets received from the KDC are cached on the local client so that it can continue to use any tickets received until they expire. In the event that a ticket expires, the LSA negotiates the renewal by communicating with the KDC.

The main drawback with using Kerberos is that it is supported only on Windows 2000, Windows Server 2003, and Windows XP Professional operating systems. If the network has any down-level clients, NTLM is required for the down-level clients to authenticate with the Active Directory domain.

The Logon Process

You can log on to a Windows network using either NTLM or Kerberos in three ways:

- Using local computer accounts authentication
- Using Windows NT 4 domain authentication
- Using Active Directory domain authentication

Using the Log On To drop-down list box in the Log On To Windows dialog box (see Figure 7.1), you can log on using the local computer database by selecting your computer name in the box, or you can select any of the domains that are available either through the computer being a member of the domain or through trust relationships established between your domain and other domains.

FIGURE 7.1 The Log On To Windows dialog box

If the Log On To drop-down list box does not appear, click the Options button to display it.

Whether the computer is running Windows NT 4, Windows 2000, Windows Server 2003, or Windows XP Professional, the local computer accounts database is on the computer itself, and Windows uses the local SAM database when logging on to the local computer. In Windows 2000, Windows Server 2003, and Windows XP Professional, Windows first attempts to use the KDC for Kerberos authentication. When the operating system fails to find the KDC, it falls back to using NTLM and attempts to log on locally using the following steps:

1. In the Log On To Windows dialog box, enter your username and password.

2. The GINA collects the username and password and then sends that information to the LSA for authentication.

3. The LSA takes the information sent by the GINA and passes it to the *Security Support Provider Interface (SSPI)*. The SSPI is works with the Kerberos and NTLM services and enables third-party developers to create security-aware applications without any in-depth knowledge of how Kerberos and NTLM work.

4. The SSPI then passes the user information to Kerberos, where it checks to see if the logon target is the local computer or the domain. If it is the local computer, Kerberos passes an error message back to the SSPI. The computer then generates an error message behind the scenes, stating that the KDC could not be found.

5. This hidden error causes SSPI to start the logon process again, and the GINA sends the user logon information to the LSA again, and then LSA sends it to the SSPI again.

6. When the SSPI receives the logon information the second time, it sends the user logon information to the NTLM driver. The NTLM driver uses the Net Logon service to authenticate the logon information against the SAM database on the local computer.

Windows 2000 and Windows Server 2003 will fail to find the KDC on the local computer unless the local computer is a domain controller.

The local logon process is quick, and it is secure because it happens within the confines of the computer. There is no network traffic to monitor and capture out on the wire.

The logon process for logging on to a domain can be of two domain types: the Windows NT 4 domain and an Active Directory domain. The steps are similar to the local computer logon discussed previously:

1. After you enter the username and password in the Log On To Windows dialog box and click OK, the LSA of the computer passes the logon information to the SSPI, which can communicate with both Kerberos and NTLM services.

2. The SSPI then passes the user information to Kerberos, where it checks to see if the logon target is the local computer or the domain. The Kerberos SSPI determines whether the target computer name is the local computer or the domain name. In this case, it identifies the name as the domain name.

3. The KDC checks for the username and password, and the Kerberos authentication process proceeds if both are valid. The logon process ends at this point if the domain is an Active Directory domain.

4. If Step 3 fails because the username is not found by the KDC, the KDC passes an error message to the SSPI. If the KDC cannot be found, a hidden error message is passed back to the LSA, letting it know that the SSPI could not find the KDC.

5. The hidden error message to the LSA causes the process to start again, and MSGINA passes the information to the LSA again, and then LSA passes the logon information to the SSPI.

6. The SSPI then passes the logon information to the NTLM driver, and it then uses the Net Logon service to finish the authentication process using NTLM authentication.

When Windows 2000, Windows Server 2003, or Windows XP Professional computers log in, they first check to see if the logon name is a computer name or a domain name. They then first try to use Kerberos and fail over to NTLM if Kerberos is not available.

 Real World Scenario

Using Active Directory to Provide Single-Sign-On (SSO)

Security in your company is becoming more important every day. A recent poll of employees showed that the security concerns of the company are beginning to affect several employees and their ability to do their jobs.

Several employees in the Publishing department of your company are upset because they have one user account and password that they have to use for the Windows Server 2003 network. They also have another user account and password for the Unix workstations that they use as part of their detailed maps in the publications. In addition, they also have a third user account and password that they have to use to access the Internet and view the World Wide Web. They complain that with three different usernames and three different passwords, it's easy to forget which password goes to which account. They often get locked out of one system or another. The security team even found that a couple of the employees have started writing down the information, and this is a major security violation.

You do some research and recommend to your manager that you eliminate this problem by providing a single-sign-on (SSO) for all users on the network. Your solution calls for a new Microsoft Internet Security and Acceleration (ISA) Server and some reconfiguration of the Unix environment.

Using ISA Server as a member server and the ability of the Unix workstations to use Active Directory for Kerberos authentication, you can then have all of your systems working with Active Directory.

As an administrator of Active Directory, you can create user accounts and passwords so that each person in the company can use one user account and password to access the Windows Server 2003 environment resources, the Unix systems, and the Internet through ISA Server.

Troubleshooting Authentication

Troubleshooting authentication is like troubleshooting anything else. The process requires some structure and a little art. So, imagine the standard help desk call in which the user complains about not being able to log in from their computer. What kind of questions should you ask?

Can you log in on a different computer?   If the answer is yes, something is probably wrong with that particular computer. Perhaps the network wire is loose, or perhaps the network port that it is attached to has been recently configured differently. Because Kerberos is time-sensitive, you might want to check the system clock to make sure it is configured to synchronize with the Active Directory domain controller that hosts the PDC emulator role.

Can others log in on your computer?   If the answer is yes to this one, perhaps something is wrong with the user's password or they are mistyping either their username or password. Maybe the password needs to be reset and the change synched to all the domain controllers before the user tries again.

What is the name of your computer?   A quick check or two can confirm whether the computer is properly attached to the network. Pinging by the name will verify whether it is registered in DNS (Domain Name Service) and will help identify any other problems that the computer might have.

What is the exact error message that you are receiving?   TechNet, `www.microsoft.com/technet`, is a fantastic source for in-depth information on error messages. Look through it for any articles that can help with troubleshooting the problem.

Have you changed your password recently?   Often, users change their password, log off the network, and try to log right back in again. They may not get back on right away if they didn't allow time for the password change to synchronize with all the domain controllers. Wait a few minutes and try again.

You can also ask the network administrator a couple of questions. After all, they may have made some changes to the configuration of the network that could be causing problems such as changing the DNS server or even making some changes to Group Policy Objects that might impact the users. For example, did the network administrator make some changes to the NTLM configurations that disable LM and NTLM version 1? If so, you need to find out what operating system the user is trying to run and try to identify the change as a potential cause of the problem.

There are some other well-known problems regarding incompatibility with NTLM version 2. This list will probably grow over time as more administrators try to tighten security and disable the less secure LM and NTLM version 1.

- Keep passwords to 14 characters or fewer. Otherwise, problems can arise when logging on from Windows 95, Windows 98, and Windows NT 4 systems.

- Remote Installation Services (RIS) servers can exhibit problems with NTLM2 and may require NTLM1.

- Windows 2000 clusters do not respond properly using NTLM2; they need NTLM1 or LM.

Configuring Authentication Protocols to Support Mixed Windows Client-Computer Environments

As we just mentioned, only two protocols are available when logging on to the domain. You can use Kerberos if you have an Active Directory domain environment, or you can use NTLM. As we discussed, only Windows 2000, Windows Server 2003, and Windows XP Professional can use Kerberos. Even if you are using only Windows 2000, Windows Server 2003, and Windows XP Professional, you need to use NTLM to avoid significant problems such as with clustering and RIS. As with any change, test it to the best of your abilities and recognize that even with testing, you might not find a problem that surfaces when the change is made in production.

NTLM version 1 really was not that much of a security concern when it was initially implemented, but when computer hardware and software improvements made it easy to break NTLM version 1, it became a concern for many in the industry. Microsoft released NTLM version 2 with Windows NT 4 Service Pack 4, and it is a considerable improvement in security over version 1.

In Exercise 7.1, you set the Group Policy Object on the domain to enforce the LAN Manager authentication level. Setting this option determines which NTLM authentication protocol is used for network logons for connections to Windows 2000, Windows Server 2003, and Windows XP Professional systems. Because Group Policies do not apply to down-level clients, they take some additional work. Remember that Windows 2000, Windows Server 2003, and Windows XP Professional use Kerberos if it is available and use NTLM only if Kerberos is not available or if you log in to the local computer. Setting the option will affect the version of NTLM authentication used by clients, the level of security negotiated, and the authentication levels accepted by servers. The following options are available, from the lowest to the most secure:

Send LM & NTLM Responses   Clients will use LM and NTLM version 1 authentication and will never use NTLM version 2 session security. Domain controllers will accept LM, NTLM version 1, and NTLM version 2.

Send LM & NTLM   Clients will use NTLM version 2 if negotiated. Clients will use LM and NTLM authentication and will use NTLM version 2 if the server supports it. Domain controllers will accept LM, NTLM version 1, and NTLM version 2 authentication.

Send NTLM Response Only   Clients will use NTLM version 1 authentication only and will use NTLM version 2 if the server supports it. Domain controllers will accept LM, NTLM version 1, and NTLM version 2 authentication.

Send NTLM Version 2 Response Only   Clients will use NTLM version 2 authentication only and will use NTLM version 2 if the server supports it. Domain controllers will accept LM, NTLM, and NTLM version 2 authentication.

Send NTLM Version 2 Response Only\Refuse LM   Clients will use NTLM version 2 only and will use NTLM version 2 if the server supports it. Domain controllers will refuse LM and accept only NTLM version 1 and NTLM version 2 authentication.

Based on these options, you can choose the most restrictive and implement it using Group Policy Objects. However, using Send NTLM Version 2 Response Only\Refuse LM may not be the best solution, especially if you have down-level clients such as Windows 95 and Windows 98, which do not support NTLM version 2 out of the box. If you want to use NTLM version 2, you need to use software that will fully support it, and that includes all operating systems. Of course, if you need to use NTLM version 2 whenever possible but have the ability to fall back to NTLM version 1 for computers that cannot support NTLM version 2, you can get that by using the Send NTLM Response Only option. You need to weigh your security needs against the capabilities of your operating systems when making these decisions.

Configuring Authentication for Windows 95 and Windows 98 Clients

If you have down-level clients, your options are to either relax security in order to support them or to use additional software components to improve their capabilities. In the case of Windows 95 and Windows 98, you can use NTLM version 2 if you install the *Directory Services client* on each system running these older versions of Windows. In Exercise 7.2, you'll install the Directory Services client.

EXERCISE 7.2

Installing the Directory Services Client

In this exercise, you will install the Directory Services client on a Windows 98 computer and configure it to use NTLM version 2. For this exercise, you need a Windows 98 system and the Windows 2000 Server CD. This exercise assumes that Windows 98 is already installed and on the network and that the latest version of Internet Explorer is also installed. (For Windows 95, you need to follow all these steps, plus install the Distributed File System (DFS) client, WinSock 2.0 Update, and the Microsoft DUN Client 1.3.)

1. Insert the Windows 2000 CD in the drive of the Windows 98 system.

2. In Windows Explorer, navigate to the CD drive, expand the Clients folder, and then click the Win9x folder.

3. In the right pane, double-click the Dsclient file to start the Directory Services Client Setup Wizard. At the Welcome screen, click Next and then click Next again to start copying files to the hard drive.

4. When the files are copied, click Finish.

5. Click Yes to restart your computer, and the Directory Services client will finish its installation.

6. After you reboot the system, the Directory Services client is fully installed.

7. Log in to the Windows 98 computer, choose Start ➢ Run to open the Run dialog box, and in the Open box, enter **Regedit** to open the Registry Editor.

8. Expand the HKEY_LOCAL_MACHINE key, expand System, expand CurrentControlSet, and then expand Control.

9.   Expand Control and verify that the LSA key exists. If the key is missing, add the LSA key. Select Control and choose Edit ➤ New ➤ Key. Enter **LSA**.

10. Click LSA to open the LSA folder and choose Edit ➤ New ➤ DWORD Value. For the value name, enter **LMCompatibility**, and for the value, enter **3**. The result should look like this:

In Step 10, the value can be either 0 or3.

   Level 0: Send LM and NTLM Response; Never Use NTLM 2 Session security. Clients will use LM and NTLM authentication and will never use NTLM 2 session security; domain controllers accept LM, NTLM, and NTLM 2 authentication.

   Level 3: Send NTLM 2 Response Only. Clients will use NTLM 2 authentication and will use NTLM 2 session security if the server supports it; domain controllers accept LM, NTLM, and NTLM 2 authentication.

11. Close the Registry Editor.

Configuring Authentication in a Windows NT 4 Environment

Following the steps in Exercise 7.2 takes care of the NTLM version 2 concerns for Windows 95 and Windows 98 clients. However, that still leaves Windows NT 4 as a potential problem. If you have Service Pack 4 or later installed, you can use NTLM version 2. To disable LM authentication in Windows NT 4, you need to use the Registry Editor and configure the changes. You'll do so in Exercise 7.3.

You have the following options for supporting down-level clients in your networks:

- Allow LM and NTLM version 1 support to handle these older client operating systems by doing one of the following:

  - Enforcing NTLM version 2 and not allowing LM and NTLM version 1 to be used at all.

EXERCISE 7.3

Disabling LM and NTLM Version 1 Authentication in Windows NT 4

In this exercise, you will disable the LM authentication in Windows NT 4. This exercise assumes installation of Service Pack 4 or later. Service Pack 6a is highly recommended.

1. Choose Start ≻ Run to open the Run dialog box, and in the Open box, enter **RegEdt32** to open the Registry Editor.

2. Select HKEY_LOCAL_MACHINE, expand System, expand CurrentControlSet, expand Control, expand LSA, and then expand MSV1_0.

3. Choose Edit ≻ Add Value and then add the following Registry value:

    Value Name: NtlmMinClientSec

    Data Type: REG_WORD

    Value: 0x00080000

4. Close the Registry Editor.

- Choosing a configuration that will attempt to use NTLM version 2 and then fail back to support older versions.
- Make the necessary changes to your down-level clients so that they can support NTLM version 2.

The decision about how to support older operating systems without sacrificing higher levels of security can be troublesome and will always be a concern. As network administrators, you will have to explain your options, the risk associated with each option, and the potential problems with each option. Of course, your recommendations will be to have the network as secure as possible, but this will come at a cost in direct dollars for new purchases and the costs of teaching everyone how to support the new environment.

The Interoperability of Kerberos Authentication with Unix

As mentioned earlier in this chapter, Kerberos is not a new authentication protocol. It has its roots in the Unix world, where it has been proven to be secure, dependable, and scalable. In the Windows world, Kerberos was first included with Windows 2000.

Windows 2000 and Windows Server 2003 support *RFC 1510* to ensure that the Kerberos in Windows will interoperate with the Kerberos used in other operating systems that also conform to the RFC. If all the operating systems in use in an organization comply with the RFC, it is possible to have a *single sign-on* implementation for the network. In a single sign-on environment, the network user has to log in only once and can gain access to all the resources on all operating systems on the network according to the permissions that have been granted.

To achieve this single sign-on, you must make a choice. Do you configure your client operating systems to authenticate against a third-party (non-Microsoft) Kerberos implementation, or do you configure all third-party operating systems to authenticate against the Active Directory domain controllers? It is possible to configure Windows XP Professional to log in to a third-party Kerberos implementation. However, to do this, you must take the computer out of the Active Directory domain and make it a member of a workgroup. This is because a Kerberos realm is not the same thing as an Active Directory domain. Although they have many things in common, Windows 2000 Professional and Windows XP Professional clients must be configured differently to support a third-party Kerberos implementation.

On the flip side, other operating systems and their applications can authenticate against a Windows 2000 or Windows Server 2003 Kerberos implementation if they are based on the *Generic Security Service Application Program Interface (GSSAPI)*. If third-party operating systems support GSSAPI, they can obtain service tickets from an Active Directory domain.

To configure Windows XP Professional to authenticate against a third-party Kerberos implementation, you need to make some changes to the normal configuration. First, the computer has to be a member of a workgroup and cannot be a member of an Active Directory domain. Second, you have to install the proper tools on the Windows client. Third, you have to run the Kerberos command-line tool `Ksetup.exe` to establish the link between the client system and the Kerberos KDC. In Exercise 7.4, you'll make these configuration changes.

EXERCISE 7.4

Configuring Windows XP Professional to Use a Third-Party Kerberos Version 5 Implementation

In this exercise, you will install the support tools on Windows XP Professional and then run Ksetup.exe to configure Windows XP Professional to use the third-party Kerberos implementation to log in, to change passwords, and to map the user account.

1. Insert the Windows XP Professional CD-ROM. In Windows Explorer, navigate to <CD Drive Letter>:\Support\Tools and double-click Setup.exe to start the installation.

2. Verify that Ksetup.exe was installed with the rest of the support tools. It should be in the <Root Drive>:\Program Files\Support Tools folder.

3. Verify that the Windows XP Professional computer is not part of a domain. Choose Start ➢ Control Panel ➢ Performance And Maintenance ➢ System to open the System Properties dialog box. Click the Computer Name tab and then click the Change button. The screen indicates whether Windows XP Professional is part of a domain or is in a workgroup. Close all the dialog boxes. If the computer is part of a domain, remove it, and then restart the computer.

4. Choose Start ➢ Run to open the Run dialog box, and in the Open box, enter CMD to open the Command Prompt window.

5. At the command prompt, type **ksetup /addkdc** *realmname.domainname*.com *kdcservername.realmname.mydomain*.com and then press Enter to add a KDC to the Windows client. You can repeat this command if you have multiple KDCs on the network for redundancy.

6. If the realm supports the change password protocol, then using the proper servers can be configured to support changes to the password with the security dialog box when pressing Ctrl+Alt+Del on the Windows client. Type **Ksetup /addkpasswd** *realmname.domainname*.com *kpasswdservername.realmname.domainname*.com and then press Enter.

7. To log on to the computer, you need a local computer account mapped to a Kerberos account using Ksetup.exe. So, first create a local computer account on the Windows client and then at a command prompt, enter **ksetup /mapuser** *username@realmname.domainname*.com *username* and press Enter. (*username* is the name of the local account.) Without an entry, the user cannot log in on this particular computer. This is one way to prevent more than one user from using a particular computer. You can use a wildcard to map all users to the same local computer account.

8. Restart the computer so that the changes can take effect.

Because Active Directory complies with the Kerberos RFCs, it is also possible for a Unix system to use the Active Directory domain controllers as realm KDCs, using the domain name as the realm name. Kerberos is flexible in that, with proper support for the RFC, it is operating system–agnostic.

Configuring Authentication in Extranet Scenarios and with Members of Nontrusted Domains

The designers of Windows 2000 and Windows Server 2003 thought about the issues involved in extending networks to business partners; this includes both suppliers and customers. In the classic *extranet* environment, you configure your networks to allow your close partners to access your data, and they set up their networks to allow you access to their data. For example, a retailer has a close relationship with some of its suppliers. As sales increase and stock starts to dwindle, the supplier can automatically ship replacement stock based on prior agreements and save the retailer from having to place the order. At the same time, the retailer can check the shipment from the supplier to see when the order was shipped, check the quantity shipped, and find the expected arrival date. The value of extranets is clear in that increased access to data can decrease the purchase cycle time and administrative costs.

The key to making an extranet environment work is finding a way to allow outside users to access internal resources in a secure fashion. In an Active Directory domain, you need an account in your domain or in a trusted domain to apply security permissions so that the account has access to the resources it needs. You need to give an extranet user an account that lets them access your resources.

✗ Extranet users access your network in a couple of ways. You need to keep in mind that extranet users are usually members of another domain that is a nontrusted domain, and often they are also members of another company. To provide them access, normally you use one of the following methods:

- Internet web access

  - Using accounts and passwords in your network. This is done using a prompt when trying to connect to the web resources that requires logon information.

  - Using certificates that map to accounts in your network. This is done using certificate mapping, which will be discussed later in this chapter.

- VPN (virtual private network) access (covered in depth in Chapter 8, "Configuring and Troubleshooting Virtual Private Network Protocols").

- Dial-up access (covered later in this chapter)

Thankfully, Active Directory can use these methods and support authentication protocols to prove the identity of external users as they enter your network. For example, you can authenticate external users over the Internet by using standard X.509 certificates. You can then map these certificates to user accounts and assign permissions to resources to these user accounts. You can also use a web front end for the external user so they can perform the tasks needed through a web browser. Of course, you want to protect this web application using SSL, as shown in Figure 7.2.

In an extranet environment, you probably don't want to distribute an application to external clients and then have to worry about supporting it. This is where the web interface is extremely valuable. (The various web authentication methods are covered later in this chapter, including certificate mapping.)

In this simple example, you can provide support for extranet users using a number of authentication protocols, including Kerberos. The process involves the following steps:

1. The extranet user connects to the web server using an SSL connection and is prompted for a username and password. You can replace the username and password prompt with a certificate mechanism.

2. Internet Information Services (IIS) looks up the user account in Active Directory. If the username is found and the password is the proper one, a credentials package is put together and a Kerberos ticket (TGT) is issued to the IIS server on behalf of the user. If a certificate was used, the information in the certificate is used to map it to an account in Active Directory and a TGT is provided. At this point, Kerberos is being used to authenticate.

3. The IIS server uses the credentials of the extranet user to request access to the database server for the data requested using the web application and also for the ability to update or add new data. The IIS server passes the credentials to the database server with its requests using Kerberos.

4. The database server authenticates the user credentials provided in the Kerberos ticket and then uses the ACLs (access control lists) to decide whether to allow or deny access to the data.

In this example, it doesn't really matter whether a certificate is presented by the extranet client or whether a username and password is used, because everything then maps to an account in Active Directory, and this account is used in the ACLs on internal resources to determine whether access is allowed or denied. In either case, the logon process to the IIS server is protected using SSL, and the authentication using Kerberos is the same. As for the VPN client and the internal network client, they can access the application in the same way; however, the VPN client will be using a much smaller pipe and will have slower performance. The VPN client and the internal client can use either fat client software or the web application.

Extranets are extremely valuable to businesses, especially when they are used to access applications and other resources remotely. Whether your personnel or your partners are accessing the network, the process is similar.

Trust Relationships

Trust relationships allow Active Directory domains to add users from one domain to the ACL for a resource that exists in another domain and for these users to access resources across the trust. Within an Active Directory forest, all trust relationships are two-way transitional relationships so that each and every domain within a forest trusts the other domains and is also trusted by the other domains through these trust relationships.

FIGURE 7.2   How an extranet works

Each trust relationship uses an authentication protocol for the trust as well as for the users across the trust. Active Directory supports only two protocols for trust relationship authentication:

Kerberos The default Windows 2000, Windows Server 2003, and Windows XP Professional authentication service

NTLM The default Windows NT 4 authentication service

The oddity here is that trust relationships between Windows 2000 forests do not use Kerberos; they use NTLM. However, Windows Server 2003 can use either NTLM or Kerberos for authentication of the trust between forests. For any trusts within a forest, Kerberos is used. Kerberos is also used for external trusts is with third-party Kerberos realms. Figure 7.3 shows the trust types and the authentication protocol for each type of relationship.

Basically, each trust relationship and the authentication used for the trust depend on the two entities joined in the trust:

Intraforest These trusts are authenticated using Kerberos.

Forest-to-forest These trusts are authenticated using NTLM between Windows 2000 forests and forest to forest trusts are authenticated using NTLM or Kerberos between Windows Server 2003 forests.

Forest-to-NT 4 domain These trusts are authenticated using NTLM.

Forest-to-realm These trusts are authenticated using Kerberos.

FIGURE 7.3 Trust relationship authentication Ctrl

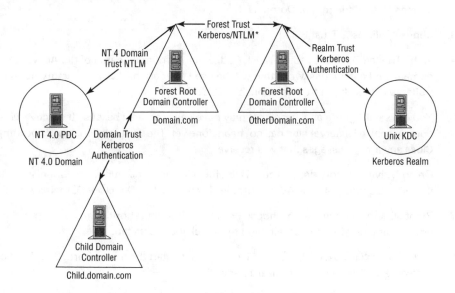

* Kerberos is used for Windows Server 2003 forests. NTLM is used for Windows 2000 forests.

At times, it is necessary to create a trust relationship between an Active Directory domain and a Windows NT 4 domain. Active Directory lets you configure a one-way trust in either direction. These one-way non-transitive trusts can be helpful when used to connect small domains such as domains in screened subnets and domains used to house specialized systems like manufacturing execution systems (MESs) that manage production lines. You can configure one-way trusts between domains. A one-way trust from the screened subnet domain or the MES domain allows accounts on the internal domain to be trusted by these other domains' external domain, but does not allow these external domain accounts to be trusted by the Active Directory domain. Exercise 7.5 demonstrates how to set up these one-way trusts.

EXERCISE 7.5

Creating a One-Way Trust: A Windows NT 4 Domain Trusts an Active Directory Domain

In this exercise, you will create a one-way trust between a Windows Server 2003 Active Directory domain and a Windows NT 4 domain:

1. Before configuring these trusts, make sure that the Windows Server 2003 Active Directory domain controllers and the Windows NT 4 domain controllers are registered in DNS and in WINS (Windows Internet Naming Service).

2. On the Windows NT 4 primary domain controller (PDC), log in as an administrator equivalent and choose Start ➤ Programs ➤ Administrative Tools ➤ User Manager For Domains to open User Manager For Domains.

3. Choose Policies ➤ Trust Relationships.

4. In the Trusted Domains section, click Add, enter the domain name of the Active Directory domain, and enter a password that will be used later on the Active Directory domain controller to establish the trust relationship. Click OK.

5. You can safely ignore any errors that may have been received because the Active Directory domain controller server side has not been done yet. The trust relationship is not complete. Close any error messages that you receive.

6. On an Active Directory domain controller, log in using an account with administrative privileges, and choose Start ➤ Administrative Tools ➤ Active Directory Domains And Trusts.

7. Right-click the domain name, choose Properties from the shortcut menu to open the Properties dialog box for the domain, and then click the Trusts tab.

8. In the Properties box, click the New Trust button to start the trust wizard. Click Next on the Welcome To The New Trust Wizard page.

9. Enter the NetBIOS name of the Windows NT 4 domain. Click Next.

EXERCISE 7.5 *(continued)*

10. Select the One-Way: Incoming Trust direction. Click Next.

11. On the Sides Of Trust page, select This Domain Only. Click Next.

12. On the Trust Password page, enter and confirm the password from Step 4. Click Next.

13. Click Next on the Trust Selections Complete page of the wizard. Click Next again.

14. On the Confirm Incoming Trust page, select the radio button to confirm the trust, enter the proper account information, and click Next.

15. Click Finish on the Completing The New Trust page to close the wizard.

16. When you receive a message verifying that the trust has been verified, click OK and close the remaining dialog boxes.

One of the keys to establishing and maintaining trusts between Windows NT 4 domains and Active Directory domains is that all the domain controllers need to be registered in WINS or the Windows NT 4 domain controllers will fail to find the Active Directory domain controllers.

Configuring and Troubleshooting Authentication for Web Users

So far, we've talked about authentication only for LANs and intranets/extranets, but eventually you'll need to configure your network for authenticating web users using the Internet. IIS supports several authentication protocols. Each protocol provides a method for a user to authenticate their identity or account to the web server using a web browser. Once they establish their identity, the account associated with that identity is used to identify the permissions to access resources such as files and web content in the case of a web server.

The following protocols are available using IIS 6 on Windows Server 2003 servers:

- Anonymous
- Basic
- Digest
- Integrated Windows
- Passport
- Certificate

The same protocols are available when using IIS 5 on Windows 2000 servers, with the exception of Passport authentication.

Web authentication involves communications between the web browser and the web server. Normal web authentication occurs upon failure of Anonymous authentication. If the site does not support anonymous access, or if the content is protected with NTFS (New Technology File System) permissions that do not include Anonymous permissions, the web server sends an error message to the web browser specifying the type of protocol to use to authenticate. For example, when Basic authentication is used, a logon dialog box pops up, asking for the username and password in most web browsers, and the browser reissues the request with the new identity information.

Each authentication protocol has different configuration requirements and has varying degrees of compatibility and security. Some of the protocols have different system requirements as well. We'll look at each one in some detail.

Anonymous Authentication

Web authentication takes place when the browser tries to access web server content. If *Anonymous authentication* is enabled and the proper file permissions are in place, all connections are allowed. This is the most common setting for web servers; after all, can you imagine having to log in on every website that you visit? That would drive everyone over the edge. So if you want others to have access to web servers that host public information, always configure those servers to use Anonymous authentication.

If you configure IIS to allow anonymous access, IIS maps all anonymous users to the account defined as the guest account for IIS. By default, this account is named IUSR_*computername* (*computername* is the name of your IIS server). The IUSR_*computername* account is created during the installation of IIS and will have logon locally user rights on the server. Without logon locally user rights, the users of the web server will not be able to connect. You can use this IUSR account to secure the web server files and restrict anonymous users to just the content that you want to make available. This IUSR account can be excluded from other files on the web server to secure them. In the event that you have content for anonymous users and content that should be restricted, you can run all this content off the same server by securing the restricted content using file and folder NTFS permissions. IIS will try anonymous authentication first; however, it will use other authentication protocols if access is restricted beyond anonymous users. If other protocols have not been configured or if the user does not have proper access to the content, IIS will send the user an "HTTP 403 Access Denied" error message.

The IUSR_*computername* account is created with a randomly generated password. Microsoft recommends that an administrator change this password using password standards for the organization so that the account can be used for troubleshooting permissions of content if needed. You reset the password in the Active Directory Users And Computers console and then change it on the Master Properties of the Internet Service Manager for each instance of IIS. The IUSR_*computername* account must be a valid user account accessible by the IIS server, but it does not have to be a local computer account. Many organizations change the accounts used for anonymous IIS access for all servers to one centralized account that can be used for all IIS servers to ease ACL administration and make auditing easier as well.

In Exercise 7.6, you'll configure a website for anonymous access.

EXERCISE 7.6

Configuring Anonymous Authentication in IIS 6

In this exercise, you will configure an IIS 6 web server to use Anonymous authentication:

1. On the IIS server, choose Start ➤ Administrative Tools ➤ Internet Information Services (IIS) Manager to open Internet Services Manager.

2. Expand Server to expose the sites, if necessary, and then right-click any site on which you want to use Anonymous authentication. For example, the Default Web Site will work just fine. Right-click the site and then choose Properties from the shortcut menu to open the Properties dialog box for the site.

3. Click the Directory Security tab.

4. In the Anonymous Access and Authentication Control section, click Edit to open the Authentication Methods dialog box.

---

5. Be sure that the Anonymous Access check box is selected and click OK to close the Authentication Methods dialog box.

6. Click OK to close the Web Site Properties dialog box and then close the Internet Information Services (IIS) Manager.

You can combine Anonymous authentication with other authentication protocols. In the event that Anonymous authentication is enabled along with other methods, the browser will always try Anonymous first. If the content does not allow anonymous access or if the content is protected using NTFS file and folder permission that require user identification, Anonymous will fail back to another method of authentication and allow the user to still access the content if they have the proper permissions.

Basic Authentication

Basic authentication is supported by most browsers and most web servers in order to comply with HTTP specifications. When Basic authentication is implemented, IIS prompts users for a valid account and password that is then used to authenticate the user and to set file security so that the user is allowed to access data only according to permissions.

A major security risk is associated with using Basic authentication: the logon information passes unencrypted. This information is sent using Base64 encoding, which is easy to decode and reveals the logon information from the captured packets. Because the logon information is not secured and can be easily captured, few organizations use Basic authentication by itself. To provide the necessary security, most organizations combine Basic authentication with SSL so that the logon information cannot be captured. This is both a secure solution and a highly compatible solution, because both technologies are Internet standards and are supported by most browsers.

In Exercise 7.7, you will enable Basic authentication.

EXERCISE 7.7

Enabling Basic Authentication in IIS 6

In this exercise, you will configure an IIS 6 web server to use Basic authentication:

1. On the IIS server, choose Start ➢ Administrative Tools ➢ Internet Information Services (IIS) Manager to open the Internet Services Manager.

2. Expand the server to expose the sites, if necessary, and then right-click any site on which you want to set Basic authentication. For example, the Default Web Site will work just fine. Right-click the site and then choose Properties from the shortcut menu to open the Properties dialog box for the site.

3. Click the Directory Security tab.

4. In the Anonymous Access and Authentication Control section, click Edit to open the Authentication Methods dialog box.

5. Select the Basic Authentication (Password Is Sent In Clear Text) check box. A warning box should appear stating that using Basic authentication will cause passwords to be transmitted without encryption. Click Yes to confirm that you are aware of this.

6. In the Authenticated Access section, enter the domain information for the Default Domain and the Realm boxes.

7. Click OK to close the Authentication Methods dialog box and then click OK again to close the Web Site Properties dialog box. If you see an Inheritance Overrides dialog box, click Select All and then click OK.

8. Close the Internet Information Services (IIS) Manager.

It is vital that you remember that Basic authentication is susceptible to intruders that can capture packets and then use Base64 decoding to gather logon information. Basic authentication is not secure, so when using it, be sure to protect the site using SSL. You need to use SSL on more than just the initial logon page because every object request that is protected with NTFS permissions will cause the logon information to be re-sent to the server. To properly protect the password, the entire session needs to be protected using SSL.

Configuring Basic authentication does not automatically configure the IIS server so that it authenticates users. The user accounts must be available, and the file and folder permissions must be set on the content. If the content does not restrict access for anonymous users and you have both Anonymous and Basic authentication configured, users can access the content without having to authenticate using Basic authentication. It is a good idea to set up a network sniffer or to use Network Monitor to monitor the network traffic and verify that the logon information is not going in and out without being encrypted.

Digest Authentication

Digest authentication is new to IIS starting with version 5. Digest authentication is similar to Basic authentication except that instead of using Base64 encoding, the credentials are hashed. This hash is known as a message digest, and it is then encrypted. It is secure in that it is encrypted, and it has protection against replay attacks.

Digest authentication works through both proxy servers and firewalls, but it requires the following:

- HTTP 1.1 support. Any browsers that do not support HTTP 1.1 will be denied access.

- Internet Explorer 5 or later.

- The web server must be an Active Directory domain member with access to Active Directory.

- Active Directory must be configured for Digest authentication.

Digest authentication does not work the same way as Basic authentication. In Digest authentication, the browser tries to access the content using Anonymous authentication. When anonymous access fails because either the content is protected with NTFS permissions that will not let the IUSR_*computername* account access the content or the site does not allow anonymous authentication, then the following steps occur:

1. The IIS server sends a response to the web browser indicating the authentication method to be used.

2. The browser takes the username, password, and some additional information and creates a hash. The additional information is sequencing information to prevent replay attacks.

3. The browser sends the hash to the web server.

4. The web server performs the same hashing operation by using the plain text password information found in Active Directory. (You need to set up reversible encryption for all accounts that will be using Digest authentication.)

5. If the hashes are equal, access is allowed to the content.

The hash is extremely secure because it is not based on information that can be guessed and brute force attacked. With the combination of the account, password, and the sequencing information, the hash is extremely difficult to break.

In Exercise 7.8, you will enable Digest authentication.

EXERCISE 7.8

Enabling Digest Authentication in IIS 6

In this exercise, you will configure an IIS 6 web server to use Digest authentication. First, though, you must configure Active Directory to support Digest authentication, and then you need to configure the IIS 6 website:

1. Choose Start ➢ Administrative Tools ➢ Active Directory Users And Computers to open Active Directory Users And Computers.

2. Double-click the account that you want to use with Digest authentication and then click the Account tab.

3. In the Account Options section, select the Store Password Using Reversible Encryption check box and click OK.

4. You must reset the password after enabling Reversible Encryption for it to take effect. Right-click the account and choose Reset Password from the shortcut menu.

5. Enter a new password and click OK.

After you configure all the accounts to support Reversible Encryption, you must configure IIS 6 to support Digest authentication:

6. On the IIS server, choose Start ➢ Administrative Tools ➢ Internet Information Services (IIS) Manager to open the Internet Information Services (IIS) Manager.

7. Expand the server to expose the sites, if necessary, and right-click any site on which you want to set Digest authentication. For example, the Default Web Site will work just fine. Right-click the site and choose Properties from the shortcut menu to open the Properties dialog box for the site.

8. Click the Directory Security tab, and in the Anonymous Access and Authentication Control section, click Edit to open the Authentication Methods dialog box.

9. Select the Digest Authentication For Windows Domain Servers check box. A warning box should appear, stating that Digest authentication requires storing passwords in clear text within Active Directory. Click Yes to continue. Enter the Realm information.

10. Click OK to close the Authentication Methods dialog box and then click OK to close the Web Site Properties dialog box. If you see an Inheritance Overrides dialog box, click Select All and then click OK.

11. Close the Internet Information Services (IIS) Manager.

Once Reversible Encryption is enabled and the password is reset, the new password is stored in Active Directory using clear text.

When troubleshooting Digest authentication, check for the following:

- Is IIS a member of an Active Directory domain?
- Is Reversible Encryption enabled for the account?
- Has the account password been reset since Reversible Encryption was enabled?
- Is IIS also using other authentication methods instead of Digest authentication?
- Is the web browser Internet Explorer 5 or later?

Remember, Digest authentication works only if the domain server for which a request is made has a plain text copy of the requesting user's password. This is a security risk in itself, because now that all domain controllers have plain text copies of passwords, they need to be secured from a variety of both physical and network attacks. Refer to the Resource Kit for information on how to properly secure an Active Directory domain controller.

Integrated Windows Authentication

Integrated Windows authentication is also known as Windows NT Challenge/Response and NTLM. Integrated Windows authentication is fairly secure, because it does not ever transmit actual passwords. Integrated Windows authentication uses either Kerberos or NTLM authentication protocols. Although Kerberos is considered secure, NTLM is no longer considered as secure as it used to be, because in the last few years it has become more feasible to break the encryption using better software and faster processors.

Integrated Windows authentication enables the browser to use the current logon information to access secured data. If the user is already logged in to the network with a valid username and password and tries to access web content that is secured using NTFS permissions, the browser can pass the logon information behind the scenes and authenticate the user without using any prompts for logon information. If the user has not logged on already, they are prompted for the logon information. When Integrated Windows authentication is used, a request for secured web content is handled as follows:

1. Anonymous access is attempted and fails, because the content is either secured with NTFS permissions that do not allow anonymous access or the website is not configured to allow anonymous access.

2. The web server sends a response to the browser notifying it of the authentication protocols it supports.

3. The browser automatically supplies the logon information if the user has logged on to the network. If the user has not logged on to the network, the browser prompts the user for the logon information.

4. With the proper credentials supplied, access is granted.

The only issue with Integrated Windows authentication is whether it is using Kerberos or NTLM. Kerberos is used if all the following conditions are met:

- The client is running Windows 2000 or later.

- The client is running Internet Explorer 5 or later.

- The server is running IIS 5 or later.

- The client and the server are in the same Active Directory domain or are in trusted domains.

- The server name matches the website name, or the server has the Server Principal Name set to be equal to the site name.

 You can set the Server Principal Name using the SetSPN tool in the Resource Kit.

If any of these conditions cannot be met, Windows Integrated authentication will use NTLM. In Exercise 7.9, you will enable Integrated Windows authentication.

EXERCISE 7.9

Enabling Integrated Windows Authentication in IIS 6

In this exercise, you will configure an IIS 6 web server to use Integrated Windows authentication:

1. On the IIS server, choose Start ≻ Administrative Tools ≻ Internet Services Manager to open the Internet Services Manager.

2. Expand Server to expose the sites, if necessary, and right-click any site on which you want to set Integrated Windows authentication. For example, the Default Web Site will work just fine. Right-click the site and choose Properties from the shortcut menu to open the Properties dialog box for the site.

3. Click the Directory Security tab.

4. In the Anonymous Access and Authentication Control section, click Edit to open the Authentication Methods dialog box.

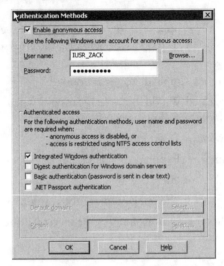

5. Choose the Integrated Windows Authentication check box.

6. Click OK to close the Authentication Methods dialog box and then click OK to close the Web Site Properties dialog box. If you see an Inheritance Overrides dialog box, click Select All and then click OK.

7. Close the Internet Services Manager.

You need to remember the following when working with Integrated Windows authentication:

- It does not work across CERN-compliant proxy servers.

- It does not work with some firewall applications, but will work with others such as Microsoft's ISA (Internet Security and Acceleration).

- It requires Internet Explorer 2 or later.

Passport Authentication

Passport authentication is a significant step for IIS 6 administration. Microsoft Passport provides another authentication method for IIS. However, with Passport, the administrators of the website do not have to maintain account information, and the users of the website do not have to remember a specific account name and password for the site. It is convenient for both the web administrator and the user. While there is increased convenience, there is also increased risk because web administrators need to trust Microsoft to protect the account data in Passport.

The basic steps for Passport authentication are as follows:

1. The user enters the Passport-authenticated site.

2. The Passport-authenticated site detects that the HTTP request is coming from a non-authenticated user. The web server sends a Passport Sign-In button to the user.

3. The user clicks the sign-in button, which creates an authentication request that is sent from the user to the Passport-authenticated site.

4. The web server forwards the authentication request to the Microsoft Passport servers.

5. The Microsoft Passport server sends the user a web page that includes username and password fields.

6. The user enters their logon information into the username and password fields and clicks the sign-in button. Clicking the sign-in button generates an authentication request to the Passport server, and it is provided the username and password entered by the user.

7. The Passport server authenticates the username and password.

8. If the user is successfully authenticated, the user is redirected to the original Passport-authenticated site.

9. The web server provides access according to the user authentication.

Configuring Passport requires that you first set up a Passport account. Once you have a Passport account, you can register your website with Microsoft's Passport Server at www.netservicesmanager.com. Once you connect to this site, you need to sign in using your Passport. The general steps for implementing .NET Passport authentication are included in Exercise 7.10.

EXERCISE 7.10

Implementing Passport Authentication

In this exercise, you will configure your web server to accept Passport authentication sign-up, and then you will create an application with Microsoft's Passport service. Configure IIS 6 to accept Passport authentication using the following steps:

1. On the IIS server, choose Start ➤ Administrative Tools ➤ Internet Services Manager to open the Internet Services Manager.

2. Expand Server to expose the sites, if necessary, and right-click any site on which you want to set Integrated Windows authentication. For example, the Default Web Site will work just fine. Right-click the site and choose Properties from the shortcut menu to open the Properties dialog box for the site.

3. Click the Directory Security tab.

4. In the Anonymous Access and Authentication Control section, click Edit to open the Authentication Methods dialog box.

5. Select the .NET Passport Authentication check box. Using the Select button, select the Default domain.

6. Click OK to close the Authentication Methods dialog box and then click OK to close the Web Site Properties dialog box.

7. Close the Internet Services Manager.

Once you have created your content and configured the website to use Passport authentication, you need to create the application at Microsoft's Passport site using the following steps:

8. Open a web browser and connect to www.netservicesmanager.com.

9. After signing in, click Create and Manage An Application. This link opens a licensing agreement; click Accept Terms after reading the agreement. Rejecting the terms means that you will not be able to use Passport for your website or application.

10. You are then required to update your Passport user information. Click the Submit button to continue.

11. Click Create Application.

12. Provide the name for your application and click Submit.

13. On the Manage Applications page, click the Add Service link.

14. You will see three selections:

    The .NET Passport

    The Kids Passport

    Microsoft Alerts

    Selecting Kids Passport enables both the standard .NET Passport and the Kids Passport. Select .NET Passport and click Next.

15. Enter the information for your website, including the title, domain name, default return URL, customer support info, and the Privacy Policy URL. Click Next.

16. Enter your cobranding information. Click Next.

17. Enter the Other .NET Passport Information and click Next.

18. Enter the .NET Passport Single Sign-in Information. Click Next.

Once the information has been submitted, Microsoft runs a compliance review to verify that your site is up and available and that all the information you entered is valid.

Passport authentication is new to IIS 6 and was not available to the general public prior to the release of IIS 6. In most cases, other authentication methods will meet the needs for your website. However, you may run into a need for .NET Passport authentication for a commercial application or internal application.

Authenticating with Client Certificate Mapping

Client certificate mapping is the process of mapping certificates on client computers to Active Directory accounts. Certificates are used in many applications, including data encryption, signing of data, and providing authentication. A certificate includes an encrypted set of authentication credentials, which includes the digital signature from the issuing certificate authority (CA). As you saw in Chapter 6, "Deploying, Managing, and Configuring SSL Certificates," the process of obtaining a certificate from a certificate authority is a process of identification authentication, so it makes sense that you can use certificates to prove your identity and authenticate for network resources.

Using certificates for authentication requires that the client computer present its certificate to the server and that the server present its certificate to the client computer for mutual authentication. The client stores its certificate on the local computer, and the browser can access the certificate when requested by the server.

On the server, client certificates are mapped to user accounts in Active Directory. These accounts can then be used and applied in ACLs on web server content. With a mapped account and a local certificate, the web browser can attach to the web server and request secured content without having to log in. All the authentication can take place behind the scenes, and the data can be downloaded without having to supply logon information like other authentication protocols. These certificate mappings can be one certificate to one Active Directory user account or multiple certificates to one Active Directory user account.

To use certificates for extranet users, you need to configure a certificate authority, which is covered in depth in Chapter 9, "Installing, Configuring, and Managing Certificate Authorities," and then you need to obtain certificates for each client from the certificate authority. Each extranet user must request and install a certificate from the CA into their browsers. After each extranet user has a certificate installed, that certificate can be used to authenticate against an IIS server once the certificates have been mapped to an account or multiple accounts. In Exercise 7.11, you will configure certificate mapping.

EXERCISE 7.11

Configuring Certificate Mapping

In this exercise, you will obtain a certificate from a local certificate authority and then map that certificate in IIS to a user account in Active Directory:

1. Log in to the client computer that will be used to connect to the IIS 6 server. In the browser, enter the URL for the local CA, for example, **http://*servername*/certsrv**.

2. Click the Request A Certificate link.

3. Click Advanced Certificate Request.

4. Click Create And Submit A Certificate Request To This CA to open the Certificate Template screen.

5. From the drop-down list box, select User, set the key size to 1024, and then click Submit.

6. Depending on how security is set on your browser, you may see a Potential Scripting Violation warning message. If so, click Yes to proceed. If not, proceed to Step 7.

7. You will see a message asking you to wait for the server to process the request, and then the certificate will be issued.

8. Click Install This Certificate to install the certificate on the local computer.

9. You should then see a message that your new certificate has been successfully installed. Close the web browser window.

Now that you have installed the certificate on the local computer, you need to configure mapping for the certificate:

10. On the certificate authority server, choose Start ➢ Administrative Tools ➢ Certificate Authority to open the Certificate Authority console.

11. Expand the left pane so that you can select Issued Certificates.

12. In the right pane, right-click the certificate that you just requested and installed on the client computer and choose Open from the shortcut menu to open the dialog box.

13. Click the Details tab and then click the Copy To File button to start the Certificate Export Wizard.

14. At the Welcome screen, click Next and select the Base-64 Encoded X.509 (.CER) radio button.

15. Enter the filename under which you want to save the exported certificate. This should be a shared file location accessible from the web server. Click Next and then click Finish.

16. Click OK in the Success Notification window, click OK in the Certificate window, and close the Certificate Authority console.

Now that the certificate has been exported, you can map it to a user in the Internet Services Manager console:

17. On the IIS server, choose Start ➢ Administrative Tools ➢ Internet Information Services (IIS) Manager to open the Internet Information Services (IIS) Manager.

18. Expand Server to expose the sites, if necessary, right-click the site that you want to configure to accept certificates, and choose Properties from the shortcut menu to open the Properties dialog box for the site.

19. Click the Directory Security tab and then click the Edit button in the Secure Communications section to open the Secure Communications dialog box.

20. Click the Accept Client Certificates radio button, click Enable Client Certificate Mapping,
and then click the Edit button to open the dialog box.

21. Click the 1-To-1 tab and then click Add to create the account mapping.

22. Navigate to the shared file location where you exported the certificate in Step 15 and click
Open to open the Map To Account dialog box.

23. Verify that the Enable This Mapping check box is selected and in the Map Name box, enter
a name for the mapping that will be easy to remember. In the Account box, enter the
account name or browse for it. In the Password box, enter the password for the account to
be mapped. Click OK to close the Map To Account dialog box.

24. Click OK again to close the Account Mapping dialog box. Click OK to close the Secure Communications window. Click OK to close the Properties dialog box for the website. (If necessary, accept Inheritance Overrides and click OK.)

25. In the left pane of Internet Information Services (IIS) Manager, right-click the server name and choose Restart IIS from the shortcut menu.

26. When the restart is finished, close the Internet Information Services console.

Using certificate mapping, you can extend your networks to enhance the relationships between customers, suppliers, and other business partners. Not only can you extend the network, but you can do so securely using extranet technologies. Stronger ties with those in your business world will result in better service to your customers and more efficient business practices. It just makes good sense all around. Of course, you need to be careful to weigh these added benefits against the added costs of deploying and maintaining this technology.

Configuring and Troubleshooting Authentication for Secure Remote Access

Remote access is one way to allow external users to access the internal network of the organization. We need to stress how important it is that you use proper authentication protocols for these connections. By proper, we mean that they should be secure. Remote access will be covered in more depth in Chapter 8 as we discuss virtual private networks. This section looks at how Remote Access authentication works and the protocols that you can use.

The scenario is simple: Your client computer dials a Routing and Remote Access Services (RRAS) server to connect to the organization's network. You use one of the following authentication protocols:

- *Password Authentication Protocol (PAP)*
- *Challenge Handshake Authentication Protocol (CHAP)*
- *Microsoft Challenge Handshake Authentication Protocol (MS-CHAP)*
- *Microsoft Challenge Handshake Authentication Protocol version 2 (MS-CHAPv2)*
- *Extensible Authentication Protocol Message Digest 5 (EAP-MD5)*
- *Extensible Authentication Protocol-Transport Layer Security (EAP-TLS)*

You can select which protocols you want to use by configuring RRAS appropriately, as in Exercise 7.12.

Configuring RRAS Authentication Protocols

In this exercise, you will configure RRAS authentication protocols on a server.

1. On the RRAS server, choose Start ➤ Administrative Tools ➤ Routing And Remote Access to start the RRAS console.

2. Right-click the server name and choose Properties to open the Properties dialog box for the server.

3. Click the Security tab and then click the Authentication Methods button to open the Authentication Methods dialog box.

4. Select the authentication protocols to be used by checking the box next to each one that you want to configure.

5. Click OK to close the Authentication Methods dialog box and then click OK again to close the Properties dialog box for the server.

6. Close the Routing and Remote Access console.

As you can see from the exercise, you can choose from several authentication protocols. By default, Windows 2000 enables MS-CHAP and MS-CHAPv2 while Windows Server 2003 also supports EAP by default. However, there are other options to consider. Some of them will be required, depending on your environment:

PAP   If you select Password Authentication Protocol (PAP), the client computer sends the logon information in clear text. The server then authenticates the client access against the information in Active Directory. This is the least secure of all the authentication protocols and is typically used only when compatibility with a large number of clients is required. Don't use PAP unless it is not possible to use a more secure authentication method, because the client cannot support it.

CHAP If you select Challenge Handshake Authentication Protocol (CHAP), the RRAS server sends a challenge to the client computer. This challenge contains session identifier information as well as an arbitrary string. The client computer sends an encrypted reply using a Message Digest 5 hash of the arbitrary string, plus the session identifier and the logon information. The server then compares the hash received by the client with the hash that it builds using the same information to see if it is valid. If the hashes are equal, the logon is considered authenticated.

CHAP is considerably more secure than PAP, because it does not send the actual password information to the server; it just proves that it knows the password by creating the hash for the server to compare to its hash. CHAP is an industry standard and is compatible with almost all third-party remote access devices.

 PAP and CHAP cannot be used if data encryption is required for dial-up or PPTP (Point-to-Point Tunneling Protocol) connections.

MS-CHAP Microsoft Challenge Handshake Authentication Protocol (MS-CHAP) is similar to CHAP, but it has been extended or enhanced by Microsoft. Just like CHAP, MS-CHAP uses a challenge-response process. The difference between the two is that MS-CHAP uses Microsoft Point-to-Point Encryption (MPPE) instead of Message Digest 5.

MS-CHAP works with all versions of Windows starting with Windows 95, but it is not compatible with many non-Microsoft remote access devices. It is installed by default as an authentication method for RRAS.

 To use MS-CHAP for Windows 95, Dial-Up Networking (DUN) version 1.3 is required.

MS-CHAPv2 Version 2 of MS-CHAP offers improvements in security. MS-CHAPv2 provides for mutual authentication, not just one way like MS-CHAP, and it provides strong encryption. Windows Server 2003 uses EAP, MS-CHAPv2, and MS-CHAP for authentication. Windows Server 2003 will attempt to use the strongest method first. Windows 2000 and Windows XP Professional use MS-CHAPv2 for both dial-up networking and VPN connections. Windows NT 4 and Windows 98 can only use MS-CHAPv2 for VPN connections. The backward compatibility is a problem if working with older client operating systems, and there is little compatibility with third-party remote access devices.

Windows 2000 uses MS-CHAPv2 as one of its default RRAS authentication protocols along with MS-CHAP. To try to improve on the security, though, Windows 2000 will try to negotiate with MS-CHAPv2 before it tries MS-CHAP so that version 2 is used whenever possible.

EAP-MD5 EAP-MD5 is an extension to the Point-to-Point Protocol (PPP). The Message Digest 5 challenge is the same type as used in CHAP, but the messages are sent using EAP, so they are even more secure.

EAP provides support for many authentication methods that might be added by third parties in the future—smart cards, token cards, one-time passwords, certificates, and biometric devices, among others. EAP offers stronger authentication methods that provide greater protection than other password-based authentication protocols against password attacks such as brute-force attacks and dictionary attacks.

In Exercise 7.13, you will enable EAP on RRAS.

EXERCISE 7.13

Enabling EAP on RRAS

In this exercise, you will enable EAP for a RRAS server and view the EAP types supported:

1. On the RRAS server, choose Start ➤ Administrative Tools ➤ Routing and Remote Access to open the Routing and Remote Access console.

2. Right-click the server name and choose Properties from the shortcut menu to open the Properties dialog box for the server.

3. Click the Security tab and then click the Authentication Methods button to open the Authentication Methods dialog box.

4. Select the Extensible Authentication Protocol (EAP) check box and click the EAP Methods button to open the EAP Methods dialog box.

Notice that the EAP methods installed are the default methods as shown here, but you can add more using third-party plug-ins to support other EAP types in the future.

EAP-TLS EAP-TLS is used for certificate-based security. When using smart cards, for example, you must use EAP-TLS authentication to support the certificate stored on the smart card. EAP-TLS authentication provides for mutual authentication of the client to the server and the server to the client. During authentication, the client computer sends its user certificate and the server sends its computer certificate. If either computer certificate is not valid, not trusted by the other computer, or expired, the authentication fails and the connection is dropped.

EAP-TLS is extremely secure because it also provides for the negotiation of the encryption method. EAP-TLS provides the strongest authentication available at this time.

EAP-TLS is supported only on Windows 2000 and Windows Server 2003 servers running RRAS that are configured to use Windows authentication and are Active Directory domain members. EAP-TLS is not supported on stand-alone servers running RRAS. A remote access server running as a stand-alone server or a member of a workgroup does not support EAP-TLS.

Multifactor Authentication with Smart Cards and EAP

The key to accessing the network is having the proper username and password combination. This is known as single-factor authentication. Anyone who happens to have your username and password, or can guess it, can easily pretend that they are you on the network. The password alone is not enough to properly secure the network and to authenticate a user with extremely high levels of confidence.

A two-factor system is a great improvement over a one-factor system. The automated teller machine (ATM) is a good example of the two-factor system. You need the ATM card with the account information on it, and you also need a personal identification number (PIN). One item is not enough. You need both to access the ATM and withdraw money from it. Of course, the weakness of a two-factor system such as the ATM card is that if you lose the card, you cannot withdraw money, and to get a replacement card is not an easy process because the old one has to be canceled and a new one created. The lost time is a major cost for many organizations.

In Windows 2000 and Windows Server 2003 networks, you can use a number of multifactor systems:

Smart cards   A smart card is a card that can store data—usually a certificate—for identification purposes. Smart cards can provide two-factor authentication by using a PIN in combination with the card.

Tokens   RSA security has the best-known token system. A small device carried by the user generates special codes that must be entered during logon along with the user name. This is also an example of two-factor authentication.

Biometric devices   Some common biometric devices are fingerprint scanners and retinal scanners. These devices are fairly expensive compared to other multifactor devices, and other issues can render them worthless such as a badly burned finger or an eye patch after getting poked with a sharp stick while doing yard work.

Generally, smart cards are the best solution for multifactor authentication. With a smart card and the PIN for the card, multiple factors must be met to prove identity to the network. Smart cards happen to have other advantages such as the ability to provide mutual authentication with the domain controller and to provide encryption keys to protect the logon information. Smart cards can be configured so that they not only require a PIN, but they also require a username and password logon as well.

Windows 2000 and Windows Server 2003, along with EAP, allow for multifactor authentication systems to be used to increase security. Soon multifactor authentication will become the industry standard, as the prices of smart cards and smart card readers come down. Not only is EAP more secure than other authentication methods because of the certificate use, but when combined with the requirement for the smart card and the PIN, the reliability of the system is much greater as well.

Summary

This chapter looked at various ways to authenticate users. We discussed the security concerns associated with some authentication methods and made some recommendations about which authentication protocols should be used and when. We discussed authentication in relationship to the following:

- Supporting older versions of Windows such as Windows NT 4 and Windows 9x clients

- Supporting Kerberos with Unix systems

- Supporting remotely located clients

- Supporting extranet environments

- Supporting web servers

- Supporting smart cards

Authentication is one of the most important concerns with security in any network. After all, without knowing for sure who is on the other side of a network connection, you cannot be sure that a user should have access to the data they are using. You need to be sure that the clients on your network belong there and did not break in, and you can help increase the security of your network by using the best authentication protocols available for the environment.

Exam Essentials

Make sure you understand the issues with older Microsoft clients such as Windows 9x and Windows NT 4. Know which authentication protocols each operating system can support and understand the benefits of the Directory Services client.

Be aware of the interoperability between Kerberos and Unix. Make sure you understand that Kerberos in Windows Server 2003 follows the RFCs and will interoperate with Unix clients and Unix servers.

Make sure that you understand the needs of most businesses to provide access to external partners.   Be aware of the tools that you need in order to provide secure authentication for those client computers.

Understand trust relationships.   Make sure you understand the authentication protocols that are used in establishing and maintaining trust relationships between Windows Server 2003 Active Directory domains and Windows NT 4 domains, as well as Unix Kerberos realms.

Make sure that you can configure authentication protocols for IIS 6 web servers.   Understand the benefits and problems with each of the following authentication protocols:

- Basic authentication
- Integrated Windows authentication
- Anonymous authentication
- Digest authentication
- Client certificate mapping

Know the authentication protocols used for secure remote access.   Make sure that you understand each of the authentication protocols used for Windows 2000 and Windows Server 2003 Routing and Remote Access Services (RRAS) servers. In particular, know when each should be used and the value of each authentication protocol, including:

- PAP
- CHAP
- MS-CHAP
- MS-CHAPv2
- EAP-MDS
- EAP-TLS

Understand multifactor authentication with smart cards and EAP.   Understand the value of multifactor authentication and the options available in Windows 2000 and Windows Server 2003 through EAP. Understand the benefits of smart cards.

Review Questions

1. Your supervisor told you to set the Default Group Policy for the domain to tighten security for LAN Manager Authentication Level to Send NTLMv2 Response Only\Refuse LM. Since making this change, Windows 98 users are unable to log in. How can you fix this problem without changing the Group Policy Object?

   A. Install the Dial-Up Network (DUN) v1.3 client on Windows 98.

   B. Install the Directory Services client and configure the Windows 98 computer's Registry to Send NTLMv2 Responses Only.

   C. Upgrade to Windows 98 Second Edition.

   D. Upgrade all Active Directory domain controllers to Windows Server 2003.

2. You implemented a peer-to-peer network in a small branch office using Windows 2000 Professional and Windows XP Professional for the client operating systems. Performing a security audit, you find that these computers are not using Kerberos. Why is Kerberos not being used?

   A. Kerberos requires an Active Directory implementation for the user to log in to.

   B. Service Pack 1 for Windows XP Professional and Service Pack 3 or later for Windows 2000 Professional are needed to support Kerberos in a peer-to-peer configuration.

   C. The local computer policies need to be configured to refuse LM, NTLMv1, and NTLMv2 in order to force Kerberos to be used.

   D. At least one Windows 2000 Professional or Windows XP Professional computer needs its KDC service set to automatic.

3. You want to implement a single sign-on solution so that all the Windows 2000 Professional and Windows XP Professional computers can access all Windows 2000, Windows Server 2003 server resources, and all Unix server resources. The Unix administrator says it is not possible. You say it is if the Unix servers and their applications support which of the following?

   A. Generic Security Service Application Program Interface (GSSAPI)

   B. Kpass.exe utility

   C. Ksetup.exe utility

   D. AddksetupAPI

4. Your co-worker changed the security requirements for all accounts so that the minimum password length is set at 15 characters. Now Windows 95 users can't log in. Why?

   A. Windows 95 computers require 7 characters or fewer for their passwords.

   B. Windows 95 computers are unable to support Group Policies.

   C. Windows 95 computers must be allowed to support passwords of all lengths and cannot be forced to use a minimum-length password.

   D. Windows 95 computers require 14 characters or fewer for their passwords.

5. You have Windows 98, Windows NT 4 Workstation, and Windows XP Professional clients. You want the Windows XP Professional computers to always use NTLMv2 only, but you still want to be able to support the other computers. What is the highest level that you can set the LAN Manager Authentication Level option in Group Policy to achieve your goals?

    A. Send LM & NTLM

    B. Send NTLM Response Only

    C. Send NTLM Version 2 Response Only

    D. Send NTLM Version 2 Response Only\Refuse LM

6. Your Unix administrator read that Windows XP Professional can be configured to use the Kerberos v5 implementation that he has for his Unix systems. He uses the `Ksetup.exe` utility to configure the KDCs in his realm and maps a local computer account to a Kerberos account in his realm. However, it doesn't work. What is the most likely reason that it is failing?

    A. The local computer account is used for more than one Kerberos mapping.

    B. Windows XP Professional clients can only use Kerberos in Active Directory domains.

    C. The Unix servers must be running Samba.

    D. The Windows XP Professional client is installed as a member of the Active Directory domain.

7. You have finally finished your migration to 100 percent Windows XP Professional client computers and 100 percent Windows Server 2003 servers and have Active Directory running in one forest. You also administer a second forest that is still running a Windows 2000 Active Directory. You set up a trust relationship between these two forests. You are preparing for a security audit by a third-party company and want to make sure that NTLM is no longer being used. Your network administrator has been capturing packets and analyzing them for you and finds that NTLM is being used, but it is only used between the domain controllers at the forest root between the two forests. How do you force the servers administering the trust relationship to use only Kerberos?

    A. Configure the LAN Manager Authentication Level option to refuse LM, NTLMv1, and NTLMv2.

    B. Make sure to physically locate a domain controller for each forest in all sites.

    C. You cannot force them to use Kerberos. Windows 2000 can only use NTLM for inter-forest trusts.

    D. Configure the routers between the two forests to filter out NTLM traffic.

8. Your public web server is configured to use Anonymous authentication. It has been working for several months. Your co-worker changed the password of the IUSR_*computername* account on the local web server, and now nobody can access the website. What is the most likely cause?

    A. The password was not synchronized with the password in the Master Properties for the web server for the IUSR_*computername* account.

    B. Somebody must have disabled Anonymous authentication.

    C. Another administrator must have added Basic authentication.

    D. Another administrator changed the NTFS permissions for the files and folders for the public website.

9. Your co-worker has enabled Basic authentication in order to allow users to access restricted content using their username and password for the domain. Users are prompted for their username and password, but it does not seem to work. What is the most likely cause?

   A. Basic authentication does not work unless it is combined with SSL.

   B. The option to set the domain name for Basic authentication was not used, and the logons fail because they need to be formatted with *domainname\username*. Users are not aware of this requirement.

   C. The SSL certificate used on the website is not a trusted certificate.

   D. Digest authentication must also be set, and it is causing a conflict.

10. Your co-worker has configured a website to use only Basic authentication and Anonymous authentication, but when testing the site, you are never prompted to enter your logon credentials. What is the most likely cause?

   A. The ACLs for the web content were not configured to restrict access to certain users and are allowing anonymous users to access the content.

   B. Digest authentication must also be set, and it is causing a conflict.

   C. Basic authentication without SSL will cause failures in most browsers.

   D. The site must also be configured with Integrated Windows authentication.

11. Your co-worker configured a website to use Digest authentication. All the users are complaining that they are not able to access the content even though they have the proper permissions. You check the ACLs on the files, and they should be able to access the content. Why is it failing?

   A. IIS 6 can use only local computer accounts for NTFS permissions.

   B. Not all the accounts were configured to enable the Store Password Using Reversible Encryption option.

   C. IIS 6 cannot use Digest authentication for external users; it works only on intranet sites.

   D. Anonymous authentication must also be set on the site, and the two methods cannot be used on the same website.

12. Your co-worker configured a website to use Digest authentication. A few of the users are complaining that they are not able to access the content even though they have the proper permissions. You check the ACLs and they should be able to access the content, and you have verified that the Store Password Using Reversible Encryption option was set and that the passwords were reset afterward. Why are some users unable to access the content?

   A. Anonymous authentication must also be set on the site, and the two methods cannot be used on the same website unless using Internet Explorer 5 or later.

   B. Users must be using a browser that does not support HTTP 1.1.

   C. The web server is a member of the Active Directory domain, and it needs to be a stand-alone web server to support Digest authentication.

   D. Their passwords must be too short. Digest authentication requires passwords of more than eight characters.

13. Your co-worker has configured a website to use Integrated Windows authentication. Users are complaining that they are unable to access it from outside the company. What is the most likely reason that they cannot access the site outside the office?

    A. The company firewall is causing Windows Integrated authentication to fail.

    B. The users are not using Internet Explorer 5 or later.

    C. The certificate mapping is not configured properly.

    D. Anonymous authentication must be set and is causing conflicts.

14. Your supervisor has requested that you come up with a solution that will enable all extranet users to access the web data on `Server1.companyname.com` from the Internet. He wants your solution to be as secure as possible but to require the minimal administration for the web administrator when setting up NTFS permissions for the content. He says that all the external users will have the same rights to content. What would you do?

    A. Configure a web-based certificate authority so that all extranet clients can get certificates, and then map all the certificates to a single account in Active Directory and use that account for the NTFS permissions.

    B. Configure the website to use Digest authentication, and make sure that all external users have the proper browsers needed to meet the requirements.

    C. Configure the website to use Integrated Windows authentication and force use of Kerberos.

    D. Configure a web-based certificate authority so that all extranet clients can get certificates, and then map all the certificates on a one-to-one basis in Active Directory and use all the accounts for the NTFS permissions.

15. Your co-worker configured a Windows Server 2003 server for Routing and Remote Access Service (RRAS) for dial-up users. Several users are complaining that they are not able to access the service, while others are not having any problems. Investigation shows that Windows 2000 Professional and Windows XP Professional systems are not having any problems, but all other Windows operating systems are unable to access the RRAS server no matter how they configure their dial-up clients. What is the most likely cause of the problems for everyone using older Windows operating systems?

    A. PAP and CHAP are both configured. Windows 9x and Windows NT 4 clients are unable to use PAP and CHAP for dial-up access; they can only use MS-CHAP.

    B. MS-CHAP is the only authentication method configured on the server. Only Windows 2000 Professional and Windows XP Professional can use MS-CHAP for dial-up access.

    C. MS-CHAPv2 is the only authentication method configured on the server. Only Windows 2000 Professional and Windows XP Professional can use MS-CHAPv2 for dial-up access.

    D. EAP has not been configured, and it is needed to properly support older Windows operating systems for dial-up access.

16. Your co-worker configured a Windows Server 2003 server for Routing and Remote Access Service (RRAS) for dial-up users. Several users are complaining that they are not able to access the service, while others are not having any problems. Investigation shows that Unix, Linux, and Macintosh users are all having problems no matter how they configure their dial-up clients. What should you do to fix the problem?

   A. Configure PAP or CHAP.

   B. Remove MS-CHAP.

   C. Remove MS-CHAPv2.

   D. Configure EAP.

17. Your supervisor has requested that you install a two-factor authentication system for remote users. What should you do?

   A. Configure thumbprint scanners on all local workstations.

   B. Implement VPNs.

   C. Remove PAP and CHAP and use only MS-CHAPv2 and EAP.

   D. Configure EAP and implement smart cards.

18. Your supervisor has asked you to implement EAP-TLS for remote network users. Your company has Windows 98, Windows NT Workstation, and Windows XP Professional installed for its remote users. What should you do?

   A. Set up a certificate authority.

   B. Work with the remote users to acquire certificates.

   C. Map the certificates to Active Directory accounts.

   D. Tell your supervisor that it is not possible.

19. Your co-worker configured a many-to-one mapping for all partners to access the extranet. One of your partners went out of business. What should you do?

   A. Create a new account for access and map all the certificates to it, except for the failed partner.

   B. Delete the account in Active Directory.

   C. Edit the certificate mapping.

   D. Change the password on the Active Directory account.

20. Your co-worker configured Integrated Windows authentication for your company's website. Some external clients are unable to log on even though they are using the correct username and password. What is the most likely reason for this failure?

   A. Integrated Windows authentication does not work for Windows $9x$ clients.

   B. Integrated Windows authentication does not work for websites.

   C. Integrated Windows authentication does not work with IE 5.5 or later.

   D. Integrated Windows authentication does not work if the remote client is behind a proxy server.

Answers to Review Questions

1. B. Installing the Directory Services client and configuring the Registry allow Windows 98 to use NTLMv2.

2. A. Kerberos requires the KDC in Active Directory. Without a KDC, Windows 2000, Windows Server 2003, and Windows XP Professional clients will fail over to NTLM.

3. A. All systems and applications supporting the GSSAPI will be able to receive tickets from the Active Directory KDC.

4. D. Windows *9x* clients support passwords of 14 characters or fewer. Longer passwords can cause logons to fail.

5. C. With this option, clients will use NTLM Version 2 authentication only, but the domain controllers will accept LM, NTLM, and NTLM Version 2 authentication. Remember that only Windows 2000, Windows Server 2003, and Windows XP Professional can apply Group Policy options.

6. D. Windows XP Professional clients must be a member of a workgroup in order to log in to a third-party Kerberos implementation.

7. C. Inter-forest trusts authenticate using NTLM only if one or both are Windows 2000.

8. A. It is important to make sure that when changing the password manually, it is also changed in the Master Properties for the web server.

9. B. Setting the default domain name for Basic authentication allows users to enter just their user-name and password.

10. A. In order for Basic authentication to happen, the Anonymous authentication must fail first. Basic authentication will never be used if the content is accessible using anonymous.

11. B. If the Store Password Using Reversible Encryption option is not set and the password is not reset afterward, Digest authentication will fail.

12. B. HTTP 1.1 is required for Digest authentication.

13. A. Many firewalls do not support Integrated Windows authentication.

14. A. Certificates are required for the highest level of secure authentication because they support mutual authentication.

15. C. Only Windows 2000 Professional and Windows XP Professional support MS-CHAPv2 for dial-up connections.

16. A. Non-Windows clients will not use MS-CHAP or MS-CHAPv2 in most cases. You need to allow PAP or CHAP, depending on the authentication that they support.

17. D. Two-factor authentication requires the use of multiple authentication methods such as a smart card and then a PIN.

18. D. Windows 9*x* and Windows NT do not support EAP-TLS.

19. C. All that needs to be done is to remove the mapping for the failed partner's certificate to the Active Directory account.

20. A. Proxy servers and some firewalls can prevent Integrated Windows authentication from working properly.

Chapter
8

Configuring and Troubleshooting Virtual Private Network Protocols

THE MICROSOFT EXAM OBJECTIVES COVERED IN THIS CHAPTER:

✓ Configure and troubleshoot virtual private network (VPN) protocols. Considerations include Internet service provider (ISP), client operating system, network address translation devices, Routing and Remote Access servers, and firewall servers.

✓ Manage client configuration for remote access security. Tools include remote access policy and the Connection Manager Administration Kit.

Most organizations are utilizing remote network connections. Business demands require keeping the field staff up-to-date with e-mail and providing access to applications and data on the intranet. Business demands also require providing proper access to business partners to improve communications and the efficiencies of doing business together.

Previously, we discussed how partners and other remote network users can access data via web interfaces and other technologies. The *virtual private network (VPN)* has made connecting remote users from any place on the planet covered by the Internet to your company network possible and cost-effective. VPNs allow you to connect computers securely across shared networks, private and public. The perfect example is a computer on the Internet, connecting to the company network and being able to access all the company network resources as if it were on the office network. Several years ago, VPN technology was rather expensive and required some specialized skills. Today, with Windows Server 2003, it has become much easier to implement and much more cost-effective.

The most popular uses of VPN technology include the following:

1. Connecting remote computers over the Internet to the company intranet

2. Connecting two or more networks over the Internet

3. Creating an extremely secure perimeter network for company network users and partners

This chapter describes how to configure VPNs and how to troubleshoot VPN connections.

VPN troubleshooting is like troubleshooting any WAN problem. The process is usually complex because data has to travel through so many links. For a VPN, the typical flow is from the client to the *Internet service provider (ISP)* router, through the ISP's *firewall*, across the ISP's network, through other ISPs, to the destination company's ISP, to the company router, to the company firewall, and to the VPN server. Then there is the trip back. This chapter discusses the VPN technology and the problems that you might encounter.

VPNs and Internet Service Providers

The ISP contact at your company will become a familiar person if you ever have problems with your VPN connections. If you receive good help and response, treat them well! Always consider the role of the ISP and the potential they have to break your VPNs. Any time you connect to the Internet, you do so through your ISP.

ISPs used to sell packages allowing completely unfiltered TCP/IP connections to everyone. The idea at the time was that people would buy an ISP package so they could send and receive e-mail, browse the Web, and download content. Then many ISP clients started getting smarter. They would keep their systems online 24 hours a day if allowed. These computers would run scripts to make it appear that the connection was alive so as not to get disconnected by the ISP. The clients started hosting their own e-mail and web servers, and then peer-to-peer networks started taking off. To combat this unexpected use, ISPs began filtering traffic to allow only basic services and to prevent their clients from hosting web and e-mail sites that consume a great deal of bandwidth. A major problem arose when ISPs started cracking down on home users. ISPs often caused problems for their business clients in their attempts to control the usage by their small home clients.

You need to consider your company needs when contracting with an ISP. Make sure that none of your ports will be filtered by the ISP, or at least those ports that you intend to use. However, don't forget the ISP used by the remote computer that you will be troubleshooting.

Of course, if the ISP is not filtering ports, you are susceptible to many attacks from the Internet. Remember to protect yourself with a firewall.

When troubleshooting any connection, you deal with multiple ISPs. After all, your VPN connection will really look something like Figure 8.1.

The VPN client computer connects to its ISP, and the company network connects to its ISP. In between the two ISPs are several other higher-level ISPs and the Internet backbones. Logically, the VPN connection travels from the client computer to the VPN server and back using the tunnel. Physically, the route is much different. In between the physical route are at least two ISPs—the company ISP and the remote-use ISP—but many more could be involved.

FIGURE 8.1   ISP connections

🌐 **Real World Scenario**

Connecting Branch Offices Using VPNs

Your company has three small branch offices and a larger headquarters office. All four offices have direct connections to the Internet. All three branch offices are connected to the headquarters office using leased line connections. The problem is that the cost of the leased lines is going up, and you need some alternatives.

Using VPNs to connect the three branch offices to the headquarters office might be the perfect solution. If you use VPNs, you can drop the leased lines completely and invest the money saved in other areas, including increasing the Internet pipes.

Be aware that some ISPs used by remote users do not support VPNs. Check with these ISPs during your troubleshooting process; doing so might save you pulling out a great deal of hair. If the ISP does not support VPNs, find another ISP for your remote client systems. Also understand that satellite providers such as DIRECWAY, a two-way satellite Internet connection provided by DirecTV, do not support VPNs because of the network latency issues when using satellite links.

Routing and Remote Access Services (RRAS) Server

Assuming you just got started and selected your ISPs for the company and for your remote network clients, the next step is to configure the VPN server. You will then need to configure the client computers (which we'll describe in the next section).

Configuring RRAS

Configuring *Routing and Remote Access Services (RRAS)* is a straightforward process. You need either Windows 2000 Server installed as a domain controller or as a member server, or Windows Server 2003 configured as a domain controller or as a member server. You should not use domain controllers as edge computing devices, because doing so increases the vulnerability of your accounts database. Microsoft recommends using a member server for RRAS deployments. You can use Windows 2000 or Windows Server 2003 as a stand-alone server, but you must create separate accounts and passwords on the stand-alone server. Although the stand-alone server deployment of RRAS is more secure, it is also more complex to manage. In Exercise 8.1, you will use a member server. Remember, you might need a more secure implementation requiring a stand-alone server in your production environments.

EXERCISE 8.1

Configuring RRAS for VPN

In this exercise, you will configure RRAS as a VPN server.

1. Choose Start ➢ Administrative Tools ➢ Routing And Remote Access.

2. Right-click the server name and choose Configure And Enable Routing And Remote Access from the shortcut menu.

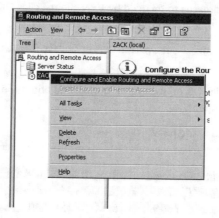

3. Click Next to start the Routing And Remote Access Server Setup Wizard.

4. In the Configuration screen, click the Remote Access (Dial-Up Or VPN) radio button and then click Next to open the Remote Client Protocols screen. (A number of selections will allow VPN services. Choose Remote Access (Dial-Up Or VPN) here to allow dial-up connections, too.)

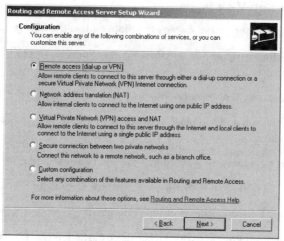

5. Enable both VPN and Dial-Up check boxes and then click Next.

EXERCISE 8.1 *(continued)*

6. Select the Local Area Connection for the external connection facing the Internet. Verify that the Enable Security On The Selected Interface By Setting Up Static Packet Filters check box is enabled and click Next (provided you have two or more network cards installed) to open the IP Address Assignment screen.

7. Click the From A Specified Range Of Addresses button and then click Next.

8. Click New, enter the addresses to be used by VPN clients, click OK, and then click Next to open the Managing Multiple Remote Access Servers screen.

9. Select the No, I Don't Want To Set Up This Server To Use RADIUS Now radio button and click Next.

10. Click Finish and then click OK on the warning message about the issue with needing to install the DHCP Relay Agent.

RRAS is now configured and ready for VPN clients.

You might have noticed that when you installed RRAS, it automatically configured 128 *Point-to-Point Tunneling Protocol (PPTP)* ports and 128 *Layer 2 Tunneling Protocol (L2TP)* ports. RRAS can support 256 connections. However, it is a good idea to create only the number of connections you need to support all your remote network clients. If your company needs only 20 PPTP connections and only 5 L2TP connections, create only those ports and delete any excess ports.

In Exercise 8.2, you will create and delete VPN ports.

EXERCISE 8.2

Creating and Deleting VPN Ports

In this exercise, you will go through the steps to create and delete VPN ports.

1. Choose Start ➢ Administrative Tools ➢ Routing And Remote Access to open the RRAS MMC console.

2. Expand the RRAS server if necessary until the Ports icon is exposed in the left pane.

3. Right-click the Ports icon and choose Properties from the shortcut menu to open the Ports Properties dialog box.

4. Highlight the port type that you want to increase or decrease and click Configure.

5. Enter the number of ports in the Maximum Ports box. Click OK.

6. Repeat Steps 4 and 5 for the other port type if needed.

7. Click OK to close the Ports Properties dialog box. Close the Routing And Remote Access window.

Because you must have enough IP addresses to support the VPN clients, you need to configure the server to assign IP addresses. The IP addresses can come from either a static address pool or from DHCP (Dynamic Host Configuration Protocol). When using a static address pool, RRAS clients receive the same DNS (Domain Name Service) and WINS (Windows Internet Naming Service) settings that the RRAS server uses. If the RRAS server can browse the network and access resources, clients should also be able to browse the network and access network resources with the same settings. You can also configure RRAS to use DHCP. Options provided by DHCP, such as the DNS and WINS addresses, can be provided to RRAS clients.

Configuring Authentication Protocols

RRAS can use various authentication protocols, as discussed in Chapter 7, "Configure, Manage, and Troubleshoot Authentication." Configuring authentication protocols for the RRAS server is a straightforward process. Simply open the Routing And Remote Access MMC console, right-click the server, select Properties, and then select the Security tab. In the Security tab, click the Authentication Methods button. Figure 8.2 shows that the default authentication protocols for RRAS are MS-CHAP and MS-CHAPv2.

FIGURE 8.2 Authentication methods

To support devices and systems other than Microsoft operating systems, you need to use one of the other *authentication methods* as supported by the VPN client that will be used. Also note that *EAP (Extensible Authentication Protocol)* is available for authentication for PPTP and L2TP tunneling. EAP requires either Windows 2000 or Windows XP clients, however.

Troubleshooting RRAS

Once RRAS is properly configured, VPN connections through RRAS are dependable and secure. However, much can go wrong with RRAS, and you need to be ready to troubleshoot.

Some basics steps for troubleshooting VPN connections from the RRAS server include the following:

- Test basic Internet connectivity from the RRAS server.

- Verify that IP addresses are available either through the static pool or through the DHCP server environment. If more IP addresses are needed, you can add them to the static pool by right-clicking the RRAS server in the Routing And Remote Access MMC console and then clicking the IP tab. To add addresses, you can click the Add button; to edit the existing pool, click the Edit button, as shown in Figure 8.3.

FIGURE 8.3   The static address pool

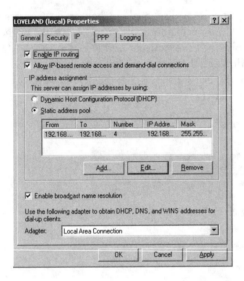

- Verify that VPN Ports are available, as shown in Figure 8.4. If all the ports are active, create more ports.

- Verify that certificate authorities used for EAP authentication are trusted by both the RRAS server and the VPN client systems. Remember, for L2TP tunnels with *IPSec (Internet Protocol Security) protocol*, you need certificates for both the RRAS server and for each VPN client system.

- You can enable or disable *PPTP filtering* in the Routing And Remote Access MMC console. Because PPTP filtering is fairly complex, it is addressed in more depth in the next section. Troubleshooting might require verifying that these filters were set properly or removing them for testing.

- *Authentication protocol* mismatches can be a problem. Make sure that the client operating system and the RRAS server are configured to use the same authentication protocols. If Unix and Macintosh computers are having problems, you might want to check to see if lower-level authentication protocols are enabled for them. Many administrators forget that other operating systems do not support MS-CHAP and MS-CHAPv2. PPTP VPNs require MS-CHAP, MS-CHAPv2, or EAP-TLS (*Extensible Authentication Protocol with Transport Layer Security*). Refer to Chapter 7 for details on authentication protocols.

- TCP/IP (Transmission Control Protocol/Internet Protocol) configuration issues often require troubleshooting:

  - DNS configuration is important at the server level because VPN clients inherit the DNS server address from the RRAS server.

  - WINS configuration is also important at the server level because VPN clients inherit the WINS server address from the RRAS server.

  - DHCP configuration can be a problem for many RRAS implementations. It is vital that the DHCP Relay Agent is properly installed on the RRAS server; if it is not, VPN clients will not be able to connect and work on the network.

  - Default gateway configurations should be left blank for the internal LAN interface, and the default gateway should be set with the ISP-provided gateway on the WAN interface.

PPTP Filtering

Configuring *PPTP filtering* requires setting up six filters. You need to configure three filters as inbound filters and three filters as outbound filters. PPTP filtering is a fantastic way to lock down the RRAS server that is exposed to the Internet. The RRAS server will not respond to any requests other than VPN connections using PPTP. In Exercise 8.3, you will manually configure PPTP filtering.

FIGURE 8.4   VPN port availability

EXERCISE 8.3

Manually Configuring PPTP Filtering

In this exercise, you will create six filters so that the external interface of an RRAS server does not allow any packets other than PPTP packets for VPN client connections.

Selecting the External Interface

1. Choose Start ➤ Administrative Tools ➤ Routing And Remote Access.

2. Expand the RRAS server and expand IP Routing.

3. Click General, right-click the external interface, and select Properties from the list in the right pane to open the network Properties dialog box at the General tab.

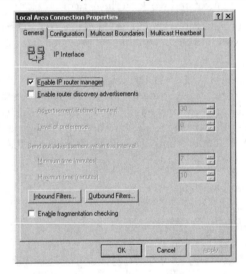

Setting the Three Inbound Filters

1. Click the Inbound Filters button and then click New to open the Add IP Filter dialog box.

2. Select the Destination Network check box and then enter the IP address and the subnet mask for the external interface.

3. In the Protocol drop-down list box, select Other. In the Protocol Number box, type **47**, and then click OK to close the Add IP Filter dialog box.

This completes the first filter.

4. In the Inbound Filters window, click New.

5. Select the Destination Network check box and enter the IP address and the subnet mask for the external interface.

6. In the Protocol drop-down list box, select TCP. In the Source Port box, enter **0**, and in the Destination Port box, enter **1723**. Click OK.

7. This completes the second filter.

8. In the Inbound Filters window, click New.

9. Select the Destination Network check box and enter the IP address and the subnet mask for the external interface.

10. In the Protocol drop-down list box, select TCP. In the Source Port box, enter **1723**, and in the Destination Port box, enter **0**. Click OK.

11. Click the Drop All Packets Except Those That Meet The Criteria Below radio button, and then click OK.

This completes the third filter. This filter is optional and is needed only if the RRAS server will also be used as an RRAS client to connect to other servers. The best example is an RRAS server that connects external clients and also connects branch offices. Step 10 is required even if the third filter is not configured.

Setting the Three Outbound Filters

1. In the Local Area Connection Properties dialog box, click Outbound Filters, and then click Add.

2. Select the Destination Network check box and enter the IP address and the subnet mask for the external interface.

3. In the Protocol drop-down list box, select Other, type **47**, and click OK.

This completes the fourth filter.

4. In the Outbound Filters window, click Add.

5. Select the Destination Network check box and enter the IP address and the subnet mask for the external interface.

6. In the Protocol drop-down list box, select TCP. In the Source Port box, enter **0**, and in the Destination Port box, enter **1723**. Click OK.

This completes the fifth filter.

7. In the Outbound Filters window, click Add.

8. Select the Destination Network check box and enter the IP address and the subnet mask for the external interface.

9. In the Protocol drop-down list box, select TCP. In the Source Port box, enter **1723**, and in the Destination Port box, enter **0**. Click OK.

10. Click the Drop All Packets Except Those That Meet The Criteria Below radio button, and then click OK.

This completes the sixth filter. This filter is optional and is needed only if the RRAS server will also be used as an RRAS client to connect to other servers. The best example is an RRAS server that connects external clients and also connects branch offices. Step 20 is required even if the third filter is not configured.

Troubleshooting PPTP filtering requires verifying that all the filters were set properly. In some cases, it will be necessary to remove one or even all the filters to get VPNs working properly.

Auditing and Event Logs

You can increase auditing to assist with troubleshooting RRAS. To set logging to the maximum level, open the Routing And Remote Access MMC console, right-click the RRAS server, and choose Properties from the shortcut menu to open the RRAS Properties dialog box. Click the Logging tab and select the options shown in Figure 8.5.

FIGURE 8.5   Event logging

You can also turn on account logon and logon events auditing though the Default Domain Controllers Policy. With auditing turned on, you can try the connection again to see if anything shows up in the Security log in Event Viewer. If the username is incorrect, if the password is wrong or is expired, or if there is no valid computer account, you will see this in the Security log. On the other side of the equation, if the user logs on properly, you will also see the success message in the Security log.

Configuring and Troubleshooting VPN Client Systems

So far, you've checked the ISPs as one of the first steps in troubleshooting your VPNs, especially when coming from the client side. Assuming that you're performing your troubleshooting correctly, you have checked your server and found that many other users are connecting without any problems. So the next step is to troubleshoot the client system.

Configuring Client Systems for VPNs

Before you can troubleshoot your client connection, you must configure the client, which you'll do in Exercise 8.4.

EXERCISE 8.4

Configuring a Windows XP Professional VPN Client

In this exercise, you'll configure a Windows XP Professional system as a VPN client and connect to an RRAS server.

1. Choose Start ➤ Control Panel ➤ Network And Internet Connections.

2. Click Create A Connection To The Network At Your Workplace.

3. If you have never set up the telephony configuration for your system, you will be prompted to enter the information, as shown in this graphic. Click OK and then click OK on Dialing Rules screen.

4. Because you want a VPN connection, click the Virtual Private Network Connection radio button and click Next to open the Connection Name screen.

5. Enter the name of your company or some other information that will help you identify the connection for later reference. Click Next to open the VPN Server Selection screen.

6. Enter the computer name or the IP address of the VPN server. In most cases, entering the IP address is preferred because it will eliminate troubleshooting later. Click Next.

7. Select the Add A Shortcut To This Connection To My Desktop check box. Click Finish.

8. Close the Network And Internet Connections window.

9. Double-click your new shortcut to open the Connect VPN ServerName dialog box.

10. Click Properties to open the Properties dialog box for this connection and then click the Options tab. Select the Include Windows Logon Domain check box. Click OK.

11. Enter the logon credentials—including the domain information—and click Connect.

At this point, you should be connected properly to the VPN server. You can further test the connectivity by pinging devices on the company network and attaching to file and printer shares. You can disconnect by double-clicking the VPN connection icon in the Taskbar and clicking Disconnect. You can also disconnect by choosing Start ➢ Control Panel ➢ Network And Internet Connections ➢ Network Connections and then right-clicking the VPN connection and selecting Disconnect.

Windows XP Professional is the best client operating system to use for VPN connectivity. The built-in features of the VPN client make it easy to configure and easy to change and troubleshoot as needed, and it is extremely secure. After Windows XP Professional, Windows 2000 Professional is probably the next best bet for a VPN client operating system. Both client operating systems make fantastic VPN clients. In Exercise 8.5, you'll configure a Windows 2000 Professional VPN client.

Configuring a Windows 2000 Professional VPN client

In this exercise, you will configure a Windows 2000 Professional system as a VPN client and connect to an RRAS server.

1. Choose Start ➢ Settings ➢ Control Panel and click Network And Dial-up Connections.

2. Click Make New Connection.

3. If you have not filled in the telephony information before, you need to fill it in at this time. Enter the area code and other information as necessary, click OK, and click OK again. If you have already filled this in before, proceed to the next step.

4. Click Next at the Welcome To The Network Connection Wizard screen to open the Network Connection Type screen.

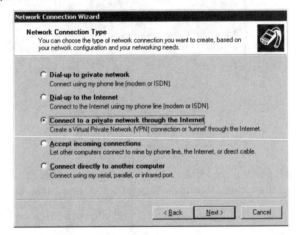

5. Click the Connect To A Private Network Through The Internet radio button and click Next.

6. Enter the hostname of the RRAS server or enter the IP address of the RRAS server. Click Next.

7. Click the Only For Myself radio button so that the VPN connection cannot be used by others on the network. Click Next.

8. Name the VPN connection with a user-friendly name that will be easy for the user to recognize. Select the Add A Shortcut To My Desktop check box. Click Finish.

This completes the basic configuration of the VPN client and will immediately open the VPN connection application so you can test it.

VPN clients can use three technologies for the tunnels:

- PPTP

- IPSec

- L2TP

PPTP is popular and has a fairly long history. PPTP supports secure encapsulation of IP, IPX (Internetwork Packet Exchange), and NetBEUI (NetBIOS Enhanced User Interface) traffic sent across private and public IP-based networks. IPSec tunneling allows only IP packets to be encrypted and sent over private and public IP-based networks. L2TP allows IP, IPX, and NetBEUI traffic to be encapsulated and sent over any IP, X.25, Frame Relay, and ATM (Asynchronous Transfer Mode) networks. Both PPTP and L2TP are Layer 2 tunneling protocols. IPSec is a Layer 3 tunneling protocol. IPSec tunneling has several weaknesses, which are not discussed in this book. However, combining IPSec and L2TP makes a very secure tunneling protocol combination. Microsoft has been recommending this combination for the last couple of years.

> *L2TP/IPSec* is considered a better solution because it supports computer authentication as well as user authentication, it provides for header compression, and authentication occurs after IPSec encryption is in place so that all credentials are encrypted. L2TP/IPSec requires Windows 2000 or Windows XP VPN clients.

Once the VPN client is installed, you can review its configuration and see that it supports both PPTP and L2TP/IPSec, as shown in Figure 8.6. Support for IPSec tunneling is not offered by itself.

In reality, a VPN client has to maintain two sets of TCP/IP information. One set is maintained for its network connection to the LAN or its connection to the ISP. The second set is maintained for the VPN connection. Because there are two routes for all IP traffic—one to the local network or ISP and the other through the VPN—the routing table must direct packets to the ISP for all Internet traffic and must also be configured to direct the traffic bound for the remote network through the VPN interface. If the default gateway is improperly configured, or if the routing table is not correctly built, ugly things will happen.

FIGURE 8.6   VPN types

Troubleshooting Client Systems

We have found the following steps to be most successful when troubleshooting client systems:

Test basic client Internet connectivity. Testing helps to verify connectivity to the ISP and the Internet. This basic testing will also tell you whether the client has proper IP configuration information and DNS entries.

Verify that the Allow Access permission is granted for dial-in users. Using Active Directory Users And Computers, check the properties for the remote user and verify that they have Allow Access permission on the Dial-In tab.

Verify that all utilized CAs are trusted by both the VPN server and the VPN clients when using L2TP with IPSec. If the certificate authorities (CAs) are not trusted by both the VPN server and the VPN client, the mutual authentication will fail. Without mutual authentication, the connection will not be established.

You might need to create computer accounts for the VPN client, depending on the operating system they are using. This is particularly important when it comes to browsing the network. If the client system is not part of the domain, it will be in a workgroup and will be tough to find. Also, because the computer account trust is reset in as little as seven days (depending on the operating system), deleting and re-creating the computer account may be required.

Make sure that the client operating system and the RRAS server are configured to use the same authentication protocols. Authentication protocol mismatches can be a problem. Refer to Chapter 7 for details on troubleshooting authentication protocols.

TCP/IP configuration issues often require troubleshooting. Be sure to consider the following TCP/IP configuration issues:

- DNS configuration is important at the client level, because VPN clients need the proper DNS configurations just to connect to the RRAS server by the server name.
- WINS configuration is also important. The VPN clients inherit the WINS server address from the RRAS server. It is a good idea to verify that WINS information was properly received.
- DHCP configuration can be a problem for many RRAS implementations. It is vital that the DHCP Relay Agent is properly installed on the RRAS server; if it is not, VPN clients will not be able to connect and work on the network.
- Default gateway configuration can be a problem. When the VPN client connects to the RRAS server, it starts using the default gateway provided by the RRAS server. To prevent this, you need to open the Properties dialog box for the VPN client. Click the Networking tab, select Internet Protocol (TCP/IP), click Properties, and then click the Advanced button. On the General tab, clear the Use Default Gateway On Remote Network check box. Click OK and then close the rest of the configuration windows.

The computer name of the RRAS server can be a problem, especially if it is not properly registered in DNS or if there are client DNS problems. The best fix is to use the IP address when possible, as shown in Figure 8.7.

FIGURE 8.7   VPN connection properties

The lists in the "Troubleshooting RRAS" and "Troubleshooting Client Systems" sections are good starting points to troubleshoot these configuration errors.

Network Address Translation (NAT) and VPNs

Network Address Translation (NAT) allows a device that supports NAT to intercept all traffic bound for the Internet from the intranet and replace the source IP address in the packet with its own source IP address. When the packet response returns from the destination and reaches the NAT device or service, NAT then replaces the destination IP address with the IP address of the internal device. Figure 8.8 illustrates this process.

NAT is a strong solution because it hides the originator's IP address from the Internet. NAT is also nice from the standpoint of ISPs that can now reduce the number of IP addresses leased to most companies because they can use NAT devices or services. Using NAT allows most companies to use private IP address ranges for all internal networks.

The major problem with NAT is that it is not able to properly handle all IP packets going from the internal network out to the Internet. One of the biggest problems with NAT is that it cannot support L2TP/IPSec tunneling because the IPSec *Encapsulating Security Payload (ESP)* packets become corrupted. VPN servers and VPN clients cannot use L2TP/IPSec tunneling if any of them are behind NAT devices or servers using NAT.

FIGURE 8.8 The NAT process

If NAT is used for remote network clients using VPNs or if the VPN server is behind NAT, the solution will require using PPTP tunnels. Although PPTP is not as secure as L2TP/IPSec, it meets the needs of most organizations.

Firewall Servers with VPNs

Firewalls can be a problem for VPN connections. Almost every company on the Internet uses firewalls to protect their internal networks from Internet attacks. Many individuals also use firewalls on their personal computers; these firewalls are often referred to as personal firewalls. And many ISPs use firewalls to protect their hosted environments, as do many users who have signed up for additional services.

In order for VPNs to work through firewalls, the proper protocol IDs and port numbers must be enabled. The following will be required (L2TP requires IKE [Internet Key Exchange] and ESP too):

Protocol	Protocol ID	Port Number
PPTP (GRE)	47	TCP 1723
L2TP		UDP 1701
IKE		UDP 500
ESP	50	

Generic routing encapsulation (GRE) is a problem with some ISPs because they use GRE to manage internal network routers. If the ISP is using GRE, they may filter it out to and from client connections for security reasons. GRE filtering is not common, but if GRE is filtered out, it will prevent a PPTP connection.

The best solution, when it comes to firewalls, is to ask the firewall vendor if they have any compatibility problems with VPN tunneling in or out of their firewall. Some older firewalls may not support L2TP/IPSec or PPTP.

 Firewalls that allow VPN clients through will fail to stop VPN clients from accessing all protocols that would normally be filtered by the firewall. Because all other traffic is encapsulated, the firewall cannot filter what it cannot see. For example, an internal user is not allowed to use instant messaging technologies. If they are going through the firewall using VPN to another location, the instant messaging packets will be encapsulated within the VPN packets and will not be visible to the firewall.

Managing Client Computer Configurations for Remote Access Security

Configuring the client side for VPN connectivity can be simple for small-scale deployments. However, properly configuring larger-scale deployments may require the use of other tools. Many organizations also have to be concerned with how VPNs are used by the general population. Resulting VPN policies often require enforcement as to who can use VPN and under what conditions. These remote access policies can be enforced with the aptly named *Remote Access Policies*.

Remote Access Policies

Remote Access Policies define and enforce which users and groups can use RRAS, when they can use RRAS, under what conditions they can use RRAS, and what levels of encryption and authentication are required for RRAS connections. RRAS policies are important, because you want to verify and ensure the following:

- Only authorized users can access RRAS and during approved times.
- Users must be using the proper authentication protocols.
- Users must be using the proper encryption levels.
- Idle time and session lengths are properly constrained.
- Only approved media types are used.
- Only approved tunneling protocols are used.

You can place other types of constraints on RRAS connections for remote network users, but these are the major constraints, and they should address most of your needs.

RRAS is configured with a default policy during its initial configuration. The default policy specifies any day of the week and any time of the day. This means that the default policy conditions will always be met. The default policy permission is Deny Remote Access Permission. Most administrators are confused when they see these settings, and then they see that the title for this policy is Allow Access If Dial-In Permission Is Enabled. The logic does not work here. However, the logic does work if you understand that the default policy allows access for all users who have been granted Allow Access permission in the Dial-In tab of their user account properties. The permissions in the policy are overridden by the Dial-In tab permissions. Many organizations use this as the very last policy in a list of policies as a final catch-all policy. Other companies delete this default policy because they want to enforce only a certain number of policies and do not want any others that might affect the environment without their expressed desires.

RRAS policies can best be described as having three sections:

Conditions   The Conditions section describes under what conditions the policy will apply. These conditions can include the day and time restrictions, security group restrictions, tunnel type restrictions, and other restrictions regarding phone numbers and IP addresses for remote connections and RADIUS servers if Internet Authentication Service (IAS) is used. Conditions are in the Specify The Conditions To Match box. Clicking the Add button displays the conditions that can be used, as shown on the right in Figure 8.9.

FIGURE 8.9   RRAS policy conditions

Permissions   After the conditions are reviewed and met, the policy applies the proper permissions. Either the connection is granted or it is denied based on whether the Grant Remote Access Permission or the Deny Remote Access Permission radio button is selected. Notice in Figure 8.9 that the Deny Remote Access Permission radio button is selected. A note underneath states that "Access will be denied. The profile you specify will be ignored unless access is overridden on a per-user basis." This means that whatever permission is granted here can be overridden in the user account attributes using Active Directory Users And Computers. With the Deny in the policy, the attributes for the Administrator account in Figure 8.10 override the Deny, and the administrator can use this policy to access the RRAS server.

Figure 8.10 shows the properties when Active Directory is in mixed mode. In mixed mode, policies are more difficult to enforce because they can be overridden. When mixed mode is changed to native mode, the Control Access Through Remote Access Policy radio button becomes available, as shown in Figure 8.11.

Profile   The profile section provides restrictions on the connection once it is made. In the policy properties, click the Edit Profile button to open the Edit Dial-in Profile dialog box (see Figure 8.12). The profile is basically a user profile for RRAS connections, whether they are dial-in or VPN connections. The Authentication tab specifies what authentication protocols can be used for the connection, and the Encryption tab specifies what level of encryption can be used (or multiple levels that will be allowed) for the connection.

FIGURE 8.10   The Administrator Properties dialog box in mixed mode

FIGURE 8.11 The Administrator Properties dialog box in native mode

A remote network user trying to connect to the RRAS server goes through several steps that take an extremely short time to happen. The process is well documented in many places, but it deserves some attention here. The high-level steps are as follows:

1. RRAS tries to match a policy with the conditions of the current connection attempt. It starts from the top of the list of policies and goes down. If it finds a policy that matches the conditions, it uses that policy to determine permissions. If no policy is found that matches the conditions, the connection is denied.

2. If a policy is found that matches the conditions, RRAS processes it for permissions. This works as follows:

   ▪ If the account Dial-In tab is set to Allow Access, the connection can proceed.

   ▪ If the account Dial-In tab is set to Deny Access, the connection is denied.

   ▪ If the account Dial-In tab is set to Control Access Through Remote Access Policies, the permissions section of the policy is evaluated and processed according to its Grant or Deny permissions.

3. The profile is applied to the connection. If the connection does not meet a parameter in the profile, the connection is denied.

As you can see, making the connection work properly involves many considerations. Troubleshooting RRAS policies can be easy if you keep these steps in mind and remember that RRAS evaluates each policy in order starting from the top and going down. If RRAS finds a match to the conditions and the connection fails because of permissions or profile constraints, RRAS does not attempt to find another policy that might also match farther down the list.

FIGURE 8.12   The RRAS profile

FIGURE 8.12   The RRAS profile

The Connection Manager Administration Kit

You can use the *Connection Manager Administration Kit (CMAK)* to distribute the service profile to remote clients and to provide information for remote clients to find updates. You can, for example, use the CMAK to generate phone books for remote clients so that they can dial up to local ISPs or local branch offices when traveling. In addition, you can use the CMAK to provide VPN server configuration information as well as dial-up information.

Many larger companies use the CMAK to make connecting easy for remote users; however, other companies create images for remote users with all the proper configuration information already input and installed. Either method will work, but using the CMAK method has some other benefits such as the ability to get updates from a web server specified in the service profile created.

You can run the CMAK Wizard on any Windows 2000 server or Windows Server 2003 server. It is probably best to run the wizard on the RRAS server that will be used. If you run the CMAK Wizard on the RRAS server, the files are automatically stored on the RRAS server. In Exercise 8.6, you'll run the CMAK.

Using the CMAK can really be helpful if you support a large number of remote network clients. Updating one package and sending it to everyone that uses remote network connections via dial-up or VPN can be extremely cost-effective. The CMAK can be used to distribute ISP phone numbers for remote users so that they can make ISP connections and then establish VPN connections once they are connected to the ISP. The CMAK can also be used to deploy the phone numbers for locally hosted modems on RRAS servers around the company.

EXERCISE 8.6

Running the Connection Manager Administration Kit

In this exercise, you will install the CMAK, run it, and then use the resulting executable to install and test the resulting service profile. You can run the CMAK processes on any Windows 2000 Server, Windows 2000 Professional computer, Windows Server 2003 server, or even Windows XP Professional machines.

Install the CMAK Wizard

1. Choose Start ➤ Settings ➤ Control Panel and double-click Add/Remove Programs.

2. Click Add/Remove Windows Components.

3. Select Management And Monitoring Tools and click the Details button.

4. Select the Connection Manager Components check box and click OK.

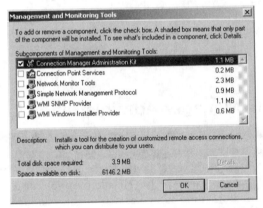

5. Click Next. If prompted, you may have to respond to the Terminal Services Setup dialog box. Verify that the proper radio button is selected and click Next again.

6. Windows copies the proper files. Be prepared to provide the latest service pack CD and the location of the Windows installation files. Click Finish when the file copy process is completed. Close the Add/Remove Programs window and any other windows that might still be open.

   At this point, the CMAK Wizard is installed on the RRAS server.

Run the CMAK Wizard

1. Choose Start ➤ Administrative Tools ➤ Connection Manager Administration Kit to start the CMAK Wizard.

2. At the Welcome To The Connection Manager Administration Kit Wizard screen, click Next to open the Service Profile Source screen.

3. Select the New Profile radio button and then click Next to open the Service And File Names screen. In the future, you can use this wizard to edit this profile as well as other service profiles.

4. In the Service Name box, enter a filename of eight characters or fewer. This name should be meaningful and self-explanatory. Click Next to open the Merged Service Pro-files screen.

5. Because this is a new profile, you will not have any others to merge. In the future, you can use this screen to merge service profiles to save time when creating new ones. Click Next to open the Support Information screen.

6. Enter support information. This information appears in the logon dialog box for users so they know where to call or send e-mail if they have problems. Click Next to open the Realm Name screen.

7. Verify that the Do Not Add A Realm Name radio button is selected and click Next. The Realm name is a nice option if you have to provide it as part of the authentication; it is not required in this case.

8. Click Next on the Merging Profile Information screen. This is not needed because this is the first profile.

9. Enable the Phone Book From This Profile check box and then enter the IP address of the VPN server in the Always Use The Same VPN Server field. Click Next.

10. In the VPN Entries page, select the existing entry and click Edit. Configure the appropriate information in the General, TCP/IP Settings, and Security tabs and click OK. Click Next.

EXERCISE 8.6 *(continued)*

11. In the Phone Book page of the wizard, enter the name of a phone book file if you want to add it to the profile and also provide additional text as per the example provided on the page. You are not required to add any information here. Click Next.

12. Click Next on the Phone Book Updates page after filling in the appropriate information for the phone book name and the URL for the Connection Point Services server.

13. Click Next on the Dial-up Networking Entries, unless you also want to create the information for dial-up networking connections to your RRAS environment. If you want to configure the information for dial-up networking, highlight the existing entry and click Edit. Make all necessary changes and click OK.

14. Click Next on the Routing Table Update page.

15. Click Next on the Automatic Proxy Configuration page.

16. Click Next on the Custom Actions page.

17. Click Next to use the default Logon Bitmap graphic. If you want to use a custom graphic, it must be 330 140 pixels or smaller.

18. Click Next to use the default Phone Book Bitmap. If you want to use a custom graphic, it must be 114 309 pixels or smaller.

19. Click Next to accept the default icons on the Icons page of the wizard.

20. Click Next on the Notification Area shortcut menu.

21. Click Next on the Help File page. You can use this page to deploy a custom help file.

22. Enter special support information such as the phone number for the help desk and click Next on the Support Information page.

23. Verify that the check box is enabled for the Install Connection Manager 1.3 With This Service Profile option. Click Next.

24. On the License Agreement page, enter the filename for any special license agreements that you want to include and click Next.

25. On the Additional Files page, use the Add button to add any additional files that you want to be part of the service profile. Click Next.

26. Click Next on the Ready To Build The Service Profile page.

27. Click Finish to complete the wizard. Note the name and location of your service file. This is the file that will be used in the next step to deploy your dial-up and VPN configurations.

The file created in these steps can now be sent out and installed on remote client systems.

EXERCISE 8.6 *(continued)*

Client Deployment and Testing

1. Copy the service profile executable to a remote client system.

2. Double-click the executable on the client system. Click Yes to install the connection.

3. Click the My Use Only radio button and verify that the Add A Shortcut To The Desktop check box is checked. Click OK.

4. The installation runs and automatically creates a shortcut to access the RRAS server on the Desktop. The VPN client automatically runs.

5. Enter your user credentials and click Connect.

You are now logged in, and the VPN is established.

Summary

Virtual private networks are secure and cost-effective, and can be deployed efficiently. To properly troubleshoot VPN connections, you must understand that the connections can be impacted in several places:

- ISPs
- RRAS servers
- Client systems
- Firewalls
- NAT servers
- Policies
- Permissions

With VPNs becoming more prevalent in network designs, it is vital to understand the basic problems that you might encounter from the server side as well as from the client side with issues such as remote access permissions, types of VPN protocols, and authentication protocols.

Deployment of VPN configurations and access control options allow administrators the ability to control who uses VPN connections, when they use VPN connections, and what configurations they must use. With these decisions made, you can also make it easy for remote users to install the VPN client by creating a service profile and sending them an installation package.

The Routing and Remote Access Service (RRAS) provided by Windows 2000 Server is an excellent platform for VPN connections, and it is a much more cost-effective solution than the third-party solutions of the past.

Exam Essentials

Understand the details of troubleshooting VPN protocols. Make sure you understand the basics of VPNs, including which protocols are available.

Make sure you understand that ISPs can impact VPNs through protocol filtering. Not all ISPs are equal, so it is important to contact the ISP from the client side as well as from the server side when troubleshooting VPN problems.

Make sure you know how to configure the RRAS server to support VPN connections. Know where to set the encryption level and when to use a stand-alone RRAS server instead of a member server. Understand how to create and delete VPN ports. Understand how to implement a static pool and understand when to use DHCP. Make sure you understand what PPTP filtering is and how it can impact troubleshooting if it is being utilized.

Make sure you understand the basics of troubleshooting the VPN client. Make sure you know how to create the client-side VPN connection and know how to force it to use L2TP/IPSec instead of PPTP.

Understand how to successfully use NAT with VPNs. Make sure you know which VPN protocol works through NAT and which does not.

Understand the use of firewall servers and VPNs. Understand which ports and protocol ID are needed to support VPN connections through firewalls. Understand that some firewalls can also use NAT. Understand why GRE might be filtered at an ISP firewall.

Know how to set RRAS policies. Make sure that you understand the components of an RRAS policy and how the permissions in the policy interact with the permissions in Active Directory. Make sure you understand how policies are applied and in what order policies are evaluated. Make sure you understand which conditions can be set in the policy and which connection requirements can be set through the profile.

Know how to leverage the Connection Manager Administration Kit (CMAK). Make sure you know what CMAK is and how it can be used to create service profiles for dial-up and VPN connections to the RRAS server. Make sure you know how to create the executable and how to use the executable file to install the VPN client configuration on a client system.

Review Questions

1. For which of the following can you use virtual private networks? (Choose all that apply.)

    A. Connecting remote client machines to an intranet

    B. Connecting multiple offices together over the Internet

    C. Building extremely secure extranets

    D. Providing secure e-mail traffic with the Internet

2. Your company has changed ISPs over the weekend. On Monday, VPN users report that they can no longer access the company network using VPN connections. What is the most likely solution?

    A. Reconfigure VPN clients to use a new IP address.

    B. Change VPN clients from PPTP to L2TP.

    C. Reconfigure VPN clients to use a new hostname for the RRAS server.

    D. Disable software compression for VPN clients.

3. Your company just started a new division in another building 20 miles away. The new division uses NetWare and Windows Server 2003. Many of the division members will be working in the new building, and others will split time between the buildings. Your supervisor is planning to purchase a leased line between the two offices. Both offices will have direct Internet connections. Both offices use private IP addresses, and the RRAS servers providing VPN services are located behind firewalls running NAT. Your supervisor asks you for options. Which of the following options will work?

    A. Build a VPN between the two offices using L2TP tunneling. NWLink and IPX can traverse the VPN. Do not purchase a leased line.

    B. Build a VPN between the two offices using IPSec tunneling. NWLink and IPX can traverse the VPN. Do not purchase a leased line.

    C. Build a VPN between the two offices using L2TP. Purchase a leased line to handle the IPX traffic.

    D. Build a VPN between the two offices using PPTP tunneling. NWLink and IPX can traverse the VPN. Do not purchase a leased line.

4. Your company installed RRAS and intends to use it for VPN access from remote clients. You set up RRAS to use DHCP. VPN clients are not able to connect. What is the most likely reason?

    A. DHCP delivers the wrong DNS address, and the VPN clients can't find the RRAS server by its hostname.

    B. It is necessary to install a DHCP relay agent on the RRAS server.

    C. RRAS needs a different DHCP scope than for internal addresses.

    D. DHCP is delivering the wrong default gateway address to RRAS clients.

5. Your co-worker configured RRAS as a Remote Access Server. It worked during testing with three different VPN users; however, it doesn't seem to be working now that it is in full production. What is the most likely reason?

    A. Your co-worker must have removed most of the ports for testing so that only a few were available during the testing timeframe.

    B. The test users must have all been using L2TP ports, and all the new users do not have certificates needed for L2TP.

    C. The RRAS server will support only five users when configured as a VPN server.

    D. The production users do not have the proper certificates to support IPSec in combination with L2TP.

6. Your company plans to put the RRAS server directly on the Internet and then connect it to the company intranet. What can be done to secure the RRAS server from Internet attacks and still allow it to provide VPN services?

    A. Configure Remote Access Policies.

    B. Disable multicasting on the external interface.

    C. Use PPTP filtering on the external interface.

    D. Configure all ports as L2TP and use L2TP/IPSec tunneling only.

7. Your company hosts critical data in a protected perimeter network. Users access the data using VPN connections from the Internet. An internal user at the company would also like to connect to this server through the company network instead of having to dial up the Internet through a local ISP. What do you tell him?

    A. He can connect directly to the RRAS server from the LAN using a VPN.

    B. He can only connect via the Internet.

    C. It will require a third-party VPN device; RRAS cannot accept intranet addresses.

    D. He can connect directly to the RRAS server, but he can use L2TP/IPSec tunneling only.

8. Your company runs RRAS to support VPN connections. One of the company VPs is working from a hotel while on vacation. The hotel filters out certain websites, one of which is your company beta site. How can you help him?

    A. Tell him he can use a VPN and connect directly to the website using the URL for the destination hostname.

    B. Tell him that he can use his VPN connection to the RRAS server and then access the beta site through the company intranet.

    C. Tell him he can use a VPN and connect directly to the company website using the IP address for the destination address.

    D. Tell him to use the Security tab in the VPN Properties dialog box to set the Require Data Encryption option and then use the VPN to connect directly to the beta site.

9. You just added five more VPN users to the network. You receive a call from a VPN user saying that he cannot connect. This is a VPN user who has never had any problems. You think that you may have run out of VPN ports and need to create more. How do you do this?

   A. Open the Routing And Remote Access MMC console on the RRAS server. Click Remote Access Clients to see how many VPN ports are in use and how many are available.

   B. Open the Routing And Remote Access MMC console on the RRAS server. Click Ports to see how many VPN ports are in use and how many are available.

   C. Open the Routing And Remote Access MMC console on the RRAS server. Click Remote Access Logging to see how many VPN ports are in use and how many are available.

   D. Open the Routing And Remote Access MMC console on the RRAS server. Click Remote Access Policies to see how many VPN ports are in use and how many are available.

10. You received a call from a remote network user. He bought a new computer and has been having trouble using his VPN client ever since he installed it. He installed the client using the service profile that you sent him earlier. Troubleshooting reveals that PPTP works, but L2TP/IPSec does not work. What is the most likely reason?

   A. The Options tab does not have the Include Windows Logon Domain check box enabled.

   B. The advanced settings on the Security tab do not include PAP authentication.

   C. He has Windows XP, and his Internet Connection Firewall is enabled.

   D. He does not have a certificate for his new computer.

11. You received a call from a remote network user. He is having trouble using his VPN client over the last few hours. Troubleshooting reveals that he can access the VPN server using the IP address but not the fully qualified domain name. Other VPN users are not experiencing this problem. What is the most likely reason for this user's problem?

   A. The DNS server he has configured for his ISP is unavailable.

   B. The company DNS server is unavailable.

   C. PPTP filtering has stopped DNS resolution of the RRAS server.

   D. The ISP firewall must be stopping external DNS from resolving.

12. You received a call from a remote network user. She is having trouble using her VPN client ever since she installed it. Troubleshooting reveals that she has configured the advanced settings on the Security tab. She has configured PAP, CHAP, and SPAP for authentication protocols. What can be done to fix the problem?

   A. Change the client to use Extensible Authentication Protocol (EAP).

   B. Configure the client to include the Windows Logon Domain in the Options tab.

   C. Add PAP, CHAP, and SPAP to the RRAS authentication methods.

   D. Remove PAP, CHAP, and SPAP from the client configuration and add MS-CHAP and MS-CHAPv2.

13. Your company has decided to deploy RRAS to support VPN connections from remote network clients. Your supervisor states that the authentication protocols must support mutual authentication. Which protocols can you configure to meet this requirement? (Choose all that apply.)

    A. CHAP

    B. MS-CHAP

    C. MS-CHAPv2

    D. EAP

14. Your company has decided to deploy RRAS to support VPN connections from remote network clients. Your supervisor states that the EAP must be used. Which client operating systems can you use to meet this requirement? (Choose all that apply.)

    A. Windows 9*x* with DUN v1.3

    B. Windows NT 4

    C. Windows 2000

    D. Windows XP

15. Your company has decided to deploy RRAS to support VPN connections from remote network clients. Your supervisor states that the L2TP/IPSec must be used. Which client operating systems can you use to meet this requirement? (Choose all that apply.)

    A. Windows 9*x* with DUN v1.3

    B. Windows NT 4

    C. Windows 2000

    D. Windows XP

16. Your company has decided to deploy RRAS to support VPN connections from remote network clients. Your supervisor states that the L2TP/IPSec must be used. Which steps must you take to meet this requirement? (Choose all that apply.)

    A. Install a computer certificate on the RRAS server.

    B. Install a computer certificate on all VPN clients.

    C. Use only Windows 2000 or Windows XP clients.

    D. Make sure that the RRAS server and the VPN clients are not behind a NAT device.

    E. Configure Remote Access Policies to enforce L2TP/IPSec.

17. You received a call from a remote network user. She is having trouble using her VPN client ever since she installed it. She states that she tried to ping the RRAS server and it didn't respond, so there must be something wrong with the server. You know that many people are connected using VPNs to the RRAS server, so it is not down. What is the most likely reason that ping fails from the client system?

    A. The ISP is filtering ICMP.

    B. The RRAS server has the wrong default gateway.

    C. PPTP filtering is enabled on the external RRAS interface.

    D. The client system has the wrong default gateway.

18. You received a call from a remote network user. He is having trouble using his VPN client ever since he installed it. He states that he is no longer able to access the website through his local ISP connection to the Internet. What is the most likely reason?

    A. You need to clear the Use Default Gateway On Remote Network check box in the VPN client configuration.

    B. You need to select the Enable IP Routing check box on the IP tab in the RRAS Properties dialog box.

    C. You need to configure the RRAS server as a router by selecting the Router check box on the RRAS General Properties tab.

    D. You need to select the Allow IP-Based Remote Access And Demand-Dial Connections check box on the IP tab of the RRAS Properties dialog box.

19. You just set up a new user in Active Directory Users And Computers. You added the user to the VPN Users security group, which has a Remote Access Policy. The Remote Access Policy for the VPN Users group has the conditions set for Monday to Friday from 6 A.M. to 8 P.M. You walk the user through setting up the VPN client for PPTP tunneling over the phone, but he is unable to connect. What is the most likely reason?

    A. The user is in a different time zone.

    B. The user needs a certificate for his computer.

    C. You need to configure DNS on the client computer.

    D. You forgot to select the Allow Access radio button on the Dial-In tab for the user account.

20. You just configured RRAS to support VPN connections. You configured a new Remote Access Policy for users to access the intranet using VPN connections during work hours. During testing, however, your test user always connects, even when the policy is set to Deny Remote Access Permission. You check the Dial-In tab on the test account in Active Directory Users And Computers. You find that the user account is set to Allow Access. You want to set the user to Control Access Through Remote Access Policy, but it is grayed out. How can you make this option available?

    A. Join the RRAS server to the Active Directory domain.

    B. Configure the RRAS server with a static IP address for both the internal and external network interfaces.

    C. Change the Windows 2000 Active Directory to native mode.

    D. Configure the Remote Access Policy profile to Server Settings Define Policy.

Answers to Review Questions

1. A, B, C. VPNs can provide secure tunnels to connect remote computers, connect branch offices over public networks, and provide secure access to perimeter network resources such as an extranet.

2. A. Changing ISPs will almost always require changing IP addresses for Internet-facing resources such as a web server. Although the hostname for the RRAS server might have been updated with the new IP through DNS, it's likely that there are statically configured VPN clients.

3. D. L2TP will not work because of NAT being in place, and IPSec tunneling will not support IPX. PPTP supports NAT and IPX, along with TCP/IP.

4. B. Even though the RRAS configuration wizard warns administrators to configure a DHCP relay, they can still forget.

5. A. When configuring RRAS as a VPN server, it creates 128 PPTP and 128 L2TP ports by default. Administrators can change the number of ports and types of ports manually.

6. C. PPTP filtering configures the external interface so it responds only to VPN connections.

7. A. VPN connections do not have to originate from the Internet.

8. B. The hotel's ISP will not be able to stop access of the website, because it cannot see the information inside the VPN.

9. B. Clicking Ports displays all ports that are currently active and all ports that are inactive.

10. D. The client computer must have a computer certificate that is trusted by the RRAS server.

11. A. The local ISP DNS is probably down or unavailable for a short time. He should call his ISP to verify, or he should configure a secondary DNS server to avoid this problem in the future.

12. D. RRAS, by default, uses MS-CHAP and MS-CHAPv2. The client and the server must match with at least one authentication protocol in order to connect.

13. C, D. Both MS-CHAPv2 and EAP provide mutual authentication. EAP requires certificates, but there is still mutual authentication.

14. C, D. Only Windows 2000 and Windows XP support EAP authentication.

15. C, D. Only Windows 2000 and Windows XP support L2TP/IPSec tunneling.

16. A, B, C, D. L2TP/IPSec requires certificates and the proper network operating systems to function. Also, L2TP/IPSec does not work through NAT.

17. C. PPTP filtering causes the RRAS server to drop all packets except VPN packets, making it look as if it is offline to users trying to ping it.

18. A. This check box is enabled by default and will prevent the VPN client from accessing the Internet directly using its Internet connection.

19. D. If the Deny Access radio button is selected, the connection will fail.

20. C. Active Directory must be in native mode to enable the Control Access Through Remote Access Policy.

Chapter

9

Installing, Configuring, and Managing Certificate Authorities

THE MICROSOFT EXAM OBJECTIVES COVERED IN THIS CHAPTER:

✓ **Install, manage, and configure Certificate Services.**

- Install and configure root, intermediate, and issuing certification authorities (CAs). Considerations include renewals and hierarchy.

- Configure certificate templates.

- Configure, manage, and troubleshoot the publication of certificate revocation lists (CRLs).

- Configure archival and recovery of keys.

- Deploy and revoke certificates to users, computers, and CAs.

- Back up and restore the CA.

Understanding public key infrastructure (PKI) and the use of certificates to secure networking is extremely important to network administrators. Certificate-based encryption and authentication provides a much higher level of security and should be used whenever security is extremely important to an organization.

Certificate authorities (CAs) are key components of a PKI. The CA issues and manages the certificates used by all users and computers involved in secure transactions. The CA has to be trusted by all parties involved in the transactions, and it must be kept as secure as possible to prevent any breaches that could compromise the integrity of the PKI. If all users and computers cannot trust the CA, there is no reason to use it. Trust is paramount.

In this chapter, you will install and configure certificate authorities, and you will go through the processes of managing a certificate authority.

Public Key Infrastructure and Certificate Authorities

Public key infrastructure (PKI) is the combination of systems and technologies used to provide the foundation of completely trustworthy and secure communications and business transactions. A true PKI includes *certificate authorities (CAs)* that provide *digital certificates* to individuals, computers, and even applications. The certificates used in the PKI are based on *public-private key pairs* used for signing and sealing communications, data, and transactions.

For a PKI to be acceptable to everyone involved in business communications and transactions, it must provide high levels of the following:

Integrity You know that the transaction has not been changed since it was transmitted.

Confidentiality You know that nobody has read the message since it was transmitted.

Authenticity You know that the message is not a replay or a fake with a spoofed origination address.

Nonrepudiation You know that the sender is who they say they are and that the message is their transaction.

A PKI must also be highly available, meaning that it must be running and it must be accessible at all times when business transactions are running that depend on its services. An example of a PKI-enabled application is an e-mail application that can sign and seal messages sent to receivers on the Internet as well as internally within the company. Another example is a fully secured website accessed using SSL-enabled sites and pages, so that all content and information sent to the site are fully encrypted. These are only two examples of many in which PKI-enabled applications provide security and confidence to business transactions. Some other major PKI-enabled applications include the following:

- 802.1x authentications

- EFS (Encrypting File System)

- IPSec (Internet Protocol Security) encryption

- Smart card logons

Installing a CA in a Microsoft network allows your CA to issue certificates to users, computers, and service accounts (after all, they are just user accounts, too). Using certificates, these objects can sign, seal, or sign and seal all communications between each other and can mutually authenticate identities.

CAs are subject to several types of threats that can diminish their value to the organization and even make them a threat to the organization. Some examples of threats include

- Attacks against systems hosting certificate revocation lists (CRLs)

- Attempts to modify the configuration of the CA

- Attempts to compromise the key pair of the CA

- Attempts to obtain unauthorized certificates

Compromising the CA allows attackers to obtain unauthorized certificates and use those certificates to authenticate with resources on the network. Once the CA has been compromised, it must have its certificate revoked and it must be removed from the network. Removing the CA can mean the loss of the entire PKI and require stopping the use of all previously issued certificates. Stopping the use of the previously existing certificates requires the stopping of many services and requires that many resources be removed from the network so they are not compromised too.

Larger organizations have a hierarchy of CAs—such as that shown in Figure 9.1—as a way of protecting against the recreation of the PKI in the event that a CA is compromised. The three-tiered structure is considered a best practice for organizations in which security is important.

Let's take a look at the three types of CAs illustrated in Figure 9.1.

Root CA   In larger organizations, a *root CA* is usually a stand-alone offline CA. The root CA is kept in a secure area and is not put on the network. The root CA provides certificates for intermediate CAs. The root CA is used to revoke the certificates of any intermediate CAs in the event that they are compromised. New CAs are then created using the root CA, as long as it has not been compromised.

Intermediate CAs   *Intermediate CAs* are used to separate classes of certificates, in many cases. For example, one intermediate CA might be used specifically for users, and another might be used specifically for computers. Or the structure might be based on geography. Intermediate CAs are usually stand-alone offline CAs just like root CAs. These are the CAs that will revoke the certificates for issuing CAs and are then used to create new CAs to replace the compromised CAs.

FIGURE 9.1 A CA hierarchy

Issuing CAs   *Issuing CAs* are used to provide certificates to users, computers, and services. In some cases, there will be multiple issuing CAs, and they will be used for separate processes much like intermediate CAs. For example, one issuing CA might be used for all computer certificates and another might be used for all user certificates. Multiple issuing CAs allow multiple CAs to share the load of issuing and managing certificates on the network.

Issuing CAs can be used in many ways. For example, an issuing CA might be located at each physical location of a company to service the network segments at the remote sites. Because issuing CAs get their certificates from intermediate CAs, they can have their certificates revoked in the event that they are compromised. If an issuing CA is compromised, all of the certificates that it has issued must be revoked, the certificate revocation list must be updated, and then the issuing CA must be shut down. It can be replaced after it has been shut down, or users can request certificates from other existing CAs that may exist on the network. We will discuss the installation and configuration of these types of CAs in the following sections.

Installing and Configuring the Root CA

The root CA is the most important CA for a PKI and is the first CA in a PKI. The root CA is used to issue certificates to subordinate CAs that are then used to issue certificates to users, computers, and services on the network. A root CA is self-signed; the root CA issues itself a certificate. This requires a great deal of confidence and trust in the CA and its processes, because you must accept that it is vouching for itself and verifying its own identity. All clients on the network must trust the root CAs; otherwise the PKI does not meet the requirement of integrity. The root CA can be added to the client's list of trusted root certificates in several ways:

- An administrator can add the root CA manually using the Certificates MMC console to add the root CA's certificate to each computer's trusted list.

- A user can add the root CA manually using the Certificates MMC console. However, any certificates added to the list of trusted root certificates apply only to that single user on the computer.

- An administrator can use a Group Policy to distribute trusted root certificates for all computers under the control of the Group Policy.

- An administrator can use *certutil.exe* to modify the Configuration container and publish trusted root certificates to the Certification Authorities container under the Public Key Services container.

- An administrator can use `certutil.exe` to modify the Configuration container and publish trusted root certificates to the AIA container under the Public Key Services container.

No matter which method is used, it takes some testing to verify that the trusted root certificates are properly updated. Also note that the first two methods work with Windows NT 4 and later; the other methods work only with Windows 2000 and later systems.

The root remains off the network so that if something happens that compromises an issuing CA, the root CA can be brought back online to revoke the certificate for the compromised issuing CA. The root CA can then be used to issue a certificate to a new replacement CA. The company does not have to scrap its entire PKI if it uses an offline stand-alone root server. Smaller organizations may have only one CA, which is the root CA as well as an issuing CA. A single CA is generally not recommended, because if it fails, the entire PKI is compromised and must be recreated.

The prerequisites for installing a stand-alone offline root CA are as follows:

The stand-alone offline root CA must be a workgroup member and not a member of any domain. Because the root CA is offline and secured, it cannot have network connections and cannot be linked to any domain. If it were a member server in a domain, it would lose its trust relationship with the domain.

The computer name must be unique for the entire forest. Even though the computer is offline, the name is part of the information published in Active Directory.

A *certificate revocation list (CRL)* must be published even though the server is offline. The *CRL distribution point (CDP)* is always included in the certificate. The CDP must be accessible to users on the network. This process is normally completed after the root CA is installed.

The root CA certificate itself should also be made available to the network for verification of the root CA and the CA chain. This process is normally completed after the root CA is installed.

The *authority information access (AIA)* distribution point needs to be configured for the intermediate and other CAs further down the chain so that the CA chain can be properly verified. This process is normally completed after the root CA is installed.

The server for the CA must be running IIS (Internet Information Services). Because the server is not online on the network, the only way to request and retrieve certificates from the offline CA is to use the web forms.

 Virtual PC 2004 and Virtual Server are great software products that you can use to create the three-server hierarchy of PKI certificate servers without multiple physical servers in your lab. You can find information about Virtual PC 2004 at http://www.microsoft.com/windowsxp/virtualpc.

In Exercise 9.1, you will install a stand-alone root CA.

EXERCISE 9.1

Installing a Stand-Alone Root CA

In this exercise, you will install and configure a stand-alone root certificate authority server.

1. Choose Start ➢ Control Panel ➢ Add Or Remove Programs to open the Add Or Remove Programs window.

2. Click Add/Remove Windows Components in the left pane to start the Windows Components Wizard.

3. Select the Certificate Services check box. Click Yes when you see the message stating that you cannot change the computer name or its domain membership.

4. Click the Details button and notice that Certificate Services installs two components: the Certificate Services CA and Certificates Services Web Enrollment Support. Click OK to close the window.

5. Click Next to start the installation and open the CA Type screen.

6. Notice that you have two choices for root CAs: the Enterprise Root CA and the Stand-Alone Root CA. If the server is not a member server, the Enterprise Root CA choice will be grayed out. Click the Stand-Alone Root CA radio button and then click Next to open the CA Identifying Information screen.

7. Fill in the CA identifying information. By default, the CA expires in five years. For an offline root CA, you might want to consider increasing it to 10 years. Click Next to open the Certificate Database Settings screen.

8. Select the location of the certificate database and its log files. It's a good idea to put the database and the log files on separate hard drives. In the event of a hard drive failure, you'll have better restore capability. Click Next.

9. Click OK when you see the warning that IIS will be stopped.

10. You may be prompted for the location of the latest service pack and the original Windows CD. Make sure that you have them available. If you are prompted, click OK and point the installation program to these files. Click Finish.

11. Close all the remaining windows.

At this point, you have a functioning stand-alone root CA. You can now remove it from the network and place it in a secure location.

Installation of a stand-alone root CA is just the first step in building a certificate authority hierarchy as part of the PKI for an organization. The next step is to properly publish information about the stand-alone offline root CA so that it can be accessed by systems that need to check for the CRL and install any intermediate CAs that might be needed for the organization.

Configuring the Publication of CRLs

Publishing the CRL is extremely important to the PKI. The users of the network and the network resources need to know when a certificate has been revoked. If a certificate is revoked, and the network users and resources do not know that it has been revoked, it still has the same value as a current certificate. This is not acceptable in most environments.

For offline CAs, publication requires some manual configuration. Exercise 9.2 will walk you through the process of publishing the CRL so that it is accessible to the users of the network. Keep in mind that if you are using a CA for external use, the CRL must be available to external users too.

EXERCISE 9.2

Creating the CDP for the Stand-Alone Offline Root CA

You can create the CDP using either a file share location, a web URL, or an LDAP (Lightweight Directory Access Protocol) directory location. In this exercise, you will create the CDP using a web URL and the file URL.

Create a Share Point for the CDP

1. Select a server on the network running IIS. This server should be a part of the Active Directory forest.

2. On the selected server, choose Start ➤ Programs ➤ Accessories ➤ Windows Explorer to open Windows Explorer. Navigate to the drive that you want to use for the CDP.

3. Click the hard drive, choose File ➤ New ➤ Folder, and enter the folder name. Name it **CDP**.

4. Right-click the folder and choose Sharing And Security from the shortcut menu. Click the Share This Folder radio button. Accept the default name of CDP.

5. Click the Permissions button and then verify that the Full Control and the Change check boxes are cleared. Only the Read check box should be enabled. Click Add, enter domain admins, and click OK. Select Domain Admins and select the Full Control check box. Click OK twice.

Create a Virtual Directory for the CDP

1. Choose Start ➤Administrative Tools ➤ Internet Information Services (IIS) Manager. Expand the Server and Web Sites objects. Right-click the Default Web Site and then choose New ➤ Virtual Directory. Click Next, name the Alias CDP, and click Next.

2. Enter the directory to the new folder that you just created or use the Browse button to select it. Click Next.

3. Accept the default virtual directory access permissions and click Next. Click Finish.

Copy the *CertEnroll* Folder Contents from the Root CA to the New Directory

1. Go to the root CA server and copy the files and folders from the %systemroot%\system32\ certsrv\certenroll folder on the stand-alone offline root CA to a floppy disk.

2. Copy the contents of the floppy disk to the new share point that you just created.

3. Write down the URL to access the virtual directory and the universal naming convention path to the file share.

Add the CDP and AIA to the CA Certificate

1. On the root CA, choose Start ➤ Administrative Tools ➤ Certification Authority. Right-click the CA server and choose Properties from the shortcut menu to open the CA Server Properties dialog box.

2. Click the Extensions tab.

3. Using the Select Extension drop-down list, select the CRL Distribution Point (CDP) option. Click the Add button and enter the URL for the CDP virtual directory configured in Steps 6 through 8. For example, enter **http://<*ServerDNSName*>/cdp/<CaName><CRLNameSuffix> <DeltaCRLAllowed>.crl** for the location. Click OK.

4. Click the Add button again and enter the URL for the CDP file share configured in Steps 1 through 5. For example, enter **file://\\<ServerDNSName>/cdp/<CaName><CRLNameSuffix> <DeltaCRLAllowed>.crl** for the location. Click OK.

5. On the Extensions tab, use the Select Extension drop-down list and select the Authority Information Access (AIA) option. Click the Add button and enter the URL for the CDP virtual directory configured in Steps 6 through 10 pointing to the certificate file. For example, enter **http:// <*ServerDNSName*>/cdp/<*ServerDNSName*>_<CaName><CertificateName>.crt**. Click OK.

6. Click the Add button and enter the URL for the CDP file share configured in Steps 1 through 5 for the certificate file. For example, enter **file://\\<ServerDNSName>/cdp/<ServerDNSName> _<CaName><CertificateName>.crt**. Click OK.

7. Click OK to close the Extensions tab.

8. Click Yes when you see the message stating that Certificate Services must be restarted for these changes to take effect.

9. Close the Certification Authority snap-in.

The CRL distribution point is now properly published, along with the certificate chain information, and the certificate itself is on the network.

Once the stand-alone offline root CA is properly installed, you must configure the publication points and place them where they can be readily found on the network. Publishing updates to the distribution point requires manually copying the `certenroll` folder files to the CDP folder. You need to remember that Certificate Services publishes a new CRL every week regardless of whether an update is needed. You need to copy and move the CRL to the publication point each week. If you fail to manually move these CRLs to the publication point, you will have a broken chain when the CRL expires and the updated CRL is not available.

After you complete this process, you can install the next level of a CA hierarchy, which means installing any intermediate CAs that might be needed for the organization.

Installing and Configuring the Intermediate CA

After an offline root CA is properly installed, you can start on the next layer of the CA hierarchy. The second layer in a three-layer model is the offline subordinate intermediate CA. The intermediate CA is often used to separate classes and types of certificates that can be distinguished by policy. Organizations that use a three-level CA configuration typically use two stand-alone offline intermediate CAs. Many organizations use one intermediate CA to support external use and a second intermediate CA to support internal use.

The prerequisites for installing a stand-alone offline intermediate CA are as follows:

The stand-alone offline intermediate CA must be a workgroup member and not a member of any domain.   Because the intermediate CA will be offline and secured, it cannot have network connections and cannot be linked to any domain.

The computer name must be unique for the entire forest.   Even though the computer is offline, the name is part of the information published in Active Directory.

A CRL must be published even though the server is offline.   The CDP is always included in the certificate. The CDP must be accessible to users on the network. This process is normally completed after the root CA is installed.

The intermediate CA certificate itself should also be made available to the network for verification of the intermediate CA and the CA chain.   This process is normally completed after the root CA is installed.

The AIA distribution point needs to be configured for the intermediate CA so that the CA chain can be properly verified.   This process is normally completed after the root CA is installed.

The root CA must be available, or it must have its CRL and AIA information properly published.   Certificate users and services must be able to verify that a certificate is still valid by referring to the CA or by referring to the CRL and AIA publication points.

The server for the CA must be running IIS.   Because the server is not online on the network, the only way to request and retrieve certificates from the offline CA is to use the web forms.

In Exercise 9.3, you will install an intermediate CA.

Once the stand-alone offline intermediate CA is properly installed, you must configure the publication information and place it where it can be readily found on the network, as you did earlier for the stand-alone offline root CA. It is vital that the CRL and the AIA information are made available to the network users to verify the certificate, verify that it is not revoked, and verify its chain. The process for the stand-alone offline intermediate CA is exactly the same as it is for the stand-alone offline root CA.

EXERCISE 9.3

Installing an Intermediate CA

In this exercise, you will install an intermediate CA using the root CA installed in Exercise 9.1 as the basis of your new CA. The intermediate CA will be much like your root CA in that it will be a stand-alone offline CA.

1. Choose Start ➤ Control Panel to open the Control Panel. Select Add Or Remove Programs.

2. Click Add Or Remove Windows Components in the left pane.

3. Select the Certificate Services check box. Click Yes when you see the message stating that you cannot change the computer name or its domain membership.

4. Click the Details button. Notice that Certificate Services installs two components: the Certificate Services CA and Certificates Services Web Enrollment Support. Click OK to close the window.

5. Click Next to start the installation and open the CA Type screen.

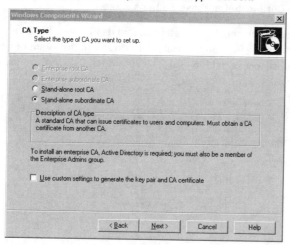

6. Notice that you have two choices for intermediate (subordinate) CAs: the Enterprise Subordinate CA and the Stand-Alone Subordinate CA. Because this is an offline stand-alone server and is not a member of a domain, the Enterprise Subordinate CA option is not available. Select the Stand-Alone Subordinate CA radio button and then click Next to open the CA Identifying Information screen.

7. Fill in the CA identifying information. Note that the Validity Period field is grayed out. Click Next to open the Certificate Database Settings screen.

8. Select the location of the certificate database and its log files. It's a very good idea to put the database and the log files on separate hard drives. In the event of a hard drive failure, you'll have better restore capability. Click Next to open the CA Certificate Request screen.

9. Click the Save The Request To A File radio button. You must use this option because the root CA is an offline CA and is not available on the network. Save the file to a floppy disk that you can then take to the root CA for processing. Click Next.

10. Click Yes when you see the warning that IIS will be stopped.

11. You may be prompted for the location of the latest service pack and the original Windows CD. Make sure that you have them available. If you are prompted, click OK and point the installation program to these files.

12. During the rest of the processing, a message appears stating that the Certificate Services installation will not be complete until you get the certificate from the root CA and then manually install it. Click OK.

13. Click Finish.

14. Close all the remaining windows.

At this point, you have a nonfunctioning stand-alone intermediate CA. To complete the installation, you need to get a certificate from the root CA.

15. Go to the root CA. Start Internet Explorer and, in the Address bar, enter **http://servername/certsrv** to open the Microsoft Certificate Services screen shown here. Click the Request A Certificate link.

16. Click the link to submit an Advanced Certificate Request.

17. Click the link to Submit A Certificate Request By Using A Base-64-Encoded PKCS #10 File, Or Submit A Renewal Request By Using A Base-64-Encoded PKCS #7 File.

18. Using Notepad, open the request file saved to the floppy disk. The content of the file is a certificate request like you used in your SSL exercises in Chapter 6, "Deploying, Managing, and Configuring SSL Certificates." Copy and paste the certificate request into the Saved Request field as shown here. Click Submit.

19. The root CA then responds with a message to the browser stating that the request has been received. However, you must wait for an administrator to approve the request and issue the certificate.

20. Go to the root CA server and choose Start ➢ Administrative Tools ➢ Certification Authority to open the Certification Authority MMC console.

21. Expand the root CA server and click Pending Requests to display the request submitted in Step 18. Right-click the certificate request in the pane on the right and choose All Tasks ➢ Issue from the shortcut menu.

At this point, the certificate for the intermediate CA is now approved and is ready to be picked up and installed on the intermediate CA.

22. Using the web browser on the root CA, go to http://*servername*/certsrv. This time, click the View The Status Of A Pending Certificate Request link.

23. In the web browser, click the Saved-Request Certificate link.

24. Click the Download Certificate and Download Certificate Chain links. Save the files to the floppy disk.

At this point, the root CA has done its part and has provided a certificate for the intermediate CA. Now, you must install it on the intermediate CA so that it is fully functional.

25. Take the floppy to the intermediate CA and insert it in the floppy drive.

26. On the intermediate CA, choose Start ➤ Administrative Tools ➤ Certification Authority. A red square indicates that the intermediate CA is not running.

27. In the Certification Authority MMC console, right-click the intermediate CA server name and then choose All Tasks ➤ Install CA Certificate.

28. Enter the filename and location of the certificate on the floppy disk and click Open to install the certificate needed for the intermediate CA. The file is a .cer file.

At this point, the intermediate CA is operational, and you can remove it from the network and place it in a secure location.

Publishing updates to the distribution point requires manually copying the CertEnroll folder files to the CDP folder. Remember that Certificate Services publishes a new CRL every week regardless of whether an update is needed. You must copy and move the CRL to the publication point each week. If you fail to manually move these CRLs to the publication point, you will have a broken chain when the CRL expires and the updated CRL is not available. You can also choose to extend the length of time between publication periods to make it much longer than a week.

After this process is completed, you can install the next level of a CA hierarchy—any issuing CAs that might be needed for the organization.

Installing and Configuring the Issuing CA

After an offline root CA is properly installed and the appropriate offline intermediate CAs are installed, you can start on the next tier of the CA hierarchy. The third tier in the three-tiered model is the enterprise issuing CA. The issuing CA is usually an enterprise CA because it is used for computers, users, and services that require rapid response for enrollment. Issuing CAs are often configured to provide automatic enrollment for certificates based on permissions. For example, Active Directory domain controllers automatically request certificates when an enterprise CA comes online. Organizations that use a three-level CA configuration typically use two or more issuing CAs for redundancy and for performance reasons.

The prerequisites for installing an issuing CA are as follows:

The server must be a member or domain controller of an Active Directory domain if it is to be an enterprise CA. It must have access to Active Directory domain controllers.

The higher level CAs in a tiered CA environment must have published their CRL and AIA information to a distribution point that is included in the CA certificate. Certificate users and services must be able to verify that a certificate is still valid by referring to the CA or by referring to the CRL and AIA publication points.

DNS must be installed.   Installing an issuing CA requires that DNS be installed in support of the Windows 2000 Active Directory.

IIS must be installed on the same computer as the CA.   The CA needs to authenticate clients to verify that they are requesting only certificates that they have permissions to request. The web enrollment process requires IIS running on the CA.

You can approach the placement of servers running enterprise CAs in different ways. One approach is to place an enterprise CA in each production domain. Another is to keep all CAs in a separate domain for CAs only. A third approach is to place CAs in the forest root domain only. Benefits and liabilities are associated with each approach:

- Placing an enterprise CA in each production domain allows for quick certificate enrollment and authentication processes. However, the resources to do this are fairly significant.

- Placing all enterprise CAs in their own domain makes management fairly easy and allows for good separation of administrative tasks, but it requires the resources for another domain and all the management tasks associated with another domain.

- Placing CAs in the forest root domain might sound good on the surface, but such an approach means having more administrators with rights to the forest root domain, which is a considerable security risk.

Probably the most common approach is to place an enterprise CA in each physical location to issue and manage certificates for that location, without having to worry about certificate enrollment failures or other problems caused by the occasional down WAN link.

Installing and configuring an enterprise issuing CA is similar to configuring an intermediate CA, because the process of requesting and retrieving a certificate from an offline CA is the same for both. The main difference is in the way you publish the information about the CA after it is installed and the type of CA you select during the installation process. In Exercise 9.4, you will install an issuing enterprise CA.

EXERCISE 9.4

Installing an Issuing Enterprise CA

In this exercise, you will install an issuing CA using the intermediate CA installed in Exercise 9.3 as the provider of the certificate for your new CA. The intermediate CA will be much like your root CA in that it will be a stand-alone offline CA too.

1. On the new issuing CA, choose Start ➢ Control Panel to open Control Panel.

2. Click Add Or Remove Windows Components in the left pane.

3. Select the Certificate Services check box. Click Yes when you see the message stating that you cannot change the computer name or its domain membership.

4. Click the Details button. Notice that Certificate Services installs two components: the Certificate Services CA and the Certificates Services Web Enrollment Support. Click OK to close the window.

5. Click Next to start the installation. If the Terminal Services Setup window opens, click Next again. The Terminal Services Setup window always opens if Terminal Services is installed on the server. Click Next to open the CA Type screen.

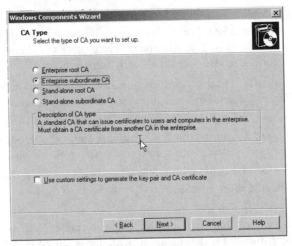

6. Notice that all four options are available this time. Because the server that is to be an Enterprise Subordinate CA is a member of Active Directory, it can take on any of the four CA roles. In this case, select Enterprise Subordinate CA and then click Next.

7. Fill in the CA identifying information. Note that the Validity Period field is grayed out. Click Next to open the Certificate Database Settings screen.

8. Select the location of the certificate database and its log files. It is a good idea to put the database and the log files on separate hard drives. In the event of a hard drive failure, you'll have better restore capability. Click Next to open the CA Certificate Request screen.

9. Click the Save The Request To A File radio button. You must use this option because the intermediate CA is an offline CA and is not available on the network. Save the file to a floppy disk that you can then take to the root CA for processing. Click Next.

10. Click Yes when you see the warning that IIS will be stopped.

11. You may be prompted for the location of the latest service pack and the original Windows CD. Make sure that you have them available. If you are prompted, click OK and point the installation program to these files.

12. During the rest of the processing, a message appears stating that the Certificate Services installation will not be complete until you get the certificate from the root CA and then manually install it. Click OK to acknowledge the statement.

13. Click Finish.

14. Close all the remaining windows.

At this point, you have a nonfunctioning enterprise issuing CA. To complete the installation, you need to get a certificate from the intermediate CA.

15. Go to the intermediate CA. Start Internet Explorer and, in the Address bar, enter **http://servername/certsrv** to display the Microsoft Certificate Services screen. Click the Request A Certificate link.

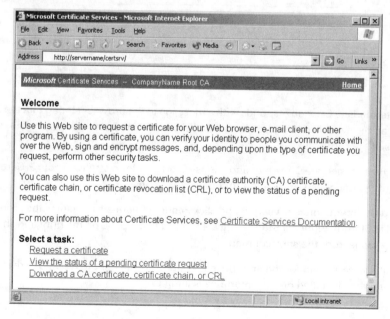

16. Click the link to submit an Advanced Certificate Request.

17. Click the link to Submit A Certificate Request By Using A Base-64-Encoded PKCS #10 File, Or Submit A Renewal Request By Using A Base-64-Encoded PKCS #7 File.

18. Using Notepad, open the request file saved to the floppy disk. The content of the file is a certificate request like you used in your SSL exercises in Chapter 6. Copy and paste the certificate request into the Saved Request field as shown here. Click Submit.

19. The intermediate CA then responds with a message to the browser stating that the request has been received; however, you must wait for an administrator to approve the request and issue the certificate.

20. Go to the intermediate CA server and choose Start ➢ Administrative Tools ➢ Certification Authority to open the Certification Authority MMC console.

21. Expand the intermediate CA server and click Pending Requests to display the request submitted in Step 18. Right-click the certificate request in the pane on the right and choose All Tasks ➢ Issue from the shortcut menu.

At this point, the certificate for the enterprise issuing CA is now approved and is ready to be picked up and then installed on the enterprise issuing CA.

22. Using the web browser on the intermediate CA, go to http://*servername*/certsrv. This time, click the View The Status Of A Pending Certificate Request link.

23. In the web browser, click the Saved-Request Certificate link.

24. Click the Download Certificate and the Download Certificate Chain links. Save the files to the floppy disk.

At this point, the intermediate CA has done its part and has provided a certificate for the enterprise issuing CA. Now you must install it on the enterprise issuing CA so that it will be fully functional.

25. Take the floppy to the enterprise issuing CA and insert it in the floppy drive.

26. On the enterprise issuing CA, choose Start ➢ Administrative Tools ➢ Certification Authority. A red square indicates that the enterprise issuing CA is not running.

27. In the Certification Authority MMC console, right-click the enterprise issuing CA name and choose All Tasks ➢ Install CA Certificate.

28. Enter the filename and location of the issued certificate on the floppy disk and click Open to install the certificate needed for the enterprise issuing CA. The file is a .cer file.

At this point, the enterprise issuing CA is now operational, and you can begin using it.

Once the enterprise issuing CA is properly installed, you must configure the publication information and place it so that it can be readily found on the network. It is vital that the CRL and the AIA information are made available to the network users to verify the certificate, to verify that it is not revoked, and to verify its chain. To verify that the information has been properly entered into Active Directory, use the Active Directory Sites And Services MMC console. In Exercise 9.5, you will view published certificates and CRLs in Active Directory.

EXERCISE 9.5

Viewing Published Certificates and CRLs in Active Directory

In this exercise, you will go through the steps to properly view the published certificates and CRLs in Active Directory.

1. Choose Start ➢ Administrative Tools ➢ Active Directory Sites And Services to open the AD Sites And Services window.

2. Choose View ➢ Show Services Node.

3. Expand the Services folder, expand the Public Key Services folder, and then click AIA to view the certificates that have their AIA information in Active Directory: the root CA, the intermediate CA, and the enterprise CA created in earlier exercises.

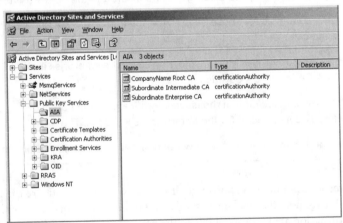

4. Click CDP to display the folders for each server used in the CA hierarchy. Clicking each folder displays which CRLs are on each server.

Not only will the CA information be published in Active Directory, but the certificates it issues can also be published in Active Directory. In the Certification Authority MMC console, right-click the CA server and choose Properties from the shortcut menu. Click the Exit Module tab and then click Configure. Notice the little check box that allows all certificates to be automatically published in Active Directory.

Now that all the CAs are installed, it's time to discuss how to work with templates.

Configuring Certificate Templates

While both Windows Server 2003 Standard and Enterprise Editions can host CAs, only Windows Server 2003 Enterprise Edition can host an online Enterprise CA that can be used to modify *certificate templates*. A certificate template is simply a rule or a profile that defines the contents and structure of a certificate based on how the certificate will be used. Think of a certificate template as a type of certificate that will be used based on the needs of the business. A good example is the certificate used for EFS. The EFS certificate has a particular use, and it meets a specific business need.

Each template is stored in the Configuration container of Active Directory. The entire forest must know about the template and its definition, and the Configuration container is replicated to all domain controllers in the forest, making it available to everyone in the forest. Along with the definitions that include the rules and profiles of the template, a discretionary access control list (ACL) is attached to each template to identify which users or groups of users have permissions to read the templates and also to identify which users and groups of users have permissions to enroll the certificate template and use its capabilities.

When the enterprise CA is installed, a default set of templates are created. These templates can be categorized according to the intended target: users and computers. Another way to view them is as either single-use or multipurpose certificates. The following templates exist, as well as others:

Administrator   Used for a variety of purposes, including authentication, secure e-mail, EFS, and certificate trust signing.

Authenticated Session   Used to authenticate clients.

Basic EFS   Used to encrypt and decrypt data files.

Computer   Used to authenticate clients and servers.

Code Signing   Used to sign applications and drivers.

EFS Recovery Agent   Used to recover encrypted files created and stored by EFS users.

IPSec   Used to establish IPSec communications.

Smart Card Logon   Allows the user of the certificate to authenticate on the network using the certificate stored on the smart card inserted in a smart card reader.

Smart Card User   Used for authentication and for secure e-mail.

Subordinate Certification Authority   Used to add a subordinate CA to a CA hierarchy.

User   Used for authentication, secure e-mail, and EFS.

Web Server   Authenticates the web server to client systems and provides SSL protection of sessions.

By default, only Administrator, Domain Controller, Computer, Basic EFS, EFS Recovery Agent, User, and Web Server templates are available on an enterprise CA. To add other templates, you must use the Certification Authority MMC console, as described in Exercise 9.6.

EXERCISE 9.6

Adding and Deleting Certificate Templates

In this exercise, you will add and delete certificate templates using the Certification Authority MMC console.

Add Certificate Templates

1. On your enterprise CA server, choose Start ➤ Administrative Tools ➤ Certification Authority to open the Certification Authority MMC console.

2. Expand the CA server name and then click Certificate Templates to display all the currently installed certificate templates in the right pane.

3. Choose Action ➤ New ➤ Certificate To Issue.

4. Select the templates that you want to add and click OK.

Delete Certificate Templates

1. Choose Start ➤ Programs ➤ Administrative Tools ➤ Certification Authority to open the Certification Authority MMC console.

2. Expand the CA name and then click Certificate Templates to display all the currently installed certificate templates in the right pane.

3. Right-click the certificate template that you want to delete and choose Delete from the shortcut menu.

Add only the certificate templates needed to meet business requirements. Adding templates for rules that you do not want to support can be a potential security problem and can lead to extra administration. For example, if there is no business requirement for EFS, removing the Basic EFS template from all CAs effectively prevents all users from using EFS within the Active Directory forest. If the template is installed, users have permissions to enroll themselves and to implement EFS, even if you do not want them to do so. If users leave the organization and you need their files, you'll run into a major problem if no recovery agent is available. It is better not to have the capability than it is to try to solve problems after the fact without any prior planning and testing.

Configuring Public Key Group Policies

Windows Server 2003, Windows 2000, and Windows XP Professional computers can use Group Policies to assist with the distribution of certificates in an organization. Normally, somebody with administrative privileges on a computer needs to request and install computer certificates. The process can be an administrative nightmare, because it requires visiting all the computers in an organization. However, with Group Policies, certificates can be enrolled by all users, and the renewal process can be automated as well.

Prerequisites for Using Group Policies to Distribute Certificates

To use Group Policies to assist with the distribution of certificates in an organization, the following requirements must be met:

- The computers must be members of an Active Directory domain.
- The users must be logged in to the domain.
- You need to know the type of certificates needed by the computers.
- You need to know which CA will be used for the process.

Computer certificates include the certificate needed for IPSec, Web Server, and Computer roles. You can install any of these certificate types using Group Policies to automate the enrollment process.

The first step is to install the required certificate template. Exercise 9.6 showed the steps required to install the certificate template. The next step in the process is to configure the Automatic Certificate Request Policy. In this case, you will install the Computer certificate template. Exercise 9.7 will walk you through the required steps.

EXERCISE 9.7

Configuring the Automatic Certificate Request Group Policy

In this exercise, you will configure the default domain Group Policy to allow the automatic enrollment of Computer certificates.

1. Choose Start ➤ Administrative Tools ➤ Active Directory Users And Computers to open Active Directory Users And Computers.

2. Right-click your domain and choose Properties from the shortcut menu.

3. Click the Group Policy tab.

4. Click the Default Domain Policy and then click the Edit button.

EXERCISE 9.7 *(continued)*

5. Expand the Computer Configuration folder, the Windows Settings folder, the Security Settings folder, and the Public Key Policies folder.

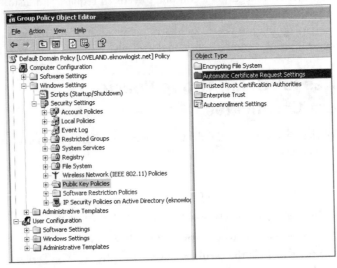

6. Right-click the Automatic Certificate Request Settings folder and choose New ➤ Automatic Certificate Request.

7. Click Next to start the Automatic Certificate Request Setup Wizard.

8. In the Certificate Template screen, select Computer in the Certificate Template list and click Next.

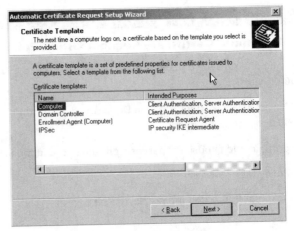

EXERCISE 9.7 *(continued)*

9. Select the enterprise CA that you want to use from the list and click Next.

10. Click Finish to complete the wizard.

11. Close the Group Policy window and click OK.

Once the Group Policy is configured to automatically enroll for certificates, the certificates are automatically requested the next time that users log on or the next time the Group Policy refreshes. As new computers join the domain, they are automatically enrolled for Computer certificates.

You can verify that certificates are installed on computers by using the Certificates MMC console. This is not installed on most client computers. To install it, enter **MMC** in the Open box of the Run dialog box, press Enter, and then use the Add/Remove snap-in to add the Certificates snap-in to the console. Use the Computer Account option with the snap-in installation.

You can use the process described in Exercise 9.7 to edit the Domain Controllers OU Default Domain Controllers Policy. However, in this case, instead of installing the Computer certificate template, install the Domain Controller certificate template. Once the template is configured for automatic enrollment, do not remove it. Doing so can cause WinLogon errors, in particular, Event ID 1010 errors.

You can also use Group Policies to distribute certificates for offline certification authorities. Using a Group Policy to distribute an offline root or intermediate certificate is good practice. Do not use Group Policies to distribute an enterprise CA certificate, because it is automatically published in Active Directory. Whenever possible, manage the Trusted Root Certification Authorities list with Group Policies. Adding a certificate to this list ensures that all Active Directory domain clients receive the certificate automatically. In Exercise 9.8, you'll use Group Policy to configure the Trusted Root Certification Authorities list.

EXERCISE 9.8

Configuring the Trusted Root Certification Authorities List Using Group Policy

In this exercise, you will add an offline root CA's certificate to the Trusted Root Certifications Authorities list using Active Directory Group Policies.

1. Choose Start ➢ Administrative Tools ➢ Active Directory Users And Computers to open Active Directory Users And Computers.

2. Right-click your domain and choose Properties from the shortcut menu.

3. Click the Group Policy tab.

4. Click the Default Domain Policy and then click the Edit button.

5. Expand the `Computer Configuration` folder, the `Windows Settings` folder, the `Security Settings` folder, and the `Public Key Policies` folder.

6. Right-click Trusted Root Certification Authorities and choose All Tasks ➢ Import to start the Certificate Import Wizard.

7. Click Next to open the File To Import screen.

8. Enter the filename and its location in the File Name field or click the Browse button to find it. Remember, this file was copied to a floppy disk in Exercise 9.2. Click Next.

9. Verify that the Place All Certificates In The Following Store radio button is selected and that the Certificate Store field shows Trusted Root Certification Authorities. Click Next.

10. Click Finish to complete the wizard. Click OK to acknowledge that the import was successful.

11. Close the Group Policy window and click OK.

Once the information is configured in the Group Policy, all affected systems receive the certificate. The root certificate becomes part of the computer policy, and all users inherit the certificate trust.

You can also automate the configuration of the Enterprise Trust list using Group Policies. First, create and install an Enterprise Trust list. You can edit it later using the Group Policy, and all the changes will be pushed out to all the computers in the Active Directory domain. In Exercise 9.9, you'll configure the Enterprise Trust list using Group Policy.

Configuring the Enterprise Trust List Using Group Policy

In this exercise, you will create an Enterprise Trust list and add it to the Default Domain Group Policy to deploy the settings using Active Directory Group Policies.

Add a Certificate with Trust List Signing Capabilities

To add the Trust List Signing certificate template, follow the steps in Exercise 9.6. Then follow these steps:

1. Choose Start ➢ Run to open the Run dialog box, enter **MMC** in the Open box, and press Enter.

2. Choose File ➢ Add/Remove Snap-In.

3. Click the Add button. Select the Certificates snap-in from the list and click Add.

4. Click the My User Account radio button and click Finish.

5. Click Close in the Add Standalone Snap-In window. Click OK in the Add/Remove Snap-In window.

6. Expand the `Certificates` folder and double-click Personal.

7. Right-click Certificates and then choose All Tasks ➢ Request New Certificate to start the Certificate Request Wizard.

8. Click Next at the Certificate Request Wizard welcome page.

9. Select Trust List Signing from the Certificate Templates list and click Next.

10. Enter a friendly name and a description for the certificate and click Next.

11. Click Finish to complete the wizard. Click OK when you see the notice that the certificate request was successful.

12. Close the MMC.

Create the Enterprise Trust List

1. Choose Start ➢ Programs ➢ Administrative Tools ➢ Active Directory Users And Computers to open Active Directory Users And Computers.

2. Right-click your domain and choose Properties from the shortcut menu.

3. Click the Group Policy tab.

4. Click the Default Domain Policy and then click the Edit button.

5. In the Group Policy window, expand the `Computer Configuration` folder, the `Windows Settings` folder, the `Security Settings` folder, and the `Public Key Policies` folder.

6. Right-click Enterprise Trust and choose New ➢ Certificate Trust List to start the Certificate Trust List Wizard.

7. Click Next to open the Certificate Trust List Purpose screen.

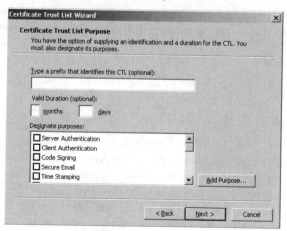

8. Enter the information for the new trust list. Select a prefix for the trust list so you can identify it later. (This is optional but recommended.) Enter a valid duration and select all the purposes required from the list. You can add more purposes using the object identifier (OID) of the purpose if you know it. Click Next when complete.

9. Click Add From Store to add the certificates from the CAs that you want to trust. This step allows you to not select CAs that you do not want to trust in your organization. Alternatively, you can add the list from a file if you have it.

10. Select the CAs that you want on the list, click OK, and then click Next.

11. You can select a certificate to sign the newly created list. You should use the certificate obtained in Steps 1 through 12 earlier. Click Select From Store. Select the certificate listed with the friendly name that you created in Step 10. Click OK.

12. Click Next. Click Next again.

13. Enter a friendly name for the new *certificate trust list (CTL)* in the Friendly Name box. Enter a description. Click Next.

14. Click Finish to complete the wizard. Click OK.

15. Close the Group Policy window and click OK.

You can edit and update this newly created CTL through Group Policy by right-clicking the CTL and choosing All Tasks ➢ Edit. To delete this CTL and remove it from the computers in the domain, right-click the CTL and choose Delete from the shortcut menu.

Configuring Certificate Enrollment and Renewals

There are basically three processes for certificate enrollment: two manual techniques and auto-enrollment. Each process has some requirements that might prevent it from being used.

Manual Enrollment

Any system can use manual enrollment processes. You can manually enroll a certificate in two ways:

- Using the Certificates MMC snap-in
- Using the Certificates Enrollment web pages

Because Windows NT and Windows 9*x* do not support auto-enrollment, you have no other option than to use a manual process. However, only Windows Server 2003, Windows 2000, and Windows XP Professional computers can use the Certificates MMC snap-in to enroll certificates. The MMC does not exist for Windows NT and Windows 9*x* computers. This means that Windows NT and Windows 9*x* computers will be required to use the Certificates Enrollment web pages.

Microsoft also recommends that you use the manual process for high-value certificates such as Web Server certificates and EFS Recovery Agent certificates. Having those certificates available for auto-enrollment is probably not a good idea and would be a great security risk. Because the entire idea of using certificates is based on the security needs of an organization, it makes sense that manual enrollment still be used for certain types of certificates. These high-value certificates should be clearly identified and documented.

The process of requesting and installing a certificate using the Web Enrollment pages has been discussed and used in a few exercises in this chapter and in previous chapters. For a Windows NT and Windows 9x user, the process is no different. In Exercise 9.10, you will use the Web Enrollment pages to manually request a certificate.

EXERCISE 9.10

Using the Web Enrollment Pages to Manually Request a Certificate

You can use either the standard or the advanced method to request a certificate from a CA. You will use both methods in this exercise.

The Standard Method

1. Using the web browser, connect to the CA at http://*CAServerName*/certsrv. You may need to provide user credentials to access the server and to authenticate your identity.

2. Click the Request A Certificate link.

3. Select the User Certificate link.

4. Fill in the information in the More Options link if needed and click Submit. Click Yes to allow the website to obtain the certificate.

5. Click Install This Certificate.

This completes the standard method of using the CA website to enroll a user certificate.

The Advanced Method

1. Using the web browser, connect to the CA at http://*CAServerName*/certsrv. You may need to provide user credentials to access the server and to authenticate your identity.

2. Click the Request A Certificate link.

3. Click the Advanced Certificate Request link.

4. Click the Create And Submit A Request To This CA link. The other requests will not apply to a Windows NT or Windows 9x user. Click Next and select the Certificate Template, then select the Key Options and any Additional Options. Click Submit.

5. Click Yes to confirm that you want the website to request the certificate now.

6. Click Install This Certificate.

This completes the advanced method for using the CA website to enroll a user certificate.

Using the advanced method you can select many more options, but only individuals with specific needs should use it. Most of the time this does not apply to any Windows NT or Windows 9*x* users. The User certificate received through the standard process can be used for secure e-mail, authentication, and EFS.

The other way to manually enroll a certificate is to use the Certificates MMC snap-in, which is used in Exercise 9.11. Remember, this snap-in can be used only by Windows Server 2003, Windows 2000, and Windows XP Professional computers.

EXERCISE 9.11

Using the Certificates MMC Snap-In to Enroll for User and Computer Certificates and for Renewing Certificates

In this exercise, you will configure a custom MMC with the Certificates snap-in and then use your new MMC to request, install, and renew certificates.

Configure an MMC

1. Choose Start ➤ Run to open the Run dialog box, enter MMC in the Open box, and press Enter.

2. Choose Console ➤ Add/Remove Snap-In.

3. Click the Add button, select the Certificates snap-in from the list, and click Add.

4. Click the My User Account radio button and then click Finish.

5. Verify that Certificates is still highlighted in the Add Standalone Snap-In window and click Add again.

6. Click the Computer Account radio button and then click Finish.

7. Close the Add Standalone Snap-In window. Click OK in the Add/Remove Snap-In window.

Request a User Certificate

1. Expand the Certificates folder and double-click Personal.

2. Right-click Certificates and choose All Tasks ➤ Request New Certificate to start the Certificate Request Wizard.

3. Click Next.

4. Select User from the Certificate Templates list and then click Next.

5. Enter a friendly name and a description for the certificate, and click Next.

6. Click Finish to complete the wizard. Click Install Certificate when you see the notice that the certificate request was successful. Click OK in the Certificate Request Was Successful message box.

EXERCISE 9.11 *(continued)*

Request a Computer Certificate

1. Expand the `Certificates` folder and double-click Personal.

2. Right-click Certificates and choose All Tasks ➤ Request New Certificate to start the Certificate Request Wizard.

3. Click Next.

4. Select Computer from the Certificate Templates list and click Next.

5. Enter a friendly name and a description for the certificate, and click Next.

6. Click Finish to complete the wizard. Click Install Certificate when you see the notice that the certificate request was successful. Click OK in the Certificate Request Was Successful message box.

Renew a Certificate

1. Right-click any certificate that you want to renew and choose either All Tasks ➤ Renew Certificate With New Key or All Tasks ➤ Renew Certificate With Same Key. It's a good idea to select the New Key option, because this recreates the certificate key. If anyone has been trying to break your certificate key, this would require that they start their attempt over again.

2. Close the MMC. You might want to save the MMC for later use.

When using the Web Enrollment forms, it is important to know that the user requesting a certificate must have administrator or power user rights on their own computer. They need these rights to install the ActiveX controls and then to install the certificate that is received. If the user does not have the proper rights, the enrollment will fail.

Auto-Enrollment

One of the bigger problems with certificate enrollment is that users make mistakes and obtain the wrong kind of certificate, or they select the wrong options and the certificate is not as strong as they would like. This process can be confusing and can take considerable time for each user on the network.

Certificate auto-enrollment can be set up using Group Policies as discussed earlier in this chapter in the section "Prerequisites for Using Group Policies to Distribute Certificates" and as detailed in Exercise 9.7. Windows Server 2003, Windows 2000, and Windows XP Professional computers can automatically receive computer certificates through auto-enrollment. Windows NT and Windows 9x computers cannot participate in auto-enrollment processes because they do not support Group Policies.

🌐 Real World Scenario

Using a Windows Server 2003 Certification Authority (CA)

You are working on three different projects for your company. The first project is to provide a new application where all Human Resources information—including timesheets, vacation schedules, and sick days—are kept on a web server. The second project is implementing EFS for all users in Accounting and Human Resources. You are also working on another project where the company is investigating smart cards for user authentication.

In all cases, you have been told by the teams that they need extra money for certificates to make their products work. You do not have any money in the budget to purchase certificates from a public certificate authority (CA).

Instead, you implement a private CA infrastructure with an offline root CA, an offline intermediate CA, and an enterprise-issuing CA.

For the first project, you use the Internet Information Server (IIS) Manager snap-in to request and install a certificate from the issuing CA. You configure the Enterprise Trusted Certification Authorities List for distribution using a Group Policy Object. You also configure publication of the certificate distribution point and the certificate revocation list using a Group Policy Object.

For the second project, you use Active Directory to automatically deploy EFS certificates and train key staff members on how to implement EFS. You also configure a data recovery agent for EFS.

For the third project, you configure a smart-card enrollment station where users can get their smart cards activated and download their certificate to their smart cards.

Managing Certificate Authorities

Managing CAs involves many day-to-day tasks and some tasks that are done less frequently such as restoring a CA that you hope you never have to restore. Microsoft has provided some tools to help you manage certificates:

Certificates MMC snap-in   Use this tool to manage the local certificate store and to request, delete, and manage certificates issued to a user or computer.

Certification Authority MMC snap-in   Use this tool to manage the CA and the certificates issued by the CA. You can also use this tool to publish CRLs.

certutil.exe   This is an extremely powerful command-line tool that you can use in scripts to create CAs, to publish CRLs and certification authority certificates, to revoke certificates, and to recover archived private keys. The online help for certutil.exe is several pages long.

certreq.exe   You can use this command-line tool to request certificates from a CA.

You should practice using each of these tools and understand how each of them is used in configuring and managing the CAs in an organization. The Certutil tool has an extremely large number of options available to it. Using `certutil.exe` is the main method of CA management from the command prompt.

Viewing Certificates

You can view certificates if you are running Windows Server 2003, Windows 2000, or Windows XP Professional. Using the Certificates MMC snap-in, you can view certificates issued to you and to your computer. The process of installing the Certificates MMC snap-in was described in Exercise 9.11 earlier in this chapter.

To view your personal certificates, open the console, expand the `Certificates–Current User` folder, expand the `Personal` folder, and then click Certificates to display all your user certificates in the right pane of the window. Double-clicking a certificate opens the Certificate dialog box (see Figure 9.2), which displays information about the certificate.

The Certificate dialog box shows all the details of the User certificate, including the following:

- The capabilities of the certificate. For example, it might show that the certificate can be used for secure e-mail.

- The date issued.

- The expiration date.

- The issuing CA.

FIGURE 9.2   The Certificate dialog box

Clicking the Details tab displays even more information about the certificate, including the following:

- Version
- Serial number
- Length of the key
- Certificate template used
- CRL publication point
- AIA publication point

The Certification Path tab of the Certificate dialog box shows the certificate chain. It illustrates which CA issued the certificate to the user, which CA issued the certificate to the issuing CA, which CA issued the intermediate CA's certificate, and so on, all the way to the root CA of the certificate chain.

You can also view the certificates issued to the computer. Open the console, expand the `Certificates (Local Computer)` folder, expand the `Personal` folder, and then click Certificates to display all certificates for this computer in the right pane of the window. Double-clicking a certificate opens the Certificate dialog box, which displays details about the computer certificate.

Using the Certification Authorities MMC console, an administrator can click the `Issued Certificates` folder, which is illustrated in Figure 9.3. The certificates are visible in the right pane of the window. Double-clicking any certificate displays details about it.

Revoking Certificates

Revoking certificates will be necessary on some occasions. Most of the time, revocation involves an employee leaving the company or a partner who is no longer a partner. In both cases, you cannot allow these certificates to be used on your network, so you must revoke them. If you do not revoke these certificates, they will be valid until they expire. Because many certificates are created for considerable lengths of time, it is important that you not let them continue to exist on the network.

To revoke a certificate, use the Certificate Authority MMC console on the CA, as described in Exercise 9.12.

FIGURE 9.3 The Certification Authority MMC

EXERCISE 9.12

Revoking a Certificate

In this exercise, you will revoke a certificate.

1. Choose Start ➢ Administrative Tools ➢ Certification Authority.

2. Expand the CA server, if necessary, to display the Issued Certificates folder in the left pane.

3. Click the Issued Certificates folder to display all the certificates issued by the CA.

4. Right-click the certificate that you want to revoke and choose All Tasks ➢ Revoke Certificate to open the Certificate Revocation dialog box.

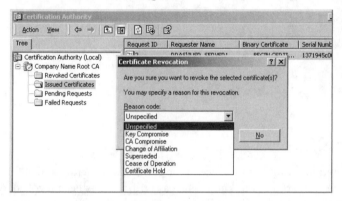

5. In the Reason Code drop-down list, select the reason for the revocation and click Yes.

Following these steps revokes the certificate, and it now appears in the Revoked Certificates folder under the CA.

Editing Certificates

You can edit certificates by using the Certificates MMC snap-in. Open the Certificate dialog box for the certificate and click the Details tab. Click Edit Properties to open the Certificate Properties dialog box (see Figure 9.4), and edit the friendly name and the description. You can also change the purposes of the certificate. You can choose to disable all the purposes, or you can choose to enable or disable any of the individual purposes for a multipurpose certificate.

FIGURE 9.4 Editing a certificate

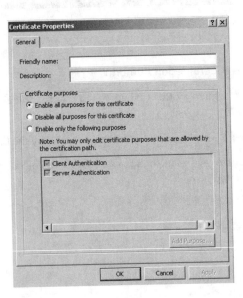

Managing CRLs

The CRL is an extremely important piece of the certificate structure and any PKI. Users and computers on the network need to know when a certificate has been revoked; otherwise, they will continue to accept it and use it just like any valid certificate. If you continue to use revoked certificates, you cannot be confident in your PKI. Security will be impaired.

We described how to manually publish the CRL in Exercise 9.2 for offline certificate authorities. You need to remember to publish all offline CRLs regularly. This should be part of your standard administrative tasks. To reduce the amount of work this takes, you can lengthen the time before a CRL expires by configuring its publication interval to a longer period of time such as every three months or even every year. After all, the only time you revoke a certificate for an offline CA is when an issued certificate has become compromised, and there should not be many issued certificates for an offline CA.

By default, each CA updates and publishes a new CRL based on a time interval. Any certificates revoked between publications of the CRL are still valid, so it's extremely important that you set the expiration time to minimize these problems. However, you do not want to set this interval to such a small number that your clients have to go to the CA and retrieve updates too often. An alternative to reducing the update time period is to manually publish the CRL after major changes.

In the Certification Authority MMC console, right-click the Revoked Certificates folder and choose Properties from the shortcut menu. In the Properties dialog box, you can set the publication interval and also view the current CRL. Right-click the Revoked Certificates folder and choose All Tasks ➢ Publish to update and publish the CRL immediately. The new CRL is updated in Active Directory, if it's an enterprise CA, and in the %systemroot%\system32\certsrv\certenroll folder of the certificate authority.

Backing Up and Restoring the CA

As with any resource, it's important that you understand and practice backing up and restoring a certificate authority. You should have documented processes before you actually have to do it, and you should be comfortable with the process. Because you may have to restore a backup that you created, it's important that you know you can trust your backups and that they will work.

CA Backup

The CA maintains information about all certificates it has issued, has revoked, or has pending in its database and its log files. Much of this information is also stored in the Registry, which is another reason to make sure you have the machine physically secured. Because the data for the CA is stored in databases and in the Registry, you need to make sure that you back up all the components necessary to properly restore a failed CA. Also, because Windows Server 2003 uses IIS 6 and Windows 2000 uses IIS 5 to issue certificates, you need to make sure that the IIS *metabase* is properly backed up.

Back up the database and log files using `certutil.exe`, which can also be used for many other functions:

- You can back up the CA certificate and the private key using Certutil–backupKey.
- You can back up the database using Certutil–backupDB.

To back up the CA configuration information stored in the Registry, use the NTbackup program that ships with Windows or use any third-party backup program that backs up the system state data of the server. Because the backups contain valuable information, properly secure and store them in a safe place.

You can use the Certification Authority MMC console to back up the Certificate Services. Open the console, right-click the CA, and choose All Tasks ➤ Backup CA to start a wizard that completes the backup process. The wizard allows you to back up the private key, the CA certificate, the issued certificate log, and the pending certificate request queue, as shown in Figure 9.5. You must send the backup to an empty folder, however. You are then prompted for a password and can complete the wizard.

FIGURE 9.5   The Certification Authority Backup Wizard

Backing up the IIS metabase requires using the Internet Information Service (IIS) Manager MMC console. Exercise 9.13 steps you through this process.

EXERCISE 9.13

Backing Up the CA

Backing up the CA requires two steps. First, you must back up the Certificate Services and then you must back up the IIS metabase.

Back Up the CA

1. Choose Start ➤ Administrative Tools ➤ Certification Authority.

2. Right-click the CA and choose All Tasks ➤ Backup CA to start the Certification Authority Backup Wizard.

3. Click Next to open the Items To Back Up screen.

4. Select the Private Key And CA Certificate check box and then select the Certificate Database and Certificate Database Log check box.

5. In the Back Up To This Location field, enter the drive and path for the location where the backup will be stored. The wizard creates the folder if needed. The folder must be empty. Click Next to open the Select A Password screen.

6. Enter and confirm the password needed for a restore. Click Next.

7. Click Finish to close the wizard.

8. Close the Certification Authority MMC console.

Back Up the Metabase

1. Choose Start ➤ Administrative Tools ➤ Internet Information Services (IIS) Manager.

2. Right-click the server name and choose Backup/Restore Configuration to open the Configuration Backup/Restore window.

3. Click the Create Backup button to open the Configuration Backup dialog box.

4. Enter a name for the backup. (It might be a good idea to use a date in the name structure.) You may also wish to include a password for encryption of the backup. Click OK.

5. Click Close when the backup is complete.

6. Close the Internet Information Services MMC console.

Exercise 9.13 is a manual process, and you cannot schedule it using the graphical user interface. To properly schedule a CA backup, use the `certutil.exe` command-line utility and the Task Scheduler. In addition, use the NTBackup utility or a third-party backup program to schedule the backup of the system state data of the server, which also properly backs up the IIS metabase.

The best practice is to use a high-quality tape drive and a third-party backup program that captures the system state data and can be used to schedule backups. Make sure to store the tapes for the CA backup in a secure area.

CA Restoration

The restore process depends on the backup method. Properly restoring the Certificate Services in the event of corruption requires a current copy of the database and the IIS metabase. If the database and certificate were backed up with `certutil.exe`, use `certutil.exe` to restore the information:

- To restore the CA certificate and the private key, use Certutil–restoreKey.
- To restore the database, use Certutil–restoreDB.

To restore the CA configuration information stored in the Registry, use the NTbackup program that ships with Windows or any third-party backup program that backs up the system state data of the server.

If the backup was done using the Certificate Authority MMC console and the Internet Services Manager MMC console, the restore should use the same tools and the steps outlined in Exercise 9.14.

EXERCISE 9.14

Restoring the CA

Restoring the CA requires two steps. First, you must restore the Certificate Services, and then you must restore the IIS metabase.

Restore the CA

1. Choose Start ➢ Administrative Tools ➢ Certification Authority.

2. Right-click the CA and choose All Tasks ➢ Restore CA.

3. Click OK when you see the message that Certificate Services must be stopped in order to continue.

4. At the Welcome screen of the wizard, click Next to open the Items To Restore screen.

5. Select the Private Key And CA Certificate check box and then select the Certificate Database And Certificate Database Log check box.

6. Enter the drive and path of your backup files. You can click the Browse button to find the folder if needed. Click Next.

7. Enter the password used during the backup. Click Next.

8. Click Finish to close the wizard. Click Yes in the Certificate Authority Restore Wizard notification window. This restarts the Certificate Services as well.

9. Close the Certification Authority MMC console.

Restore the Metabase

1. Choose Start ➤ Administrative Tools ➤ Internet Information Services (IIS) Manager.

2. Right-click the server name and choose Backup/Restore Configuration from the shortcut menu to open the Configuration Backup Restore dialog box.

3. Select the backup files that you want to restore and click the Restore button.

4. Click Yes in the IIS Manager window that tells you that restoring is a lengthy process and requires stopping and restarting services.

5. Click OK when the restore is completed. Close the Configuration Backup/Restore dialog box.

6. Close the Internet Information Services (IIS) Manager MMC console.

You can use the steps in Exercise 9.14 to restore only a corrupted database. If the server itself has failed, you'll need to restore the entire server from backups. Hopefully you have recent backups of the server and the system state data. If you have these backups, use the normal restore process for your backup software. The best practice is to use a high-quality tape drive and a third-party backup program that captures the system state data and can be used to schedule backups. You can then use this same program to restore the server in the event of a failure.

Summary

With the new focus on security for networking, it's clear that you'll have to deploy and support a PKI in the future, if not right away. To properly deploy a PKI, you need a trustworthy CA hierarchy and the processes to properly support Certificate Services. To support the PKI and the CA hierarchy, you need to be able to do the following:

- Install and configure three types of CAs:
  - Root
  - Intermediate
  - Issuing certificate
- Configure and utilize certificate templates
- Configure publication for the following:
  - CRLs
  - AIA

- Utilize Group Policy Objects to automate certificate processes
- Configure enrollment and renewal of certificates
- Manage CAs

Certificates are an increasingly important part of securing networking today. We need stronger and better methods of authentication, and we need these methods to be standards that will work with many operating systems on both servers and client systems. Not only do you need to know how to use certificates, you need to know how to support the structure to issue and manage certificates.

Exam Essentials

Know how to install and configure the root CA.   Make sure you understand how to install an offline stand-alone root CA. In particular, know how to use the Web Enrollment pages to request and receive certificates and how to publish CRL and AIA information so that it is available on the network even if the CA is not available.

Know how to install and configure the intermediate CA.   Make sure you understand how to install an offline stand-alone subordinate CA. In particular, know how to use the Web Enrollment pages to request and receive certificates and how to publish CRL and AIA information so that it is available on the network even if the root CA is not available.

Make sure you understand how to apply a certificate to the CA server from the offline stand-alone root CA.

Know how to install and configure the issuing CA.   Make sure you understand the prerequisites for installing an enterprise subordinate CA. Make sure you understand how to publish the CRL and AIA for an enterprise CA.

Understand how to configure certificate templates.   Make sure you understand how to add and delete certificate templates from the list of templates serviced by the enterprise CA. Make sure you understand the difference between a computer and a user certificate template. Make sure you understand how to disable parts of a multifunction template.

Understand how to configure the publication of CRLs.   Make sure you understand how to publish offline and enterprise certificate authority CRLs. Understand how to change the publishing interval and when it is appropriate to manually update a CRL for publication.

Know how to configure public key Group Policies.   Make sure you understand how to use Group Policies to automatically enroll certificates, to provide Trusted Root Certification Authorities lists, and to provide Enterprise Trust lists.

Make sure you can configure certificate renewals and enrollment.   Make sure you understand how to manually enroll certificates and how to manually renew certificates. Make sure you understand how to use both the Certificates MMC snap-in and the Web Enrollment pages to manually enroll certificates. Make sure you understand how to use auto-enrollment for Windows Server 2003, Windows 2000, and Windows XP Professional computers on the network.

Know how to deploy certificates to users, computers, and CAs.   Make sure you understand how to issue certificates as an offline stand-alone CA and as an enterprise CA. Make sure you can issue certificates to users who manually request certificates and that you can use the auto-enrollment capabilities to automatically distribute certificates.

Understand the activities involved in managing CAs.   Make sure you understand how to do the following:

- Enroll and renew certificates.
- Revoke certificates.
- Manage and troubleshoot CRLs.
- Back up and restore the CA and the IIS metabase.

Review Questions

1. To which of the following can certificates be issued? (Choose all that apply.)

   A. Computers

   B. Users

   C. Services

   D. Certificate authorities

2. Knowing that the sender is indeed who they say they are is an example of which of the following?

   A. Confidentiality

   B. Nonrepudiation

   C. Availability

   D. Sealing

3. Which services utilize certificates? (Choose all that apply.)

   A. 802.1x

   B. EFS

   C. IPSec

   D. NTLMv2

4. Using a card-sized hardware device with a certificate installed on it to identify the holder of the card is an example of which of the following?

   A. Smart cards

   B. One-time passwords

   C. Biometric device

   D. Scanning devices

5. Which of the following are encrypted protocols?

   A. Telnet

   B. SMTP

   C. FTP

   D. HTTPS

6. Which of the following are often implemented as stand-alone offline services? (Choose all that apply.)

   A. Root CAs

   B. Intermediate CAs

   C. Enterprise CAs

   D. Issuing CAs

7. Which methods can be used to add a new CA to the list of trusted root certificates on a computer? (Choose all that apply.)

    A. A local administrator can add the CA manually using the Certificates MMC console to add the CA's certificate to each computer's trusted list.

    B. A user can add the CA manually using the Certificates MMC console. Any certificates added to the list of Trusted Root Certificates apply only to that single user on the computer, however.

    C. An administrator can use a Group Policy to distribute Trusted Root Certificates for all computers under the control of the Group Policy.

    D. An administrator can use the Certification Authorities MMC console to add the CA to all computers in the Active Directory domain.

8. A single-level CA hierarchy contains which of the following?

    A. An enterprise root CA

    B. An intermediate CA

    C. An enterprise subordinate CA

    D. A stand-alone subordinate CA

9. Stand-alone root CAs often have which of the following? (Choose all that apply.)

    A. Short publication intervals

    B. Large numbers of certificates issued

    C. Long publication intervals

    D. Manual CRL publication processes

10. Stand-alone CAs must have which of the following? (Choose all that apply.)

    A. DNS installed

    B. Unique computer names from the rest of the computers in the forest

    C. IIS running

    D. Self-issued certificates

11. Certificate revocation list distribution points can be published using which of the following? (Choose all that apply.)

    A. HTTP

    B. FTP

    C. LDAP

    D. File shares

12. Which CA requires DNS to be installed in the network?

    A. Enterprise root CA

    B. Enterprise subordinate CA

    C. Stand-alone root CA

    D. Stand-alone subordinate CA

13. Which tool is used to verify that the CRL and the AIA have been properly published in Active Directory?

    A. Certificates MMC console

    B. Certification Authority MMC console

    C. Active Directory Users And Computers

    D. Active Directory Sites And Services

14. Which of the following are default certificate templates? (Choose all that apply.)

    A. Trust List Signing

    B. CEP Encryption

    C. User

    D. Computer

15. You need to back up the CA for your domain. What should you do? (Choose all that apply.)

    A. Back up the system state data.

    B. Back up the certificates database.

    C. Back up the DNS database.

    D. Back up the CDP.

16. You need to manually publish the CRL. Which node or folder do you use in the Certification Authority MMC console?

    A. `Revoked Certificates`

    B. `Issued Certificates`

    C. `Pending Requests`

    D. `Failed Requests`

17. Your company has installed an enterprise CA and has just configured Group Policies to automatically enroll all computers to receive computer certificates. You check your certificates store and do not find a computer certificate. What is the most likely reason?

    A. You need to log out and then log back in to receive the new GPO.

    B. The root CA is an offline CA.

    C. The GPO should be applied to the Domain Controllers OU.

    D. The Enterprise Trust list was not updated with the new CA.

18. You receive a call from a user who wants to enroll for a computer certificate. You try to walk them through the process of using the Certificates MMC snap-in to request a certificate, but they say that they cannot start the MMC. What is the most likely reason?

    A. The Enterprise Trust list has not been added to the Group Policy.

    B. The computer template is not available on the CA.

    C. The user does not have permissions to the Certificates snap-in.

    D. The user's computer is running Windows 95 or 98.

19. You receive a call from a user. They are looking at the Certificates MMC snap-in but do not see the computer certificate that they enrolled yesterday. You check the CA and see that it was issued yesterday. What is the most likely problem?

    A. The Group Policy permissions stopped the certificate from being applied.

    B. The root CA was not online when their request went to the enterprise subordinate CA.

    C. They are looking at the Certificates–Current User instead of Certificates (Local Computer) node.

    D. They need Service Pack 3 for Windows 2000 to view computer certificates.

20. You are trying to configure a new automatic certificate request for user certificates. The user template is not listed in the Certificate Template screen in the wizard, and you cannot complete your task. What is the most likely reason?

    A. You tried to apply the setting to the Domain Controllers OU instead of to the domain.

    B. The User certificate template has not been installed, and it needs to be installed first.

    C. Windows 2000 does not support distribution of User templates through Group Policies.

    D. You need to be an Enterprise Admin in order to deploy User certificates through Group Policies.

Answers to Review Questions

1.   A, B, C, D. Certificates can be issued to computers, users, services, and CAs. Many people forget that a CA must receive a certificate from either another CA or from itself.

2.   B. Nonrepudiation is referred to in authentication as providing proof of the integrity and the origin of the message that can be verified by a third party (the CA).

3.   A, B, C. Certificates are used by 802.1x in authentication, in EFS for encryption of files, and in IPSec in encryption of network traffic.

4.   A. A smart card is a plastic card with an integrated chip or embedded integrated circuit that can store information such as a certificate.

5.   D. HTTPS is SSL-enabled HTTP (web traffic) and requires a certificate for encryption.

6.   A, B. Root and intermediate (sometimes called policy) CAs are often implemented as offline CAs and are not connected to the network. Enterprise and issuing CAs are online and need to be online to handle all the transactions necessary.

7.   A, B, C. Certificates can be added using the Certificates MMC Console or using Group Policies. They can also be added using the `certutil.exe` command-line tool.

8.   A. A single-level CA hierarchy always contains an enterprise CA.

9.   C, D. Stand-alone root CAs often have long publication intervals and require a manual CRL publication process, because they do not issue many certificates and they cannot automatically update CRL publication points because they are offline.

10. B, C. The name must be unique because it is used within Active Directory and throughout the forest, and IIS must be installed to manage offline certificate requests. Only the root needs a "self-issued certificate"; offline intermediate CAs receive a certificate from the root CA.

11. A, C, D. CDPs can be published using web servers, file shares, and Active Directory (LDAP).

12. A, B. Enterprise CAs require DNS to support Active Directory, which is required for an enterprise CA.

13. D. ADSS is used with Show Services Node enabled to verify that the CRL and AIA have been properly published.

14. C, D. By default, only the templates for Administrator, Domain Controller, Computer, Basic EFS, EFS Recovery Agent, User, and Web Server are installed.

15. A, B. Backing up the system state data gets the configuration information in the Registry, including the IIS 5 metabase, and then backing up the database itself works. You should also back up the CA certificate and its private key.

16. A. Right-click the `Revoked Certificates` folder and choose All Tasks ➢ Publish.

17. A. You need to either log out and log back in again or wait for the GPO refresh interval to pass.

18. D. MMC is not available on Windows 95 and 98 clients. To enroll, the user must use the Web Enrollment pages.

19. C. Only user certificates can be seen using the Certificates–Current User node.

20. C. Windows 2000 and 2003 only supports distribution of computer-based certificates through the Automatic Certificate Request Settings in Group Policies.

Chapter

10

Managing Client-Computer and Server Certificates and EFS

THE MICROSOFT EXAM OBJECTIVES COVERED IN THIS CHAPTER:

✓ **Plan requirements for digital signatures.**

✓ **Install, manage, and configure Certificate Services.**

- Install and configure root, intermediate, and issuing certification authorities (CAs). Considerations include renewals and hierarchy.

- Configure certificate templates.

- Configure, manage, and troubleshoot the publication of certificate revocation lists (CRLs).

- Configure archival and recovery of keys.

- Deploy and revoke certificates to users, computers, and CAs.

- Back up and restore the CA.

Chapter 9, "Installing, Configuring, and Managing Certificate Authorities," discussed installing, configuring, and managing the certificate authority (CA). This chapter focuses on certificates from the perspective of the client computer and the server. Although it might seem that we are repeating concepts and issues and objectives, we're going to explore many new ones in this chapter while reinforcing some of the previous discussions by looking at them from the client-computer side. We're also going to discuss the Encrypting File System (EFS) and its reliance on certificates.

As you saw in Chapter 9, installing and configuring a PKI (public key infrastructure) is vital to properly securing networks. However, you might forget that the whole purpose of a PKI is to properly provide certificates to computers and users on the network.

If you use the driver's license analogy for authentication, it makes a great deal of sense. It does no good to have top-quality driver's licenses with the ability to provide third-party verification if the driver's license office is open only on Friday for three hours. It does no good to have great identity-verification tools if nobody can get the identifications and if nobody uses them as proof of identity.

So, this chapter puts the pieces together. You will use certificates for securing data storage and messaging. You will also look at troubleshooting certificate usage from the client side.

Managing Client Certificates

Computer certificates are also known as *machine certificates*. Server certificates are exactly the same thing as client-computer certificates. Computer certificates authenticate computers, whether they are client computers or server computers. Well, it really isn't that simple, but you can use this to get started.

However, client computers generally use different *certificate templates* than servers. For example, a client computer would most likely never need to enroll a web server certificate for *SSL (Secure Socket Layer)*. So there's a difference between the two, and it all comes down to the tasks and how certificates are used. In the following sections, you'll look at how certificates are used for specific tasks on client computers.

Securing E-mail with Secure MIME

Secure Multipart Internet Mail Extension (S/MIME) has been used for years to sign and seal e-mail across the Internet as well as within organizations. Chapter 5, "Implementing Security for Wireless Networks," talked about using SSL-enabled SMTP (Simple Mail Transfer Protocol) to send e-mail to an SMTP server out on the Internet and to secure the e-mail during the travel from the client computer to the server. Once the e-mail hits the server and is sent to another SMTP server (the destination) on the Internet, the e-mail is traveling in the clear. A good analogy is the postal system. The best way to think of these messages is that there are three classes of messages or mail service:

- Totally open and in the clear, like a postcard. Standard SMTP is like a postcard.
- Signed with a clear and recognizable signature. Signed SMTP is like a signed postcard.
- Signed with a clear and recognizable signature and sealed in an envelope. Signed and sealed SMTP is like a signed letter in a sealed envelope.

Normally, SMTP traffic is all in the clear, like a postcard. You write your message on the back and put on a stamp for postage. While the postcard is being processed by the postal service, every person who handles it can read it. What prevents everyone from reading it? Absolutely nothing, other than the fact that people have better things to do with their lives. Because post-cards are not secure, you generally don't use postcards for sending private information to friends and relatives.

Think about office memos. What is the one item in a memo that really proves who wrote it? It is either a clear *signature* or some initials. If you want to ruin somebody's day, write a memo telling them that they will be laid off in four weeks and put it on their desk. The only way to know it's not real is to verify the signature.

It's the same with SMTP e-mail. The problem with e-mail is that not everyone uses *digital signatures* to *sign* their messages. Similar to verifying a person's real signature by asking them if it is their signature or comparing it to a previous one, a digital signature can actually be checked with a third party: the certificate authority that issued it. If the e-mail is signed, the signature can be checked, and you can be sure that the e-mail was not replaced en route and that it was not tampered with during the journey.

When you want to send confidential correspondence (private letters), you fold them and put them in envelopes. The receiver can look at an envelope and can verify the letter was not opened and replaced with another letter by verifying the *seal*. This is the same thing as a sealed e-mail. The seal hides the content from prying eyes. Unlike memos lying on desks and postcards, a sealed letter cannot be viewed without some evidence of it being opened.

In standard business correspondence, letters are both signed and sealed. To do the same thing in e-mail is a good practice for messages that need this type of security.

S/MIME is based on *public-private key pairs* and requires certificates. As you know from previous chapters, you can use either a private CA or a public CA to get certificates. In the case of e-mail, which will be sent all around the world as well as inside the company, it makes good sense to use a public CA. After all, the receivers are going to want to verify the signature, and a public CA is best suited to handle that task.

NOTE Remember one nice thing about postcards: They are cheaper to send. Security has a cost, and that is the expense of acquiring, maintaining, and managing certificates and the expense of encryption when it comes to CPU time.

The process involves three main steps:

1. Obtain a certificate for e-mail.

2. Send a signed e-mail message to everyone who will send you encrypted e-mail messages.

3. Receive a signed e-mail message from everyone who wants to send encrypted e-mail.

   In Exercise 10.1, you'll see how to use S/MIME to sign and seal e-mail.

EXERCISE 10.1

Using S/MIME to Sign and Seal E-mail

In this exercise, you will go through all three steps using Outlook Express.

Acquire the Certificate

1. Go to the web page of your favorite public CA. The process will vary slightly depending on the CA. If you do not have a favorite, select one from Microsoft's recommended Digital ID provider list at http://office.microsoft.com/assistance/2000/certpage.aspx? &helplcid=1033&path=outldigid.asp. For this exercise, you will use Comodo Group at www.comodogroup.com.

2. Click the Products link, click Certificate Services, and then click Free Secure Email Certificates. Click Sign Up Now.

3. Enter the information as shown in the following graphic for the application form. Click Advanced Security Options if you want to choose the *Cryptographic Service Provider (CSP)* and the key size. You can choose a CSP that will work with a smart card if you want and use the default options. Click Submit & Continue.

4. You may receive a Potential Scripting Violation warning screen such as the one shown in the following graphic, depending on how your web browser security is configured. Click Yes to request the certificate.

5. Instructions on how to download and install your certificate are then e-mailed to the address you entered in Step 3.

6. Click the link in your e-mail to collect and install your certificate.

7. In the web page that is displayed in the following graphic, click Collect & Install Certificate.

8. Enter the e-mail address and the password provided by Comodo Group in the web form as shown in the following graphic. Click Submit & Continue.

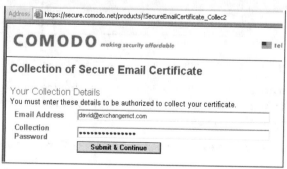

9. You may again receive a Potential Scripting Violation warning screen. Click Yes if you receive the warning. You should then receive a message that your certificate is now installed.

Install the Certificate Using Outlook Express

1. Open Outlook Express.

2. Choose Tools ➢ Accounts to open the Internet Accounts dialog box.

3. Click the Mail tab and select the e-mail account for the certificate. The e-mail address for the account must match the e-mail address that you used to acquire the certificate.

4. With your account highlighted, click the Properties button to open the Properties dialog box for that account.

5. Click the Security tab.

6. In the Signing Certificate section, click Select, as shown in the following graphic. Select the certificate from the list and click OK.

7. In the Encrypting Preferences section, click Select, select the certificate, and click OK.

8. In the Algorithm drop-down list box, select the algorithm that you want people to use when they send you encrypted e-mail. *3DES,* or triple DES, is the default and is the strongest algorithm available on the list.

9. Click OK to close the Properties dialog box and then click Close to close the Internet Accounts dialog box.

Send Signed E-mail Using Outlook Express

1.   Open Outlook Express.

2.   Click Create Mail.

3.   Create an e-mail message as you would normally do.

4.   Click the Sign button.

5.   Click Send.

Add Received Certificates in Outlook Express

As we discussed, before you can send encrypted e-mail to somebody, you must have their certificate. If they e-mail you a signed message, you can get their certificate from that message. The best way is to configure Outlook Express to automatically add the certificate.

1.   Open Outlook Express.

2.   Choose Tools ➤ Options to open the Internet Options dialog box.

3.   Click the Security tab.

4.   Click the Advanced button to open the Advanced Security Settings dialog box.

5.   Enable the Add Senders Certificates To My Address Book option.

6.   Click OK to close the Advanced Security Settings dialog box. Click OK to close the Internet Options dialog box.

Send Encrypted E-mail Using Outlook Express

Again, remember that you cannot send encrypted e-mail unless you already have the receiver's certificate that contains their *public* key.

1.   Open Outlook Express.

2.   Click Create Mail.

3.   Create an e-mail just as you would normally do.

4.   Click the Encrypt button.

5.   Click Send.

Configuring S/MIME enables improvements in messaging and heightens your confidence that messages are from whom the sender says they are. Knowing that your messages were not altered or even read by others allows for more confidential communications through e-mail. Although these e-mail certificates are actually *personal certificates* and not machine certificates, we cover this topic here because the certificates are stored on the computer. To change computers requires *exporting* the certificates from the current computer and then *importing* them to the new computer.

We'll cover exporting certificates later in this chapter. However, you can use Outlook Express to export certificates. Choose Tools ➢ Options to open the Internet Options dialog box. On the Security tab, click Digital IDs. In the Certificates dialog box, you can select a certificate and then click the Export button to copy the certificate to a file and then store it in a safe place. You can also remove a certificate by selecting it and then clicking the Remove button.

 Real World Scenario

Signing E-Mail

I was recently at a client site helping them plan their Exchange 2003 upgrade strategy. While on site, the administrator asked if I knew anything about digital signatures because she was having a problem she couldn't solve.

This client is a U.S. Department of Defense (DoD) contractor. All official contract documents require a digital signature when sending via e-mail. Recently, the administrator said the DoD customer was reporting that the e-mail messages were coming in with an invalid signature.

My first thought was the certificate had expired. We went to one of the contracting officer's computers to look at the certificate (remember, e-mail certificates are stored on the computer). The certificate was fine. I checked the certificate revocation list (CRL) to see if the root CA had been compromised. It too was fine.

We called the customer and asked them to forward a copy of the invalid message. Sure enough, it indicated the message had been tampered with. We signed a message and sent to an internal mailbox so we could see all headers. Interestingly, the signature was valid! After a coffee break, we sent a message to my personal e-mail account (external to the client). I fired up my VPN and connected back to the office to look at the message. Outlook reported the message had been tampered with! I told Outlook to ignore the error and open the message. Sure enough, the message had more text than we had typed in the test message, so indeed it had been tampered with. The external mail gateway had added a disclaimer. The disclaimer program had tampered with the message. The message on the receiving end was different from the message as it existed when we signed.

Later we discovered that one of the junior administrators had incorrectly changed the group membership on the disclaimer application. In addition to illustrating how certificates can sign e-mail messages and can show tampering, this also demonstrates how simple change management can impact your security configurations.

Securing Files and Folders with the Encrypting File System (EFS)

Now that you're confident that your e-mail is not being read by everyone on the Internet and everyone internally in the company, let's move on. You can use the *Encrypting File System (EFS)* to encrypt all the folders and files that you have to protect from prying eyes. You can use EFS to encrypt files stored on Windows 2003 NTFS-formatted drives. EFS uses key pairs in combination with a symmetric key to perform *encryption* and *decryption*.

Using EFS is simple from the user perspective. Certificate enrollment and implementation is completely hidden from the network user. In fact, the user doesn't even need a certificate for EFS in order to encrypt files. When the user sets the encryption attribute for a file or folder, EFS attempts to locate a certificate in the user's personal certificate store. If EFS finds a certificate with the EFS template or another template that allows file encryption, it uses that certificate. If the user does not have a certificate for EFS, EFS gets one. It tries to use *auto-enrollment*, if it has been set up as you did in Chapter 9. If EFS cannot automatically enroll a certificate, it creates its own self-signed certificate and begins the encryption process. Even though a self-signed certificate is not trusted, it is still valid for use to encrypt files.

If you are a proactive administrator, you will consider the needs for EFS in your company, and you will set up the automatic enrollment process for your enterprise-issuing CA. It is a good idea to do this, because you can also set up and configure *recovery agents* for EFS and have them ready. Without recovery agents, you can run into situations in which you can't recover encrypted data because the user's key is lost. You can avoid this problem through some planning and implementation work.

The process of encrypting files using EFS is illustrated in Figure 10.1. The steps are as follows:

1. A network user chooses to encrypt a file. When encryption is required, the user's computer generates a *file encryption key (FEK)*.

2. The computer then uses the FEK and a symmetric encryption algorithm to encrypt the file. At this point, it has not used the certificate.

3. The file is now encrypted using the FEK. The computer attempts to retrieve the user's EFS certificate from the personal certificate store. If it finds the certificate, it extracts the public key from the certificate. If it can't find the certificate, it attempts to enroll one. If it can't find an Enterprise CA to enroll the certificate, it creates its own. Once EFS has the certificate, it extracts the public key.

4. The computer uses the public key to encrypt the FEK using an asymmetric algorithm. EFS then places the encrypted FEK in the *data decryption field (DDF)* located in the file's header. Windows XP Professional allows multiple entries in the DDF so that EFS files can be shared with other users.

5. The computer retrieves the EFS recovery agent certificate for each recovery agent and extracts its public key. The public key is used to encrypt the FEK, and the encrypted FEK is put into the *data recovery field (DRF)* located in the file's header. This process is repeated for each EFS recovery agent.

6. The encrypted file is stored with the DDF and the DRF entries in its header in the filesystem.

FIGURE 10.1 The EFS process

Once the encrypted file is stored on the hard drive, the only user who can open the file and read its contents is the user who stored the file using their public key to encrypt the FEK or an account that has the recovery agent's certificate. In both cases, the private key from the certificate is required to decrypt the file using these steps:

1. The user attempts to open the encrypted file. The computer retrieves the user's certificate and extracts the user's private key from the certificate.

2. The computer uses the private key to decrypt the DDF to get the FEK from the document header.

3. The computer then uses the FEK to decrypt the file.

The process of encrypting the file uses *symmetric* encryption followed by *asymmetric* encryption. The process of decrypting the file uses asymmetric encryption followed by symmetric encryption. While the file is traveling across the network from the client computer to the file server and from the file server to the client computer, it is not encrypted.

We used a couple of terms that can be confusing, so let's define them right now:

Symmetric key A symmetric key is like a secret password. If you were to send a file encrypted with a special password, the recipient would have to know that special password to decrypt it. Symmetric keys are used in many security products. Symmetric encryption uses the secret key (or password) that is generated to encrypt the contents. The exact same secret key is used to decrypt the contents. Symmetric keys are used for bulk encryption processes, because the encryption is between 100 and 1000 times faster than using asymmetric keys.

Public key   A public key (so called because it is available to the general public) is part of an asymmetric key pair. The other half of the pair is the private key. An asymmetric key pair consists of a private key and a public key that are used together. When you send e-mail using the person's public key, the only way to decrypt the e-mail is to use the private key of the key pair. One key can do only half the work. The other key of the pair is required to do the other half of the work. So if one key encrypts, the other is required to decrypt. The order of use is not important. What is important is that the user or owner of a certificate is the only one who should have the private key. The public key can be given out freely without any worries if the private key is properly maintained.

In Exercise 10.2, you will use EFS to encrypt files.

File and folder attributes are applied to each file and folder in the NTFS file system. One of those attributes is the EFS *attribute* showing whether a file has been encrypted. When you copy files and folders, you do not copy their attributes too. They inherit their attributes from their new location. The EFS attribute is an exception to the rule. If the file was encrypted before the copy or move, it will remain encrypted even if the destination folder is not encrypted. If the file or folder is moved to an encrypted folder, then it will become encrypted.

EXERCISE 10.2

Using EFS to Encrypt Files

In this exercise, you will encrypt a folder and its contents.

1. Choose Start ➢ All Programs ➢ Accessories ➢ Windows Explorer to open Windows Explorer.

2. Navigate to the folder that you want to encrypt.

3. Right-click the folder and choose Properties from the shortcut menu to open the Properties dialog box for the folder.

4. In the Attributes section, click the Advanced button to open the Advanced Attributes dialog box.

5. Enable the Encrypt Contents To Secure Data check box. Click OK to close the Advanced Attributes dialog box.

6. Click OK to close the Properties dialog box.

7. The Confirm Attribute Change dialog box opens, asking whether the change (enabling encryption) should be made to the folder only or to the folder, its subfolders, and any files underneath the folder and subfolders. Click the Apply Changes To This Folder, Subfolders, And Files radio button. Click OK.

EFS encrypts the folders and files required. It may take a couple of minutes or more, depending on how many files are involved and their sizes.

Think of it as cloning. If you were to clone a human child, the clone would get many attributes from the donor such as physical characteristics like the eye and hair colors of the donor. The clone would also have to get new attributes from his new parents in his new home such as clothes, toys, and pets.

It's the same with files and folders. They gain many attributes (clothes, toys, pets, and NTFS attributes) from their new parents. So if you copy a file from one location to another, it acquires the attributes of its parent folder.

Moving the file or folder is different, though. If you move the child, he will pack up all his attributes and take them with him because he owns them. So if you move a file from one location to another, it will still have the same attributes (encryption). This rule applies only if it is moved to another location on the same logical hard drive partition. If you move the file to another logical hard drive, it's a different story. NTFS uses a *transactional file system*. This means it has to have the ability to roll back in case of a failure during a transaction such as a copy or a move. To protect itself, NTFS actually copies the folder or file to the new location (if it's on another drive). After the operating system successfully copies the file, it deletes the original. Because it's really a copy, the object inherits its permissions from the new parent.

Some tips on implementing EFS are probably in order right about now:

Back up and secure EFS certificates.   EFS users should export their keys to a floppy disk (maybe multiple floppies) and store them in a secure place. The private key is required to decrypt the FEK and then decrypt the file. Microsoft Support lists this as one of their top 10 phone calls: Users call to report that they cannot decrypt their encrypted files because they have lost their private key.

Do not use the administrator account as the default recovery agent account.   Create a special account for the recovery agent. The administrator account's well-known SID is a prime target for intruders, and you do not want to expose the recovery agent to intruders who might succeed in damaging the administrator account or compromising it.

Properly back up and restore the EFS recovery agent certificates.   Without the private key from these certificates, you will not be able to save the files for users who have lost their private keys.

Although EFS certificates are actually personal certificates and not machine certificates, we cover this topic here because the certificates are stored on the computer. To change computers requires exporting the certificates from the current computer and then importing them into the new computer.

It is unlikely that you'll ever need to move a computer certificate or copy a computer certificate to another machine. After all, that's the whole purpose when it comes to computer certificates—they are used to authenticate a computer. To have the same certificate applied to multiple computers defeats the purpose and actually breaks the PKI. The only reason to export computer certificates is for disaster recovery.

Importing and Exporting Certificates

The main reason to export a certificate is to back it up and store it or to use the exported file to import the certificate on another computer. As you have seen with S/MIME and EFS, the user that the certificate is assigned to actually moves around in the organization, and they need the certificates available wherever they are working.

Exporting Certificates

You want to export a certificate from a certificate store to a file for the following primary reasons:

- So that you can recover from a disaster. Along with the certificate, also back up its private key.
- So that a user can use another computer to perform tasks that require certificates.
- So that you can install the certificate on a replacement computer.

Part of the export process requires selecting the file format in which to store the certificate information. The file format is important because each format has different features that need to be considered. This is especially true for exporting certificates with their private keys, because not all file formats support exporting and storing the private key.

The available formats include the following:

DER Encoded Binary X.509 *(.cer)*   DER (Distinguished Encoding Rules) is a compatible certificate file format adhering to the X.509 standards. This encoding method is used for encoding objects such as messages and, of course, certificates that need to be transferred to other systems. Many applications use DER encoding because the certification request information has to be DER-encoded in order to be signed by a certificate authority. This encoding format is used by many certificate authorities that do not run Windows certification authorities.

Base64 Encoded X.509 (.cer)   Base64 was developed to be used for S/MIME. S/MIME is used in many e-mail systems to encode attachments sent over the Internet. All files that are encoded with Base64 are converted into ASCII format. MIME is covered by RFCs and is an Internet standard for attachments. Its purpose is to reduce the errors and corruption in transferring file attachments—particularly binary attachments—through Internet gateways. Because MIME is a well-established standard, all standard clients can decode Base64 files. It is provided for compatibility with other operating systems.

Cryptographic Message Syntax Standard - PKCS #7 Certificates *(.p7b)*   PKCS #7 allows the certificate and the certificate chain to be transferred from one computer to another or for the information to be stored in a .p7b file. This file format adheres to the X.509 standard.

Personal Information Exchange - PKCS #12 *(.pfx)*   This format is another industry-standard format. However, this format supports the exporting of certificates and private keys to a file. The private key can only be exported in certain situations. In particular, the certificate must have been requested using the Windows 2003 certificate authority's advanced method. The key can be marked as exportable when using the advanced method. The private key can also be exported if the certificate is an EFS certificate or an EFS recovery agent certificate. This is the only format supported in Windows XP Professional for exporting a certificate and its associated private key.

Generally, if you plan to import the certificate into a Windows system, the preferred format is PKCS #7. This format is preferred because it also exports the certificate chain information. It's important to maintain the trust path for the certificate. Other operating systems may not support the PKCS #7 format. If you find that the target system to which you need to restore the certificate does not support PKCS #7, you'll want to use DER Encoded Binary or Base64 Encoded formats. These two formats are compatible with many operating systems. In Exercise 10.3, you will export a certificate.

EXERCISE 10.3

Exporting a Certificate

In this exercise, you will export a certificate to PKCS #7 format and then you will use this file in Exercise 10.4 to import a certificate.

Create a Certificates MMC Console

1. Choose Start ≻ Run to open the Run dialog box. In the Open box, type MMC to open the MMC.

2. Choose Console ≻ Add/Remove Snap-In to open the Add/Remove Snap-In window.

3. Click the Add button.

4. Select Certificates from the list of available snap-ins and click Add.

5. Click the My User Account radio button to manage user account certificates and then click Finish.

6. Select Certificates from the list of available snap-ins again and click Add.

7. Click the Computer Account radio button this time. Click Next.

8. Click the Local Computer radio button. Click Finish.

9. Click Close in the Add Standalone Snap-In window.

10. Click OK in the Add/Remove Snap-In window.

11. Choose Console ≻ Save. In the File Name field, enter `Certificates.msc` and click the Save button to save this console into the Administrative Tools menu of your computer.

Export a Certificate

Because you used EFS and previously created an Enterprise CA in Chapter 9, there should be a certificate on the computer used for EFS.

1. Open the Certificates MMC that you just created. Expand the Certificates - Current User node in the MMC.

2. Expand the Personal folder and click Certificates. In the right pane of the window, you see the certificate issued for EFS. You can identify it by looking at the Intended Purposes column.

3. Right-click the certificate and choose All-Tasks ≻ Export to start the Certificate Export Wizard.

4. Click Next.

5. Click the Yes, Export The Private Key radio button. Click Next to open the Export File Format screen.

EXERCISE 10.3 *(continued)*

6. Because you are exporting the private key, the only option for the file format should be the PKCS #12, as shown in the following graphic. Enable the check boxes for Include All Certificates In The Certification Path If Possible and Enable Strong Protection. Make sure the Delete The Private Key If The Export Is Successful check box is cleared. Click Next to open the Password screen.

7. Enter a password and then confirm the password using the proper fields. This password will be required when you try to import the certificate in the next exercise. Click Next.

8. Enter the filename and the path for the file in the File Name field or click Browse to navigate to the location and then enter the filename. The filename needs a .pfx extension. Click Next.

9. Click Finish in the summary screen to complete the wizard.

10. Click OK on the success message.

Importing Certificates

You will need to import a certificate for a few reasons. In particular, you will need to import a certificate

- When it is delivered or received from the certificate authority in a file format

- To restore a corrupted or deleted certificate that was previously backed up

- To install a certificate, its chain, and its private key from a computer previously used by the certificate user

Importing a certificate is the same as copying the certificate from a file in a standard certificate format to a certificate store on your computer. The certificate store used depends on whether it is a user certificate or a computer certificate.

Using the Certificates MMC snap-in tool is the best way to import a certificate. The import process can also import the private key if it was originally exported to the file, or if the file being imported is the certificate file provided by the certificate authority. You can also import the certificate chain. It is important for the certificate chain to be able to properly follow the certificate to its root certificate authority. If any CA in the chain is compromised, you will likely have to replace the certificate.

Certificates, their chains, and their private keys can be imported from the following file formats:

- PKCS #12
- PKCS #7
- Binary-encoded X.509

In Exercise 10.4, you will import a certificate.

EXERCISE 10.4

Importing a Certificate

A user can obtain a certificate by downloading it from a certificate authority or through some other means. Often, you can retrieve the file from the certificate authority through a retrieval program on a website. Once the file is available, you can import it. For this exercise, you will import the file exported in Exercise 10.3.

1. Choose Start ➤ All Programs ➤ Administrative Tools ➤ Certificates.

2. Expand the Certificates - Current User node of the MMC.

3. Expand the Personal folder. Right-click the Certificates folder and choose All Tasks ➤ Import to start the Certificate Import Wizard.

4. Click Next.

5. Enter the file path and filename in the File Name field or click the Browse button to navigate to the file location. Click Next to open the Password screen.

6. Enter the password used to export the file in the previous exercise. Enable the Enable Strong Private Key Protection and Mark The Private Key As Exportable check boxes, as shown in the following graphic. Click Next.

7. Click the Place All Certificates In The Following Store radio button. The Personal store should already be selected. If it's not, click the Browse button to select it. Click Next.

8. Click Finish in the summary screen to complete the wizard.

9. Click OK in the Importing A New Private Exchange Key message box.

10. Click OK in the success message.

The file format makes a difference, as you can see in Exercise 10.4. Properly test and document the recovery of certificates. Also, properly document the exporting of certificates. After all, you can't recover what you have not backed up. It is a really good idea to properly export all the major certificates used in the organization such as the certificate used to create the CA. You never know when they might be needed. That's the real reason for the many administrative tasks necessary for disaster recovery. You never know when the disaster will hit and what kind of a disaster it will be.

Certificate Storage

When a user acquires a certificate, it is stored in the *certificate store*. This store holds the computer certificates, and it also holds the user certificates that were requested while the user was logged in on the computer. You can view certificates using the Certificates MMC snap-in, as installed in Exercise 10.3. The store has two views: the certificate purpose and the logical certificate stores, as shown in Figure 10.2. Each view can also display the *physical certificate stores* and the archived certificates. The logical view combines all the storage locations into one view. A certificate can appear in the list twice if it is stored in separate physical locations. The logical view combines these separate physical locations into one view.

FIGURE 10.2   The View Options dialog box

The logical view provides the following locations:

Personal   Certificates associated with personally held private keys. These certificates have been issued to the currently logged-on user or the computer that the user is currently logged on to.

Trusted Root Certificate Authorities   Includes self-signed certificates for explicitly trusted CAs. This list includes the prepopulated list of CAs provided by Microsoft, root certificates from internal CAs, and any other third-party CAs that may have been added.

Enterprise Trust   Includes self-signed root certificates from other organizations and the purposes for which you will trust these certificates.

Intermediate Certificate Authorities   Includes all the certificates issued for intermediate CAs.

Trusted People   Includes all certificates for people that you explicitly trust. These are manually added.

Other People   Includes certificates that are implicitly trusted as part of a trusted certification hierarchy.

Trusted Publishers   Includes certificates from CAs that are trusted according to software restriction policies.

Disallowed Certificates   Includes certificates that are explicitly not trusted. Normally, certificates are added through applications such as Outlook.

Third-Party Root Certificate Authorities   Includes certificates for CAs outside the company.

Certificate Enrollment Requests   Certificates that are pending approval.

Active Directory User Object   User certificates published in Active Directory.

Certificate storage is an important issue. Certificates can be stored in three physical locations:

The default store   The profile is the main store for certificates. It is important to keep this in mind when working with roaming profiles or when deciding not to use roaming profiles. With roaming profiles, the same user certificates can be used on multiple computers without having to manually export and import them. Certificates are stored in the user's profile in the `Application Data\Microsoft\SystemCertificates\My\Certificates` folder.

Smart cards   Gemplus and Schlumberger smart cards can store certificates along with other data. Users can then carry their certificates with them.

Active Directory   Enterprise CAs automatically publish certificates to Active Directory by default. To confirm this, open the Certificate Authority MMC, right-click the CA, and choose Properties from the shortcut menu to open the Properties dialog box. Click the Exit Module tab and then click the Configure button to verify that the Allow Certificates To Be Published In The Active Directory check box is enabled.

If certificates are not properly published in Active Directory and if they are not properly stored using either smart cards or *roaming profiles*, considerable administrative work can be required to maintain certificates. If you store certificates in roaming profiles, you need to maintain high levels of security on the folders where the profiles are stored, because the user's certificates contain the private keys. If the certificates are ever compromised, the files secured using EFS can also be compromised using the private key from the certificate.

Publishing Certificates through Active Directory

As discussed in the last section, enterprise CAs automatically publish certificates in Active Directory by default. If this configuration is ever disabled, you can reset it in the Certificate Authority MMC. However, there are a couple of issues with using Active Directory to publish certificates. You need to consider how stand-alone root CAs publish their information in Active Directory. Also, you need to look at the use of child domains. Although the certificates are properly published in Active Directory in the parent domain, they are not properly published in the child domain.

Publishing Certificates from a Stand-Alone Online CA

Chapter 9 went through the process of publishing the *CRL (certificate revocation list)* information for a stand-alone offline root CA. However, this process does not publish the certificates. If you remember, you walked through the steps in a couple of exercises to manually publish the information to the network. If you have a stand-alone CA that is online, the process is quite different. To publish the certificates, you must take two additional steps. First, you need to properly configure the CA, and then you need to set up the certificate enrollment. Exercise 10.5 takes you through this process.

EXERCISE 10.5

Configuring and Publishing a Certificate from a Stand-Alone CA

In this exercise, you will configure the CA and set up certificate enrollment to properly publish certificate information in Active Directory. This requires that the stand-alone CA is online and that the server is a member server.

1. On the CA computer, choose Start ➤ Run to open the Run dialog box. In the Open box, enter **cmd** and press Enter to open the command console.

2. At the prompt, enter `certutil -setreg exit\publishcertflags exitpub_activedirectory` and press Enter.

3. Choose Start ➤ All Programs ➤ Administrative Tools ➤ Internet Services Manager.

4. Expand the server in Internet Information Services and expand the Default Web Site.

5. Right-click the CertSrv virtual directory and then choose Properties from the shortcut menu to open the CertSrv Properties dialog box.

6. Click the Directory Security tab.

7. In the Anonymous Access And Authentication Control section, click Edit.

EXERCISE 10.5 *(continued)*

8. Clear the Anonymous Access check box.

9. Enable the Basic Authentication check box.

10. Enable the Integrated Windows Authentication check box. Click OK. Click OK again to close the CertSrv Properties dialog box. Close the Internet Information Services MMC.

The CA can now publish the information properly to Active Directory even though the certificates are enrolled using the Web Enrollment pages. There is one caveat, though. The user must select the Advanced Request type and submit the request using the Submit A Certificate Request To This CA Using A Form as shown in Figure 10.3.

FIGURE 10.3   Using a form option

The requestor must also type **CertificateTemplate:User** in the Attributes field as shown in Figure 10.4.

FIGURE 10.4   The Attributes field

This is probably a little much to expect for the user population, though, which is why we still recommend using enterprise CAs for all issuing CAs in an organization. The automatic publication capabilities of the enterprise CA is just one of the many benefits.

Using Certificates in a Child Domain

If you have a parent and a child domain in your Active Directory structure, and the enterprise CA is in the parent domain, you may have problems publishing certificates so that they are visible in the child domain. The difficulty arises because of the permissions on the CA. Generally, the CA allows read and write permissions for users in its domain. This does not include trusted domains such as a child domain, though. To fix this problem, you need to allow child domain members to enroll certificates, and then you must configure the publication of the certificates to Active Directory, as outlined in Exercise 10.6.

EXERCISE 10.6

Enabling Child Domain Users to Enroll Certificates and Configure Publication to Active Directory

By default, a Windows certification authority does not also include support for child domains in the same forest without some additional configuration. This exercise will guide you through configuring the certification authority and the child domain to support access to the certification authority.

Configure CA Permissions

1. On the CA, choose Start ➤ All Programs ➤ Administrative Tools ➤ Certification Authority.

2. Right-click the CA and choose Properties from the shortcut menu to open the Test Enterprise Root CA Properties dialog box, as shown in the following graphic.

3. Click the Security tab and verify that Authenticated Users are allowed to enroll certificates.

EXERCISE 10.6 *(continued)*

Configure Active Directory Sites and Services

1. Choose Start ➤ Programs ➤ Administrative Tools ➤ Active Directory Sites And Services to open the AD Sites And Services window, as shown in the following graphic.

2. Choose View ➤ Show Services Node.

3. Expand the Services node, expand Public Key Services, and then expand Certificate Templates.

4. In the right pane, right-click the certificate template that you want to be used for automatic enrollment and choose Properties. Most organizations configure auto-enrollment for EFS, Machine, and User certificates.

5. Click the Security tab. Grant Enroll permissions to Authenticated Users. Verify that the same group also has Read permission. Click OK to close the Properties dialog box for the certificate template and then repeat this step for all certificate templates that you want to configure for auto-enrollment.

Configure the Exit Module to Publish to Active Directory

1. On the CA computer, choose Start ➤ All Programs ➤ Administrative Tools ➤ Certification Authority.

2. Right-click the CA and then choose Properties from the shortcut menu.

3. Click the Exit Module tab.

4. Click the Configure button.

5. Verify that the Allow Certificates To Be Published In Active Directory check box is enabled. If it isn't, check it. Click OK to close the Certificate Publication Properties dialog box and click OK again to close the CA Properties dialog box.

Configure the Child Domain

1. On a domain controller in the child domain, choose Start ➤ All Programs ➤ Administrative Tools ➤ Active Directory Users And Computers.

2. Right-click the domain name and choose Delegate Control from the shortcut menu to start the Delegation Control Wizard.

3. Click Next to open the Users Or Groups screen.

4. Click Add. Select Cert Publishers From The Parent Domain. Click OK. Click Next.

5. Click the Create A Custom Task To Delegate radio button. Click Next.

6. Click the Only The Following Objects In The Folder radio button. Enable the check boxes for User Objects. Click Next to open the Permissions screen.

7. Enable the Property-Specific check box. Enable the Read UserCertificate and Write User-Certificate check boxes, as shown in the following graphic. Click Next.

8. Click Finish on the summary screen. Close Active Directory Users And Computers.

9. Choose Start ➤ Run to open the Run dialog box. In the Open box, enter **cmd** and press Enter.

10. At the command prompt, type **dsacls** "cn=adminsdholder,cn=system,dc=*child*, dc=*domain*,dc=*com*" /G "*CADomain*\Cert Publishers:WP;userCertificate" and press Enter.

11. At the command prompt, type **dsacls** "cn=adminsdholder,cn=system,dc=*child*, dc=*domain*,dc=*com*" /G "*CADomain*\Cert Publishers:RP;userCertificate" and press Enter. *CADomain* is the domain name where the CA is installed, and *dc=child,dc=domain,dc=com* is the domain name of the child domain.

After you configure all the permissions in the parent domain and in the child domain, users in the child domain can enroll certificates using the parent domain's CA, and the CA can automatically publish the certificates in Active Directory for the child domain.

Enrolling Certificates

As discussed in Chapter 9, you can enroll certificates in three ways:

- Using the Certificates MMC snap-in on the client computer
- Using the *Web Enrollment* pages on the CA
- By configuring auto-enrollment on the CA and in Active Directory

Obviously, the preferred method is to use auto-enrollment, which requires the least amount of day-to-day administration. It's also really nice to be able to set the permissions up to allow only certain security groups to auto-enroll. Using auto-enrollment, you can also exclude certain groups of users through the Deny permission for the Enroll right.

The Certificates MMC Snap-In

Using the Certificates MMC snap-in to enroll certificates is covered in previous chapters. The process is basic and straightforward. You use the Certificates MMC snap-in when auto-enrollment is not configured. You can only use the Certificates MMC snap-in to request certificates from online enterprise CAs. In Exercise 10.7, you'll use the Certificates MMC snap-in.

EXERCISE 10.7

Using the Certificates MMC Snap-In

The Certificates MMC Snap-In is the easiest tool to use for requesting and receiving a certificate from a local certification authority.

Configure the MMC

1. Choose Start ➢ Run to open the Run dialog box. In the Open box, enter **mmc** and press Enter to open the MMC.

2. Choose Console ➢ Add/Remove Snap-In.

3. Click the Add button.

4. Select Certificates from the list of available snap-ins and click Add.

5. Click the My User Account radio button to manage user account certificates and click Finish.

6. Select Certificates from the list of available snap-ins again and click Add.

7. Click the Computer Account radio button and then click Next.

8. Click the Local Computer radio button. Click Finish.

9. Click Close to close the Add Standalone Snap-In window.

10. Click OK in the Add/Remove Snap-In window.

11. Choose Console ➢ Save, and in the File Name field, type **Certificates.msc**. Click the Save button to save this console into the Administrative Tools menu of your computer.

Not all users will have permissions to request computer certificates or to manage computer certificates.

Request a User Certificate

1. Choose Start ➢ All Programs ➢ Administrative Tools ➢ Certificates.

2. Expand the Certificates - Current Owner node. Expand the Personal node.

3. Right-click Certificates and choose All-Tasks ➢ Request New Certificate to start the Certificate Request Wizard.

4. Click Next.

5. Select the certificate template that you want from the list of available templates. Click Next.

6. Enter a friendly name and a description for the certificate. For example, if the certificate is an EFS certificate for a user, enter **EFS** in the Friendly Name field, and in the Description field, enter **For encrypting and decrypting personal files**. This will make it easier to identify the certificate later.

7. Click Finish to complete the wizard. Click Install Certificate to install the requested certificate. Click OK to close the success message window.

The Certificates MMC snap-in is easy to use with a little practice. However, it's not necessarily the best tool for acquiring certificates.

Web Enrollment Pages

Many CAs are not enterprise CAs, and they are not integrated with Active Directory. These CAs require a Web Enrollment page to request and receive a certificate. The Web Enrollment process can also be used for enterprise CAs, but it is not the simplest method available.

Because Windows 95, Windows 98, and Windows NT 4 Workstation clients do not support the Certificates MMC snap-in or the auto-enrollment process, these systems will have to use the Web Enrollment process, as outlined in Exercise 10.8.

The Web Enrollment form is flexible and supports all operating systems that use certificates. However, we do not recommend its use unless it's required. Users tend to make many mistakes and request certificates that they cannot properly use.

EXERCISE 10.8

Using Web Enrollment

In many cases, it is not possible to use the Certificates MMC Snap-In to obtain a certificate. The operating system, for example, may not support the use of the MMC. In cases where you can not use the MMC, you will need to use the Web Enrollment tool to obtain certificates.

Standard User Certificate

1. Open your web browser and, in the Address bar, enter **http://*servername*/certsrv**, using the name of your CA server.

2. On the Welcome screen, click the Request A Certificate link and then click Next.

3. To request a user certificate, click the User Certificate link and click Next to open the User Certificate - Identifying Information screen.

4. Click Submit. You can click the More Options link if you want to select the Cryptographic Service Provider or if you want to enable strong private key protection.

   Depending on your browser security configuration, you may receive a Potential Scripting Violation warning. If you receive the warning, click Yes to proceed.

5. Click the Install This Certificate link to download the certificate and install it on your computer.

Advanced Certificate Request

1. Open your web browser and, in the Address bar, enter **http://*servername*/certsrv**, using the name of your CA server.

2. At the Welcome screen, click the Request A Certificate link and then click Next.

3. Click the Advanced Certificate Request link and click Next.

   You have three choices on this screen. You can submit the request using a form, or you can submit a request using a PKCS file. Normally, you use the PKCS file when a program of some kind generates a Certificate Signing Request. You use the third option only if you are requesting a certificate for a smart card on behalf of another user and you need special permissions to perform this task. So this leaves the form option as the best selection for the majority of requests.

4. Click the Create And Submit A Request To This CA link.

5. From here, you can select the certificate template to be used, the Cryptographic Service Provider, the key length, and several other options. Using the Advanced form, you can select the Mark The Keys As Exportable option. After selecting all the options, click Submit.

   Depending on your browser security configuration, you may receive a Potential Scripting Violation warning. If you receive the warning, click Yes to proceed.

6. Click the Install This Certificate link to download the certificate and install it on your computer.

Auto-Enrollment

One of the bigger problems with manual certificate enrollment processes such as the Certificates MMC snap-in and web enrollment is that users make mistakes. They obtain the wrong kind of certificate, or they select the wrong options and the certificate is not as strong as you would like. The process can be confusing, and it takes considerable time for each user on the network to enroll certificates.

You can set up certificate auto-enrollment using Group Policies, as discussed in Chapter 9. Windows Server 2003 provides even greater support for auto-enrollment with Windows XP Professional client computers. Exercise 10.9 will walk you through the steps of configuring Group Policies to support auto-enrollment.

Windows 2000 and Windows XP Professional computers can automatically receive computer certificates through auto-enrollment. Windows NT and Windows 9x computers cannot participate in auto-enrollment processes. Windows NT and Windows 9x systems must use the manual Web Enrollment forms process.

EXERCISE 10.9

Configuring Group Policies to Support Auto-Enrollment

In this exercise, you will configure the default domain Group Policy to allow the automatic enrollment of computer certificates.

1. Choose Start ➤ All Programs ➤ Administrative Tools ➤ Active Directory Users And Computers to open Active Directory Users And Computers.

2. Right-click your domain and choose Properties from the shortcut menu.

3. Click the Group Policy tab.

4. Click Default Domain Policy and then click the Edit button.

5. Expand the Computer Configuration folder, expand the Windows Settings folder, expand the Security Settings folder, and then expand the Public Key Policies folder.

6. Right-click the Automatic Certificate Request Settings folder and choose New ➤ Automatic Certificate Request to start the Automatic Certificate Request Setup Wizard.

7. Click Next to open the Certificate Template screen.

8. Select Computer and click Next.

9. Select the enterprise certificate authority that you want to use from the list and click Next.

10. Click Finish to complete the wizard.

Managing and Troubleshooting EFS

Security is really the topic of this entire book. Security is the focus of the associated Microsoft exam. So it makes sense that after looking at the security around authentication, looking at the security around network traffic, providing secure access to remote network users, and securing services, you'll have to address storage. EFS is extremely useful when security is extremely important. Although we addressed EFS earlier in this chapter, there is more to know about managing and troubleshooting EFS.

Implementing EFS

EFS is another layer of security. If an intruder does manage to work through all the other defenses, their next step is to defeat EFS. Mobile computers also benefit greatly from EFS. If they are lost or stolen, the data is not easily compromised. Because EFS is tightly integrated with NTFS, the process of encrypting and decrypting files is all done in the background and is transparent to the user.

The user can implement EFS in three ways:

- By setting the advanced properties for existing files and folders

- By adding new files and folders to an existing EFS-enabled folder

- By using the *cipher.exe* command-line tool

You can also configure the computer so that the shortcut menu includes the ability to encrypt or decrypt files and folders, which you'll do in Exercise 10.10.

EXERCISE 10.10

Configuring the Shortcut Menu

In this exercise, you will edit the Registry. It's good practice to back up the Registry before you start. Be careful and follow the steps exactly. There is no Undo function in the Registry Editor.

1. Choose Start ➢ Run to open the Run dialog box. In the Open box, type **regedit** and press Enter to open the Registry Editor.

2. Expand HKEY_LOCAL_MACHINE.

3. Expand Software, expand Microsoft, expand Windows, expand CurrentVersion, expand Explorer, and then select Advanced.

4. Choose Edit ➢ New ➢ DWORD Value and enter **EncryptionContextMenu** for the value name.

5. Double-click the new value and enter **1** in the Value Data field. Click OK.

6. The change will be effective the next time Windows Explorer is opened.

Windows XP Professional includes several new features for EFS:

- More than one user can access EFS-encrypted files and folders. After a file is encrypted, additional users can be given permission to access it. You specify this setting on a per-file basis, but not on a folder. To add another user, right-click the file, choose Properties from the shortcut menu to open the Properties dialog box, click the General tab, and then click Advanced. Click the Details button and then click Add. You can then search for a user by name and add them to the file.

- *Offline files* can be encrypted. Configuring this support for offline folders is an extremely good idea. Any data in the offline folders will be encrypted and cannot be recovered by just anyone who happens to find or steal a laptop computer. To enable this feature, in Windows Explorer, choose Tools ➢ Folder Options to open the Folder Options dialog box. Click the Offline Folders tab, click the Enable The Offline Files and Encrypt Offline Files To Secure Data check boxes, and then click OK. This secures all offline files on portable computers.

- Encrypted files can be stored in *web folders*. Web folders are actually more secure than file shares when used with SSL. Traffic to and from the SSL-protected web folder is protected twice. SSL encryption is available, and EFS encryption and decryption take place on the client computer. Normally, files stored on a remote drive, such as a file share, are encrypted and decrypted at the file share and travel across the network without any protection. Of course, the files are protected while stored in the web folder using EFS. Web folders can be used over the Internet as well as on LANs and WANs, which gives web folders an added advantage.

- 3DES is available. Windows 2000 Professional clients use DES-X, which is not as heavily encrypted as Windows XP Professional's 3DES. Windows Server 2003 also uses 3DES.

The difference between EFS in Windows 2000 Professional and Windows XP Professional clients may lead many organizations to expedite their Windows XP Professional deployments. The value is hard to ignore, and in security-conscious organizations, it makes good sense to deploy the most secure client operating system available.

EFS Encryption for Domain Members

EFS encryption is the same for file shares on a domain member server as it is for local resources, with one major difference. Instead of the client computer doing the encryption, the file server actually does the encryption on behalf of the client computer. For this to work, the file server must *impersonate* the client computer by using Kerberos delegation.

If *Kerberos delegation* works like it's supposed to (which requires that the client be logged on to a Windows 2003 domain controller and authenticated using Kerberos), the file server works with EFS on the client computer to determine if the profile is local or roaming. If the profile is a roaming profile, EFS loads it and retrieves the EFS certificate. If the profile is a local profile, EFS loads it and retrieves the EFS certificate from the local profile. If, for some reason, EFS cannot locate the profile, it creates a new one.

Once EFS either locates or creates a profile, EFS searches for an EFS certificate. If no EFS certificate is available, EFS attempts to enroll a certificate with a trusted enterprise CA on the network. If EFS is unable to find a trusted CA on the network to enroll a certificate, EFS create its own self-signed certificate. If EFS has to create its own self-signed certificate, it stores the certificate in the user's profile with both the private and public keys. Once EFS has the profile and the certificate, it verifies the existence of a private key (thus verifying that it can later be decrypted) and then it extracts the public key from the certificate.

Once EFS has the public key from the EFS certificate, the FEK is created and is used to encrypt the file's data. After the file is encrypted using the FEK, the FEK is encrypted using the user's public key, and the encrypted FEK is stored in the file header. EFS recovery agent public certificates are also used to encrypt the FEK, and the recovery agent-encrypted FEK is stored in the file header as well.

Decryption involves a similar process. Again, of course, EFS on the remote file server must impersonate the client computer using Kerberos delegation. Once impersonation takes place, EFS can obtain the user's private key from the certificate. However, before it can do that, it must find the profile and then find the certificate stored in the profile. Once the private key is retrieved, it is compared to the public key to verify that they have the same thumbprint value associated with the key pair. Public-private key pairs share a common *thumbprint* value to show that they belong together. This is an important step because some users may actually have more than one EFS certificate.

Once EFS has verified that the private key is the correct one, EFS uses the private key to decrypt the FEK. Once EFS has the unencrypted FEK, it uses the FEK to decrypt the file data. The file data is then transmitted across the LAN to the client computer.

EFS and Workgroup Members

In a workgroup environment, there is no enterprise CA, so EFS automatically creates its own certificates any time a user attempts to encrypt a file for the first time. After the certificate has been created and stored in the profile, that same certificate is used for later encryption and decryption. There is one major drawback to EFS in a workgroup environment: the lack of a recovery agent. It's possible to configure a recovery agent for stand-alone computers, though. In Exercise 10.11, you will configure a recovery policy on a stand-alone Windows Server 2003 computer.

EXERCISE 10.11

Configuring a Recovery Policy on a Stand-alone Windows Server 2003 Computer

In cases where you want to support EFS in a workgroup environment, you need to obtain a certificate for the user that you want to configure at the Data Recovery Agent before beginning the process.

1. Choose Start ➢ Run to open the Run dialog box. In the Open box, type **mmc** and press Enter.

2. Choose File ➢ Add/Remove Snap-In. Click Add to open the Add Standalone Snap-In dialog box.

3. Click Group Policy Object Editor and then click Add.

4. Verify that Local Computer is displayed in the Group Policy Object field and click Finish.

5. Close the Add Standalone Snap-In dialog box. Click OK to close the Add/Remove Snap-In dialog box.

6. Expand Local Computer Policy, expand the Computer Configuration node, expand Windows Settings, expand Security Settings, expand Public Key Policies, and then expand Encrypting File System.

7. Right-click the Encrypting File System node and click Add Data Recovery Agent. Click Next to start the Add Recovery Agent Wizard.

8. Click Browse Directory and find the account that you want to add as a data recovery agent. Click OK and then click Next.

9. Click Finish on the summary page of the wizard.

The process is similar for a Windows XP Professional computer. In all cases, you need to verify that you are logged on as a local administrator.

If a stand-alone server or client is later joined to a domain, you can replace the self-signed EFS certificates with CA-issued certificates. Run the `cipher.exe` utility with the /k argument to archive the computer's existing EFS certificate and request a new EFS certificate from an available CA. It's a good idea to leave the archived EFS certificate alone. If you delete the archived certificate, it will be impossible to decrypt any files that were encrypted with the old certificate unless that is a valid recovery agent. As old encrypted files are opened, the archived certificate decrypts them and the new certificate is used to encrypt the files as they are re-saved.

Disabling EFS

You can disable EFS for individual files a couple of ways:

- Enable the System attribute on the file or move the file into the system root folder or any of its subfolders. System files cannot be encrypted.

- Remove write permissions. Users cannot encrypt files when they do not have write permission.

You can disable EFS on an entire folder by creating a `desktop.ini` file and placing it in the folder. The *desktop.ini* file must have two lines in it:

```
[Encryption]
Disable=1
```

With those two lines in the `desktop.ini` file, no file in the folder can be encrypted. Any attempts to encrypt the file will result in an error message stating that the folder has been disabled for encryption.

You can disable EFS on a stand-alone computer in two ways:

- Delete all recovery agents from the computer local policy.

- Create a DWORD value in the `HKEY_LOCAL_MACHINE\Software\Microsoft\Windows NT\CurrentVersion\EFS` subkey. The DWORD value to create is EfsConfiguration, and the value is 1. If you enter 0, EFS will work again.

Troubleshooting EFS

EFS, like many new technologies, requires that administrators get some experience with it so they can fix problems. Here are some guidelines:

- Using `copy` and `xcopy` commands to copy EFS files to a non–EFS-capable volume, local or network, will fail with a message stating that the files cannot be copied or moved without losing their encryption. You do have the option of continuing the copy, though. Windows XP Professional, however, has some new switches for `copy` and `xcopy` that allow files to be copied to non–EFS-capable locations. `Copy /d` works with Windows XP Professional to decrypt the file during the copy to the new location, and `xcopy /g` works in the same way in Windows XP Professional.

- Antivirus programs will fail to scan encrypted files. If possible, scan all files before encrypting them.

- When users report that they are unable to encrypt files, the most common errors are that the location of the files is not an NTFS partition or that they do not have write permissions.

- When users report that they are unable to decrypt files, the most common error is that the user's profile is not available on the computer they are using. To solve this problem, you may need to export and then import the EFS certificate to the computer, making sure that you also get the private key during the process. Another solution is to convert the user to a roaming profile. It is also fairly common that the computer account or the user account is not trusted for delegation. Check the trust for delegation rights on the object properties.

- Archive keys have been deleted. This happens when older keys have been used to encrypt files and folders, but the user has deleted the archived certificate. Without the private key from the certificate, EFS will be unable to open files and folders encrypted using the older key.

If a user receives an error message stating that there is no valid key set, that error would seem to map closely to a problem with the archived certificates. If a user receives an error message saying the directory has been disabled for encryption, it's likely that the `desktop.ini` file is in place. An error message stating that the disk partition does not support file encryption sounds much like a FAT partition is being used.

The infamous "Access Is Denied" message is a little tougher to troubleshoot because it could be a permissions issue (remember, the user needs write permissions); it could also be an attempt to encrypt a system file or a file with the system attribute enabled on it. It could also be that the private key is not available, or it could be that it's not a file that you have encrypted and the file has not been configured for sharing with another user.

Troubleshooting takes lots of experience with the technology, and it really is an art form. EFS is difficult to troubleshoot because so many of its processes happen behind the scenes and are transparent to users.

Summary

Managing certificates is a little more cumbersome than most administrators would like. However, with Active Directory and the improvements with auto-enrollment, it's getting much better. Microsoft has worked hard over the last several years to improve on Windows NT 4 and take the extremely large leap to Windows 2000. Windows 2003 has further improved the ease of certificate administration. Along the way, Microsoft has greatly increased the security of network computing. Many security improvements have centered on encryption capabilities that use certificate keys.

This chapter described how to manage and use certificates. We covered several topics, including the following:

- Securing e-mail using digital signatures to provide proof of identity and using certificates to encrypt e-mail
- Securing data files using EFS to encrypt and decrypt files and folders
- Changes in capabilities with the Windows XP Professional clients that improve on Windows 2000 clients
- Using export and import to provide disaster recovery for vital certificates
- Understanding certificate storage
- Understanding common problems and issues and some solutions to potential problems

The exercises in this chapter gave you an opportunity to practice enrolling certificates and using them to secure both data and messaging. You practiced backing up certificates using the export feature and then recovering certificates using the import feature.

This chapter also discussed the business needs involving file security and messaging concerns and described some ways to provide protection.

Exam Essentials

Know how to manage certificates. Make sure you understand how to use certificates to provide security for messaging.

Understand the steps involved in using EFS and how it uses certificates. Be able to properly export certificates, including private keys. Make sure you understand how to properly back up important certificates and how to safeguard them.

Be able to import certificates, including private keys. Make sure you understand how to move certificates from one computer to another.

Understand how and where certificates are stored. Make sure you know how to store certificates so they are available to network clients.

Understand how to publish certificates with Active Directory. Understand how to publish certificates issued by stand-alone certification authorities and how to make the CA available to multiple domains at the same time.

Make sure you understand the ways that certificates can be issued and which methods need to be used by different operating systems. Make sure you understand how to use the different processes to enroll certificates for clients.

Know how to recover certificates. Make sure you understand how to recover certificates for standard CAs as well as for Exchange key management servers.

Make sure you understand EFS and know how to fully leverage its capabilities. Understand the improvements in Windows XP Professional. Make sure you know how EFS works in domain and workgroup environments. Make sure you understand the basics of troubleshooting EFS.

Review Questions

1. You receive a phone call from a friend asking you to test his new e-mail system by sending him an encrypted e-mail message. You create the message and attempt to send it using encryption. When you click the Send button, you receive an error message stating that the message can't be sent encrypted because of a missing or an invalid certificate. What is the most likely reason?

    A. Your friend's e-mail system does not support S/MIME.

    B. You do not have a copy of his public key.

    C. His certificate authority is offline.

    D. Your e-mail system does not support S/MIME.

2. Your co-worker is configuring a stand-alone Microsoft CA to issue certificates for secure e-mail. She says she is doing it to save money for the company so they will not have to get public CA certificates for everyone. What's wrong with her plan?

    A. She needs to configure auto-enrollment.

    B. She needs to use an enterprise CA so that certificates are published in Active Directory.

    C. A private CA will not be trusted by other organizations.

    D. She needs to configure the Exchange certificate templates.

3. You want to get a secure e-mail certificate so you can start digitally signing e-mail. Which CAs can supply these certificates?

    A. Only private CAs can provide secure e-mail certificates.

    B. Only public CAs on Microsoft's recommended list.

    C. Only public CAs that use Microsoft certificate authorities.

    D. Almost any public CA can supply secure e-mail certificates.

4. You have been signing your e-mail for several months after installing a secure e-mail certificate. While preparing for a security audit, you notice that your e-mail can be read using a packet sniffer. What is the most likely cause?

    A. Signed e-mail is not encrypted. This is expected behavior.

    B. Your e-mail system does not support digital IDs.

    C. The CA you used for the certificate is not supported by Microsoft.

    D. Your certificate has expired.

5. One of your co-workers recently left the company. While going through his files, you find that many of them are encrypted. Your company does not have a CA installed. What is the most likely explanation?

    A. EFS can be used regardless of whether there is a CA.

    B. Your co-worker used a third-party application.

    C. Your co-worker installed a temporary CA to issue an EFS certificate.

    D. Your co-worker used a public CA for the EFS certificate.

6. One of your co-workers recently left the company. While going through her files, you find that many of them cannot be opened. The error message states that you do not have access privileges. You take ownership of the files and reset the NTFS permissions to allow you full control. You still receive the error. What is the most likely cause?

    A. You need to reconfigure the share permissions.

    B. The files are encrypted using EFS.

    C. The files are corrupted.

    D. You need to remove the expired account from the NTFS privileges.

7. One of your co-workers recently left the company. While going through his files, you find that many of them cannot be opened. You know that they are encrypted with EFS. Your company does not have a CA installed. How can you access the files?

    A. Use a domain recovery agent.

    B. Use the domain administrator account.

    C. Use the local recovery agent account.

    D. You can't access the files.

8. You receive a call from a network user who is trying to configure an EFS encrypted file to be shared with a co-worker. You walk her through the process, but there is no Details button. What is the most likely reason for the missing button?

    A. She needs to install the latest service pack.

    B. The CA is offline.

    C. The person that she wants to share the file with does not have an EFS certificate.

    D. The client computer must be a Windows XP Professional client.

9. You receive a call from a network user who is trying to configure an EFS-encrypted file to be shared with a co-worker. You walk him through the process and click Add to add a user. The Find User button is grayed out, and there is no way to add another user. What is the most likely cause of this problem?

    A. Nobody else in the company has an EFS certificate.

    B. Nobody else has NTFS permissions to read the file.

    C. The domain controllers are offline.

    D. Your co-worker's computer is not a member of the domain and is in a workgroup.

10. You need to encrypt all files for a special project at work. You don't want to encrypt any other files. All the files have been named with the project code with the first four letters of the filename: trvt. You need to encrypt the files as quickly as possible. What should you do?

    A. From a command line, run `cipher.exe /d trvt*.*`.

    B. From a command line, run `cipher.exe /k trvt*.*`.

    C. From a command line, run `cipher.exe trvt*.*`.

    D. From a command line, run `cipher.exe /e trvt*.*`.

11. You receive a call from a user. She moved several of her files from her local hard drive to her home folder on the file server as you requested. She is upset, though, because she was told that moving encrypted files would not be a problem and that they would still be encrypted after they were moved. She says that all the files are now unencrypted. What should you tell her?

    A. Moving files between drives causes them to inherit the encryption status of the new folder.

    B. The files should have stayed encrypted. The home folder must be on a FAT drive that does not support EFS.

    C. Moving EFS-encrypted files to a remote file server is not possible because the file server does not have the user EFS certificate.

    D. Windows 2000 file servers do not support EFS-encrypted files for multiple users. Somebody else must be using EFS encryption already.

12. You receive a call from a user. He regularly uses two different computers. He can encrypt and decrypt files on one computer, but he cannot decrypt the files on the other computer. What should you do? (Choose all that apply.)

    A. Decrypt and re-encrypt all files from both computers.

    B. Export his EFS certificate and the private key from his working computer and then import the certificate and the private key on the other computer.

    C. Change his user profile to a roaming profile.

    D. Obtain an EFS certificate from a different CA.

13. You receive a call from a user. She regularly uses two different computers. She exported her certificate and the private key from her main computer and then imported the certificate and the private key on the second computer. Now, she can encrypt files from either computer, but she can only decrypt files from the second computer. What should you do?

    A. Use `cipher.exe` with the /K switch on the main computer that will not decrypt.

    B. Use the EFS file-sharing capability in Windows XP Professional to share the EFS files between both computers.

    C. Re-export the EFS certificate from the main computer and then re-import it on the second computer.

    D. Export her EFS certificate and the private key from the second computer and then import the certificate and the private key on the main computer.

14. You purchased a new computer for the company's production web server that is used on the Internet for receiving web orders for company products. The old server will be retired. You do not want to purchase a new SSL certificate for this server if it is not required. What should you do?

    A. Export the SSL certificate and import it on the new server.

    B. Replacing servers requires purchasing a new SSL certificate.

    C. Back up the entire web server, take it offline, and then restore it to the new computer.

    D. Back up the system state data from the web server and restore it on the new server.

15. You need to export an SSL certificate with its private key from a web server for disaster recovery. What file format should you use?

   A. DER Encoded Binary X.509 (`.cer`)

   B. Base64 Encoded X.509 (`.cer`)

   C. Cryptographic Message Syntax Standard - PKCS #7 Certificates (`.p7b`)

   D. Personal Information Exchange - PKCS #12 (`.pfx`)

16. Where can you find the S/MIME and the EFS certificates when looking in the Certificates MMC snap-in when organized by the Logical Certificate Stores option? (Choose all that apply.)

   A. Certificates - Current User node under the `Personal` folder

   B. Certificates (Local Computer) node under the `Personal` folder

   C. Certificates - Current User node under the `Active Directory User Object` folder

   D. Certificate (Local Computer) under the SPC folder

17. One of the web server administrators needs to renew an SSL certificate for an intranet server. Which tools can he use to renew a certificate?

   A. The Certificates MMC snap-in

   B. Web Enrollment

   C. Auto-enrollment

   D. Internet Services Manager

18. You receive a call from a user who wants to know how to use EFS to encrypt files. Which of the following methods will work? (Choose all that apply.)

   A. Use the Advanced Properties dialog box to enable encryption for individual files.

   B. Use the Advanced Properties dialog box to enable encryption for folders.

   C. Copy files into a folder already configured for encryption.

   D. Run the `cipher.exe` command with the `/e` switch.

19. You receive a call from a user. He has been using EFS for several months and has heard that the company is now running its own enterprise CA to support EFS encryption. He wants to know if he can get a new EFS certificate and still decrypt all his old files. What should you tell him?

   A. Use the `cipher.exe /k` command to get a new EFS certificate. Remind him not to delete the previous key that will be archived. He will be able to open all newly encrypted files, as well as previous files.

   B. He needs to decrypt all his files that are currently encrypted and then delete their EFS certificate. He should then get a new EFS certificate and re-encrypt all his files.

   C. He can get a new EFS certificate and EFS.

   D. If he requests a new certificate, he can use the new certificate to access his old files as well as his new files.

20. You receive a call from your supervisor. She is extremely concerned that many of the network users are using EFS to encrypt files in their home folders. She does not want them to have this ability. What should you do?

A. Delete all recovery agents from the home folders local policy.

B. Remove write permissions on all home folders.

C. Run the `cipher.exe /d` command on all home folders.

D. Create a `desktop.ini` file with the appropriate information in it. Set NTFS permissions on the file so users cannot delete it. Copy it to all home folders.

Answers to Review Questions

1. B. In order to send encrypted e-mail to anyone, you must first have their public key, which you can get from an e-mail message that they have previously sent with a digital signature.

2. C. Every external person who wants to use the certificate to send encrypted e-mail has to manually trust the certificate if it is issued by a private CA. This is too much to expect from non-employees and non-technical users.

3. D. The only limiting factor in choosing a CA is the compatibility of their certificates with others.

4. A. Signed e-mail is not the same as sealed e-mail. If you need e-mail encrypted so that it cannot be read, you must send it encrypted, not just signed.

5. A. EFS issues a self-signed certificate if it cannot find a CA.

6. B. EFS encryption generates an access privilege error message that almost sounds like an access denied error. Having NTFS permissions does not allow access.

7. C. D might be correct if there is no local recovery agent account. However, if there is a local recovery agent, it can be used. Okay, this is not a fair question. Remember that, without a CA, there is no domain EFS recovery agent by default or by intended creation.

8. D. Only Windows XP Professional can support sharing EFS-encrypted files.

9. D. Workgroup computers cannot search for and find others to add to share the file.

10. D. The /e switch is used to encrypt files.

11. A. Moving files between drives is similar to copying files. The files inherit their encryption status from the new folder.

12. B, C. Exporting and importing the certificate makes it available on both computers, and the user can use EFS from either one. Giving him a roaming profile moves his EFS certificate to the server, where it can be used by any computer that he logs on to in the future.

13. D. Exporting the private key can cause it to be removed if the Delete The Private Key If The Export Is Successful option is chosen when using the Certificate Export Wizard. The private key is required to decrypt, and the public key is used to encrypt. Without the private key, the computer will not be able to decrypt.

14. A. Because the server will have the same name (such as WWW) on the Internet, it can use the same certificate without any problems.

15. D. Personal Information Exchange - PKCS #12 (.pfx) supports the exporting of private keys.

16. A, C. The S/MIME and EFS certificates can be found under both folders in the Certificates - Current User node.

17. A. Only the Certificates MMC snap-in can renew a certificate.

18. A, B, C, D. You can encrypt files in all these ways.

19. A. The `cipher.exe /k` command archives the old EFS certificate and gets a new one from the CA. It's important that the user not delete the archived certificate, because it will be used to decrypt all the old files. However, opening and resaving encrypted files causes the new certificate to be used.

20. D. Although answer B might work, users who can't save to their home folders will be upset. The correct answer in this case is D. With the proper information in the `desktop.ini` file, users will not be able to encrypt files in their folder.

Chapter

11

Configuring & Managing Groups, Permissions, Rights, & Auditing

---

THE MICROSOFT EXAM OBJECTIVES COVERED IN THIS CHAPTER:

✓ **Plan and configure auditing and logging for a computer role.** Considerations include Windows events, Internet Information Services (IIS), firewall log files, Netlog, and RAS log files.

✓ **Plan group structure.**

- Decide which types of groups to use.
- Plan security group scope.
- Plan nested group structure.

✓ **Plan and configure authorization.**

- Configure access control lists (ACLs).
- Plan and troubleshoot the assignment of user rights.

In any secure environment, you should monitor and record significant events. It's a bit foolish to deploy a system that is supposed to be secure and yet not attempt to monitor and understand significant events that occur on that system.

This chapter looks at how to configure and manage auditing and logging. Of course, in order to audit access to files, you have to grant or deny access to those files. You'll get a quick review of Windows Server 2003 security group structure and how to use security groups to grant access. You'll learn how to read and understand the various log files in Windows Server 2003. There's much to learn here, so let's get going.

Windows Server 2003 Security Groups

This section gives a brief review of the Windows Server 2003 group structure. A complete discussion of groups is beyond the scope of this book and exam.

Group structure is tested extensively on exam 70-290. If you feel weak on this subject, please refer to *MCSA/MCSE: Windows Server 2003 Environment Management and Maintenance Study Guide* by Lisa Donald, Suzan Sage London, and James Chellis (Sybex, 2003).

Windows Server 2003 provides two group categories: a distribution group and a security group. A distribution group is really an e-mail distribution list. A security group is a group of users who share a common access requirement. Groups can be further broken down. This breakdown defines a group type. The three types of groups are as follows:

Domain local   A domain local group is limited in scope to the local domain when applying permissions to objects. Domain local groups are used to grant access to local resources, files, and printers in their domain, for example. Domain local groups can host global groups from any domain in the forest, universal groups from the forest, and individual user accounts in any domain in the forest as members.

Global   Global groups are limited in scope to the local domain for membership, but they can be a member of other groups and they can be granted access permission in any trusting domain. The "global" in the name goes back to the Windows NT 3.1 era, when global groups were the only group type that could be used anywhere in the domain. Global groups can only contain user accounts from the local domain or other global groups when Windows Server 2003 is in Windows 2000 native mode, or Windows Server 2003 functional mode.

Universal   Universal groups extend beyond the local domain boundary. Universal groups are available to any domain within an Active Directory forest. This makes them useful for managing security across domains. Universal groups can have individual users as members as well as global groups—from any domain in the forest—as members. Universal groups are available only when your domain is in Windows 2000 native mode or Windows Server 2003 functional mode; in other words, universal groups are not available when running in any mixed mode.

Group Nesting

Group nesting is a tool to help minimize future administration. When you define access to resources, grant access only to local groups. The local group can then have global or universal groups as members. In the future, when you need to change access to a resource, you can do it via Active Directory Users And Computers and not have to change individual resources.

An example will probably make this clearer. Let's use a nested example that's built into every Active Directory installation and is very near and dear to your hearts as administrators.

Let's review the nesting of administrator groups. On a Windows Server 2003 member server, user rights (discussed later in this chapter) to manage the server are granted to the local administrators group. The local administrator account is automatically a member of this group. When the server joins a domain, two other groups are automatically inserted into this local administrators group: the global group Domain Admins and the universal group Enterprise Admins. This nesting allows any member of Domain Admins or Enterprise Admins to be an administrator of every server in the domain. Now imagine that one of the administrators gets reassigned and no longer requires administrative permissions. You simply need to remove the user account from the appropriate group and almost immediately the user is no longer able to manage any server in the domain.

The administrators example in this section is also an example of how you can use security groups for granting access to resources and the proper nesting of groups. The recommended method is as follows:

- User accounts go into global groups.
- Global groups are members of universal groups.
- Universal groups are members of domain local groups.
- The domain local group is granted or denied access to a resource.

In most cases, the proper method for utilizing groups is to use the A-G-DL-P paradigm and not use universal groups. For example, if you have a color printer that you want to make available only to select people across multiple domains, you should create global groups in each domain, add the user accounts to the new global groups, and then add each global group in the domain local group located in the domain where the printer is located. You should then grant the domain local group permissions to the printer. User accounts go into the global groups, global groups go into the domain local group, and then permissions for the object are assigned to the domain local group.

Understanding Windows Events

When Windows Server 2003 boots up, logging begins automatically in several logs. A *log* is a file that holds event information for later review. *Auditing* is the process of extrapolating events from a log file to ascertain what has happened on the network. An *event* is a significant occurrence in the system or in an application that should be recorded for later review. Events can be recorded in the following logs:

Application The Application Log is the location where applications record their events. For example, a database program might record a file error in the Application Log.

System Operating system components are coded to record their event messages in the System Log. Events such as services failing to start or disk quota limits exceeded appear in this log.

Security Failed or successful logon attempts are a prominent type of entry that appears in the Security Log. In addition, the events that you specify in your audit policy also appear in this log.

DNS Server Events from the Domain Name Service (DNS) server are recorded in this log.

File Replication The File Replication log records events from the File Replication Service (FRS) on computers running Windows 2000 and later.

Directory Service The Directory Service log records events related to the functioning of Active Directory (AD). Messages are generated only by domain controllers.

In addition to events that are recorded in the logs just described, other events are also recorded by some applications in their own text log files. These applications include Internet Information Services (IIS), the World Wide Web Service, the File Transfer Protocol Service, the Internet Locator Service, and Microsoft SQL Server.

Some events are considered *missing events*, meaning that an event was supposed to occur but did not. You can use the filtering reporting options in Event Viewer to see whether the event occurred. For instance, if you have an automated backup procedure that is supposed to run at a certain time, you can check the logs to see if the procedure ran. If the event is not recorded, you can safely assume that the procedure did not run as scheduled and is a missing event.

The next section describes the event types that appear in a Windows Server 2003 event log and discusses how to enable auditing and the information that auditing yields after it is implemented.

Event Messages in Event Viewer

Figure 11.1 shows a typical message in an event log. The point of this particular illustration is not the specifics of the message, but rather the structure of how the information is presented. Regardless of the logs, certain characteristics are always present if the event is viewed in Event Viewer. Understanding how to read an event is important for understanding the event's message.

FIGURE 11.1   An event message from the System Log

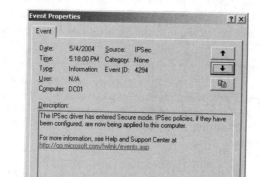

A typical message in an event log displays the following information:

The date and timestamp   The date and time that the message was generated is in the upper portion of the Event tab in the Event Properties dialog box.

The message type   Messages can be of five types:

Information   An Information message is meant to simply inform you that an important event has taken place. Usually, no action is required because there is no problem to fix. An example of an Information message is a print job message that merely informs you that a document was printed.

Warning   A Warning message means that a serious event has taken place and that it's considered critical enough to warn you about it. For example, a Warning message might tell you that a driver has disabled a write cache on a hard disk. You might not want the cache disabled, so Windows Server 2003 informs you of this event even though it is not necessarily an error.

Error   An Error message means that something has gone wrong—an unexpected event took place that Windows Server 2003 considers an error. A common example of this is shown in Figure 11.1, in which the Win32 time system is not synchronizing with an external time clock. Other types of Error messages from SQL to Exchange to IIS to Windows Server 2003 will all appear and should not be ignored. Once in a great while, you'll receive an Error message that, after being researched, is found to be benign and can be safely ignored. But these scenarios are few and far between. Never ignore Error messages. Research and correct them as soon as possible.

Success Audit   You will see Success Audit messages only in the Security Log. This message means that a request to access a secured resource was granted. A common example of this is a message that tells you a user has successfully logged on to the network.

Failure Audit   You will see a Failure Audit message only in the Security Log. This message means that a request to access a secured resource was not granted. A common example of this is a message that tells you that a user has entered the wrong password when logging on to the network. A Failure Audit message is entered into the Security Log for later review.

Event log entries in the Application and System Logs include the blue *i* for informational messages, a yellow exclamation mark (!) to designate warnings, and the red *x* sign for error messages. In the Security Log, you'll find entries that include either a locked or unlocked padlock icon to indicate the failure or success of security events.

The user   This is the user account under whose security context the event took place. System-generated messages may not be applicable, so in some cases, as in the example shown in Figure 11.1, you will see the N/A designation.

The computer   This is the computer at which the event occurred.

The source   The source is the actual service on the computer that generated the message. When performing a search in TechNet or the MSDN (Microsoft Developer Network) library, it's often helpful to include the source name along with the event ID. Doing so helps refine the initial search so that the result set is more manageable and meaningful.

Another useful resource when researching events in the event logs is the website www.EventID.net.

The category   This is the category for the event message. In large logs, the category may be useful for filtering. For example, if you're trying to determine who recently changed a policy, you can filter the Security Log for the category "policy change."

The event ID   This is a numeric ID that is associated with the message. It is not uncommon in the Microsoft literature to find tables of event ID messages and their associated numbers. Each message has its own number, and the ID helps identify the message. The event ID can also be used by Microsoft's Product Support Services (PSS) to help diagnose a particular error message.

Description and Data fields   These fields contain the messages and any associated data. This is really the heart of the event message. Often, you can use the phrases in the Description field as search strings in TechNet and MSDN. Doing so helps locate Knowledge Base articles that help you think about how to solve a problem.

Messages in an event log are presented in a one-line-per-message format, meaning that each line in the event log indicates a different message (see Figure 11.2). As you can see, each event begins with an icon indicating the type of message, the date, the time, the source, the category, the event, and user information for the message. If you want to view the entire message, simply double-click it to open it.

FIGURE 11.2   The System Log file viewed through Event Viewer showing an event on each line in the log file

Pay particular attention to the Failure Audit, Warning, and Error message types. If you ignore these messages, small problems can snowball into large ones, and possible attacks against your network will continue without a response from you. Investigate and resolve each of these message types in all event logs.

You can manage event logs through the shortcut menu when you right-click a log in the left pane of Event Viewer. From the shortcut menu, you can do the following:

- Open the log file.
- Save the log file for later review.
- Create a new log file view.
- Clear all the events in the log file.

There is no way to recover deleted events when you choose to clear the events in a log file. Use this option only when you have no need to recover any of the events in the log file, or after you have saved or exported the current log file.

- Rename the log file.
- Refresh your view of the log file to include new events.
- Export the log file to a `.csv` or a `.txt` file format.
- Open the Properties dialog box for the log file.
- Open online help for Event Viewer.

The Properties dialog box for a log file contains two tabs: General and Filter. On the General tab (see Figure 11.3), you can make several configuration changes, including the display name for the log file, the maximum log file size, and the method for overwriting events. Generally speaking, the more actions and activities you plan to audit, the larger your Security Log will be. Hence, you need to come to this General tab to increase the log file size and select how you want old events to be overwritten (if at all).

You use the options on the Filter tab (see Figure 11.4) to instruct Event Viewer to display only those events that you want to view. Notice that you can filter the events based on any combination of the following criteria:

- Event type
- Event source
- Category
- Event ID
- User
- Computer
- Date and time

Hence, if you're looking for a specific event that you know is supposed to run at midnight with a certain event ID number, you can filter the event log to display this single event.

Filtering options available with Event Viewer affect only the log of collected events and the displayed results; filtering options do not affect the actual events that are collected.

FIGURE 11.3   The Security Log Properties dialog box, open at the General tab

FIGURE 11.4   The Security Log Properties dialog box, open at the Filter tab

Implementing and Configuring Auditing

A part of any security strategy is determining the events to be audited on your network. Auditing should identify successful and unsuccessful attacks. Moreover, auditing should identify events that pose a threat to your network or sensitive resources. There may also be legal, contractual, or regulatory reasons driving your auditing strategy.

When you implement auditing in Windows Server 2003, those events are recorded in the Security Log. The more events you select to audit, the more event messages will be generated, and the more difficult it can be to spot the messages that are of greatest benefit to you. Fortunately, you can use event filtering to yield only the most important messages in the Security Log.

Audit events can be categorized as success or failure events. A successful event indicates that the action was committed successfully, such as logging on to a network or gaining access to a resource. A failed event indicates that the action was not successful, such as when a person is denied access to a resource or is unable to print to a particular printer.

If auditing is enabled, attacks that fail on your network indicate that an attempted attack occurred but was unsuccessful. This information can be useful in understanding when the attack occurred, the source location, and so on. Successful attacks can be more difficult to track than failed attacks for any number of reasons:

- Perhaps you are not auditing for successful events on the selected vector.

- The attacker used impersonation to gain entrance, so the successful audit event message looks normal and expected.

- The successful event message fits the user's normal pattern of activity.

- The successful event message is not connected to a series of preceding failed messages.

Audit messages provide information about important events, but always interpret these messages in light of a larger context and picture. Combine audit events with other information that you have to properly interpret these event messages.

How to Enable Auditing

You enable auditing through Group Policies in AD. You can enable auditing on the site, the domain, organizational unit (OU) objects in AD, or on the local machine. The audit policy settings are inside the Local Policies node of the Security Settings node.

Unless you have a specific reason to do otherwise, enable auditing at the highest levels in AD to ensure consistency across servers and workstations. For machines that are not members of any domain, you can enable auditing in Local Policies. In Exercise 11.1, you will enable auditing using a Group Policy.

EXERCISE 11.1

Enabling Auditing Using a Group Policy

1. Choose Start ➤ Administrative Tools ➤ Active Directory Users And Computers to open the Active Directory Users And Computers (ADUC) MMC.

2. Right-click the domain object in the left pane and choose Properties from the shortcut menu to open the Properties dialog box.

3. Click the Group Policy tab.

4. Select the Group Policy that you want to use to enforce auditing in your domain.

5. Click Edit to open the Group Policy.

6. Under Computer Configuration, expand Windows Settings, expand Security Settings, expand Local Policies, and then select the Audit Policy node. The right pane should now be populated with the individual audit policies that you can configure.

7. In the right pane, double-click Audit Logon Events to open the Security Policy Setting dialog box.

8. Click the Define These Policy Settings check box.

9. Click the Success and Failure check boxes.

10. Click the OK button to close the Security Policy Setting dialog box.

11. In the right pane, you should now see that the computer setting for Audit Logon Events is Success, Failure.

12. Close the Group Policy window.

13. Click OK to close Properties dialog box for the domain.

14. Choose Console ➤ Exit to close the ADUC MMC.

You have now implemented auditing for logon events that are both successful and unsuccessful. If you have installed the Group Policy Management Console (GPMC), you will need to use the GPMC interface to edit group policies rather than the ADUC MMC.

To enable auditing on a resource such as a file, a folder, or printer, you use the Properties dialog box for the resource. By way of example, create a mock `Payroll` folder as an illustration. Suppose you want to audit everyone who attempts to access this folder, both successfully and unsuccessfully. Follow these steps:

1. Right-click the `Payroll` folder and choose Properties from the shortcut menu to open the Payroll Properties dialog box:

2. Click the Security tab, click Advanced to open the Access Control Settings For Payroll dialog box, and then click the Auditing tab.

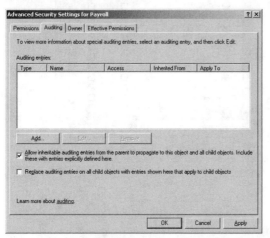

Now things can get a bit complicated. Let's assume that you want to ensure that you're tracking all failed attempts to access the Payroll folder. What this means is that you want to know about *any* attempt to connect to this folder, regardless of which share is used on the payroll server. You'll want to throw a broad net over auditing for failed attempts. The broadest group that's available in Windows Server 2003 is the Everyone security group. This group could easily be renamed to *Anyone* because that's who it includes: Anyone who connects to the server is automatically made a member of the Everyone group. Hence, auditing for the Everyone group is the best practice for failed attempts.

The steps continue:

3. In the Access Control Settings For Payroll dialog box, click Add to open the Select User, Computer, Or Group dialog box:

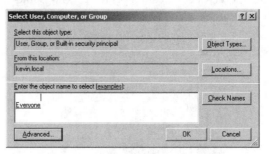

4. Type **Everyone** in the selection box and click the Check Names button. (You could also use the Advanced button to query AD for specific names, and then click OK to open the Auditing Entry For Payroll dialog box.)

Notice that the Auditing Entry For Payroll dialog box lets you audit access to the `Payroll` folder at two granular levels. First, in the Apply Onto drop-down list box, you have the following choices as to how pervasive you want to apply this auditing policy:

- The folder only
- The folder, subfolders, and files
- This folder and subfolders
- This folder and files
- Subfolders and files only
- Subfolders only
- Files only

You can apply this auditing policy only to folders, only to files, or to both folders and files. And you can bypass the folder that you're working on and work with only subfolders and files. Very flexible and very nice.

The other granular level is what type of access you can audit. In the Access section, you can select either the Successful or Failed check boxes (or both) for the following actions:

- Traverse Folder/Execute File
- List Folder/Read Data
- Read Attributes
- Read Extended Attributes
- Create Files/Write Data
- Create Folders/Append Data
- Write Attributes
- Write Extended Attributes
- Delete Subfolders And Files
- Delete
- Read Permissions
- Change Permissions
- Take Ownership

The idea here, of course, is flexibility and granularity: You can audit for individual actions or for a plethora of actions. Whatever your audit needs, you can accomplish them here. In this example, you're set up an audit policy to record the Everyone security group for failed attempts, so you select all the Failed check boxes, because you want to know whenever anyone attempts any of these actions that failed.

You also want to know who has successfully accessed this folder. To successfully implement this portion of the audit policy, you must first block permissions inheritance on the Security tab in the Payroll Properties dialog box. Blocking inheritance means that you explicitly assign permissions to this object and don't want the object's parent's permissions inherited. To block inheritance, follow these steps:

Chapter 11 · Configuring & Managing Groups, Permissions, Rights, & Auditing

1. In the Payroll Properties dialog box, click the Security tab, click the Advanced button to open the Advanced Security Settings dialog box, and then clear the Allow Inheritable Permissions From Parent To Propagate To This Object check box to open the Security dialog box.

Notice that you can either copy or remove inherited permissions. The Copy function lets you block inheritance but retain the inherited permissions as explicit permissions. This is best selected when you want to block inheritance but want to simply add more security configurations to the existing configurations. The Remove function lets you clear all security assignments and configurations so that you can start with a clean slate and configure your own permissions. This is best used when the explicit permissions that you want to assign are so different from the inherited permissions that it's easier and/or cleaner to simply start over.

2. Click Remove to remove all permissions from this item.

Back in the Payroll Properties dialog box, clicking OK locks everyone out of the object (see Figure 11.5).

FIGURE 11.5 The Payroll folder's security configurations after removing all inherited permissions

> **NOTE** Depending on your company's security policies, it's recommended that you enable Allow for the Administrators group Full Control permission before leaving the Security dialog box for administrative purposes.

1. To add the Payroll Users security group, click Add to open the Select Users, Computer, Or Groups dialog box, type **Payroll Users** in the selection box, click Check Names, and select this group.

2. Click OK to close the Select Users, Computer, Or Groups dialog box and return to the Security tab in the Payroll Properties dialog box:

3. To audit the Payroll Users security group's access to the Payroll folder, click Advanced to open the Advanced Properties dialog box and then click the Auditing tab.

4. Click Add to open the Select User, Computer, Or Group dialog box, type **Payroll Users** in the selection box, click Check Names, and select the Payroll Users security group.

5. In the Auditing Entry For Payroll dialog box, select to apply this auditing policy to This Folder, Subfolders, And Files.

6. In the Access selection box, select all the Successful check boxes to ensure that you have a complete record of which members of the Payroll Users security groups have successfully accessed the Payroll folder and what actions they exercised successfully, as shown in Figure 11.6.

7. Click OK to close the Auditing Entry For Payroll dialog box.

8. Click OK again to close the Payroll Properties dialog box.

Now, whenever anyone attempts to access the Payroll folder, you will see events to this effect recorded in the Security Log.

FIGURE 11.6 Auditing the Payroll Users security group for successful access to the folder

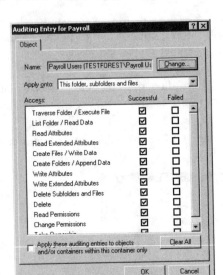

Types of Events to Audit

This section describes the categories of events that you can audit on a system-wide basis.

Logon Events

When you audit for logon events, you capture the timing of when a user logged on and off an individual computer. These events are always logged in the logs of the local computer. At a technical level, an event is logged in the Security Log whenever an access token (AT) is either generated or destroyed.

Tracking such events is useful when an attacker attempts to connect to a particular server from a particular location. You can use the logs to investigate attacks that originated at a specific location. Successful attempts result in a successful event being entered in the event log. Failed attempts result in the opposite: a failed event is entered in the event log.

When auditing logon events, you see messages from both user and computer accounts. This is by design. Only Windows NT and later operating systems generate logon events for the computer. Windows 9x machines do not generate such events.

You often see events 529 ("The logon attempt was made with an unknown username or a known username with a bad password") and 534 ("The user attempted to log on with a logon type that is not allowed, such as network, interactive, batch, service, or remote interactive") when an attacker attempts to log on to your network by guessing either (or both) the username or password. However, these events do not distinguish between a valid user who forgets their password and an attacker who is guessing at a password. The point of the messages is to inform you that the attempted logon failed and the reason that it failed.

Other events, such as 530 through 533, indicate a misuse of a user's account. The user was able to enter a valid username and password, but other restrictions prevented the user from successfully being authenticated in the domain. These event numbers indicate a potential compromise of at least one user account, so don't ignore them. Always investigate failed logon events with these event ID numbers.

Event 539 indicates that an account was locked out for logon purposes. Depending on your account policies, this can indicate that a logon attack failed. Use event ID 539 along with event 529 to establish the timing, pattern, and location from which the attack occurred.

Account Logon Events

Account logon events record when a user attempts to log on or off using a domain account, and the request is serviced by a domain controller. Such activity is recorded in the domain controller, not on the local computer. Because account logon events can be recorded at any domain controller, you need to consolidate the server's logs before analyzing possible attack activities. This activity applies to logon attempts at domain controllers, member servers, and member workstations.

As with logon events, account logon events record both computer and user account activities.

Event IDs 675 and 677 indicate failed domain logon attempts. Also, if a client's computer is off by more than five minutes from the domain controller that services the logon request, a 675 message is generated.

Account Management Events

Account management auditing is used to discern when users or groups are created or modified. Who performed the task is also tracked as part of the event message.

Event IDs 624 and 626 report that a user account was created or enabled. If only certain people are allowed to create user accounts in your domain, you can use these events to determine if unauthorized personnel have created user accounts.

Event IDs 627 and 628 indicate that a user's account password was successfully changed by someone other than the individual user. You can review the event detail to ensure that the account that changed the password is an approved account such as a member of the Help Desk or Administrator team.

Event IDs 629 and 630 indicate that an account was successfully deleted. An attacker can use these event IDs to cover their tracks after performing malicious activities under a certain account. Look also for Event ID 626 followed shortly by a 629 event. This succession indicates that a disabled account was enabled, used, and then disabled again.

The lockout of an account is recorded at the PDC Emulator domain controller.

Object Access Events

Nearly every object in Windows Server 2003 can be audited for object access. Audit events on object access are created when a handle to the object is opened. For instance, when a user attempts to open a file, a message is passed to the system kernel requesting a handle to the file, along with the type of access requested such as Read or Write. The system then compares the user's token to the entries in the DACL (discretionary access control list). If there's a match, the system compares the user's token to the entries in the SACL (system access control list), which generates messages based on whether the user was granted access or denied access. Of course, the entries in the SACL tell the system what kind of message to generate. If auditing is turned on only for success events, the SACL will contain no entry for requests that are denied, and thus no failure event messages are generated.

When an event message is generated in this category, nothing has happened to the object at the time the message is generated. The system merely generates the requested audit failure or success message. Hence, write audit messages are generated *before the write operation is performed*, and read audits are generated before the object is exposed for reading.

When attempting to audit for nontrusted accounts, use the Everyone group. This group is broad and includes everyone who can connect to your system, regardless of their method.

Member server and domain controller installations are preconfigured to audit for success and failed object access. Use Group Policies to configure objects that need to be audited that exist on multiple computers. You can configure auditing for a single object on a single computer using either a Group Policy or the Properties dialog box for the object itself.

Event ID 560 indicates that access was granted to an existing object. If you're looking to see who has access to which objects, you'll be looking primarily for 560 event messages:

- Event ID 562 reports that a handle to an object was closed.

- Event ID 563 indicates that an attempt to open an object with the intent of deleting that object was recorded.

- Event ID 564 indicates that a protected object was deleted.

- Event ID 565 records access to existing object types.

If you want to see who has accessed a particular file, look for 560 events, and in the details, look for the full path to the file. If you want to see what a specific user has accessed, filter for both 560 events as well as for the user's account name. Finally, if you want to find out which actions have been performed at a specific computer, filter for that computer and look for 560 events associated with that computer.

Directory Service Access Events

This message type is used to audit access to objects that don't exist in the domain partition. For instance, if you want to audit access to objects in the configuration or schema naming contexts, you enable Directory Service access auditing. For the configuration partition, you enable auditing using the Active Directory Service Interface Edit (ADSIEdit) program from the Windows Server 2003 Resource Kit.

Because the configuration partition is constantly accessed, you're advised to use failure audit configurations. Success audits result in large log files that may or may not be useful, even when filtered. Failed access messages to naming contexts other than the domain naming context result in Event ID 565. You need to read and filter these events before they yield much useful information.

Privilege Use Events

Some users will be given special rights or privileges on your network. You can track the exercising of these rights for future reference. Not all uses of privileges are tracked using this method. The following user rights are excluded from this category type:

- Bypass traverse checking

- Debug programs

- Create a token object

- Replace process-level token

- Generate security audits

- Back up files and folders

- Restore files and folders

You can override the default behavior of not recording backup and restore user rights by enabling the Audit Use Of Backup And Restore Privilege security policy setting in the Security Options node, which is inside the Security Settings/Local Policies node in a Group Policy (see Figure 11.7).

When you choose to audit successful message types on privilege use, you create a large number of messages in the Security Log. Make sure that you have increased the log file size significantly to accommodate these messages.

Event ID 576 indicates that specific privileges have been added to a user's access token. This event is only generated at the time that a user logs on to the system. Event 577 indicates that a user attempted to perform a privileged system service operation. This does not necessarily indicate whether the user was successful.

Here are some examples of how these event IDs are recorded:

- If a user changes the system time on a server, look for event ID 577 or 578 with the `SeSystemtimePrivilege` privilege indicated. This event can indicate a user's attempt to change the system time to hide the true time that another event took place.

- When a device drive is loaded or unloaded, look for event ID 577 or 578 with the user right `SeRemoteShutdownPrivilege`. Such an event can indicate that a malicious drive has been loaded that is intended to cause harm to your server or system.

FIGURE 11.7   The Audit Use Of Backup And Restore Privilege policy setting

- When the ownership of files or objects is changed, look for event ID 577 or 578 with the `SeTakeOwnershipPrivilege` user right indicated. Knowing who has taken ownership of critical files may indicate a (perhaps successful) attempt to copy or modify these files. Other privileges to look for associated with the 577 or 578 IDs include `SeShutdownPrivilege`, which indicates a successful shutdown of a server, or `SeTcbPrivilege`, which can indicate an attempt to elevate the user account's privileges to act as part of the operating system.

Process Tracking Events

Event messages for process tracking indicate when a process was created and ended on a Windows Server 2003 Server machine. It also records when a process attempts to generate a handle to an object or obtain indirect access to an object.

If you choose to enable process tracking, be sure to increase the size of your log considerably. Process tracking creates a large number of audit entries:

- Event ID 592 indicates that a new process was created.
- Event ID 593 indicates that a process exited.
- Event ID 594 indicates that a handle to an object was duplicated.
- Event ID 595 indicates that indirect access to an object was obtained.

You can keep track of every program and process that is run on your network by using process tracking. For instance, if you want to know how often your users are running FreeCell, enable process tracking on your users' desktops. From there, you can filter the logs and see how often your users are opening FreeCell. From a security standpoint, you can discern every process that runs on your network and pinpoint when a malicious program was started and when it was stopped. However, the amount of material to wade through to pinpoint such a program might be voluminous; therefore, implement process tracking only when necessary.

System Events

When aspects of a computer's environment are altered, system events are generated. These include such activities as shutting down the computer or changing the system time. Auditing system events also audits when the Security Log entries are cleared. This is important to know because good hackers (if there is such a thing) will attempt to cover their tracks after making an environmental change. Member servers and domain controllers are set to audit for system events automatically.

Several event IDs are associated with system events:

- Event ID 512 indicates that the Windows operating system is starting.
- Event ID 513 indicates that it is shutting down.
- Event ID 517 indicates that the Security Log was cleared. If you feel that your system has been compromised, be sure to check the Security Log for event 517. This may indicate that the attacker cleared the Security Log to cover their activities.

Policy Change Events

Your audit policy defines which changes to your environment will be recorded for later review. The more you audit, the more information you'll have on hand to understand the nature and timing of an attack on your system. However, you'll also have more information through which you'll have to wade to glean the necessary information.

If you audit for policy change, you will record attempts to change your audit policy. By default, member servers and domain controllers audit policy change for both success and failure. Policy change events include the following:

- Event ID 608 records when a user right was assigned.
- Event ID 609 records when a user right was removed from the user account.
- Event ID 610 records when a trust relationship with another domain was created.
- Event ID 611 records when a trust relationship was removed.
- Event ID 612 indicates when your audit policy was changed.

The two most important events to note are IDs 608 and 609. Most attacks will need elevated privileges, and it's important to note when a user account is given a new right and when it is taken away. In addition to privilege use, you'll find that an account that was given the Act As Part Of The Operating System privilege will have Event ID 608 recorded too. When the attack is finished, the attacker may remove this privilege and return the user account to a "normal" state. The removal of this privilege generates a 609 ID. Table 11.1 lists and describes assigned right names. This table is a handy reference for 608 and 609 IDs.

T A B L E 11.1   Assigned Right Names for Events 608 and 609

Assigned Right Name	Description
SeTcbPrivilege	Act as part of the operating system.
SeMachineAccountPrivilege	Add workstations to the domain.
SeBackupPrivilege	Back up files and folders.
SeChangeNotifyPrivilege	Bypass traverse checking.
SeSystemtimePrivilege	Change the system time.
SeCreatePermanentPrivilege	Create permanent shared objects.
SeDebugPrivilege	Debug programs.
SeRemoteShutdownPrivilege	Force shutdown from a remote system.
SeIncreaseBasePriorityPrivilege	Increase scheduling priority.
SeSecurityPrivilege	Manage auditing and Security Log.
SeAssignPrimaryTokenPrivilege	Replace a process-level token.
SeRestorePrivilege	Restore files and folders.

TABLE 11.1   Assigned Right Names for Events 608 and 609 *(continued)*

Assigned Right Name	Description
SeShutdownPrivilege	Shut down the system.
SeTakOwnershipPrivilege	Take ownership of files or other objects.

Configuring Access Control Lists

The access control list (ACL) is where you as administrators basically provide users access to some network resources and prevent other users from gaining access. You do this by inserting an access control entry (ACE) into the ACL. This is a basic function of a network administrator, and Microsoft covers ACLs on most of the operating system exams. This section presents just a quick review of the topic.

File and Directory Permissions

In order to control access to files and directories, the disk volume must be formatted as NTFS. To view or set permissions, simply right-click the object and choose Properties where there will be a Security tab. NTFS allows you to set several different types of permissions, as shown in Table 11.2.

TABLE 11.2   NTFS Permissions

Permission	Access Rights
Full Control	Traverse folders and execute files (programs) in the folders. List the contents of a folder and read the data in a folder's files. See a folder's or file's attributes. Change a folder's or file's attributes. Create new files and write data to the files. Create new folders and append data to the files. Delete subfolders and files. Delete files. Change permissions for files and folders. Take ownership of files and folders.
Modify	Traverse folders and execute files (programs) in the folders. List the contents of a folder and read the data in a folder's files. See a folder's or file's attributes. Change a folder's or file's attributes. Create new files and write data to the files. Create new folders and append data to the files. Delete files.

TABLE 11.2   NTFS Permissions *(continued)*

Permission	Access Rights
Read & Execute	Traverse folders and execute files (programs) in the folders. List the contents of a folder and read the data in a folder's files. See a folder's or file's attributes.
List Folder Contents	Traverse folders. List the contents of a folder. See a folder's or file's attributes.
Read	List the contents of a folder and read the data in a folder's files. See a folder's or file's attributes.
Write	Change a folder's or file's attributes. Create new files and write data to the files. Create new folders and append data to the files.

As you can see, you have quite a bit of granularity in designing your file structure ACLs. Another feature that may help in creating your structure is inheritance. In Windows Server 2003, permissions are inherited by default from the parent folder to every child folder. For many cases, that allows you to set the permissions once at the root folder. There may be times, however, when you don't want permissions inherited. You can disable this by deselecting the Allow Inheritable Permissions For The Parent To Propagate To This Object And All Child Objects on the Advanced Security Settings dialog box.

If there are multiple ACEs in an ACL, the permissions are combined into a user's effective permissions. In Windows 2000, you had to manually add all of a user's permissions and then subtract all denied permissions to determine the effective permissions. Windows Server 2003 added a new tab to the Advanced Security Settings dialog box for Effective Permissions. Remember that any denied permission always wins when compared to allowed permissions. Explicit denies can be used quite productively. When at all possible, you want to use domain local groups for setting permissions to minimize future maintenance.

User Rights

User rights are similar in nature to file ACLs. While file ACLs grant access to objects, user rights give users permissions to perform certain actions. The ability to change the system time, for example, is a user right. Generally, user rights apply to a particular computer.

To modify user rights for a user or group, on a non-DC, open Local Security Policy from the Administrative Tools menu, or on a DC, open the Domain Security Policy. Table 11.3 lists the various user rights you have to work with to secure your systems.

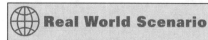

Real World Scenario

Using Explicit Deny

You work for a multinational company that performs some contract work for the U.S. Department of Defense (DoD). A large percentage of your employees are not U.S. citizens. That does not preclude the non-citizen employees from working on the DoD projects; they are just limited to viewing a small portion of each project.

You set up the project directories in a fashion that helps minimize administrative effort. The further down the directory structure you go, the more restrictive the access becomes. This allows you to use inheritance for a majority of the directories. Then, on the sensitive directories, you should put in an explicit deny on a security group that contains non-citizens as its members.

TABLE 11.3   User Rights

User Right	Description
Access this computer from the network	Connect over the network to a computer.
Act as part of the operating system	Act as a trusted parrot of the operating system; some subsystems have this privilege granted to them.
Add workstations to the domain	Make machines domain members.
Back up files and directories	Back up files and directories. This right supersedes file and directory permissions.
Bypass traverse checking	Traverse a directory tree even if the user has no other rights to access that directory. Allows a user to have permissions and access to a child directory when they don't have permissions to the parent directory.
Change the system time	Set the time for the internal clock.
Create a page file	Create a system page file.
Create a token object	Create access tokens. Only the Local Security Authority should have this privilege.
Create permanent shared objects	Create special permanent objects.

TABLE 11.3   User Rights *(continued)*

User Right	Description
Debug programs	Debug applications.
Deny access to this computer from the network	Revoke the right to users/groups to access a computer.
Deny logon as a batch job	Revoke the right to log in as a batch job.
Deny login as a service	Revoke the right to log in as a service.
Deny logon locally	Revoke the right to log in locally.
Enable computer and user accounts to be trusted for delegation	Designate accounts that can be delegated.
Force shutdown from a remote system	Allow a computer to be shut down from a remote system.
Generate security audits	Generate audit log entries.
Increase quotas	Increase object quotas.
Increase scheduling priority	Boost the scheduling priority of a process.
Load and unload device drivers	Add or remove drivers from the system.
Lock pages in memory	Lock pages in memory to prevent them from being paged out to the page file.
Log on as a batch job	Log on to the system as a batch queue.
Log on a service	Allow a process to log in and run as a service.
Log on locally	Log on at the server console.
Manage auditing and security log	Specify what types of events and resource access are to be audited and allows viewing and clearing of the Security Log.
Modify firmware environment variables	Modify system environment variables.
Profile single process	Use profiling capabilities to observe a process.

TABLE 11.3   User Rights *(continued)*

User Right	Description
Profile system performance	Use profiling capabilities to observe the system (e.g., Perfmon).
Remove computer from docking station	Remove a laptop from its docking station.
Replace a process-level token	Modify a process's access token.
Restore files and directories	Restore files and directories. This right supersedes file and directory permissions.
Shut down the system	Shut down Windows Server 2003.
Synchronize directory service data	Update Active Directory information.
Take ownership of files or other objects	Take ownership of files, directories, and other objects that are owned by other users.

As you can see, like NTFS file permissions, user rights assignments are quite granular. This affords you the flexibility to implement security to meet most security designs. User rights can be assigned locally on a system or can be enforced via GPO. Using GPO allows you even more flexibility in determining which systems receive specific rights assignments.

Using Event Logs

This section looks at the particular logs available to you, how they work, and how to interpret the information they provide.

IIS Logs

IIS writes its events to a text file in the `%systemroot%/system32/logfiles` folder. Each website that is run by IIS has its own folder under which the log files are generated. The default website's folder name is `W3SVC1`. If you installed a second website, its folder name is `W3SVC2`. The default log format is the W3C Extended Log File Format.

These log files generate the following required information:

- Software version
- Date and time of the entry
- Client IP address
- Client username
- Port number

- Method
- URI (uniform resource identifier) stem and query
- Any status messages returned to the user

Windows Server 2003 does not include any user interface (UI) to these logs. They are best opened in Notepad and read manually (see Figure 11.8). Otherwise, you can purchase third-party tools such as WebTrends to read and present the information in these files in a more intuitive and helpful format.

From a security standpoint, it's imperative that you understand these logs, even though they can be difficult and boring to read. Port 80 is the most often attacked port, and IIS is one of the most often attacked software packages on the Internet today. Knowing who has attacked and from which IP address can help pinpoint the attacker and stop future attacks.

If you don't want to store the logs in a text file, you can configure IIS to store the logs in a SQL Server database. In Exercise 11.2, you'll configure IIS for this task.

Once the information is stored in a SQL database, you can have a SQL developer write a UI to the information so that you can more easily view and interpret it.

FIGURE 11.8 IIS logs in Notepad

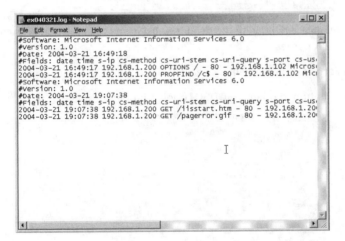

EXERCISE 11.2

Changing the Logging Option for a Website to Log Its Events to a SQL Database

1. Choose Start ➢ Administrative Tools ➢ Internet Services Manager.

2. Expand the Server object in the left pane to reveal the websites and services offered by this IIS server.

EXERCISE 11.2 (continued)

3. In the left pane, right-click the website, and then choose Properties from the shortcut menu to open the <Name_of_Website> Web Site Properties dialog box.

In this example, you are working with the default website, so the name of this dialog box is Default Web Site Properties.

4. In the Active Log Format drop-down list, select ODBC Logging.

5. Click the Properties button to open the ODBC Logging Properties dialog box:

6. Enter the correct information and click OK to close the ODBC Logging Properties dialog box and return to the Web Site Properties dialog box.

7. Click OK again to close the Web Site Properties dialog box.

8. Close the IIS window.

Firewall Log Files

Internet Security and Acceleration (ISA) Server provides logs for packet filters, the ISA Server Firewall Service, and the ISA Server Web Proxy Service. By default, logs are stored in the W3C Extended Log File Format but can be stored in a SQL Server as well. By default, these logs are stored in the `%systemroot%\program files\microsoft isa server\isalogs` folder.

Firewall logs are important to monitor, because they can tell you when your router or firewall is under attack. Moreover, they can help you figure out who is doing the attacking. Because most firewalls are the first point of entry into a network, it's important to record the packets that flow in and out. Moreover, you can use log file retention to track trends. For example, hackers send a single `ping` to potential targets and then wait for several months before sending another `ping` packet. Patient hackers can often infiltrate a network through the firewall over many months by stealth, most often because the log files are not read with a long-term view and because many organizations don't retain them for any length of time.

Reading and understanding the firewall logs gives you up-to-date information on who is performing port scanning, who is sending suspicious packets to your network, and who is sending information out of your network.

Network Monitor Logs

Network Monitor is a nifty tool that captures and displays all the packets that have run between two devices. The version that ships with Windows Server 2003 can capture (sometimes called trace) packets between itself and a remote machine. The version of Network Monitor that ships with Systems Management Server can capture packets between two remote hosts.

When using this tool, you can view each packet that comes in and goes out of a specific device like a router or a Windows Server 2003 server. The value of this tool is that you can use it to track exactly what has happened on your network and servers. For example, you can use Network Monitor (sometimes referred to as NetMon) to capture all the packets from your firewall and then filter the list to view the exact packets you want to view.

Packet traces can reveal immense amounts of information such as the originating IP address of the attacker, the exact methodologies the attacker used, the servers and workstations the attacker connected to, and the information downloaded or compromised.

In Figure 11.9, you can see that each line in Network Monitor is a distinct packet that includes the source and destination MAC (Media Access Control) address, the protocol used, and a description of what the packet was intended to accomplish. This is where it is good to know the Server Message Block (SMB) commands discussed in Chapter 4, "Configuring IPSec and SMB Signing." Once you know the SMB commands and other commands for HTTP or SMTP, you can read these packets and have a pretty good idea about what exactly happened on your network.

Learning to use Network Monitor is not easy, and it takes some time. But once you've mastered this tool, you'll find it indispensable in learning what information and commands have passed between two devices on your network.

In Exercise 11.3, you will run a packet trace on your computer.

FIGURE 11.9   A Network Monitor packet trace

Running a Packet Trace on Your Windows Server 2003 Server Machine

1. Choose Start ➢ Administrative Tools ➢ Network Monitor to open Network Monitor. (If Network Monitor does not appear under Administrative Tools, you need to add this service inside the Windows Components section of the Add/Remove Programs utility in Control Panel.)

2. If this is the first time you have run Network Monitor, you're prompted to select the network that you want to monitor. Click the plus sign (+) to expand Local Computer, then highlight Local Area Connection. (If you have multiple network cards in your server, you need to select the card using the MAC address.) Then click OK to start Network Monitor.

3. Choose Capture ➢ Start to begin capturing packets. You'll be able to see this activity.

4. Wait a short period of time and then choose Capture ➢ Stop And View to stop the capture of packets and automatically display all the packets.

5. Look through the description of each packet. What does the description tell you?

6. Look through the Src MAC Addr, Dst MAC Addr, and Protocol columns. Between which two machines were these packets flowing?

7. To close this view, choose File ➢ Close.

8. To close Network Monitor, choose File ➢ Exit.

9. If prompted to save the capture, click No.

RAS Logs

Remote Access Service (RAS) events are recorded in the System Log and can be viewed in Event Viewer. You can enable event logging on the Logging tab in the Properties dialog box of the remote access server (see Figure 11.10). On this tab, you can select which level of logging you want to employ. Logging Point-to-Point Protocol (PPP) packets is configured on this tab as well, by selecting the Log Additional Routing And Remote Access Information option.

Event logging isn't the only type of logging available for RAS servers. As just mentioned, you can enable PPP logging, which allows you to record the series of programming functions and control messages that pass between two devices during a PPP session. By default, PPP logs are stored in the %SystemRoot%\tracing folder.

In addition to logging events to the System Log, RAS can be configured to record accounting type of information to a text log file or to a SQL server. In Exercise 11.4, you will configure text logging for your RAS server.

FIGURE 11.10   The Logging tab in the RAS Properties dialog box

---

EXERCISE 11.4

Configuring RAS Logging on Your Windows Server 2003 Server Machine

1. Choose Start ➤ Administrative Tools ➤ Routing And Remote Access.

2. Click the plus sign (+) sign next to your server name to expand the options.

3. Highlight the folder in the left pane named Remote Access Logging.

4. In the right pane, double-click Local File to bring up the Local File Properties page.

5. On the Settings tab, notice the options you have. Place a check mark next to Authentication Requests.

6. Click the Log File tab and notice the file location and retention options.

7. Click OK to close the Properties page.

8. To close Routing and Remote Access, choose File ➤ Exit.

9. Make a VPN connection to your RAS server from another client.

10. Navigate to the directory listed in Step 6 and open the log file and review its contents.

You can also use Network Monitor to trace packets between a dial-up connection and an RAS server. Not only can such a packet trace be useful for troubleshooting, but it can also yield information about the attacker and what the attacker did to your server and/or network.

From a security standpoint, it would be a best practice to ensure that Network Monitor is used to trace packets when a dial-up connection is established between your network and a remote computer or network. Obviously, you must do this with some forethought because such a trace could become large rather quickly. But in certain specific situations—such as when your network is directly exposed via a dial-up connection—it might be a good idea to trace all the packets that flow over that dial-up connection.

Managing Log Retention

In addition to ensuring that you have set each log's properties in Event Viewer correctly, you should be aware of some other best practices for auditing:

- Be sure to schedule regular reviews of your event logs. This is the most often missed part of using the audit logs. It is one thing to set up the audit policy and enforce it. But if the logs are never read, they are of little value to you.

- Obviously, the more often you review logs, the faster you can detect vulnerabilities and patch them. If your policy is to regularly review logs, your company will be forced to include the review of these logs in at least one person's job description. This is good thing, because it defines exactly who is responsible for reading and understanding these logs.

- Configure log retention to dove-tail with the reading and understanding of the logs in question. For example, if logs are read only once each week, your log retention policy should be such that events are held for longer than seven days. If logs are exported and then retained, there is no industry standard for how long these .csv or .txt files should be retained. The best practice is to consult with your manager and your company's legal advisors on what logs should be retained and for how long.

- As a rule of thumb, once the information becomes unimportant, the files and events should not be retained. For example, logs that contain no remarkable events might be retained for only 14 days, but those that contain evidence of an attack might be retained for years, especially if a legal action is involved. Your log retention policy should account for these scenarios and then specify how long each log file should be retained.

- Associated with this is your event-overwriting policies. Remember that some logs can be configured to overwrite events as needed. This may not be the best policy to enforce because there is the potential for critical events to be overwritten simply because the log file is too full. If you need to ensure that you always have every event generated by the system, do not configure the logs in Event Viewer to overwrite older events.

Managing Distributed Audit Logs

In a large environment with many servers, reviewing the event logs looking for signs of trouble can be tedious. Reviewing the logs routinely could be a full-time job. In large environments, you'll probably need some automated help. Help is available from several third-party vendors. Microsoft has an application that you can purchase called Microsoft Operations Manager (MOM), which monitors an entire network. Utilization of MOM is well beyond the scope of this book.

Fortunately, Microsoft also provides a free utility that can be used to parse event logs from multiple servers—EventComb.

EventComb is a multithreaded tool that parses event logs from multiple servers simultaneously so that you can find event messages across a range of servers. This tool has tremendous value in that you can aggregate your log data and then analyze it from an enterprise perspective.

Using EventComb, you can perform the following administrative acts:

- Define single or multiple event IDs as search criteria.

- Define a range of event IDs as a single search criteria.

- Limit the search to specific event logs.

- Limit the search to specific event message types.

- Limit the search to specific event sources.

- Search for specific text within an event description.

- Define time intervals to scan back from the current date and time.

The EventComb tool is available as part of the overall scripts downloaded from TechNet for the Security Operations Guide for Windows Server 2003.

 You can download EventComb free of charge from Microsoft's website. Simply go to www.microsoft.com/technet, enter **Security Operations Guide for Windows Server 2003** in the Search box, and then click Search. On the home page for this guide, click the Downloads link and download all the scripts associated with this guide. Then extract the downloaded file. Once extracted, you'll find the EventComb tool inside the `EventComb` folder. There is no installation per se for this tool. It's merely an executable that runs when invoked.

To run EventComb, double-click the `evencombmt.exe` file to start the tool. Figure 11.11 shows EventComb's opening screen.

FIGURE 11.11   The opening screen for the EventComb tool

After starting this tool, the first step is to add the computers that you want to include in the event log search. To add computers to the search, follow these steps:

1.   In the EventComb utility, ensure that the correct domain appears in the Domain box. If it does not, enter the correct domain name.

2.   Right-click in the Select To Search/Right Click To Add box to open a shortcut menu that gives you the choices shown in Figure 11.12. Notice that you can select from a variety of servers based on their role, name, domain affiliation, or a list derived from a file. You can also select servers that appear in this box and remove them from the target list.

FIGURE 11.12   The shortcut menu for adding servers to the inclusion list for an event log search

Once the desired servers are added, you must select the servers in the list against which to perform your search. Hence, servers can appear in the list but not be searched for a particular query. What this means is that when the tool is initially run, you need to select the servers that you wish to mine two times: once to get them into the list and a second time to include them in the search query. To select multiple servers, use the Ctrl+click combination.

After you select the servers to be included in your search, you are ready to specify the search criteria, which includes the following:

- Log files to search

- Event ID numbers

- Source of the message

- Specific text

- Scope of time

By combining these elements, you can pinpoint your search to yield the best and most helpful information possible. While the search is running (see Figure 11.13), you'll see the number of threads that are being employed to conduct the search. Moreover, you'll see the cached DLLs (dynamic link libraries), which means that the DLL has been cached and is being accessed in the cache instead of being called numerous times to execute the search. Finally, the SIDs cached are also displayed. Looking up a SID (security identifier) is a rather expensive process, so once a SID has been extracted from the security database, it is cached to improve performance of the EventComb tool.

Near the bottom of the EventComb main window is a Status box that indicates the start and end times of the search and how many records matched the search criteria. The actual listing of these records is in the default folder in a simple text file.

When the EventComb tool runs, it places its findings in a set of result files that have a `.txt` extension. There is a summary file named `EventCombMTMT.txt`, and for each computer included in the search query, there is a separate text file named *`computername-eventlogname`*`_LOG.txt`. Figure 11.14 contains a sample text file.

FIGURE 11.13   The EventComb tool while running

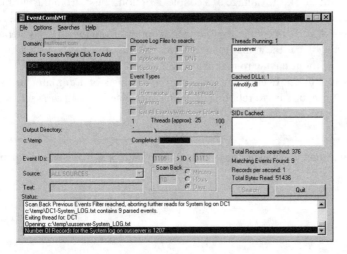

FIGURE 11.14   A sample text file generated by EventComb

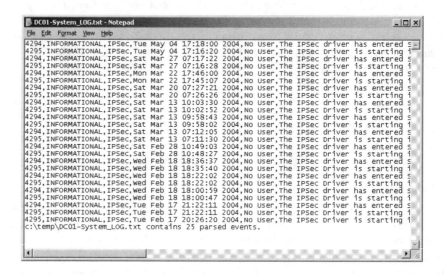

Some built-in searches ship with the EventComb utility. You can find these searches in the Searches menu. There are built-in searches for

- File Replication Service (FRS Health)
- Account Lockouts
- Active Directory
- Hardware
- DNS Interface Errors

You can also create a customized search and then save that search by choosing Searches ➤ Save This Search.

Finally, you might want to take advantage of a couple of options. First, from the File menu, you can change the output location from the default `c:\temp` to some other location (choose File ➤ Set Output Directory). Second, you can configure a number of options from the Options menu. One in particular that may interest you is the ability to save the text files as `.csv` files, which allows you to open these files in Excel without having to manually change their extension first.

In Exercise 11.5, you will use EventComb to search for restarts of a domain controller. Before you run this exercise, be sure to reboot a domain controller that you can search using the EventComb utility.

Remember, you will not be tested on the operations of EventComb in this exam.

Real World Scenario

Using EventComb to Understand a Recent Attack Vector

Let's assume that you are managing 14 Windows Server 2003 machines, 3 of which are domain controllers and 11 of which are member servers. Let's further assume that all your servers were operating as expected on Monday morning when you came to work and when you went home.

On Tuesday morning, you start to receive a steady stream of calls from your users indicating that Internet access is slow. Moreover, when you check your real-time firewall logs, you find an immense number of files being copied to the Internet—all to the same IP address.

You immediately suspect that you have been compromised. As an emergency measure, you shut down the firewall to kill all inbound and outbound traffic. Then you decide to figure out just exactly what happened on your servers during the night so that you can block future attempts to exploit this vulnerability.

What you would do, among other things, is use the EventComb utility to read the event logs of all your servers to determine which server was first compromised and how the attacker was able to log on to your network. By using this utility, you find that the attacker, after authenticating in your domain, was able to create a new user account, give that account pervasive permissions and privileges, run a program to copy sensitive data to their hard drive, and then delete the user account that was created. The only mistake the attacker made was in *not* clearing the logs before logging off.

Now, you obviously need to take other actions as part of a larger incident response, but using EventComb can play a key role in understanding how an attacker worked on your network to achieve malicious ends.

EXERCISE 11.5

Searching for Domain Controller Restarts Using the EventComb Utility

1. Open the EventComb tool.

2. Make sure that the correct domain name appears in the Domain box.

3. Right-click inside the Select To Search/Right Click To Add box and select Get DCs In Domain.

4. In the Select to Search/Right Click To Add box, select the domain controller that you rebooted before starting this exercise.

5. In the Choose Log Files To Search section, select the System check box only. Make sure that all other check boxes are cleared.

6. In the Event Types section, select both the Error and Information check boxes. Make sure that all other check boxes are cleared.

7. In the Event IDs box, type the following Event IDs: **1001 6005 6006 6008**. Type these ID numbers without commas (,) or other symbols between them.

8. Leave the other settings at their default values.

9. Click the Search button.

10. After the tool finishes its search, a folder list box focused on `c:\temp` automatically opens.

11. Right-click a file and choose Open from the shortcut menu to open the text files that are named after the servers in your list.

12. Find and read the messages in the text file.

13. Close the text file by selecting Exit from the File menu.

14. Choose File ➢ Close to close the folder list box.

15. Click Exit to close the EventComb utility.

Summary

In this chapter, you learned about event logs and the meanings of the different message types. You learned that security messages do not appear in the Security Log unless you audit activities and resources. You also learned a bit covering the Network Monitor tool, IIS logs, and RRAS logs—how to read them and how to configure them.

You learned that logging is a vital part to any successful security implementation, but particularly on a network. Learning how to read and interpret logs from an enterprise perspective helps ensure that you are able to respond to a security incident faster and better informed.

This chapter also reviewed Windows group structure and how to control access to resources via ACLs and user rights.

Exam Essentials

Understand the difference between an Information, Warning, and Error message. Remember that you cannot safely ignore Warning and Error messages.

Understand that missing events can indicate a security breach. Missing events are those events that never occurred. As part of your overall security plan, decide which events should occur on a regular basis, such as a weekly, full backup of your server or daily downloads of the latest virus definitions. Missing events can create vulnerabilities on your network that hackers can exploit.

Understand the different group scopes and types. Group scopes include distribution and security groups. Group types are domain local, global, and universal. Recall that groups can be nested to ease your administration.

Understand how to grant permissions to resources. Access to resources is controlled by modifying the resource's access control list (ACL).

Review Questions

1. You have installed a new, customized, web-based application on your Windows Server 2003 machines. You want to view messages that this application generates. In which log should you look for messages from this application?

   A. System Log

   B. IIS Log

   C. Application Log

   D. RAS Log

2. You have installed a new, customized application on your Windows Server 2003 machine that has also installed its own set of services. You want to view messages that this application and its services generate. In which two logs should you look for messages from this application?

   A. Application Log

   B. System Log

   C. Security Log

   D. DNS Server Log

3. You created an audit policy for both success and failure messages to ensure that all print jobs sent to the payroll printer are recorded in the Security Log. After the next batch of payroll checks printed, you discover that there are no success or failure messages for the payroll printer. You verify that the audit policy has been correctly implemented. What should you do?

   A. Verify that the printer is online.

   B. Verify that the printer has printed the checks.

   C. Verify that auditing has been enabled on the printer.

   D. Verify that the audit policy has been correctly implemented.

4. You enabled the Distributed File System (DFS) feature on your network. You find that some files are not being automatically synchronized between your domain controllers. You want to diagnose the problem. Where should you look to find DFS error messages?

   A. Directory Service Log

   B. File Replication Log

   C. System Log

   D. Application Log

5. Of the following, which log accepts messages only from Windows Server 2003 domain controllers?

   A. System Log

   B. Security Log

   C. File Replication Log

   D. Directory Service Log

6. You are the system administrator for a Windows Server 2003 Active Directory network. You have three domain controllers on your network: DC1, DC2, and DC3. You enabled auditing for both success and failure events for logon events on DC1 (Domain Controller 1). Later, you discover that no logon events are recorded in the Security Log for DC2 and DC3. What should you do?

   A. Configure the audit policy to audit account logon events.

   B. Check the Directory Service Log instead of the Security Log for success and failure account logon messages.

   C. Enable auditing on each user account.

   D. Configure a new Group Policy. Have that Group Policy configure the Registry of each workstation to log on at DC1.

7. You notice in your Security Log a number of Event ID 529 error messages from the same workstation between the hours of 8:30 P.M. and 10:30 P.M. Your users do not work in the office during this time period. What do you suspect is happening?

   A. The workstation is attempting to reset its trust relationship password with the domain controller.

   B. The workstation is repeatedly shutting down.

   C. Someone is trying to log on to your network and is unable to do so.

   D. The domain controllers are detecting an IP address conflict.

8. You enabled a success and failure audit policy for account logon events on your network. You have 500 Windows XP workstations and 50 Windows 98 workstations. You notice that the Windows 98 workstations are not recording their workstation logon events in the Security Log. What should you do?

   A. Reset the trust relationship password for each Windows 98 workstation.

   B. Enable Bypass Traverse Checking on the `Syslog` folder.

   C. Move the Windows 98 workstation accounts in Active Directory to their own organizational unit. Reapply the auditing Group Policy to the new OU.

   D. Do nothing. This is expected behavior because Windows 98 workstations do not have workstation accounts in Active Directory.

9. You want to audit access to a sensitive research folder on your network. You want to know who has attempted to access this folder, both from trusted and untrusted domains. Which account should you use for auditing purposes?

   A. Authenticated Users group

   B. Everyone group

   C. Domain Users group

   D. Domain Administrators group

10. You have a sensitive folder named Payroll that only three users are supposed to access. You have correctly enabled auditing on this folder. Upon reviewing the Security Log for this folder, you find that a user in the Engineering department has been opening the files in the Payroll folder. What should you do to ensure that this user does not access these files again?

    A. Verify that you have secured the folder and file correctly.

    B. Remove the Bypass Traverse Checking right from the Engineering user's account.

    C. Enable auditing on the files in the Payroll folder.

    D. Use the Loopback process mode of the auditing Group Policy to reapply the policy to the Payroll folder.

11. You suspect that one of your users is engaging in malicious behavior on the network. You want to isolate that user's activities in the Security Log to help confirm your suspicions. For which two elements should you filter in the Security Log?

    A. Event ID 564

    B. Event ID 560

    C. The user's account name

    D. The user's workstation account name

12. You suspect that one of your network administration team members is maliciously changing configurations on objects in the configuration partition. You know this person is leaving your company soon, but this has not become public knowledge yet. You want to provide evidence to your superiors that the current network problems you are experiencing are a direct result of this person's actions. What should you do?

    A. Use ADSIEdit from the Windows Server 2003 Resource Kit to enable auditing on the configuration partition in Active Directory.

    B. Create a new Group Policy object. Enable object access for the configuration partition in this new Group Policy object. Create a new organizational unit and link the new Group Policy object to the new OU. Move your team member's user account into the new OU.

    C. Use Schema Manager to create a new object in the folder and enable auditing in the object's Properties dialog box.

    D. Enable Bypass Traverse Checking and Generate Security Audits for the local system account.

13. You want to audit the backup and restore activities on your network. Before you can begin to audit these activities, there is something you must do. What is it?

    A. Enable privilege use auditing on the domain object.

    B. Create a new Group Policy. Enable audit use of the backup and restore privilege security policy.

    C. Create a new Group Policy. Enable audit use of the backup and restore privilege security policy. Then, enable privilege use auditing on the domain object.

    D. Enable Generate Security Audits on the organizational unit that hosts the user's accounts in Active Directory.

14. You are the administrator of a Windows Server 2003 domain. You are considering using groups to ease your administrative overhead. Which of the following are proper group implementations? (Choose all that apply.)

   A. Global in a domain local

   B. Domain local in a global

   C. Universal in a global

   D. Global in a universal

15. You are one of the administrators of a multi-domain Windows Server 2003 forest. There is a resource domain and an account domain. The company's Accounting department has external auditors in the office, and you need to grant the auditors read-only access to files on a member server in the resource domain. Auditing is an annual occurrence, but the individual auditor may change from year to year. You want to set up access to minimize effort and mistakes in future years. What is the best way to accomplish your goal?

   A. Create an entry in each directory ACL for a generic auditor account for each required auditor.

   B. Create the user account in the account domain and place it in a universal auditors group. On the resource domain, create an ACL granting the universal group read-only access.

   C. Create the user account in the account domain and place it in a global auditors group. Create an auditors domain local group with a membership of the global group in the resource domain. Create an ACL granting the domain local group read-only access.

   D. Create the user accounts in the resource domain. Create an auditors domain local group in the resource domain and add the user accounts to this group. Create an ACL granting the local group read-only access.

16. Remote Access Service (RAS) events are different from Remote Access Logs. Which of the following statements are true? (Choose all that reply.)

   A. Remote Access Service events are recorded in the System Log.

   B. Remote Access Service events are recorded in the RAS text-based log files.

   C. You can use Network Monitor to trace packets over a dial-up connection.

   D. You cannot use Network Monitor to trace packets over a dial-up connection.

17. Network Monitor logs are useful for which of the following?

   A. Determining the TCP/IP address for all servers in the domain

   B. Determining what services are running on your network

   C. Capturing and logging packets between two machines

   D. Monitoring your network for intrusions

18. Your security policy states that event logs must be archived for a period of one year. What formats do you have available to archive the logs? (Choose all that apply.)

    A. Text (tab-delimited)

    B. ODBC

    C. Event Log

    D. CSV (comma-delimited)

19. What factors should you consider when determining your log-retention policies? (Choose all that apply.)

    A. Legal or regulatory requirements

    B. Disk space available

    C. Frequency of review

    D. The default domain GPO

20. What is a common problem with regard to auditing?

    A. It is difficult to implement correctly.

    B. Audit logs are not read regularly, and thus the auditing process loses its value.

    C. Auditing is resource-intensive and can eat up server resources.

    D. Auditing is necessary only in high-security environments.

Answers to Review Questions

1. C. Even though this application is web-based, its messages appear in the Application Log. Messages generated by IIS appear in the IIS Log.

2. A, B. The application itself generates messages and places them in the Application Log. Services associated with the application generate messages and place them in the System Log. The Security Log hosts messages generated by the auditing policy, and the DNS Server Log hosts messages generated by the DNS service.

3. C. When auditing a resource such as a file, a folder, or a printer, not only do you need to create and apply an audit policy, but you also need to go to the resource and enable auditing on the resource. Remember that auditing resources always involves two administrative acts: creating the audit policy and enabling auditing on the resource.

4. B. The File Replication Log records events generated by the File Replication Service. The Directory Service Log records events related to the functioning of Active Directory. Only domain controllers can place messages in the Directory Service Log.

5. D. Because the Directory Service Log records events about Active Directory, it stands to reason that only Windows Server 2003 domain controllers can actually generate messages for this log. Hence, if you find something wrong with your Active Directory, the place to start troubleshooting this issue is not in the System Log, but in the Directory Service Log.

6. A. The Logon Events audit policy captures events only for local accounts that are created on the local computer. The Account Logon Events audit policy captures logon events for domain accounts. When applied to the domain controllers OU, this enables auditing of all domain logon events across all the domain controllers, and thus you will see logon events in the Security Log from all your domain controllers.

7. C. Event ID 529 indicates that a logon attempt was made with an unknown username or a bad password. A host of these events from a single workstation in a defined time period outside your normal business hours means that a malicious user was attempting to log on but failed to do so.

8. D. Windows 98 workstations cannot participate in workstation account security. This is why it is best to use only Windows XP workstations in those environments that require high security.

9. B. You want to use the Everyone security group because this group has the widest reach. Think of it this way: Anyone who can connect to your network is automatically made a part of the Everyone security group. Hence, if you want to audit any type of access to sensitive information, audit the Everyone security group.

10. A. All that auditing can tell you is *what* has happened. Now that you've learned that the user in the Engineering department has accessed the payroll files, you'll need to verify (and perhaps reapply) the security settings on the `Payroll` folder and its files. For example, it could be that the right security settings were configured on the folder, but never applied to the files. Or it could be that the Engineering user's account was inadvertently included in the list of accounts on the Security tab in the `Payroll` folder's Properties dialog box. In any event, the solution here is not more auditing or a removal of user rights, but a reconfiguration of the permissions themselves.

11. **B, D.** Event ID 560 indicates that access to an object was granted. If you want to determine actions that have been performed at a specific computer, filter for that computer and look for 560 events associated with the computer. Of course, this means that object access auditing needs to be configured on your servers before this method can yield any meaningful data.

12. **A.** To enable auditing on either the schema or the configuration partition, you must use ADSIEdit and configure auditing the properties of the root-naming context for the configuration partition. What this means is to open up the root object in the configuration partition and then enable auditing in that object's properties.

13. **B.** Of the answers given, this is the most correct. Answer C is not correct because privilege use auditing does not include tracking the backup and restore activities. After you create the Group Policy in answer B, you'll want to apply it to the OUs that host the backup and restore servers on your network.

14. **A, D.** The recommended methods of group implementations include A-G-DL-P and A-G-U-P. Domain local groups can contain other domain local groups (from the same domain). Domain local groups cannot be members of a universal group. Universal groups cannot be members of a global group. Global groups can be members of a universal group.

15. **C.** All answers technically work, but the best answer is C. The recommended method is as follows: User accounts go into global groups, global groups are members of domain local groups, and the domain local group is granted or denied access to a resource.

16. **A, C.** RAS events are recorded in the System Log and can be viewed by anyone who has access to the logs. There are no separate RAS logs as there are for IIS. Network Monitor is a great tool for recording the packets that flow between a dial-up connection and a server. You can use this method to find out if a dial-up connection was the vector used by an attacker to compromise your network.

17. **C.** Network Monitor is a packet-logging application. It can neither be used to determine the TCP/IP addressing scheme in your network, nor determine all the services running on a network. An intrusion detection server is what you need to monitor for network intrusions.

18. **A, C, D.** Event logs can be saved to a new file, but they retain their native Event Log format. They can be saved as tab-delimited text files. Event logs can also be saved in comma-delimited CSV files. There is no option to export event logs to an ODBC database.

19. **A, C.** Legal or regulatory issues may be the biggest influence on your event log retention policy. The frequency with which you review the logs is also a factor. Disk space should not be a factor in determining the policy; rather, the policy may dictate additional disk space. The default domain GPO may be the mechanism that you use to enforce your chosen policy.

20. **B.** One of the most common problems with auditing is that the logs are rarely read. Without the regular reading of the logs, there is little sense in performing logging in the first place. Although these logs can be of help immediately after an attack, they are of equal value in understanding normal behavior on a network. Learning to spot abnormal behavior and what might constitute an attack depends on knowing what normal behavior looks like from a logging perspective. Regular reading of the logs also helps you detect problems that are brewing and gives you an opportunity to fix them before they become a big problem that hurts user productivity.

Appendix

A

Responding to Security Incidents

After you discover that a vulnerability on your network has been exploited, you need to respond immediately. The actions you take in response to a security incident are important. This appendix is dedicated to ensuring that you know how to respond appropriately to security incidents.

Knowing what to do when a security event occurs is essential to good security management. Most organizations learn how to handle a security incident only after an event has occurred. To mitigate risk, think through *in advance* how to handle various events and train yourself and others in the IT department on the correct procedures to follow should an event occur. This appendix will help you do that.

How to Recognize a Security Incident

You might be wondering just how you'll know if a security incident has occurred on your network. Well, here are some common indicators that your network has been compromised or is under attack:

Network irregularities If your network performance is decreasing for (seemingly) no reason or if accounts are being used at irregular times, your network could be under attack or could have been compromised. Another sign is the inability to connect to one or more servers while being able to connect to other servers without difficulty.

System irregularities System irregularities include a marked increase in audited events, system performance degradation, and computers crashing or rebooting without explanation.

Direct reporting of events You might be tipped off that a security event is happening if a user reports these events directly to you. Of course, if you have good intrusion detection software, you might be alerted to an intrusion by this software.

Physical indicators Obvious signs of an intrusion include missing servers, broken locks, and videotape of people removing disks and hardware from the premises.

Business indicators Confidential information about your organization on the Internet or in a public location, such as a magazine or television, can indicate that your information has been compromised.

Although many abnormal events on a network are harmless, some indicate a security event. You'll probably find that, using your detection tools, determining when a real security breach has occurred is still as much art as it is science. However, investigate all events to find their causes and to determine whether the events represent a security incident.

There are several third-party monitoring applications that can help monitor the network infrastructure and report any problems. Many applications also help establish baselines for the infrastructure performance. Microsoft Operations Manager (MOM) can be huge help for you as a network administrator as well as a server administrator.

Microsoft Operations Manager (MOM)

MOM is an application that was licensed from Net IQ. MOM provides many benefits to an organization, including the following:

- Event log consolidation: MOM can consolidate and correlate events across multiple servers. For example, MOM can help identify potential network break-ins by correlating failed logon attempts on multiple servers. One failure on a server may not raise alarms, but if it's followed by failures on other servers in a short time period, it's an indication of an attempted break-in.

- Service level agreement (SLA) monitoring: MOM can identify problems that have not been resolved within established SLAs by providing an exception list.

- Performance monitoring: MOM can monitor performance objects and protocol logs to help establish baselines and to provide notification of potential problems. MOM can also provide trend analysis using performance objects and protocol logs.

- Alerting: MOM can provide alerts to notification groups about performance problems and failed services.

- Reporting: MOM provides extensive reporting on network infrastructure status, performance, capacity planning, and replication monitoring, as well as other information, depending on what applications are running on each server.

- Knowledge base information: MOM comes with built-in knowledge base information provided by Microsoft experts and allows for company-customized knowledge base information to be added.

MOM can be enhanced by installing management packs that cover certain types of applications. There are also many third-party management packs—including those provided by Net IQ—that allow MOM to monitor and manage non-Microsoft products and services.

For more information, see www.microsoft.com/mom.

Planning Your Response

This appendix's outline provides a roadmap for you to use when planning responses to security events, but you also need to bear some other issues in mind.

First, there is a strong need for clearly established security policies that are written, understood by all in the organization, and enforced without bias. Some security events are created by those of us—the technology people—who have not followed or understood change management procedures or security configurations. These policies should be clear, practical, and tested.

Second, it really does no good to have a well-written set of security policies if upper management routinely ignores and violates them for their own convenience. Gaining management support for security policies and incident handling is necessary to implement any good security program.

Third, ensure that you routinely monitor and analyze the following:

- Event logs
- Network traffic
- System performance
- Intrusion detection logs
- Security training for end users
- Releases of updated patches for all your software
- Backup processes to ensure that they are successful

To ensure that you stay on top of the security game, give regular attention to each of these areas. A lapse in any one of them can potentially create an attack vector that a hacker can exploit. User training is vital, because each user of the network services and resources is a potential point of vulnerability.

Fourth, ensure that at least once each quarter you take the time to run a trial backup and restore of your more important data. Why? Because the time to learn restore skills is not when the battle is raging after a system compromise. You don't learn how to throw a football in the fourth quarter, you don't learn how to drive a car during the Indianapolis 500, and you don't learn how to do system state and other restore procedures after a disaster has occurred.

As part of preparing to restore a server, you should build an emergency pack for each and every server in your organization. Emergency packs should include the operating system CD, all application CDs, antivirus applications, and all support codes and phone numbers, as well as any knowledge base articles and procedures used during the installation and maintenance of the system. The best practice is to perform these activities once each quarter so that you are assured of three things:

- Your backup hardware is working properly.
- You get regular practice in how to perform restore operations.
- You have all the resources you need at your fingertips.

Fifth, create a Computer Security Incident Response Team (CSIRT). Train and use this team to handle responses to all security events. Using a team approach ensures that no area is left unattended during the response phase.

Finally, place all emergency and contact information in a central offline location. Obviously, this information must be kept in a physically secure location, but it must also be readily available. This emergency information should include the following:

- Passwords
- IP addresses
- Router configuration information
- Firewall rule sets
- Copies of certificate authority keys
- Contact names and phone numbers
- Escalation procedures

The CSIRT should develop an Incident Response Plan so that everyone in the organization is aware of what to do in the event of an incident. This plan should include methods of reporting new events from users and lower-level IT staff. Moreover, regularly review this plan to ensure that it meets the ever-changing environment of your business and network. At a minimum, this plan should cover the following areas:

- How to detect a security event
- How to communicate this event to the CSIRT
- How to contain and minimize the damage
- How to identify the type of attack and the severity of the damage
- How to protect and keep evidence of the attack
- When and whom to notify regarding external agencies
- How to recover each system
- How to compile incident documentation
- How to assess the cost of the damage
- When and how to review and update the response policies

Having such a plan in place will give all IT staff and the CSIRT members a working blueprint with which to guide their actions during an incident response. Having a well-defined, well-rehearsed set of responses that you can put in place if a successful attack does occur will enable you to close unknown vulnerabilities and perhaps apprehend the attacker for criminal and civil prosecution.

Creating the First CSIRT in Your Company

After reading the rest of this appendix, you decide to create a new CSIRT in your company. What should you do to be successful? The tips that follow should help you get started. You might also want to check out www.cert.org, a great website that has excellent information on security management.

Here are the steps for creating a new CSIRT:

1. Discuss your plan with your manager and get them to buy into this idea. Outline why it is a good idea and a good use of some people's time to get involved with this team.

2. Ask your manager to obtain upper management approval for a CSIRT.

3. After receiving approval, try to get the following positions placed on this team:

   - Yourself as system administrator

   - Your firewall person

   - Help desk representative

   - Desktop support representative

   - Other IT department members as needed

   - Legal department representative

   - Business group representatives

4. Develop a plan for responding to the following:

   - Worms, viruses, and Trojan horses

   - Intrusions

   - Physical compromise

   - DoS attacks

   - Web services attacks

   - Internal violations of security policies

   - Internal attempts to hack confidential information

   - Unknown system failures or application failures

5. Practice your responses with the team members. Don't wait for a real attack to teach each team member how to do their job.

6. Enlist legal advice to ensure that you are complying with all federal and state laws.

7. Develop lines of communications and procedures for how you will communicate with upper management and the different business units during a response cycle.

8. Evaluate the plan every six months to ensure that the plan is up-to-date and to ensure that new team members know what their responsibilities are and how to act during a response.

Understanding the Types of Attacks

Viruses vs. denial of service attacks vs. natural disasters vs. Trojans vs. worms? Although this is a bit like splitting hairs, it's important to understand what motivates hackers and the differences between these types of attacks.

This section discusses each of these types of attacks, and you'll find questions about all these on the exam.

Natural Disasters

Natural disasters include such common occurrences as earthquakes, hurricanes, floods, lightning, and fire. Disasters that humans instigate fall into this category too, including riots, wars, and terrorism. All these events can cause severe damage to computer systems. Information can be lost, downtime or loss of productivity can occur, hardware can be damaged, and other essential services can be disrupted. You need to include in your plan non-natural disasters such as broken pipes, cut power lines, and severed intranetwork and internetwork connections.

Few safeguards can be implemented against disasters. The best course of action is to have disaster-recovery and contingency plans in place. These plans help an organization restore itself to normal business operations as soon as possible. They may include alternative worker placement scenarios and even complete relocation of the business to a new site.

Hacker Attacks

To paraphrase Sun Tzu, the author of *The Art of War*, if you don't know your enemy, you are doomed to be defeated by your enemy. Although there is much literature on the technical aspects of securing a resource, a firewall, or even a network, not much has been written about who your enemies are and what motivates a hacker. If you understand who would want to do you harm and what they would gain from such harm, you can better protect yourself and your organization.

Hackers are often motivated, in part, by their invisibleness. Have you ever wondered what it would be like to be invisible? Being able to go wherever you want and do anything you'd like without fear of detection or apprehension is something that all of us would like now and then. Well, on the Internet, you can peek into someone else's private world—their network—and learn many things about them while remaining anonymous. This, in and of itself, is a strong motivation—just the pure thrill of being invisible.

However, hackers often have other motivations. For example, some are just curious individuals who commit violations in the process of learning or exploring a system. Mostly without malicious intent, they are unaware that their actions violate security policy or criminal code.

Other hackers are simply trying to help: in their zeal to be helpful, they bypass security policies to fix problems or accomplish their assignments. Often, they believe that their efforts are more efficient than following established guidelines and policies.

Finally, some hackers act with malicious intent, engaging in acts of sabotage, espionage, or other forms of criminal activities. They steal information, sabotage a competitor, or cause outages to facilities to achieve their own ends. *Why* they do this can be as varied as the individuals themselves. It may be to further their own company's ends, it may be the result of a strongly held belief system, or it may be even an antisocial personality who simply enjoys destroying others and their work.

Within all these groups, you might also find certain other personality traits. For instance, they might have a sense of entitlement; they should be treated differently because they perceive themselves as being "special" and "above the rules." You might also find that some hackers act out of revenge for a real or perceived wrong that was committed against them. Others are more methodical and hardened and turn hacking into a career; they might even take employment just to commit theft, fraud, or other illegal acts against a certain company. Some might even become moles, stealing information from the inside and selling that information to competitors or foreign groups.

But in almost all hackers, you will find certain characteristics. For instance, you will likely find a personality whose curiosity sometimes consumes them. In addition, they are usually bright, intelligent people who can out-think most others in their field and in technology. More often than not, these folks are individualistic and anti-conformist, preferring to carve out their own path instead of following the prescribed path that was given to them. You'll also find that these individuals are stimulated by an array of vast and diverse subjects and that they enjoy the challenge of breaking into a system. A few hackers even enjoy the public attention and social recognition that comes with hacking a website or starting a new virus or worm that "brings down" the Internet.

The primary targets of most hackers are either e-mail lists or websites. Internal hackers can be interested in financial databases or spreadsheets, marketing plans, research and development information, and the reputation of individuals or companies.

So who is your enemy? Well, the answer is anyone who wants to do you or your organization harm *and* who has the ability and will to carry out their plans against you. On this point, you must think worldwide. It's not enough to consider only your own locale. You must think worldwide, because the Internet bypasses nearly all national and international boundaries. Your enemies might be people living halfway around the globe.

Virus Attacks

A *virus* is a piece of code that replicates itself by attaching itself to other programs or files. When these files run, the code is invoked and begins replicating itself. Some of the first computer viruses were found in 1981 on an Apple II computer. Nearly every platform now has viruses that can exploit its vulnerabilities. Microsoft platforms seem to be the focus of many virus creators because they represent such a large target and of other virus creators because they hold ill will toward Microsoft and its success in the marketplace.

Some viruses reside in memory after the original program is shut down. Then when other programs are executed, they become infected with the virus until the computer is shut down or turned off. Some viruses have a dormant phase and appear only at certain times or when certain actions are performed.

Variants can be produced by modifying a known virus. Examples of variants are modifications that add functionality or evade detection. Usually, the modifications are minor, such as changing the trigger date.

There are many types of viruses. Some viruses overwrite existing code or data. Others recognize whether an executable file is already infected. Self-recognition is required if the virus is to

---

Antivirus Solutions

Most administrators agree that antivirus solutions need to be deployed at several levels in the company. For example, antivirus applications should be installed on the following:

- Client computers

- File servers

- E-mail servers

- Firewalls and proxy servers

- SMTP gateways

The hope is that if the firewall antivirus application fails, then the file server or the client computer antivirus software will catch any virus infections and cure or delete the infected files before they can infect the client computer or network services and resources.

Antivirus software providers market themselves as the single-point solution for all of the company needs. If you buy their suite of products, you can install antivirus software at all points in the company and protect all the potential points of infiltration and infection.

There is a failure in the logic of a single vendor solution. The problem is that if the vendor has not discovered the problem and written an update to protect against a new virus, then no matter in how many layers the software is implemented, it will not be able to protect against the infection. The best solution might be to utilize multiple vendors for antivirus software so that if a virus is not caught by one vendor, maybe the other vendor will catch it.

---

avoid multiple infections of a single executable, which can cause excessive growth in the size of infected executables and corresponding excessive storage space, contributing to the detection of the virus.

Resident viruses install themselves as part of the operating system upon execution of an infected host program. The virus remains resident until the system is shut down. Once installed in memory, a resident virus is available to infect all suitable hosts that are accessed.

A stealth virus is a resident virus that attempts to evade detection by concealing its presence in infected files. For example, a stealth virus might remove the virus code from an executable file when it is read (rather than executed) so that an antivirus software package will see only the non-compromised form of the executable.

Some viruses are encrypted, rendering them difficult to disassemble and study since the researcher must decrypt the code. Along the same lines, a polymorphic virus creates copies of itself during replication that are functionally the same but have distinctly different byte streams. This variable quality makes the virus difficult to locate, identify, or remove.

Computer viruses spread mainly through e-mail. In earlier days, some viruses spread by writing themselves to the boot sector of disks and transferred themselves to new computers when the disks were inserted into the floppy drive. These days, it is not uncommon to find viruses in programs that are downloaded from the Internet. E-mail and the Internet are the two primary methods for distributing a virus.

The damage that viruses can cause ranges from nominal to critical. Some viruses cause little or no damage. Others destroy the file system tables. In all cases, do not ignore viruses. Treat them as a major, potential threat to the server, workstation, and/or the network.

Spyware

Spyware is a type of program installed without your knowledge in most cases, and it causes poor performance and compromises the security of the system and the network where the system resides. Spyware is code that is installed on a system to gather information about the user and the user's actions and then relays it to advertisers or others who might be interested in the information.

Spyware can infect a system in the same ways that a virus can infect a system. Usually, spyware is installed by a user without their knowledge or as part of an application that they want to install. Spyware is often installed without the known consent of the user.

Spyware ranges from advertiser-supported software used to collect buying habits of users to the surveillance tools that can allow a malicious user to monitor all activity on a system and capture proprietary information. Malicious spyware can capture activity on a system, including all keystrokes, websites visited, e-mails sent and received, chat logs, and many other activities. These applications can compromise security on the network.

Many antivirus vendors also provide spyware detection and removal software. You should purchase and deploy this software on all systems on your network to provide the proper protection.

Denial of Service Attacks

A *denial of service (DoS)* attack overloads an individual service on a target server to the point where the service either is totally consumed by the attack or actually stops responding. The purpose of a DoS attack is to prevent legitimate use of a service and to prevent the server or hosts on a network from communicating over the network. A DoS attack exploits the fact that services exist and that they must be up and running to be of any value to an organization.

Attackers implement a DoS attack by flooding a network or server with more traffic than it can handle. Routers and servers eventually become overloaded by attempting to service each packet or request. The attacker's system is usually masqueraded because the sender's IP address is spoofed in the sending packet. This makes it difficult to trace who the attacker really is. Often, the IP address that is spoofed is the address of another victim on the network, creating congestion between two targets that use each other to self-destruct.

A variation of the DoS attack is a distributed DoS (DDoS) attack, which is an attack that involves breaking into hundreds or thousands of computers across the Internet, installing DDoS software on each one that allows the attacker to control all these computers, and launching coordinated attacks on victim sites. Usually, bandwidth is completely saturated, router processing capacity is exhausted, and network connectivity is broken.

DoS attacks are a growing trend on the Internet because websites in general are open doors ready for abuse. People can easily flood the web server with communications in order to keep it busy. Therefore, companies connected to the Internet should prepare for DoS attacks. They are also difficult to trace and allow other types of attacks to be conducted simultaneously.

Trojan Horse Attacks

Also known as a *Trojan horse*, a *Trojan* is a malicious program embedded inside a normal, safe-looking program. When the normal program is run, the malicious code is run as well and can cause damage, steal critical information, or both. An example of a Trojan is a birthday executable file that, when executed, pops up with an animated figure that wishes the reader "Happy Birthday," while in the background, malicious code is running that deletes files or destroys other programs.

> The term *Trojan horse* comes from a myth in which the Greeks gave a giant wooden horse to their foes, the Trojans, seemingly as a peace offering. After the Trojans dragged the horse inside the city walls of Troy, Greek soldiers sneaked out of the horse's hollow belly and opened the city gates, allowing their compatriots to pour in and capture Troy.

Trojans generally are spread through e-mail or worms. The damage that these programs can cause is similar to that of a virus: from nominal to critical. The part that is the most frightening is that in most cases, users are unaware of the damage the Trojan is causing because the malicious work is being masked by the Trojan effect of the program.

Worm Attacks

A *worm* is a program that runs independently and travels from computer to computer across network connections. Worms may have portions of themselves running on many computers, or the entire program can run on a single computer. Worms do not change other programs, although they can carry code that does. In addition, some worms take on the virus aspect of self-replication.

Believe it or not, worms were first used as a legitimate mechanism for performing tasks in a distributed environment. Network worms were considered promising for managing network tasks in a series of experiments at the Xerox Palo Alto Research Center in 1982. However, that all changed when worms were used to perform unwanted and unapproved tasks on multiple computers.

The main difference between a virus and worm is that a worm is self-contained code and does not require a host file to which it must attach. In addition, most worms require a multitasking system and can replicate themselves across network links, unlike a virus.

Both worms and viruses are designed to self-replicate, and both perform a variety of additional tasks. The first network worms took advantage of system properties to perform useful actions. However, a malicious worm takes advantage of the same system properties for malicious ends. The facilities that allow such programs to replicate do not discriminate between malicious and good code. Worms exploit vulnerabilities in the operating system and use a variety of methods to replicate. Release of a worm usually results in brief outbreaks, shutting down entire networks.

The damage that worms can cause, like Trojans and viruses, range from the nominal to the critical. You must assess the type and extent of the damage individually for each worm. However, worms can install viruses and Trojans that then run their own code. An attack that combines a worm, a Trojan, and/or a virus can be a difficult attack to survive without significant damage being inflicted.

Isolating and Containing the Incident

Most organizations are not adequately prepared to deal with intrusions. They are likely to address the need to prepare and respond only after a breach occurs. The result is that when an intrusion is detected, many decisions are made in haste and can reduce an organization's ability to engage in the critical activities necessary to ensure that the chain of evidence is preserved, the source of the intrusion is understood and resolved, and future plans are created to reduce the likelihood that an intrusion will occur again.

Even if you have sophisticated prevention measures in place, intrusions can happen. When they do, make sure to implement certain practices independent of the size, type, or severity of an intrusion or the methods used to gain access to your sensitive data. You need a strategy for handling intrusions that covers three broad areas: preparation, detection, and response. And you will not know what to do when an intrusion occurs if you have not defined your procedures and then practiced your responses in advance.

Flying at a very high level, here are the actions that your plan should include:

- Establish policies and procedures for responding to intrusions.
- Maintain the tools necessary to respond to an intrusion.
- Analyze the information to best characterize the intrusion.
- Communicate with all parties the nature of the intrusion and provide them with regular updates.
- Collect and protect information associated with the intrusion.
- Eliminate the methods that the intruder used to gain access.
- Return your systems to normal operations.
- Review the lessons learned and implement new policies and procedures if necessary.

Having the plan won't be enough. You'll also need to ensure that you have trained your team members on the plan, that *you have practiced the plan in advance of an intrusion.* As we've said, you don't learn to shoot a basketball in the fourth quarter of a championship game, you don't learn to swim while trying to save another person, and you can't learn how to use your response tools during a crisis.

Preserving the Chain of Evidence

If you intend to pursue criminal prosecution, the evidence that an investigator may need might reside in a Word document, on a spreadsheet, or in some other file. Evidence may also reside on erased files, file slack (that area of a sector that is hosting a file but is not filled with any data), or even in a Windows swap file, all of which are volatile and easily changeable if not properly accessed. Sometimes, simply booting up a computer can alter and even destroy data fragments that can potentially make an investigation a success or failure. In addition, it is also possible to activate a Trojan program that a user left on the computer on purpose, which potentially could modify or destroy the file structure.

To ensure that this doesn't happen, create a mirror image of the drive in question. A mirror image is a byte-by-byte, sector-by-sector duplicate of a hard drive, which should be authenticated by a cyclic redundancy check (CRC) at the initial image and restore process.

To support this type of activity, you need to develop a firm policy and a set of procedures to ensure that no action is taken that can potentially damage the chain of evidence and cause an otherwise good examination to be inadmissible in a civil or criminal court proceeding.

Here are some steps you can take to ensure that you have adequately preserved your chain of evidence:

Collect all information associated with the intrusion.   This information will include the following:

- The name of the system
- The date/time of the intrusion
- What was compromised
- What actions were taken
- What you said
- What you did
- Who was notified
- Who had access
- What data was collected
- What information was disseminated to whom, for what purpose, by whom, and when
- What was submitted to legal counsel, by whom, when, and for what purpose

Collect and preserve the evidence.   Develop your collection procedures in conjunction with your legal advisors so that you know you are following all laws and regulations that affect the strength of your case against the intruder. Also, be sure to get a replica of the server as fast as possible so as to preserve the state of the server at the time of the compromise. In all cases, document meticulously all actions performed by all participants from detection through analysis, response, and recovery that preserve the chain of evidence.

Ensure that evidence is captured and preserved securely.   Ensure that all log files containing information regarding an intrusion are retained for at least as long as normal business records are kept, and even longer if your legal counsel advises you to do so. Furthermore, ensure that all critical information is duplicated and preserved, both onsite and offsite.

Preserve the chain of custody of the evidence.   Document who handled the evidence and in what sequence, for what purpose, and for how long. In other words, the evidence must be accounted for at all times, the passage of evidence from one person to another must be fully documented, and the passage of evidence from one location to another must be fully documented.

Be sure to contact law enforcement officials immediately if you decide to pursue and prosecute an intruder. Be aware, however, that if you decide to keep your systems up and running to gather more information about the intruder, you and your organization can be held liable if the intruder is successful in using your servers as a launch point for attacking another site. Be sure to consult with your legal counsel about this.

Implementing Countermeasures

When you first hear the term *countermeasure*, you might initially associate it with revenge or getting back at the intruder. Actually, this is not the case. In most instances, if you try to hurt the intruder, most of your actions will probably be illegal, and you could be held liable for them.

When considering countermeasures, think about proactive actions that you can implement to make it more difficult for the intruder to attack your network or use your servers in a malicious manner. Another way of conceptualizing a countermeasure is to say that a countermeasure is a method of mitigating risk. For example, the e-mail program Sendmail has a feature called "tarpitting," which is a process that slows down connection response times between e-mails. The theory is this: If a junk mail sender wants to send you many e-mails, the longer it takes for the sender to send each e-mail, the more likely it is that the sender will remove you from their junk mail list because it's too expensive for them to spend time trying to send you one e-mail when they could be sending that e-mail to 10 or 50 or even 100 other recipients. Hence, tarpitting is a type of countermeasure.

Throughout this book, we've discussed some administrative activities that you could rightly term countermeasures. For instance, in the section on hardening the TCP/IP stack in Chapter 2, "Configuring Security Based on Computer Roles," we discussed ways to make a DoS attack more difficult to execute against a Windows server. Hardening the TCP/IP stack against DoS attacks is a countermeasure that minimizes the risk of exposure to such an attack.

What other types of countermeasures can you implement to mitigate intrusion and risk on your network? Although not exhaustive, the following table lists some common attacks and possible countermeasures that you might want to implement:

Type of Attack	Possible Countermeasures
Physical access to the server	Locked doors Biotech authentication
E-mail flooding	Tarpitting Content filters Spam filters
Virus, Trojan, and worm	Antivirus software Regular scanning
Loss of data	Regular backups
Use of user accounts	User training Network security policies
DoS	TCP/IP hardening Router hardening
Operating system vulnerabilities	Installing all software patches Service offering minimization
Web service attacks	Require authentication Isolate server in demilitarized zone Use SSL Use unique port number
General intrusion	Install a honeypot Use a network-wide intrusion detection software product

This table contains one item—honeypots—that we've not discussed yet. A *honeypot* comes from the analogy of a plate of sugar that attracts bees. If you put out something sweet on a plate or in a bowl such as sugar water, you'll find it has attracted bees after a while.

By the same token, a honeypot is a server that is designed to look like a real production server, but it's not. It is basically a decoy, something that you make available to intruders that they think is a real production server and that you allow them to intrude and compromise. Why do this? Well, for two reasons. First, it attracts intruders to a decoy server, thus ensuring that your real production servers are left alone. But the second reason is even more instructive: If you can analyze the server, you can figure out how the intrusion took place and patch those holes *before* the attacker attacks your real production servers. In larger or more secure environments, a honeypot server is a good way to trap attackers before they get at your more important production servers.

Developing and installing countermeasures is an ongoing process. As your network and information changes over time, so will your need to update countermeasures that protect your information.

Restoring Services

Restoring services means bringing the server(s) back online so that they can return to normal service. Don't attempt this step until you have finished analyzing and patching the vulnerabilities in your systems, preserving the evidence, and ensuring that any changes in policy and procedures have been implemented.

Our comments here reflect a bit of idealism: In many environments, the longer a compromised server is down, the more money is lost to the organization. In these environments, it's still best to at least understand the full nature of the attack and close the avenues that the attacker used to access the information before bringing the servers back online.

The timing of all these actions—analysis, vulnerability patching, preserving evidence, and updating policies and procedures—takes time, and if you are pressed for time because your servers need to be up and running, it really makes sense to use a team of people to respond to security incidents. It makes no sense at all to try and do this by yourself.

Upper management needs to be informed and consulted on a realistic response time to a network disaster. Their input into the balancing act between running an appropriate response to an intrusion versus the need to have servers up and running so that the economic impact is minimized is essential to using intrusions as an opportunity to improve security rather than playing a game of "duck and blame" between your team members and managers. In other words, the planning process for a solid response to an intrusion should be a collaborative effort.

Summary

This appendix explained the differences between a worm, a Trojan, and a virus. Worms are independent programs that cause damage and use the underlying network to replicate themselves. Trojans are pieces of malicious code that embed themselves inside legitimate programs and execute when the host code is executed. Viruses are malicious code that attach themselves to other code and replicate themselves when the code is run. In all three cases, these code bits can cause serious damage and loss of productivity to an organization.

You also learned about the motivations of a hacker and how different factors motivate hackers for different reasons. We took a brief look at the personality types and at what hackers hope to accomplish. Understanding your enemy is paramount in being able to defend yourself.

This appendix also discussed the need to isolate an intrusion, understand the nature of the attack, close the methods or avenues the intruder used to gain access, and preserve the chain and custody of the evidence during this entire time. Preserving the evidence is crucial if you want to press legal or civil charges against the intruder.

Finally, we briefly discussed what countermeasures are and why they should be implemented. We also noted that trying to get revenge on an intruder will probably expose you legally, something you really don't want.

Glossary

3DES (Triple DES)   A more secure variant of DES, Triple DES encrypts each message using three different 56-bit keys in succession. 3DES extends the DES key to 168 bits.

802.11a   IEEE wireless networking standard using the 5GHz radio frequency band. 802.11a covers up to approximately 165 feet in distance under ideal conditions and is capable of up to 54Mbps data transfer.

802.11b   IEEE wireless networking standard using the 2.4GHz radio frequency band. 802.11b is capable of up to 11Mbps data transfer and covers up to approximately 300 feet in distance under ideal conditions. It is often referred to as Wi-Fi.

802.11g   IEEE wireless networking standard using the 2.4GHz radio frequency band. 802.11q is capable of up to 54Mbps data transfer and covers up to approximately 300 feet in distance under ideal conditions.

802.1x   IEEE wireless security protocol using EAP to send messages to authentication servers such as RADIUS. A standard that defines port-based network access control. When 802.1x clients attempt to connect to the network, they are not allowed to proceed past the wireless access point to the wireless or the wired networks until they have been authenticated.

A

access control entry (ACE)   An entry in the access control list of an object that specifies one or more user, group, or computer account(s), and their level of access to an object such as Read, Write, or Full Control.

access control list (ACL)   Contains the discretionary access control list (DACL) and the security access control list (SACL) for each object and resource on a Windows network. Each list comprises one or more access control entries (ACEs). See also *access control entry, discretional access control list*.

access point (AP)   Also known as a wireless access point (WAP). All wireless clients connect to wireless access points, and the wireless access point either relays signals to another wireless access point or puts the packets onto the wired network.

access token   An object that is used to describe the security context of user-spawned processes. A token contains the security identifier (SID) of the user account and all group accounts for the user.

ACE   See *access control entry*.

ACL   See *access control list*.

Active Directory   A proprietary name given to Microsoft's X.500-compliant directory structure hosted by domain controllers. Active Directory is composed of three partitions: schema, configuration, and domain. Active Directory is a distributed, yet hierarchical database used to host user, computer, and group accounts as well as domain, application, and object configuration information.

Active Directory Sites and Services   The Microsoft Management Console snap-in that is used to manage the configuration partition in Active Directory.

Active Directory Users and Computers   The Microsoft Management Console snap-in that is used to manage the domain partition in Active Directory.

AIA   See *authority information access*.

Anonymous authentication   Authentication as an anonymous user. Anonymous authentication is often used for web servers on the Internet when individual users do not have accounts on the server.

AP   See *access point*.

asymmetric   The opposite of *symmetric*. Asymmetric operations do not use the same processes in both directions. See also *symmetric*.

asymmetric keys   Two keys that are used to perform opposite processes. For example, one key might be used to lock a lock, but it cannot be used to unlock it. The unlock process requires a different key. Asymmetric keys are used in private/public key pairs using for encryption and decryption.

attribute   A descriptor of an object. For example, an attribute of an object such as a user account includes the full name of the user. Another attribute is a permission or right associated with the object.

auditing   The process of recording a sequence of events on servers, workstations, and other networking devices. Audited events are recorded in one or more logs. The audit policy is configured in a Group Policy in Active Directory.

authentication   The process of verifying the identity of a user. For example, a user might be authenticated by providing a username and password combination.

Authentication Header (AH)   An AH does not encrypt the data, but instead provides integrity and authentication for the packet. The AH contains several items: Payload Length field; Security Parameters Index (SPI) field that identifies a specific IP Security (IPSec) security association (SA); Sequence Number field that provides anti-replay protection; and Authentication Data field that contains an integrity check value (ICV). The ICV provides data authentication and integrity. AH can be used with Encapsulating Security Payload (ESP), which provides data encryption.

authentication methods   Processes used to authenticate a user. For RRAS, the methods include the following: Extensible Authentication Protocol (EAP); Microsoft Encrypted Authentication Version 2 (MS-CHAPv2); Microsoft Encrypted Authentication (MS-CHAP); Encrypted Authentication (CHAP); Shiva Password Authentication Protocol (SPAP); Unencrypted Password (PAP); and Unauthenticated Access.

authentication protocol   See *authentication methods*.

authenticator   A system or a device capable of receiving authentication requests and either responding with an allowed or denied message or passing on the request to another system or device.

authority information access (AIA)   Specifies locations where a user can obtain information about a certificate. The information can be found in LDAP directories, on web servers, and on file servers in many configurations. AIA needs to be specified for a certificate so that users of the certificate can check information for the certificate.

auto-enrollment   The process of obtaining a certificate from a certificate authority without having to specifically request the certificate. For example, all computers can be configured to receive computer certificates from a CA without having to use any specific interfaces to make the request.

B

Base64 Encoded X.509 (.cer)   Base64 was developed for encoding attachments sent over the Internet. All files that are encoded with Base64 are converted into ASCII format. Its purpose is to reduce the errors and corruption in transferring file attachments, particularly binary attachments through Internet gateways. All standard clients can decode Base64 files. Base64 is provided for compatibility with other operating systems.

beacon   A broadcast of information. Wireless access points can beacon their configuration information to potential wireless clients.

C

CA   See *certificate authority*.

canonicalization   The process of making something conform to a specification. To canonicalize is to ensure that data conforms to canonical rules and is in an approved format. Canonicalization may also mean generating canonical data from noncanonical data.

CDP   See *CRL distribution point*.

certificate   An electronic piece of identification received from a certificate authority. The certificate contains information about the certificate holder, including the public keys used for signatures and encryption.

certificate authority (CA)   A certificate server that has the authority to issue certificates for security purposes. Some CAs are considered root CAs, while others, called *subordinate CAs*, derive their authority from a root CA.

certificate revocation list (CRL)   A list of all certificates that have been revoked by the certificate authority.

Certificate Signing Request (CSR)   A file generated and submitted to a certificate authority. The CSR file contains information about the requestor and is used to create the certificate.

certificate store   A location where certificates, certificate revocation lists (CRLs), and certificate trust lists (CTLs) are permanently stored.

certificate templates   Templates used to define the role and capabilities or purposes of a certificate. For example, a user certificate contains the ability to encrypt data using EFS, to use secure e-mail, and to authenticate a user. Certificate templates save the certificate requestor from having to make multiple low-level decisions when requesting a certificate.

certificate trust list (CTL)   A list of certificates that have been signed by trusted certificate authorities.

certutil.exe   A command-line utility used to display information about certificates, to install and configure certificate authorities, and to manage certificate authorities.

CHAP   See *Challenge Handshake Authentication Protocol.*

Challenge Handshake Authentication Protocol (CHAP)   A challenge-response authentication protocol. This protocol uses Message Digest 5 (MD5) hashing to authenticate user identities. CHAP is an industry-wide standard used to authenticate non-Windows clients. See also *Message Digest 5.*

child server   Servers that have downstream or subordinate roles to another server are sometimes referred to as child servers. Upstream or root servers can be referred to as parent servers. See also *parent server.*

CIFS   See *Common Internet File System.*

cipher.exe   A command-line utility used to display the current encryption status of files and folders and to alter the encryption status of files and folders.

client certificate mapping   A process used to map a certificate to an account in Active Directory. When a certificate is presented to a resource, the resource can use the mapping in Active Directory to identify the proper account to test for permissions and rights.

cluster   There are two types of clusters that can be created using Windows Server 2003. One type is the Server Cluster, which is a server cluster containing two or more servers that share the same disk storage space for application data. With a server cluster, a node can run an application and use the shared storage for application data. In the event that a node fails, another node can take over the application and access the shared data. Shared data is stored on shared drives that are either SCSI or fiber attached. The other type is the Network Load Balancing (NLB) Cluster, which is a cluster of two or more servers that provide the exact same service or services and do not require shared disks for data. For example, two web servers with exactly the same content can be part of the same NLB cluster and they can balance the load between them. NLB clustering is often used to horizontally scale applications such as web applications. Additional nodes can be added to increase performance as needed.

CMAK   See *Connection Manager Administration Kit.*

Common Internet File System (CIFS)   CIFS is a method for implementing a common file-sharing system across multiple servers. CIFS is a remote file system access protocol that enables users to share documents over a network.

condition   In remote access policies, a section that specifies states such as day, time of day, and security group membership that are evaluated to decide if the policy should be applied to the remote client.

Connection Manager Administration Kit (CMAK)   A tool used to build a service profile for remote access. The service profile contains all the files needed to create and install the remote access software on the remote access client and to configure the settings for the remote access user.

countermeasure   Anything that makes it more difficult for a would-be attacker to compromise the physical or logical security of a network. Examples include locks on doors, firewalls, security policies, the use of passwords, and shutting down unnecessary services.

CRL   See *certificate revocation list.*

CRL distribution point (CDP)   A place (or places) on a Windows network where users and resources can check to see if certificates have been revoked. Every time a new CRL is published, it is placed in the CDP specified in the certificate.

Cryptographic Message Syntax Standard - PKCS #7 Certificates (.p7b)   A file format used to export and import certificates and the certificate chain. The file uses a .p7b file extension. This file format adheres to the X.509 standard.

Cryptographic Service Provider (CSP)   The algorithm that generates keys and uses the keys to authenticate, encode, and decode. Some providers offer stronger algorithms than other providers.

CSP   See *Cryptographic Service Provider.*

CSR   See *Certificate Signing Request.*

CTL   See *certificate trust list.*

D

DACL   See *discretionary access control list.*

data decryption field (DDF)   Used in EFS encryption to store the file encryption key (FEK). The FEK is encrypted in the DDF using the user's public key, which allows the user to decrypt the FEK using their private key and then decrypt the file using the FEK. See also *file encryption key, Encrypting File System.*

Data Encryption Standard (DES)   Adopted in 1977, the DES is the official encryption standard for the U.S. Department of Defense. DES is based on a 56-bit key, and the chosen key is applied in 16 rounds of permutations and substitutions to each 64-bit block of data in the message. DES was cracked in 1997 by using the ideal processing cycles of 14,000 computers cooperating on the Internet.

data recovery field (DRF)   Used in EFS encryption to store the symmetric key used to encrypt and decrypt a file stored with the encryption attribute enabled. The DRF contains the file encryption key used to encrypt a file and is encrypted using the recovery agent's public key. Only the recovery agent can then decrypt the DRF and retrieve the file encryption key and decrypt the file.

DDF   See *data decryption field*.

decryption   The process of taking an encrypted file and decoding the encryption so that it can be read in its original format.

Delegated authentication   Delegated authentication occurs when a Windows service impersonates clients to access resources on the clients' behalf. The Kerberos protocol has a proxy mechanism that allows a service to impersonate its client when connecting to other services.

de-militarized zone (DMZ)   Usually existing logically between two firewalls, a DMZ is considered a neutral area that is neither part of the local network nor part of the Internet. Servers are placed in the DMZ that should be accessed from the Internet but still need to be managed from locations on the local network. The DMZ prevents outside users from getting direct access to a server that has company data on the local network. The term comes from the geographic buffer zone that was set up between North Korea and South Korea following the United Nations "police action" in the early 1950s.

denial of service (DoS)   A form of attack conducted against a system or a network that occurs when a malicious user consumes so many resources on a server that few or none are left to service legitimate requests.

DER Encoded Binary X.509 (.cer)   A highly compatible certificate file format adhering to the X.509 standards. This encoding method is used for encoding certificate information and can be used to import or export certificates. This encoding format is used by many certificate authorities that do not run Windows.

DES   See *Data Encryption Standard*.

desktop.ini   This file is used to customize a folder. You can customize folders to provide different views of their data and to apply special properties to the data in the folder.

Diffie-Hellman Algorithm   A method for passing information between two parties. The key agreement is not based on encryption and decryption, but instead relies on mathematical functions to generate a shared secret key for exchanging information in a confidential manner online. Diffie-Hellman works by having each party agree on a public value g and a large prime number p. Next, one party chooses a secret value x, and the other party chooses a different secret value y. Both parties use their secret values to derive new public values that are different from g. They exchange their new public values. Each party then uses the other party's public value to calculate the shared secret key that is used by both parties for confidential communications. A third party cannot derive the shared secret key because they do not know either of the secret values, x or y.

Digest authentication   An authentication protocol used to overcome many of the weaknesses in Basic authentication. It requires using reversible encryption for account passwords in Active Directory. Digest authentication is used to send cryptographic hashes of the password for the user account that are extremely difficult to break.

digital certificate   See *certificate*.

digital signature   A certificate used to prove the identity of the user or company. Digital signatures are often used for signing e-mail or for code signing, and they provide non-repudiation.

Directory Services Client   An application installed on Windows 95 and Windows 98 computers to allow the older operating systems to provide Active Directory awareness to the client computers. With the Directory Services installed, Windows $9x$ computers become aware of Active Directory sites, can use any Active Directory domain controller to change their passwords, and can select domain controllers within their site to identify DFS locations. This application also allows Windows $9x$ clients to use NTLMv2.

discretionary access control list (DACL)   That part of the access control list (ACL) that can be modified using the Security tab in the resource's Properties dialog box. The DACL lists user and group SIDs that have access to the resource, along with each SID's level of access. Each entry is called an access control entry (ACE). The Deny Access permission is also listed at the top of the DACL. Together with the security access control list (SACL), the DACL forms the overall ACL. See also *access control entry*, *access control list*, *security access control list*.

DMZ   See *de-militarized zone*.

DoS   See *denial of service*.

DRF   See *data recovery field*.

dynamic rekeying   A method used by IPSec to determine how often a new key pair is generated during a communication. IPSec sends communications in blocks, and each block can be encrypted using a different, new key pair. Even if an attacker obtains the whole communication, each block's key pair needs to be cracked in order to obtain the message of the communication. The exchange of these key pairs is made possible by the Internet Key Exchange (IKE).

E

EAP-MD5   See *Extensible Authentication Protocol Message Digest 5*.

EAPOL   See *Extensible Authentication Protocol Over LANs*.

EAP-TLS   See *Extensible Authentication Protocol Transport Layer Security*.

EFS   See *Encrypting File System*.

Encapsulating Security Payload (ESP)   Encrypts the data of a packet and can be used alone or in conjunction with Authentication Headers (AHs). In an IP packet, ESP is inserted after the IP header and before an upper layer protocol such as TCP, before any other IPSec headers that have already been inserted. Everything following the ESP header—including the data—is encrypted. When ESP is used, the IP header is not signed and therefore is not protected from modification.

Encrypting File System (EFS)   The EFS is unique to Windows products and is a core technology of Windows. It is used to store files in an encrypted format on an NTFS file system.

encryption   Encryption is the process of changing data from its native format to a ciphered format that cannot be read by unauthorized users.

ESP   See *Encapsulating Security Payload*.

event   An occurrence or lack of an occurrence that is noteworthy.

EventComb   A utility provided by Microsoft that filters and searches multiple event logs and coalesces the results for faster analysis and response.

Exchange Installable File System (ExIFS)   A method for exposing data held in an Extensible Storage Engine or Web Storage System database as a virtual file system.

ExIFS   See *Exchange Installable File System*.

exporting   The process of taking data from its native format and storing it in another format that can be used by other systems or applications.

Extensible Authentication Protocol Message Digest 5 (EAP-MD5)   An authentication protocol that uses a challenge-handshake authentication process that sends message digests through EAP messages to authenticate passwords. EAP-MD5 is typically used for RRAS authentication. See also *Message Digest 5*.

Extensible Authentication Protocol Over LANs (EAPOL)   A method for encapsulating EAP messages so that they can be sent over Ethernet or wireless networks.

Extensible Authentication Protocol Transport Layer Security (EAP-TLS)   An authentication protocol used with certificate-based authentication. Smart cards use EAP-TLS to authenticate the user. EAP-TLS provides mutual authentication and is the strongest authentication and key exchange method in use for remote access clients. See also *Transport Layer Security*.

extranet   An extension of the internal network or intranet that allows access for remote clients or partner networks. An extranet usually involves connections over the Internet.

F

FEK   See *file encryption key*.

file encryption key (FEK)   A random symmetric key generated by the computer for the bulk encryption of files and folders for EFS.

firewall   A system with special security configurations used to protect the company network from untrusted networks such as the Internet. A firewall is used to filter out undesirable network traffic.

G

Generic Routing Encapsulation (GRE)   A protocol used to embed a network protocol in another network protocol. GRE is often used in tunneling applications.

Generic Security Service Application Program Interface (GSSAPI)   An application program interface that is used for client-server authentication. GSSAPI is included with most Kerberos 5 distributions, including the MIT Kerberos 5 distribution.

GINA dynamic-link library   The dynamic-link library that is responsible for generating the graphical interface for username and password input when logging in to Windows operating systems. This dynamic-link library is also responsible for passing the information to the security systems for processing.

GPC   See *Group Policy container.*

GPO   See *Group Policy/Group Policy Object.*

GPT   See *Group Policy template.*

Graphical Identification and Authentication dynamic-link library   See *GINA dynamic-link library.*

GRE   See *Generic Routing Encapsulation.*

Group Policy container (GPC)   That portion of a Group Policy that contains computer and user configuration information.

Group Policy template (GPT)   The container in which administrative template-based policy settings, security settings, applications available for software installation, and script files are stored.

Group Policy/Group Policy Object (GPO)   In Active Directory, a method for grouping Registry configurations into a single policy that can then be applied to one or more objects to control user settings, computer behavior, and audit events on your network.

GSSAPI   See *Generic Security Service Application Program Interface.*

H

honeypot   A honeypot is a decoy designed to look like a production server but one that is really a server that can be compromised without any loss to the organization. Honeypots are designed to be attractive to hackers and keep them away from the real, production servers.

hotfix Usually a small executable file that is distributed by Microsoft to fix a specific security vulnerability. The hotfix file expands and then overwrites certain .dll and .exe files to fix the vulnerability.

I

IAS See *Internet Authentication Service.*

IIS metabase Registry configurations for Internet Information Service (IIS) that are held in RAM for faster access and better response times.

IKE See *Internet Key Exchange.*

impersonation A process in which one computer or user pretends or acts as another through Kerberos delegation of the permissions. For example, a user might connect to a server such as an RRAS server and then connect from there to other systems using impersonation.

importing Transferring information from a file or other storage into a different program or application or even a different computer.

initialization vector (IV) The IV is a part of the encryption used in WEP. The IV is a 24-bit value transmitted in the clear.

Integrated Windows authentication An authentication method using cryptographic exchanges of challenges and responses using Internet Explorer.

intermediate CAs Second level CAs that exist between the root CA and the issuing CA. Intermediate CAs are stand-alone offline servers that are used to generate certificates for issuing CAs.

Internet Authentication Service (IAS) Microsoft's implementation of RADIUS in Windows.

Internet Key Exchange (IKE) Dynamic rekeying is made possible by the Internet Key Exchange. This service provides on-demand security negotiation and automatic key management between two computers. IKE provides a standard method for creating a security association (SA) between two computers and the exchange of keys so that each block in an IPSec stream can be encrypted with different key pairs.

Internet Protocol Security (IPSec) A method for exchanging information between two computers such that different portions of the overall communication are encrypted using different key pairs. Packets are encrypted and sent either directly to the receiving computer where they are decrypted or through a tunnel for decryption at the end of the tunnel. IPSec packets are encapsulated and directly sent to the receiving computer, or they are tunneled between two computers using Layer 2 Tunneling Protocol (L2TP). See also *Layer 2 Tunneling Protocol.*

Internet service provider (ISP) An organization that provides connections to the Internet for its clients.

IPSec See *Internet Protocol Security.*

ISP   See *Internet service provider.*

issuing CA   A certificate authority that issues certificates to users and computers on the network.

IV   See *initialization vector.*

K

KDC   See *Key Distribution Center.*

Kerberos delegation   Allows the use of the same user credentials across multiple layers of systems or physical layers of an application.

Kerberos V5   An authentication protocol developed for use with multiple operating systems.

Key Distribution Center (KDC)   Only found on an Active Directory domain controller in a Windows 2000 or Windows Server 2003 environment, the KDC is a service that installs with Active Directory to generate session keys between domain members for authentication purposes. You do not need to install Certificate Services in order for the KDC to operate correctly.

key management server (KMS)   Used by Exchange 5.5 to provide keys for secure e-mail.

KMS   See *key management server.*

L

L2TP/IPSec   A tunneling protocol combined with IPSec to provide encryption. See also *Layer 2 Tunneling Protocol.*

LAN Manager (LM)   An authentication protocol used for older Microsoft operating systems such as Windows 3.11.

Layer 2 Tunneling Protocol (L2TP)   An extension of the Point-to-Point Protocol (PPP) used for VPNs.

LDAP   See *Lightweight Directory Access Protocol.*

Lightweight Directory Access Protocol (LDAP)   An Internet standard for accessing directory information based on X.500 standards, but simpler.

LM   See *LAN Manager.*

Local Security Authority (LSA)   A protected Windows subsystem used to authenticate users onto the local computer.

log   A file that holds records of noteworthy events.

LSA   See *Local Security Authority.*

M

MAC   See *Media Access Control*.

MAC filtering   Using Media Access Control (MAC) addresses that are assigned to hardware devices to control which computers may or may not access a device or a network beyond a device. For example, MAC filtering can be used to limit which computers are allowed to access a wireless network by setting the filter on the wireless access point. See also *Media Access Control*.

machine certificates   A certificate assigned to a specific computer. See *certificate*.

MD5   See *Message Digest 5*.

Media Access Control (MAC)   An address encoded on most network devices that consists of an assigned number that identifies the manufacturer and a serial number assigned by the manufacturer.

Message Digest 5 (MD5)   An algorithm used to verify data integrity through the creation of a 128-bit message digest from the data itself. Because the message digest is derived from the contents, each message digest is thought to be unique. MD5 is used with digital signatures and is the fifth iteration of the Message Digest algorithm.

metabase   A database that holds information about other data and other databases.

Microsoft Challenge Handshake Authentication Protocol version 2 (MS-CHAPv2)   An authentication protocol that provides mutual authentication through the exchange of encrypted challenge and response strings.

Microsoft Challenge Handshake Authentication Protocol (MS-CHAP)   An authentication protocol that provides authentication through the exchange of encrypted challenge and response strings. Considerably weaker than MS-CHAPv2.

Microsoft Graphical Identification and Authentication (MSGINA)   A dynamic link library that provides the logon prompt for Windows and then collects the username, password, and domain name from the user logging on to the network.

missing event   An event that was to have occurred but did not. Sometimes, missing events indicate a security event or a security vulnerability.

MS-CHAP   See *Microsoft Challenge Handshake Authentication Protocol*.

MS-CHAPv2   See *Microsoft Challenge Handshake Authentication Protocol version 5*.

MSGINA   See *Microsoft Graphical Identification and Authentication*.

N

NAT   See *Network Address Translation*.

Network Address Translation (NAT)   An Internet standard process that allows the use of one set of IP addresses internally for a company and a completely different set of IP addresses for the perimeter devices exposed to the Internet. All internal addresses are converted to an external address before any information or requests are sent out of the network.

NT LAN Manager (NTLM)   An authentication protocol used primarily with Windows NT 4 and earlier operating systems.

NTLM version 2   An authentication protocol used primarily with Windows NT 4 with the release of Service Pack 4.

NTLM   See *NT LAN Manager*.

O

offline files   Offline files allow users to have local copies of network resources on their hard drives. While offline, off the network, users can open, modify, delete, and create new files that can then be synchronized with the network resource once the client computer is reconnected to the network.

Outlook Web Access (OWA)   Microsoft's web-based interface to the public and private stores on an Exchange Server.

OWA   See *Outlook Web Access*.

P

PAP   See *Password Authentication Protocol*.

parent server   An upstream or root server. Parent servers usually have some type of root or authoritative relationship to other servers, called child servers. See also *child server*.

passport authentication   Microsoft passport authentication is a centralized authentication service provided by Microsoft so that Internet users do not need to remember usernames and passwords for multiple websites on the Internet. Passport authentication is considered a single sign-on service for websites.

Password Authentication Protocol (PAP)   A plain-text authentication method. The username and password are transmitted in the clear without any encryption.

PEAP   See *Protected Extensible Authentication Protocol*.

PEAP with MS-CHAP v2   A combination of protocols used for securely transferring authentication data over 802.11 networks.

Perfect Forward Secrecy (PFS)   When used with IPSec, Perfect Forward Secrecy determines how a new key pair is generated, not when a new key pair is generated. PFS ensures that a key used to encrypt a data block cannot be used to generate a new key pair. If a master PFS key is used for dynamic rekeying, the Internet Key Exchange (IKE) needs to re-authenticate identities in order to generate a new key pair. This adds noticeable overhead on computers that use PFS to communicate.

personal certificate   A certificate issued to the user and stored in the user's profile. See *certificate*, *digital certificate*.

Personal Information Exchange - PKCS #12 (.pfx)   A file format used for importing and exporting certificates. This format supports the exporting of certificates and private keys to a file. The private key can only be exported when the key is marked as exportable. The private key can be exported if the certificate is an EFS certificate or an EFS recovery agent certificate. This is the only format supported in Windows XP for exporting a certificate and its associated private key.

PFS   See *Perfect Forward Secrecy*.

physical certificate stores   Locations where the certificates are actually stored and saved on a certificate authority.

PKI   See *Public Key Infrastructure*.

Point-to-Point Tunneling Protocol (PPTP)   A tunneling protocol used in VPNs that encapsulates Point-to-Point Protocol (PPP) in IP traffic.

PPTP   See *Point-to-Point Tunneling Protocol*.

PPTP filtering   A process used by RRAS servers to prevent the server from receiving and processing any IP traffic that is not related to VPN communications. See also *Point-to-Point Tunneling Protocol*.

private certificate authorities   Certificate authorities that are not available to the general public to request or verify certificates. See also *certificate authority*.

private key   Half of the public-private key pair issued with most certificates. The private key is held and protected by the user of the key. It is not published or made available to others. See also *public key*.

profile   A storage location for many configuration settings for a user account. It contains many folders and files specifying how the computer desktop should be configured on a client computer.

Protected Extensible Authentication Protocol (PEAP)   A protocol used for securely transferring authentication data over 802.11 networks.

public certificate authorities   Certificate authorities available to the general public. Anyone can purchase a certificate provided they meet the requirements of the certificate authority when proving their identity. See also *certificate authority*.

public key   Half of the public-private key pair issued with most certificates. The public key is made available to everyone to verify the user or computer. See also *private key*.

public key cryptography   The use of private-public key pairs to provide encryption and decryption as well as authentication by breaking the key into two pieces that work together. The public key is published and made available to everyone, while the private key is held and kept secret. Actions taken with the public key require other actions to be taken with the private key. See also *private key*, *public key*.

Public Key Infrastructure (PKI)   Consists of protocols, services, and standards that support public key cryptography. A PKI consists of applications and services that use public-private key pairs provided by certificates issued by either public or private certificate authorities.

public-private key pairs   Asymmetric key pairs issued to the holder of a certificate. The private key is held and secured from others, while the public key is published and made available to everyone. See also *private key*, *public key*.

R

RADIUS   See *Remote Authentication Dial-In User Service*.

recovery agent   Used to recover EFS-encrypted files when the user is not available to decrypt the files.

remote access policies   Conditions, permissions, and profiles for remote users that control who can access the resources remotely, when they can access them, and what changes will be made to their profile while they are connected to the remote access server.

Remote Authentication Dial-In User Service (RADIUS)   Defines a standard used for maintaining and managing remote user authentication and validation. The new Routing and Remote Access Service (RRAS) in Windows 2000 and Windows Server 2003 can operate as a RADIUS client. This allows RAS clients and dial-up routers to be authenticated against a RADIUS server instead of being authenticated by an Active Directory domain controller. See also *Routing and Remote Access Service*.

replay   The process of capturing a session between systems and then retransmitting the session in an attempt to break in to another computer or trick it into believing the intruder is another person or computer.

reverse polarity threaded naval connector   See *RP-TNC*.

RFC 1510   The RFC covering Kerberos implementations.

roaming profile   A profile stored in a central location that can be accessed from any computer on the network.

root CA   The initial certificate authority that issues its own certificate. Other certificate authorities and certificates are issued by the root certificate authority to support the rest of the certificate authority hierarchy.

Routing and Remote Access Service (RRAS)   A Windows service that provides access to LAN resources to remote users through dial-up or VPN connections.

RP-TNC   Reverse polarity threaded naval connector. A connector type used for external antennas on some higher-end wireless access points (WAPs) to improve their range. See also *wireless access point.*

RRAS   See *Routing and Remote Access Service.*

S

SA   See *security association.*

SACL   See *security access control list.*

SAD   See *Security Account Delegation.*

SAM   See *System Account Manager.*

seal   The process of encrypting data and data flows so that others cannot open the packets and view the contents.

Secure Multipurpose Internet Mail Extension (S/MIME)   A security standard for e-mail messages using public key encryption.

Secure Sockets Layer (SSL)   Also called Transport Layer Security (TLS), SSL is used to encrypt data at the Transport layer when that data flows between a web server and a web client. See also *Transport Layer Security.*

security access control list (SACL)   That portion of the access control list that contains entries that specify what actions and user, group, or computer accounts will be audited.

Security Account Delegation (SAD)   The ability to pass security credentials from one computer to another. With each hop between computers, the user's security credentials are preserved. Kerberos uses SAD to provide better security. SQL Server 2000 fully supports Kerberos, including the ability to accept delegated Kerberos tickets and to delegate these tickets further (when running on the Windows 2000 or Windows Server 2003 operating system) with Active Directory domain controllers.

security association (SA)   The end result of a negotiation between two computers, wherein they agree on a key pair to encrypt their data, determine how the data will be tunneled between the two computers, and specify other session information. An SA must be established before two computers using IPSec can begin to send messages.

Security Configuration and Analysis tool   Provides a graphical interface that allows you to edit security configuration files. This tool allows you to import security templates and either apply them to the local computer or use them to analyze the current computer's security settings against those in the template.

security principal   A user, computer or group account that can engage in authentication and access resources in Active Directory.

Security Support Provider Interface (SSPI)   A security services API used for user authentication. Applications can use this API to tie to the Windows security model and use security services.

security template   A predefined set of security configurations that can be used to create a new Group Policy Object. Windows 2000 and Windows Server 2003 install with a set of security templates, but you can use the Security Configuration and Analysis tool to create your own security templates as well. See also *Security Configuration and Analysis tool.*

Server Message Block (SMB)   The series of commands that are passed between two computers to execute file, folder, and directory commands.

service set identifier (SSID)   The network name of a wireless network. All wireless access points (WAPs) have defined SSIDs to help distinguish them as belonging to a specific wireless network and to distinguish them from other wireless networks. See also *wireless access point.*

sign   Apply a digital signature to data or data transfers to verify the point of origin and that the content has not been altered.

signature   See *sign.*

single sign-on   The process of logging on one time and being able to access resources throughout the network, including resources on different operating systems.

slipstreaming   The process of upgrading a Windows operating system package of original installation files with updated versions of those files so that after the installation of Windows (or later), you do not need to install the latest service pack because it is part of the initial installation.

SMB   See *Server Message Block.*

SMB signing   The process of inserting digital signatures into the SMB packets as they are passed back and forth between two computers. SMB signing verifies packet integrity and authentication. See also *Server Message Block.*

S/MIME   See *Secure Multipurpose Internet Mail Extension.*

Software Update Services (SUS)   Free software from Microsoft that is designed to download updates and hotfixes from Microsoft and then internally distribute these updates to all your Windows 2000–based (and later) servers and workstations. There is an SUS client that interacts with the SUS server.

SSL   See *Secure Sockets Layer.*

SSID   See *service set identifier.*

SSPI   See *Security Support Provider Interface.*

SUS   See *Software Update Services.*

symmetric   Processes that utilize a single key. Unlike asymmetric processes that require two different keys, a symmetric process requires only a single key to encrypt and decrypt a file. Many symmetric keys are simple passwords. See also *asymmetric*.

System Account Manager (SAM)   A protected Windows subsystem used to manage user and group account information. SAM is found in local resources such as domain member servers and network clients, as well as in Windows NT 4 and earlier domain controllers.

T

TGT   See *ticket-granting ticket*.

thumbprint   A hash used to identify a particular certificate.

ticket-granting ticket (TGT)   A ticket issued to a user by the Kerberos Key Distribution Center (KDC). The user presents the TGT to the KDC to request session tickets for services on other servers in a network.

TLS   See *Transport Layer Security*.

transactional file system   A file system that treats all processes as transactions that must be completed. If they are not completed, they are undone or rolled back.

Transport Layer Security (TLS)   A protocol used for secure communications over IP networks. The protocol is used to authenticate servers and even client computers. See also *Secure Sockets Layer*.

Transport mode   As opposed to Tunnel mode, Transport mode ensures security from end to end. Because the encryption occurs at the Transport layer, routers can pass encrypted packets without needing to decrypt the entire packet.

Triple DES   See *3DES*.

Trojan/Trojan Horse   A malicious program or software code hidden inside what looks like a normal program. When a user runs the normal program, the hidden code runs as well. Trojans are normally spread by e-mail attachments.

trust relationship   A relationship between domains that allows user and computer authentication in a multidomain environment. Accounts can potentially be used from one domain, while a resource may physically exist in another domain. User accounts and global groups created in a trusted domain can be given access to resources in a trusting domain.

Tunnel mode   As opposed to Transport mode, Tunnel mode provides security to a predefined point in the traversal path, but not necessarily to the endpoint of this path. For instance, Tunnel mode can provide security of a packet to the next router, but not between that router and the packet's final destination. Tunnel mode is normally used when security is provided by a device that did not originally generate the packets.

U

URL normalization See *canonicalization*.

V

virtual private network (VPN) A connection to an existing network from a remote location through private or public IP networks using encapsulated packets that are encrypted and difficult to decrypt by unauthorized users.

virtual server A resource (or resources) that exists on a server that may have a different name or logical structure than the physical server.

virus A piece of self-replicating code attached to some other piece of code. This code can be harmless or harmful, depending on what the developer wrote the code to do. The virus code searches users' files for an uninfected executable program for which the user has security write privileges. The virus infects the file by putting a piece of code in the selected program file. When a program that is infected with a virus is executed, the virus immediately takes command, finding and infecting other programs and files. Unlike Trojans, viruses spread either through program invocation or by e-mail.

VPN See *virtual private network*.

W

WAP See *wireless access point*.

war driving Using a wireless network sniffer while driving around a neighborhood and capturing all wireless traffic and analyzing it for security failures. Building a database of insecure wireless networks.

web enrollment The process used to obtain certificates from a certificate authority through the use of a web browser connecting to a web server.

web folders A file system that can be accessed using a web browser.

WEP See *Wired Equivalent Privacy*.

Wi-Fi See *802.11b*.

Wi-Fi Protected Access (WPA) WPA is a replacement for the WEP standard for wireless security. WEP had many flaws and was not as secure as the needs of many businesses. WPA has removed the flaws in WEP and has yet to be cracked. There are two types of WPA implementations. The first type, Enterprise Mode, requires the use of RADIUS (Internet Authentication Service – IAS) and an Active Directory domain for authentication. The second type, Pre-Shared Key Mode (PSK) doesn't require Active Directory and RADIUS. In PSK, a secret password is used to authenticate the initial connections between wireless clients and wireless access points.

Windows Update Synchronization Service   A service installed on Windows operating systems that can be configured to automatically download security and operating system updates and install those updates. As an alternative, there is server-based software, Software Update Services, which internally distributes these updates.

Wired Equivalent Privacy (WEP)   The encryption specification that provides the same security to a wireless network that is provided on a wired network. In wireless networks, because the data is broadcast using an antenna, the signals can be intercepted, and if not encrypted, viewed by an intruder to the system. WEP provides encryption services to protect authorized users of a wireless LAN from eavesdroppers by encrypting a data frame and its contents.

wireless access point (WAP)   A physical device much like a hub or switch that is used to connect multiple wireless systems together using radio transmissions.

wireless LANs   Networks and network devices using radio devices to communicate with each other and pass network traffic between each other in place of network cables.

worm   A program that runs independently and travels from computer to computer across network connections. Worms can be distributed programs that have portions of themselves running on many different computers. Worms do not change other programs and do not attach themselves to other programs, and they do not rely on code invocation to spread.

WPA   See *Wi-Fi Protected Access*.

Index

N

TELL US WHAT YOU THINK!

Your feedback is critical to our efforts to provide you with the best books and software on the market. Tell us what you think about the products you've purchased. It's simple:

1. Go to the Sybex website.
2. Find your book by typing the ISBN or title into the Search field.
3. Click on the book title when it appears.
4. Click **Submit a Review.**
5. Fill out the questionnaire and comments.
6. Click **Submit.**

With your feedback, we can continue to publish the highest quality computer books and software products that today's busy IT professionals deserve.

www.sybex.com

SYBEX Inc. • 1151 Marina Village Parkway, Alameda, CA 94501 • 510-523-8233

Sybex Offers the Complete Solution

SYBEX®

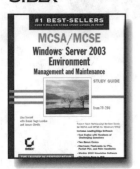

MCSA/MCSE: Windows Server 2003 Environment Management and Maintenance Study Guide
ISBN 0-7821-4260-5 • $49.99

MCSA 2003 Track

Choose ONE Client OS Requirement	
Exam #	**Exam**
70-210	Installing, Configuring and Administering Microsoft Windows 2000 Professional
70-270	Installing, Configuring and Administering Windows XP Professional

2 Network Operating System Requirements	
Exam #	**Exam**
70-290	Managing and Maintaining a Microsoft Windows Server 2003 Environment
70-291	Implementing, Managing, and Maintaining a Microsoft Windows Server 2003 Network Infrastructure

Choose ONE Elective	
Exam #	**Exam**
70-086	Implementing and Supporting Microsoft Systems Management Server 2.0
70-227	Installing, Configuring, and Administering Microsoft Internet Security and Acceleration (ISA) 2000
70-228	Installing, Configuring and Administering SQL Server 2000
	CompTIA A+ and Network+ combo
	CompTIA A+ and Server+ combo

MCSA/MCSE: Windows XP Professional Study Guide, Second Edition
ISBN 0-7821-4241-9 • $49.99

MCSA: Windows 2003 Core Requirements
ISBN 0-7821-4264-8 • $119.99

For a list of all Sybex products that will help prepare you for any of the MCSA exams, visit **www.sybex.com**.